The HABSBURG GARRISON COMPLEX *in* TREBINJE

The HABSBURG GARRISON COMPLEX
in TREBINJE

A LOST WORLD

Cathie Carmichael

CEU PRESS

CENTRAL EUROPEAN UNIVERSITY PRESS

Budapest–Vienna–New York

Published in 2024 by

CENTRAL EUROPEAN UNIVERSITY PRESS
Nádor utca 11, H-1051 Budapest, Hungary
Tel: +36-1-327-3138 or 327-3000
E-mail: *ceupress@press.ceu.edu*
Website: *www.ceupress.com*

ISBN 978-963-386-770-9 (hardback)
ISBN 978-963-386-771-6 (ebook)

Library of Congress Cataloging-in-Publication Data

Names: Carmichael, Cathie, author.
Title: The Habsburg garrison complex in Trebinje : a lost world / Cathie
    Carmichael.
Description: New York : Central European University Press, 2024. | Includes
    bibliographical references and index.
Identifiers: LCCN 2024030494 (print) | LCCN 2024030495 (ebook) | ISBN
    9789633867709 (hardback) | ISBN 9789633867716 (adobe pdf)
Subjects: LCSH: Trebinje (Bosnia and Herzegovina)--History, Military. |
    Garrisons--Bosnia and Herzegovina--Trebinje--History. | Military
    towns--Bosnia and Herzegovina--Trebinje--History. | Bosnia and
    Herzegovina--History--1878-1918. | Orthodox Eastern Church
    members--Persecutions--Bosnia and Herzegovina--History--19th century. |
    Insurgency--Bosnia and Herzegovina--Herzegovina--History--19th century.
    | Herzegovina (Bosnia and Herzegovina)--History--Insurrection, 1882. |
    Austria--History, Military--19th century. | BISAC: BIOGRAPHY &
    AUTOBIOGRAPHY / Military
Classification: LCC DR1785.T74 C37 2024 (print) | LCC DR1785.T74 (ebook)
    | DDC 949.742/01--dc23/eng/20240712
LC record available at https://lccn.loc.gov/2024030494
LC ebook record available at https://lccn.loc.gov/2024030495

Contents

Acknowledgments

The idea for this book was planted over a decade ago by reading the work of Mark Levene, whose work completely transformed the way in which we thought about the First World War. Many thanks to Petr Kostrhun, who allowed me access to the correspondence of Karel Absolon at the Pavilon Anthropos and who gave me permission to reproduce the stunning images in the Moravian Museum in Brno. Thanks to Želimir Kovačina and Aleksandar Vukanović for introducing me to the beautiful city of Trebinje. Ivana Grujić and Jelena Pujić gave me access to the collections in Muzej Hercegovine in Trebinje. Raymond Neutra generously sent me material from his father's portfolio. Piero Budinich and Elisa Vladilo kindly shared personal archives with me. Thanks to the many other friends and colleagues who helped me or gave me advice while preparing and writing the book: Aviel Roshwald, Robert Knight, Marie-Janine Calic, Konrad Clewing, Bojan Aleksov, Omer Bartov, Saša Pajević, Božidar Jezernik, Anina Carkeek, Mark Cornwall, Gareth Bish, John Paul Newman, Alex Drace Francis, Laurence Cole, Rok Stergar, Bojan Baskar, Irena Weber, Becky Jinks, Helen Graham, Nebojša Čagorović, Karen Gainer, Jeremy Walton, Nina Vodopivec, Peter Vodopivec, Adriano Vinale, Vanni D'Alessio, Roland Kostić, Dirk Moses, Miloš Jovanović, Tamara Scheer, Sanja Thompson, Norman M. Naimark, Oded Steinberg, Pamela Ballinger, Marta Verginella, Anja Nikolić, Vojislav Pavlović, Goran Kovačević, Marko Živković, Mesut Idriz, Aliye Mataracı, Wendy Bracewell, Djordje Stefanović, Robert Gerwarth, Jovo Miladinović, Hannes Grandits, Vladislav Lilić, Tomislav Dulić, Dejan Djokić, Sabrina Ramet, Celia Hawkesworth, Catherine Baker, Cornelia Sorabji, Kenneth Morrison, James Gow, Milena Michalski, and Christine Hassenstab.

My friends, colleagues, and research postgraduates at the University of East Anglia were great companions. Thanks to Richard Mills, Mark Thompson, Chris Jones, Nadine Willems, Rachel Ainsworth, Kirsten James, David Gilks, Emma Griffin, Thomas Otte, Jayne Gifford, Francis King, Dan Rycroft, Elliot Short, Jack Pitt, Oren Margolis, Alex Cruikshanks, Jovana Backović, Mohammed Al-Mutairi, Yasin Coskun, Kate Tremain, Tony and Cathy Howe, Bowden Granville, Shinjini Das, Anamika Bhattacharjee, Kate Ferguson, Geoff Hicks, Nicholas Vincent, Jakob R. Avguštin, Sam Foster, Matthew D'Auria, Jan Vermeiren, Rachel Cole, Hugh Doherty, Susan Hodgett, Claire Jowitt, Lee Jarvis, Sarah Barrow, Yvonne Tasker, Lyndsey Stonebridge, and Matthias Neumann for everything. Richard Deswarte sadly passed away in 2021, but he listened to all my stories, and was wonderfully insightful.

I am deeply grateful to the authors of the articles and monographs cited, as well as for the efforts of people in Bosnia and Hercegovina to keep so much of their heritage alive, despite everything. Archival work for this book commenced in 2017 and took me across Central Europe in the following years. I received Faculty and School Funding from UEA, as well as a grant from the British Academy/Leverhulme Trust for which I am extremely thankful. The digitization of historic newspapers by the Österreichische Nationalbibliothek has been a major contribution to the study of European history, and I thank those librarians very warmly for making a past world more accessible, especially during the Covid lockdown years. Many thanks to Jen McCall, József Litkei, Michael Cragg, and Linda Kunos from Central European University Press. Thanks to my family, as always: Mike, Una, John, David x 2, Christina, Simon, Val, Roz, and to the Browns, the Bowkers, and the Horners for their constant love and support.

A Note on Language

Within the book, the modern Latin script spelling of surnames and proper names (i.e., Bileća rather than the German-language form Bilek, Matulić rather than Matulich, Dubrovnik rather than Ragusa, and Jovanović rather than Jovanovics), has been adopted. Trebinje is described as a city or citadel throughout the book, although it did not officially gain that status until 2012. I have retained the spelling Hercegovina, as opposed to the modern US spelling of Herzegovina. We are shaped by language to anticipate state formation and national loyalty, but there were also very significant regional identities in Hercegovina. By 1918, many Orthodox people in Hercegovina regarded themselves primarily as Serbs (as did many Montenegrins): a distinct and separate Croat and Bosniak consciousness was also discernible by this time. In this book, the terms Muslim, Catholic, and Orthodox have been used for the local people in and around Trebinje before 1918, but in the historical sources there is very little consistency: Turk, Bosniak, Serb, and Croat were also used. I have used the term Habsburg for Austro-Hungarian but have also opted for regional or urban designations such as Viennese, Triestine, Moravian, Carniolan, Hercegovinian, and Dalmatian so as not to overly anticipate emerging national identities, all the more so because many of the sources I have used were conspicuously *kaisertreu* and multilingual. There were characteristic orthographic irregularities in German texts, especially with adopted words: insurrection was variously spelled either with a c or with a k, Zubci was sometimes spelled Zupci or Zubcsi—the citations in footnotes reflect the original text. German spellings were somewhat different from the modern standard and I have adhered to the spelling in the text, e.g., *Culturarbeit, Feldzugmeister, Tagebuche*, etc. Loanwords rarely had standard forms. For example, occupation was also spelled Okkupation or Okkupazion in German-language sources and I have preserved the spellings as they were. The local language (also sometimes known as Montenegrin, Serbian, *naški*, Bosnian, Croatian, or Serbo-Croat) is referred to here as either "the local Slavonic language" or "Hercegovinian" for the sake of brevity and not as a political statement about whether

South Slavonic idioms spoken in this region should always be regarded as a single language. Where there is a common English-language version of a place name (i.e., Vienna), I have opted for that. The introduction of official German names such as Cepelica Most for Čepelica, or Orien Sattel for Orjen, quickly unified Bosnia and Hercegovina with the rest of the monarchy by making place names more comprehensible or knowable to first- or second-language German speakers. Within quotations, I have usually adhered to the original spelling of names (e.g., Castelnuovo rather than Herceg Novi). Dates in the Gregorian calendar have been used, except in places where the dates in the Julian calendar were also important to add. In the bibliography and in footnotes, I have transliterated titles that were originally published in Cyrillic into the Latin script.

Figures

Brief Chronology

1698–1728: Extensive additions to the Trebinje citadel under the auspices of Osman-paša Resulbegović.

1815: Habsburg rule established in Dalmatia, which lasted until 1918.

1857: Anti-Ottoman rebellion in Hercegovina led by Luka Vukalović. They demanded the right to bear arms.

1867: *Ausgleich* between Austria and Hungary, followed in 1868 by universal male conscription in the Habsburg Monarchy. Selective conscription had existed before this date.

1869: Krivošije Uprising in Southern Dalmatia against conscription.

1875–6: Uprising in Hercegovina against Ottoman authority.

1878: Congress of Berlin recognized Serbian and Montenegrin statehood and allowed the Habsburg Monarchy to occupy the Ottoman territories of Bosnia and Hercegovina. Habsburg authorities also garrisoned Sandžak from 1878 until 1908.

September 8, 1878: Habsburg troops took Trebinje peacefully and troops from the Ottoman garrison departed.

September 1878: Resistance in Klobuk and defeat of the "insurgents."

November 1881: Extension of male conscription to Bosnia and Hercegovina, followed by rebellion in Bosnia, Hercegovina, and Southern Dalmatia.

April 1882: Amnesty proclaimed at the end of the anti-conscription rebellion.

1886: Visit of Crown Prince Rudolf to Trebinje.

1889: Skirmishes on the Montenegrin border, resulting in the death and mutilation of two officers and five men from the 58th regiment based at Trebinje.

1898: Sigmund Freud's visit to Trebinje garrison doctor Alois Pick.

July 1901: Hum-Trebinje railway branch line opened amid festivities.

June 1903: Death of soldiers from heat exposure on a march from Trebinje to Bileća.

January 1904: Insubordination and rioting by troops in Trebinje and Bileća.

1906: Visit of Habsburg heir Franz Ferdinand to Trebinje.

1908: Formal annexation of Bosnia and Hercegovina by the Habsburg Monarchy and withdrawal of Habsburg garrisons from Sandžak.

1910: Visit of Emperor Franz Joseph to Bosnia and Hercegovina.

1910: Nikola Petrović proclaimed King of Montenegro.

1911: Appointment of Oskar Potiorek as Governor of Bosnia and Hercegovina.

1912–1913: The Balkan Wars and final loss of Sandžak by the Ottoman Empire.

June 28, 1914: Assassination of Franz Ferdinand and Sophie Chotek in Sarajevo. Attempted assassination of Oskar Potiorek, also by Gavrilo Princip.

July 28, 1914: Declaration of war by Habsburg Monarchy against Serbia.

August 6, 1914: Montenegro declares war against the Habsburg Monarchy.

August 1914: Execution of civilians in Trebinje.

1914–1915: Montenegrin attacks on several frontier posts near Trebinje. Hercegovina-Montenegro border villages destroyed on the orders of Oskar Potiorek. Deportation of civilians from border regions.

December 1914: Appointment of Stjepan Sarkotić as Governor of Bosnia and Hercegovina.

October–November 1915: Defeat of Serbia by the troops of the Habsburg Monarchy and their allies.

January 1916: Troops from Trebinje and other garrisons in Hercegovina form part of the invasion of Montenegro, followed by seizure of Mount Lovćen and Cetinje.

1916–1918: Shortages in food supplies in the Habsburg Monarchy.

October–November 1918: Collapse of Habsburg power and establishment of an enlarged Karadjordjević state.

THE LONG GAZE OF REINHOLD OESER

In January 1915, Reinhold Oeser submitted a report about his visit to the small fort at Vrbica in Hercegovina at the end of July 1914: it was an important station for regional telecommunications. A remote spot close to the mountain of Vardar, the fort had been built decades earlier to guard the state border. Oeser had been based in Trebinje and then Sarajevo for many years as an officer in the postal service, so this was certainly not unknown territory for him. He witnessed the detonation of land mines which destroyed one of the frontier posts and was close enough to the event to see the reaction of the Montenegrin border guard who crouched under his horse. Oeser explained that the Montenegrins just over the border were communicating via light signals, but despite his fluency in their language, he had not been able to decipher the messages. Like so many of his contemporaries, Oeser had built up the figure of the adversary—either an Orthodox man from Hercegovina or his kinsman from Montenegro—into an almost superhuman figure. This man could slither almost unheard in his *opanci* (leather shoes) and take a Habsburg soldier by surprise. At the border post, there was a "good-tempered and clever" guard dog that would prick up his ears at the sound of the foe approaching. Despite his foreboding, Oeser had time to view the hills around him and to look at the routes taken by shepherds, and the blood-red, rose, and lilac shades of the sunset. He could see Mount Orjen and the peak of Vučji zub, which to him looked like theatri-

FIGURE 1. Geological Map from 1880 showing Trebinje, Bileća (Bilek), and Dubrovnik (Ragusa). "Geologische Übersichtskarte von Bosnien-Hercegovina," Wikimedia Commons.

cal props against a deep blue background. He also had time to share his humble rations with others: inevitably, small portions could bring men together as they broke bread in a "brotherly manner" and shared a cup of wine.[1] This reinforced a very twentieth-century view that comradeship was "the best thing about war."[2] By the time the report was submitted in January 1915, people in the border region, both soldiers and civilians, had experienced months of fighting.

Reinhold Oeser's range of feelings were typical of Habsburg officers of this era in Hercegovina. He loved the land with a deep passion, was a pillar of the state, and had been a bicycle enthusiast who often published accounts of his escapades in magazines. In his official role, Oeser had asked fellow cyclists to send their photographic

---

[1] "anschleichenden Opankentritten," in Reinhold Oeser, "Die Kriegsmassige Sprengung des Kordonspostens Vardar bei Bileća in der Hercegovina," Sarajevo, January 5, 1915, AT-OeS-tA/KA FA NFA Feste Plätze Festung Bileća 1309, Kriegsarchiv, Vienna.

[2] Yuval Noah Harari, *Renaissance Military Memoirs: War, History, and Identity, 1450–1600* (Woodbridge: Boydell, 2004), 147.

equipment to him before they toured the region, which was deemed a necessary security precaution to stop visitors from using their cameras around military installations.[3] In 1902, in his capacity as a garrison official, Oeser had been present at a splendid dinner at the Hotel Naglić and dined with Trebinje notables including Abdulrahman Resulbegović. The Naglić guests were treated to performances of folk music while they sat in the shade of paper lanterns and flags. The hotel served rainbow trout that Oeser himself had caught in the Trebišnjica river before dawn.[4] But despite his ardent enthusiasm for the land and his own levels of intimacy and local integration, this officer, like many of his peers, was alienated from and fearful of rural people in Hercegovina. In this book I will attempt to recreate some of the life of Reinhold Oeser's contemporaries, along with the generation that preceded them within the formidable garrison complex around Trebinje that they helped to build, maintain, and then resoundingly lost.

FIGURE 2. The old city of Trebinje and the side of Leotar in 2018. Photo by Saša Pajević.

---

3   "Vom Reise und Touren-Comité," *Club-Organ des Oesterreichischen Touring-Club*, no. 10 (1902): 11.
4   Dr. Oransz, "Die Gesellschafts-Radreise des 'Ö. T.-C.' nach Kroatien, Dalmatien, Herzegowina und Bosnien im Juli 1902," *Club-Organ des Oesterreichischen Touring-Club*, August 15, 1903, 7–8.

Chapter One
PLACE AND PEOPLE

Introduction

Habsburg power was imposed upon Bosnia and Hercegovina in 1878, a land in which the people had revolted against Ottoman authority, against Islamic power, and against an unequal system which had left them as poor subjects in their ancestral homes. At the same time, Bosnia and Hercegovina had only recently become a haven for Muslims escaping persecution in Serbia. Divisions between Muslim and Orthodox people, already existent at the rural and urban level, were exacerbated by a quick and decisive military action in 1878 which people of both religions resisted. The Catholic population had joined the anti-Ottoman rebellion in 1875, but generally welcomed the 1878 occupation. Although Trebinje surrendered peacefully to Habsburg soldiers, there were pockets of fierce resistance elsewhere.

Conscription had been imposed on young men in the Habsburg Monarchy after 1868, bringing them to the newly occupied regions. Through harsh labor conditions, they built a new garrison complex in Eastern Hercegovina, with Trebinje its most significant part. Although they built upon the foundations of an established Ottoman fortress, Trebinje was rapidly transformed into a modern, airy city: cafés, guest houses, and shops sprung up in the center. Urban life was wrapped around an army hierarchy that shaped and decided upon almost everything. For example, the first child of former sol-

dier Ivan Müller and his wife Terezija, born in 1883, had been baptized by a military chaplain in the absence of another available Catholic priest.[1] The army top brass played a divide and rule game between
the "civilized" space of the city and the unruly countryside. They
had arrived with readymade ideas about the *hajduk* or insurgent
bands they would face.[2] In 1882, local people, fighting in guerrilla
formations, targeted the new regime's vulnerabilities. Small in numbers, the rebels were quickly defeated, and their captured supporters were paraded in Trebinje. Subsequently, a small elite in the army
distrusted the Orthodox, while still admiring their fortitude, clothes,
traditions, and bravery in combat. Many peaceful years ensued after
1882, during which time hospitals and schools were created, roads
built, and national institutions founded. A railway line that linked
Hum with Trebinje, thereby speeding up the links between Catholic and Orthodox Hercegovina, was constructed. Soldiers made the
most of the opportunity, producing significant scientific knowledge
about geology, botany, and archaeology in their spare time. In 1914,
the assassination of the heir apparent Franz Ferdinand and outbreak
of war led to a rapid campaign of persecution against the Orthodox
by the army and government in Sarajevo, led by the Bosnian Governor Oskar Potiorek.[3] This was understood by the many subjects of
the emperor as harsh but justified, or as war correspondent Richard
Bermann (writing under the pseudonym Arnold Höllriegel) put it:
"the whole country was in rebellion and Austrian military law was
no laughing matter."[4] Border villages were burned, scores of people
were executed in public, while many were deported to internment
camps which had very high death rates especially among children

1   Valentin Miklobušec, "Od Trebinja do stratišta: O. Josip Müller DI (1883–1945)," *Obnovljeni
    Život: časopis za filozofiju i religijske znanosti* 69, no. 2 (2014): 194.
2   "Wie Insurgenten entstehen," *Epoche*, October 3, 1878, 2. By the 1870s, the term *hajduk* was
    commonly used to indicate bandits and plunderers operating within the Ottoman Empire
    and its borderlands.
3   Oskar Potiorek (1853–1933) originally from Bad Bleiberg in Carinthia, had a long career as
    an army officer before taking on the role of governor in Sarajevo.
4   "verstand keinen Spaß," Richard A. Bermann [Arnold Höllriegel pseud.], *Die Fahrt auf dem
    Katarakt: Eine Autobiographie ohne einen Helden*, ed. Hans-Harald Müller (Vienna: Picus, 2021),
    151.

and adolescents.[5] People within Trebinje were encouraged to witness and support the persecution of Orthodox country people within the confines of the city. Slowly the infrastructure around the garrisons began to fail, not least because shepherds and farmers had been attacked or deported; shortages of food and news of military defeats elsewhere left the population of Trebinje beleaguered. As the Habsburg regime fell, those soldiers left behind in the city rapidly dismantled the gallows that had come to symbolize Habsburg power. They then witnessed the jubilation of the people who rapidly reclaimed the land and put their stamp upon it. For them, the era of the *Švabe* and rule by incomers from Central Europe was over.[6]

Although short-lived, Habsburg military civilization made an enduring mark on Hercegovina. It left behind a vast extensive complex of buildings and fortifications, which included forts at Kravica, Čepelica, Vrbica, Visoka glavica, Zubci, and numerous other smaller installations. For the forty years before the end of the First World War, these military buildings were connected to the Mostar garrison, to Sarajevo, to the coast at Gruž, to the fortifications at Bileća, and to Crkvice in Boka Kotorska.[7] The personnel of the Habsburg regime left Hercegovina over a hundred years ago, but the impact of just four decades of rule by the Emperors Franz Joseph and Karl was immense. If Habsburg power meant change, it also meant control often of the smallest aspects of life via bureaucratic mechanisms, rules, and military ubiquity. Cities like Trebinje were so full of soldiers that they often outnumbered the civilian population. Although that sense of being just an occupation army did disappear with time, it never subsided completely. In 1906, the writer Radovan Perović-Tunguz depicted Bosnia and Hercegovina as a "land of wailing" where the "foreigner" ruled everything: "the ox in the plough, and the seed in the furrow, and the wheat in its ear, and the shepherd with his

5   Alan Kramer, *Dynamic of Destruction: Culture and Mass Killing in the First World War* (Oxford: Oxford University Press, 2007), 67.
6   *Švabe* (literally "Swabians"), a derogatory term used for Central Europeans during the Habsburg period, was originally meant to denote Germans, but it was used for all Habsburg incomers after 1878.
7   "Die Befestigungen in der Herzegovina," *Pester Lloyd*, March 23, 1883, 2.

flock, and the flute in his mouth, and the wind in the caves."[8] Although the wind was free to blow into the cave at Vjetrenica, it appears that tourists could not just turn up spontaneously for a visit because the metal grate at the entrance was habitually locked: to get the key, they had to travel on a train to Trebinje, a half-hour away.[9]

Ultimately it would be tempting to see the Habsburg "civilizing mission"[10] as a failure: but to paraphrase Zhou Enlai, it might just be too early to say. Certainly, the Viennese monarchy was no worse than other contemporary colonial powers in terms of human rights abuses.[11] Many individuals flourished during the reign of Franz Joseph and Vienna was the center of a great fin de siècle culture. Some reforms the Habsburg state introduced to Bosnia and Hercegovina were unambiguously positive, such as primary schools, fresh water supplies to cities, and increasing freedom for women.[12] The Habsburg state also protected the remaining Muslim population from the kind of wrath they had experienced during the 1870s. The amendments to the conscription laws of 1881, which allowed Muslim soldiers to make their ablutions in copper basins, to prepare food separately, to receive new cooking utensils, to pray at the mosque on Friday or on religious festivals, and to be buried without music, now look like a model of thoughtful religious integration.[13] The population of Trebinje still walk on shady paved streets built in the late nineteenth century and still travel on those straight, if rather treeless roads designed by Central Europeans. And individuals benefitted from the

8   Edin Hajdarpašić, *Whose Bosnia? Nationalism and Political Imagination in the Balkans, 1840–1914* (Ithaca, NY: Cornell University Press, 2015), 85-86.
9   Reinhard Günste [Rifat Eff. Gozdović pseud.], "Zavala, das herzegowinische Athoškloster und die Vjetrinicahöhle [sic]," *Deutsches Volksblatt*, December 2, 1906, 21.
10 Robin Okey, *Taming Balkan Nationalism: The Habsburg "Civilizing Mission" in Bosnia 1878-1914* (Oxford: Oxford University Press, 2007). It was sometimes referred to as *Zivilisationswerk*, see Theodor Friedrich, "Bosnische Eindrücke I," *Pester Lloyd*, July 20, 1901, 3.
11 Ferdinand Hauptmann, *Die Österreichisch-ungarische Herrschaft in Bosnien und der Hercegovina, 1878–1918: Wirtschaftpläne und Wirtschaftsentwicklung* (Graz: Institut für Geschichte an der Universität Graz, 1983); Anja Nikolić, "Similarities and Differences in Imperial Administration: Great Britain in Egypt and Austria-Hungary in Bosnia-Herzegovina 1878–1903," *Balcanica* 47 (2016): 177–95.
12 Charles St John (1831–1897) contrasted the freedom for women that he had seen in Trebinje with the absence of freedom in Prizren, where he had been in 1880; Charles St John to Earl Granville, Dubrovnik, March 24, 1881, FO 7/1023, National Archives, London.
13 Zijad Šehić, "Vojni imami u bosanskohercegovačkim jedinicama u okviru austrougarske armije 1878-1918," *Godišnjak BZK Preporod*, no. 1 (2006): 310.

knowledge economy that went alongside the garrisons: in 1905, it was reported that a villager, Zorka, was cured of blindness by a "philanthropic" regimental doctor in Trebinje.[14] Nevertheless, the people of Hercegovina also spent the following century dealing with the legacy of practices that set Muslims and Catholics against the Orthodox population. Rather than giving or subtracting virtue points, what we can say with more certainty is that the Habsburg regime helped to create a new and unique culture which fused different worlds and brought peoples together: "the Vienna-born waiter serves a rice pilaf for the hodja with one hand and with the other puts a frothy Pilsner on the table for the European," as Georg Lukas put it in 1909.[15] That Habsburg government failed rapidly and spectacularly after 1914 may be attributed primarily to the mutual radicalization between the Orthodox community and the military personnel and politicians that were in power at that time. But as I will also argue here, a culture of tough military values and a concentration of power in the hands of army commanders, many of whom held deep and long-term prejudices against Orthodox people, was inauspicious.

This book focuses on the leaders who were responsible for the actions that led to the demise of the Habsburg Monarchy, but also the incomers who used their time within the garrison complex around Trebinje to make new lives, acquire knowledge, and understand the country, its natural wealth, its people, and their history. Looking at their lives also allows us to get a "decent view of the life of (local) people."[16] The garrison complex was led by officers but supported by a parallel workforce of postal workers, medical staff, lawyers, and other reliable professionals who were preferred under the new regime. Across Bosnia and Hercegovina, their numbers grew rapidly as the state settled in. The army was supported by the manual work of soldiers and paid laborers. Conscripts moved around the monarchy with their regiments, but professionals stayed in situ for much longer, often decades. Boredom, entitlement, high levels of education, and curiosity often turned Habsburg officials into accomplished

14 H. W., "Wilde Rosen: Skizze aus der Herzegowina," *Reichspost*, July 30, 1905, 1–2.
15 Georg A. Lukas, "Bosnische Eindrücke," part 1, *Grazer Tagblatt*, October 9, 1909, 2.
16 Ninoslav Ilić, "Revitalisation of k.u.k. fortifications in Trebinje: Design sample; Fort Kličanj" (Diploma Arbeit, Institut für Architektur und Entwerfen, Vienna, 2017), 39.

scientists, ethnographers, and historians. Gradually, service and duty
turned into a genuine love for the land, which is a striking theme
running through many of the extant accounts. Like Reinhold Oeser,
Carniolan officer Jernej Andrejka demonstrated a sentimental, almost poetic attachment to his posting and described his view at
breakfast:

> The sunrise on Visoka glavica is beautiful. The golden sun floats
> up from above in the morning sky and shines first on the tops
> of the fuller beech trees, as if to show its admiration for the
> winged singers who jump from branch to branch, warbling in
> honor and glory of the creator and to delight human society after
> dawn. Far away in the south, the wide surface of the Adriatic Sea
> glistens in the morning sunlight.[17]

The idea for writing this book came originally from Mark Levene's
concept of "rimlands," namely the contested regions of Europe
where new national identities started to displace complex or multiethnic imperial allegiances.[18] Montenegro emerged as a strong na-
tion-state and its new territory after 1878 included parts of old Hercegovina. Habsburg occupation and then annexation of the rest of
Hercegovina temporarily halted the attacks on local Muslims, but
left many Orthodox people with deep loyalties which extended beyond the new state boundaries. Habsburg attempts to suppress "insurgency" in 1878 and again in 1882 along the border with Montenegro created one of the fault lines along which the Habsburg
Monarchy started to unravel. The long-term result of border changes
and political instability was stark population decline. After 1875,
both Muslim and Orthodox people left their rural homes and fled
to the towns and cities. Habsburg soldiers found settlements burned
or deserted in 1878 and as many as five thousand people escaped
over the border with Montenegro in 1882.[19] Further depopulation

17 Jernej Andrejka, *Slovenski fantje v Bosni in Hercegovini 1878* (Klagenfurt: Družba sv. Mohorja, 1904), 348.
18 Mark Levene, *The Crisis of Genocide*, vol. 1, *Devastation: The European Rimlands 1912–1938* (Oxford: Oxford University Press, 2014), 5–8.
19 Charles St John to Earl Granville, Dubrovnik, March 3, 1882, F07 1041, National Archives, London.

occurred with emigration to the New World and to big cities in the Balkans. After the summer of 1914, Hercegovina was drastically depopulated again because of the actions of the Habsburg army and its local proxies. As Heiner Grunert has observed, "in a 20-kilometre-long strip of land along the eastern border, the army arrested almost every adult Serb man who had not fled to Montenegro or Serbia."[20] In the first few months of 1914, Orthodox people were "routed and reduced to silence … their villages sacked, houses … burned and destroyed, families dispersed, the men hanged or imprisoned."[21] Like many other rimlands, some parts of the region between Trebinje and the border with Montenegro have never recovered their population levels of 1870. Some settlements also disappeared when the Trebišnjica river was flooded in 1967 and the artificial Lake Bileća created. Indeed, some places referred to in this book no longer exist as such.[22]

To try to understand how this region around Trebinje became part of a rimland, I have opted for a micro-historical approach and a particular focus on the Habsburg military presence.[23] Hercegovina has already been endowed with significant studies including Safet HadžiMuhamedović's work on Gacko,[24] the research of Hannes Grandits on the post-Tanzimat era,[25] Heiner Grunert's work on the Orthodox Church,[26] and a history of Trebinje by Vojislav Korać.[27]

20 Heiner Grunert, "The Inner Enemy in Wartime: The Habsburg State and the Serb Citizens of Bosnia-Herzegovina, 1913–1918," in *Sarajevo 1914: Sparking the First World War*, ed. Mark Cornwall (London: Bloomsbury, 2020), 258.

21 Antonio Budini, *Le memorie di guerra di papà* (Trieste: Beit Storia, 2013), 62.

22 The monastery at Kosijerevo that was damaged between 1914 and 1915 was moved to a nearby location in Montenegro. Zupci Rapti is now a deserted village.

23 For a micro-historical approach combined with a focus on the army, see Peter Melichar, "Ästhetik und Disziplin: Das Militär in Wiener Neustadt 1740–1914," in *Die Wienerische Neustadt: Handwerk, Handel und Militär*, ed. Sylvia Hahn and Karl Flanner (Vienna: Böhlau, 1994), 283–336.

24 Safet HadžiMuhamedović, *Waiting for Elijah: Time and Encounter in a Bosnian Landscape* (Oxford: Berghahn, 2018).

25 Hannes Grandits, *Herrschaft und Loyalität in der spätosmanischen Gesellschaft: Das Beispiel der multikonfessionellen Herzegowina* (Vienna: Böhlau, 2008).

26 Heiner Grunert, *Glauben im Hinterland: Die Serbisch-Orthodoxen in der habsburgischen Herzegowina 1878–1918* (Göttingen: Vandenhoeck and Ruprecht, 2016).

27 Vojislav Korać, *Trebinje: Istorijski pregled*, vol. 2, parts 1 and 2 (Trebinje: Zavičajni muzej, 1971).

Milorad Ekmečić,[28] Hamdija Kapidžić,[29] Esad Arnautović,[30] and Srećko Džaja[31] wrote insightful and very detailed research on the late Ottoman and Habsburg periods in Hercegovina. Articles in journals such as *Prilozi* and *Tribunia* add a substantial amount of local depth. Drawing heavily on the accounts written by Habsburg soldiers themselves, I have also taken great interest in the literature on the social history of the army, especially Rok Stergar's pioneering work on Slovene-speaking regiments,[32] Tamara Scheer on the Sandžak,[33] John Paul Newman on Habsburg army veterans,[34] Jiří Hutečka on Czech soldiers during the First World War,[35] and Christa Hämmerle on gender and masculinity.[36] Insight into the army combined with observations about the particularities of Hercegovina should help to explain why this region was so violent in the decade after 1875 and again in 1914. A focus on detail might also avoid reproducing a litany of war crimes and attributing collective responsibility for any violence to only distantly related contemporary entities such as Austria, Bosnia and Hercegovina, Serbia, or Montenegro or, indeed, to their current citizens.

Within this book, and by using a range of sources, I have described tragic violence alongside stories of everyday life in Trebinje and its garrison complex and the idyllic long summers before 1914. The deliberate juxtaposition of personal reminiscences, exuberance, and celebrations with humiliation and cruelty might be judged to be disruptive. Although it is tempting to construct violence as adjacent,

---

28 See, for example, Milorad Ekmečić, "Ustanak u Hercegovini 1882. i istorijske pouke," *Prilozi*. no. 19 (1982): 9–74.

29 Hamdija Kapidžić, *Hercegovački ustanak 1882 godine* (Sarajevo: Veselin Masleša, 1958).

30 Esad Arnautović, "Austrougarska okupacija Trebinja," in *Prilozi za istoriju Trebinja i XIX stoljeću*, ed. Esad Arnautović (Trebinje: Opštinska zajednica kulture, 1986), 9–23.

31 Srećko Džaja, *Bosnien-Herzegowina in der österreichisch-ungarischen Epoche (1878–1918): Die Intelligentsia zwischen Tradition und Ideologie* (Munich: Oldenbourg, 1994).

32 Rok Stergar, *"Vojski prijazen in zaželen garnizon": Ljubljanski častniki med prelomom stoletja in prvo svetovno vojno* (Ljubljana: Zveza zgodovinskih društev Slovenije, 1999).

33 Tamara Scheer, *"Minimale Kosten, absolut kein Blut!": Österreich-Ungarns Präsenz im Sandžak von Novipazar (1879–1908)* (Frankfurt: Peter Lang, 2013).

34 John Paul Newman, *Yugoslavia in the Shadow of War: Veterans and the Limits of State Building, 1903–1945* (Cambridge: Cambridge University Press, 2015).

35 Jiří Hutečka, *Men Under Fire: Motivation, Morale, and Masculinity among Czech Soldiers in the Great War, 1914–1918* (Oxford: Berghahn, 2020).

36 Christa Hämmerle, *Ganze Männer? Gesellschaft, Geschlecht und Allgemeine Wehrpflicht in Österreich-Ungarn (1868–1914)* (Frankfurt: Campus, 2022).

exceptional, and extreme, this constructs an artificial distance. Furthermore, it unjustly separates the reader from the human side of these practices. In my view, conflict and violence should be considered as part of life, and not as an incomparable practice outside of "normal" experience. While it is true that human behavior *in extremis* deserves to be studied independently, terrible events often coincide with the dull, the banal, and the everyday. Individuals still experience heat, cold, hunger, thirst, greed, envy, desire, euphoria, disgust, love, and anger even when the basic structures of life have been altered. In Hercegovina, executions were carried out in tree-lined parks and indeed oaks were used as gallows.[37] Flowers still bloomed on battlefields; people still sunbathed,[38] laughed, ate, and drank beside execution sites. Witnessing hangings of local men formed a key part in recollections of military service by soldiers even in the 1880s, and sometimes it was one of very few details in their accounts.[39] Arriving in Trebinje during the First World War, the journalist Karl Nowak was struck by the proximity of six gallows "in front of the best guesthouse" in the city.[40] Writing in 1915, Nowak added the minimal but equally telling reflection, "but they were not just in Trebinje."

By personalizing the occupation and annexation of Bosnia and Hercegovina, I have attempted to show some empathy for the ordinary soldier, condemned "insurgent," career officer, chef, shepherdess, hotelier, or journalist, as well as those with more command responsibility. This conscious strategy of "humanization" has meant the inclusion of copious, sometimes devilish detail in order to extend our "purview of empathy ... across traditional social boundaries."[41] Within these sources, the detail about life in Trebinje and its envi-

---

37 Budini, *Le memorie di guerra*, 89.
38 This juxtaposition has been discussed by Andrew Charlesworth in "The Topography of Genocide," in *The Historiography of the Holocaust*, ed. Dan Stone (Basingstoke: Palgrave Macmillan, 2004), 223.
39 See for example, "Soldatenleben in der Herzegowina," *Freie Stimmen*, June 17, 1887, 6–7.
40 "In Trebinje stehen heute noch vor dem besten Wirtshaus des Ortes sechs Galgen. Aber nicht bloß in Trebinje standen sie," Karl Nowak, "Bosnische Grenzfahrt," *Prager Tagblatt*, December 8, 1915, 11. Ratko Parežanin thought that the proximity of the gallows to the Orthodox Church was intentional; see *Die Attentäter: Das junge Bosnien im Freiheitskampf* (Munich: L. Jevtić, 1976), 144.
41 Lynn Hunt, *Inventing Human Rights: A History* (New York: Norton, 2007), 40.

rons is sometimes merely incidental, but some immersed themselves in local life. Trebinje and its garrison quickly became their world, which they desperately missed after 1918. Many were also loyal to the Habsburg Monarchy through thick and thin, even after its demise. The use of first-hand accounts is intended primarily to let "those who lived that history lend their own words to the telling of it."[42] Although this account is decidedly one-sided, reconstructed largely from the words of the incomers, the occupation and annexation of Bosnia and Hercegovina involved people from very different civilizations with different modes of dress, worldviews, and ways of thinking coming face to face (and sometimes staring at one another). Individual human interaction matters for men in uniform and nuance is often submerged or lost when the state they served collapses in military defeat.[43] We can say that the state demanded a great deal from its young conscripts, and it seems important to remember that they were also collateral damage in the maintenance of the Habsburg regime. When soldiers died of heat exposure in July 1903, it matters that they had been ordered to march along unshaded roads denuded of trees from Trebinje to Bileća in full parade uniform in more than 40 degrees Celsius heat while carrying heavy backpacks.[44] Oppressive states usually practice on the bodies of their own population long before they export violence. The British Consul Charles St John reported on Habsburg army abuses from his Dubrovnik office as the locally billeted soldiers moved toward Hercegovina in 1878. Five of these men died in the campaign. He even questioned the legality of the execution of an exhausted soldier when "not absolutely before the enemy. A similar case happened a short time since not two miles from Ragusa. A man of the Landwehr complaining of fatigue and inability to proceed any further was immediately run through the body by the officer in charge."[45]

---

42 Omer Bartov, *Anatomy of a Genocide: The Life and Death of a Town Called Buczacz* (New York: Simon and Schuster, 2018), 4.
43 Robert Gerwarth, *The Vanquished: Why the First World War Failed to End, 1917–1923* (London: Penguin, 2017).
44 "Manöverunglück bei Bilek," *Mährisches Tagblatt*, July 27, 1903, 3.
45 "Run through" is an archaic term for bayoneted. Charles St John to the Marquis of Salisbury, Dubrovnik, September 4, 1878. FO7 940, National Archives, London.

How can we reach this distant world shaped by different values? And what remains in terms of existing records? Thanks to the state military archive (*Kriegsarchiv*) in Vienna, which contains personal as well as official papers, we can assemble at least some of the available evidence about the Trebinje garrison complex. The typewriter, first invented in the mid-nineteenth century, was becoming increasingly important and by 1914, many letters and reports were hastily typed rather than being carefully inscribed, but with characteristic corrections and hand-written asides. This was a highly literate era of letters, diaries, as well as a multitude of reports and forms; several personal archives are also available. Diaries kept by soldiers were often embellished with royal postcards, photographs, business cards, funeral notices, drawings, menus, musical scores, concert tickets, and newspaper clippings. Wilhelm Sauerwald cut out and kept the story about the accident that led to the loss of his own leg while stationed in Hercegovina,[46] while Leo Weirather kept the clippings about the skeletons he discovered in Sovica jama (but apparently not those relating to his 1914 trial for espionage).[47]

Many soldiers were quite accomplished artists, and watercolors survive of Trebinje and its environs. The emerging skill of photography also gives us enduring images of local men and women, sometimes in color. The vivid work of photographer Marie Marvánková[48] was admired by the Serbian geographer Jovan Cvijić.[49] This was also an era of multiple newspapers, and editors were keen to publish all kinds of personal accounts from soldiers as an act of moral support and to fill newspapers with palatable copy. Consular papers, especially from Dubrovnik, add a lot more individual detail and human

46 "Ein verunglückter Generalstabs-Officier," *Die Presse* (*Abendblatt*), March 8, 1884, 3. Wilhelm Ritter Sauerwald von Hochland, AT-OeStA/KA NL 1554 (B,C) 1554 (B,C), Kriegsarchiv, Vienna.

47 "Ein Aussehen erregender Höhlenfund," *Volksblatt für Stadt und Land*, December 29, 1912, 7; Collections Leo Weirather, Muséum d'histoire naturelle de Genève.

48 Marie Absolonová (nee Marvánková) (1888–1972) visited Hercegovina with her husband before the First World War and before their divorce. Their joint work was published as Karel Absolon, "Z výzkumných cest po krasech Balkánu: S 33 původními obrázky dle snímků a mikrofotografií pí. Marie Absolonové," *Zlatá Praha* 33, no. 48 (1916): 574–76; no. 49: 586–88; no. 50: 597–600; no. 51: 609–12; no. 52: 622–24.

49 Jovan Cvijić to Karel Absolon, Belgrade, September 15, 1913, Sbirka Karla Absolona, Pavilon Anthropos, Moravské zemské muzeum, Brno.

FIGURE 3. Women in Rural Bosnia and Hercegovina, 1913. Photo by Marie Marvánková, Moravské zemské muzeum, Brno.

perspective. I have also relied on official papers such as memoranda and telegrams. Some records from the pre-1918 era were destroyed in a fire at the state archives in Sarajevo in February 2014, including important court records from the Trebinje garrison from 1914–1916.[50] These records were used extensively by Vladimir Ćorović and the empirical detail in his 1920 monograph *Crna Knjiga: Patnje Srba Bosne i Hercegovine za vreme svetskog rata 1914–1918. godine* aligns closely with the content in surviving documents.[51]

Occasionally, regional newspapers published anonymous "letters from soldiers" from the local regiments to record successes, privation

---

50 Adelheid Wölfl, "Wiederherstellungsprojekt: Aufruf zu Hilfe für bosnisches Archiv; Brand vor einem Jahr—Österreichische Akten vernichtet," *Der Standard*, February 10, 2015.

51 Vladimir Ćorović, *Crna knjiga: Patnje Srba Bosne i Hercegovine za vreme svetskog rata 1914–1918. godine* (Belgrade: Izdanje I. Đurđevića, 1920), 6. Ćorović (1885–1941), originally from Mostar, was a prolific historian of the national question.

or low-level discontent.[52] After arriving in Trebinje at the time of the Habsburg takeover in 1878, one soldier reflected in the *Nordböhmisches Volksblatt* on the lack of personal space: "we lay down to sleep like herrings and it was a difficult night."[53] In 1909, a newspaper published a letter from a soldier who recalled sleeping on straw in the barracks at Trebinje, long route marches, and running to drink melted snow because the distance between cisterns was too great.[54] Publishing correspondence allowed newspapers to air sensitive subjects such as living conditions among soldiers without apparently taking sides.[55] Habsburg soldiers came from regions with developed education systems and were encouraged to keep personal accounts.[56] Diaries, usually not intended for general consumption, record the most personal of details alongside other matters that seemed important at the time. Postcards can be valued as pictorial evidence and their survival has helped to preserve elements of life in Bosnia and Hercegovina of this era,[57] often in vivid and sometimes even lurid color. Soldiers wrote on the blank part but also doodled on the pictures, adding their own explanations. The utility of the postcards as insightful historical texts is less than obvious, especially as so many were stamped *"Zensuriert"* during wartime; conveying content required levels of ellipsis, but after the rapid conquest of Montenegro in January 1916, wartime censorship seems to have loosened a little. Although postcards are necessarily brief, their themes and images give us a good insight into the values of the time. Sending "splendid colorful"[58] images home fulfilled

---

52 See for example, "Die Meuterei in Bilek und Trebinje," *Villacher Zeitung*, January 10, 1904, 2.

53 "Aus einem Feldpostbriefe," *Nordböhmisches Volksblatt*, October 4, 1878, 1.

54 N. N., "Brief eines Grenzsoldaten," *Österreichische Volkszeitung*, January 12, 1909, 2.

55 For example, reproduction of an anonymous soldier's letter from Bileća allowed *Pester Lloyd* to discuss incipient Hungarian nationalism: see "Angebliche Unruhen in der Bileker Garnison," *Pester Lloyd* (*Abendblatt*), January 2, 1904, 1.

56 Ursula Reber, "The Experience of Borders: Montenegrin Tribesmen at War," in *Doing Anthropology in Wartime and War Zones: World War I and the Cultural Sciences in Europe*, ed. Reinhard Johler, Christian Marchetti, and Monique Scheer (Berlin: De Gruyter, 2014), 191–206.

57 Dieter J. Hecht, "Bosnische Impressionen: k.k. Soldaten als Tourismuspioniere vor dem Ersten Weltkrieg," in *Zwischen Exotik und Vertrautem: Zum Tourismus in der Habsburgermonarchie und ihren Nachfolgestaaten*, ed. Peter Stachel and Martina Thomson (Bielefeld: Transcript, 2014), 201–16.

58 Aristides von Arensdorff commented on the utility of postcards for keeping in touch during his military posting, see "Erinnerungen: Sarajevo und Plevlje 1906 bis 1910," AT-OeStA/KA NL 782 (B,C), Kriegsarchiv, Vienna.

an important role. Firstly, it reminded Habsburg subjects that doing military service was an important aspect of the "civilizing mission," and secondly, it presented an upbeat image which was likely to be a contrast to the reality of war or conscription. During the war years, soldiers were still sending cheerful images from before 1914. Dalmatian officer Antonio Budinich wrote to his infant daughter so that she would have an aide-mémoire if he were killed in combat.[59]

Feuilletons were short personal sketches in regional newspapers which tended to follow the progress of local battalions as they were posted around the Monarchy. They were a popular genre with officers who wanted to set down memories or tell tall stories. They allowed the authors some freedom in terms of style, composition, and content.[60] As texts, they present both advantages and pitfalls: they are sometimes hackneyed or misleading, written for an audience who wanted to hear good news. Although they clearly fulfil a function, feuilletons also brim with both local anecdotes and unfiltered ethnographic detail, and were provincial enough to convey the importance of regional connections. The style of these short pieces is often quite formulaic, but feuilletons give us insight into how enduring tropes were transmitted across the Habsburg Monarchy: generations of soldiers, officials, and so-called carpetbaggers (kuferaši)[61] arrived in Hercegovina with a rather complete set of preconceptions and prejudices about local people. The feuilleton genre survived across Central and Southern Europe, complementing habitual and devoted letter writing.

---

59 Letter to Miriam, dated July 30, 1916, personal collection of his grandson, Piero Budinich, Trieste. At the time of his military service, Antonio Budini (1880–1974) was registered with the surname Budinich. He later changed his name to Budini in line with the Italianization of names during the Mussolini era. His memoir was published under his Italian name.

60 Borut Rudolf Standeker, "Die Rolle des Feuilletons während des Zweiten Weltkrieges in der deutschsprachigen Presse in Oberkrain und der Untersteiermark, Fallbeispiele Marburger Zeitung und Karawanken Bote" (BA thesis, University of Ljubljana, 2020), 10. See also Petra Zagmajster, "Flucht aus der Realität: Das Feuilleton der Laibacher Zeitung im Ersten Weltkrieg (1914–1918)" (MA thesis, University of Ljubljana, 2019).

61 This term which denoted quick movement across the monarchy with light and easily portable bags was sometimes rendered as Kofferschlepper in German, see Reinhard Günste [Rifat Gozdović Pascha pseud.], "Heitere Erinnerungen aus ernster Zeit," Pilsner Tagblatt, January 17, 1915, 3.

Many accounts written after 1918 record a nostalgia for the lost monarchy, but often also a genuine and continuing concern for Hercegovina and its inhabitants. Writing in 1942, the Carinthian playwright Friedrich Perkonig[62] went back to the scenes of his youth: "I still think about the small Herzegovinian city of Trebinje, on the threshold between the Occident and Orient … bathed in the glow of the crescent moon, I suddenly remember it, as if some magical force had conjured it up from oblivion."[63] In 1936, the scientist Karel Absolon confessed that his "love for the caves in Hercegovina has not died."[64] Actual lived experience, daily knowledge, and familiarity broke down prejudice and complacency, promoting instead a kind of respect, interest, and empathy.[65] It is a great paradox of colonialism or territorial annexation that it opens up genuine knowledge transfer and opportunities, but this is primarily achieved at the expense of local people who become the subject either of ethnographic interest, "concern," or contempt, rather than agents of their own destinies. Holding power can either be interpreted as requiring some responsibility and reciprocity or as a series of privileges and opportunities to seize and take. Often uneven power relationships involve a complex mixture of entitlement and duty that contemporaries sometimes referred to as *Culturarbeit*[66] or *Zivilisationswerk*.[67]

At first sight, the Trebinje garrison complex would seem like an overwhelmingly masculine milieu, but it also relied on the labor and support of women, including domestic and ancillary roles in the kitchens, serving in local cafés and hotels, doing laundry, and sell-

---

62 (Josef) Friedrich Perkonig (1890–1959) was a German-language teacher, poet, and writer from Borovlje/Ferlach in Carinthia, whose distant family were Slovene speakers.
63 Josef Friedrich Perkonig, "Zwischen Abend und Morgen," *Neues Wiener Tagblatt*, December 10, 1942, 2.
64 Karel Absolon to Johann (Ivan) Čadek, Brno, April 30, 1936, Sbirka Karla Absolona, Pavilon Anthropos, Moravské zemské muzeum, Brno. Karel Absolon (1877–1960), a Moravian polymath and friend to so many in the Trebinje garrison, spent his summers in Hercegovina both before the First World War and afterwards.
65 Empathy for the "beleaguered" peoples of Bosnia and Hercegovina may already have existed in 1878; see Dragan Damjanović, "Austro-ugarska okupacija Bosne i Hercegovine gledana očima hrvatskog slikara: Prijelaz Save kod Broda Ferdinanda Quiquereza," *Radovi Instituta za povijest umjetnosti* 41 (2017): 208.
66 F. von M., "Die Culturarbeit der österreichischen Armee (Hercegovina) III," *Wiener Zeitung*, June 12, 1886, 2–3.
67 Theodor Friedrich, "Bosnische Eindrücke I," *Pester Lloyd*, July 20, 1901, 3.

ing cheese or fruit in the marketplace. It was reported in the press when Marija, the mother of the Trebinje chief of police Luka Petković, had died at the age of 117. She had done her own housework until the end.[68] Outside the domestic sphere there were female insurgents: recalling the violence in 1878, one soldier recorded "tales of cold vengeance and bloody hate ... in that haunted mountainous land of combatants.... Stories of women maiming the wounded, murdering the sick, of women risking their lives without hesitation just to harm the enemy."[69] Habsburg soldiers uncovered women's clothes when they found an insurgent "nest" in the late summer of 1882.[70] An officer called Monari sent two women up to the insurgents in May 1882 to tell them about the amnesty proclamation: "These two women who had brought the provisions from Vrbanje, took on this diplomatic mission only reluctantly and for good payment, but the insurgents did not harm them, and ... sent them back with the answer that their decision would be made at noon."[71] This was an era when some women were experiencing greater physical and intellectual autonomy through writing and traveling.[72] The intrepid Josephine Pichler persuaded the innkeeper in Lastva to take her and her husband on horse over the border close to Klobuk to Vilusi in Montenegro, but first they had to wait for three ladies from Sarajevo who had taken the last available animals for a pilgrimage.[73] Muslim men tended to travel on Friday after midday because they considered it lucky and "some men allowed their wives to go for a walk on Friday afternoon."[74] Except in times of crisis, routes in Hercegovina were safe for solo women travelers.[75] As one writer for the *Contemporary Review* observed in 1894:

68 "Hohes Alter," *Lavanttaler Bote*, February 29, 1891, 5.
69 Hugo von Martiny, "Wie Mihalcic es erzählte," *Die Quelle: Sonntag- Beiblatt der Reichspost*, May 1, 1932, 18.
70 "Die letzten Kämpfe in der Herzegowina," *Welt Blatt*, September 10, 1882, 2.
71 Gustav Ritter Hubka von Czernczitz, *Geschichte des k. und k. Infanterie-Regiments Graf von Lacy Nr. 22 von seiner Errichtung bis zur Gegenwart* (Zadar: Verlag des Regiments, 1902), 493.
72 Clotilde N. and her friend Maria from Bregenz preferred to travel to Trebinje by day because of rumors that the local population "cut the noses and ears off their enemies"; see Clotilde N., "Erinnerung an Dalmatien," *Vorarlberger Landes-Zeitung*, June 13, 1888, 2.
73 Josephine Pichler, "Quer durch Montenegro: Trebinje- Draga Obrenov Han," *Agramer Zeitung*, December 23, 1905, 19.
74 Andrejka, *Slovenski fantje*, 377.
75 Mary Edith Durham, *Through the Lands of the Serb* (London: Edward Arnold, 1904), 2–3.

A child or maiden might wander safely from Brod to Metkovitch[76] ... in the most desolate wilds of Herzegovina, where extreme poverty and fancied impunity constitute a powerful temptation to crime, life and property are literally and in sober truth considerably more secure than on the streets of London...[77]

Female writers, including Maude Holbach, Milena Preindlsberger-Mrazović, Dora Münch, and Edith Durham tended to be interested in what women in Hercegovina were doing. Their work broke some of the silence regarding the representation of women. The utility of impressions left by travelers usually depended on either the expertise of the writer or the accuracy of the detail. Many of these sources confirm or expand what was written by soldiers, especially as men in uniform were often their main sources of local stories. When Trebinje experienced security crises (or royal visits), reporters arrived on the scene. Vivid articles were produced by journalists and war correspondents, who often wrote anonymously and in the heat of the moment. The articles represent quite a stylistically free genre with a lot of detail: for example, the Viennese writer Alice Schalek was opinionated, but genuinely interested in the detailed insight given by her informants. She was also one of the very few female war correspondents of her era, which gave her "a degree of cultural purchase in the crystallizing heroic narrative."[78] A correspondent for the *Neue Freie Presse*, named only as C. M., sent a remarkable series of cables from the theater of the insurrection against conscription in 1882, most of which appeared in the evening edition of the newspaper.[79]

Memoirs, including several book-length accounts, allow a level of character development that is missing from feuilletons and war reports, as well as a greater chronological range. Some felt it was imperative to record what they were living through. Writing from the

---

76 Towns on the borders of Bosnia and Hercegovina from North to South, approximately.
77 E. B. Lanin [Emile J. Dillon], "Bosnia and Herzegovina," *Contemporary Review* 65 (May 1894): 738.
78 Samuel Foster, *Yugoslavia in the British Imagination: Peace, War and Peasants before Tito* (London: Bloomsbury, 2021), 96.
79 See for example, C. M., "Aus Trebinje," *Neue Freie Presse* (*Abendblatt*), February 24, 1882, 2; C. M., "Die Kämpfe von Korito," *Neue Freie Presse*, February 3, 1882, 9–10.

train in Hum in February 1915, the Carniolan officer Josip Wester wondered if "maybe fate intended for me to write about military events and experiences to preserve them."[80] Military reminiscences were perhaps set down by the authors as justifications for their own role in tumultuous events or, as Jiří Hutečka suggests, through reexperiencing service "in a way that better fits its outcomes."[81] Some regiments had official or semi-official histories commissioned which contain quite a lot of human detail.[82] Other memoirs were written by men who happened to be in the army at an important juncture in their life and wanted to reconnect with the world as it was in 1914. Rereading his own diary accounts of time spent in military service in Trebinje as he prepared to write his memoir *Life and Shape*, the Viennese former soldier Richard Neutra confessed: "(h)alf a century later, I found confused notes, puzzling even to myself, who once penciled them down in little books."[83]

There were years of long summers, good food and company, even idyll before 1914. Reinhard Günste had picnics of "bread, ham, and sparkling water" during one of the many sunny days in 1902.[84] Jovan Dučić shared his happiness with his friend and fellow poet Aleksa Šantić in 1901: "Trebinje is wonderful. On clear nights the Trebišnjica reflecting the poplars in its glassy surface resembles some mystic paintings from Berlin."[85] On rare days off, soldiers would walk around the city. After 1901, they were joined by an increasing number of civilians and tourists. Friedrich Perkonig remembered the scenes vividly: "It is said that Trebinje's market is one of the most remarkable under the sky. It was a market for livestock and pigeons, for fruit from gardens and farmers, for honey, wax, pelts, tools, copperware, earthenware, jars, brandy, vinegar, wine. A good deal could

---

80 Josip Wester. "Dr. Sketova pisma iz Bosne," *Ljubljanski Zvon* 35, no. 3 (1915): 139. Wester (1874–1960), originally from the Carniolan village of Dolenje Radulje, taught and translated Slavonic languages.

81 Hutečka, *Men Under Fire*, 17.

82 See, for example, Rudolf Pfeffer, *Geschichte des k. u. k. Infanterieregiments Freiherr Kray Nr. 67: Erster Band 1860–1910* (Vienna: Im Selbstverlage des Regiments, 1912).

83 Richard Neutra, *Life and Shape* (Los Angeles: Atara Press, 2009), 117.

84 Reinhard Günste [Rifat Gozdović Pascha pseud.], "Schloß Starislano: Eine hercegowinische Spukgeschichte," *Pilsner Tagblatt*, March 3, 1912, 2.

85 Dušan Puvačić, *Balkan Themes: Tradition and Change in Serbian and Croatian Literature* (Paris: Éditions Ésopie, 2013), 42.

be sealed by a steaming bowl of coffee from one of the nearby cafes."[86] Nevertheless, despite the pleasure of reminiscence in many accounts, the politics of national or religious identity and rivalry were never too far from the surface. Most were individuals trying to get along as best they could, rather than bearers of a national ideal; some were burdened by their prejudices, but many showed compassion and decency through their words and actions.

It cannot be denied that the construction of the Habsburg garrison complex around Trebinje involved great personal cost to individuals on all sides, and the comprehensive use of gunpowder and steel. A sense of anger and grief pervades many accounts, whether they were written by soldiers who had lost comrades in fighting (and only later found their bodies),[87] by officers who had been outsmarted by rebels and insurgents, by Orthodox mountaineers who had lost an opportunity for self-rule after centuries of abuses, or by Muslims who had been driven by violence from their settlements and had lost their long connection to the Ottoman Porte. Traveling through Hercegovina toward Montenegro in 1916, one military correspondent wrote: "why even wage war in this land ... when all there is to gain is a few goats and sheep?"[88] But of course, the stakes were very high, and control of the land meant more than just notional ownership for all the people involved.

The narrative in this book only leans very slightly into the 1920s and 1930s and focuses on the fate of a few individuals. This is not because what happened after the Habsburg period was not significant. Mitja Velikonja was undoubtedly right that the events of 1914 were an "ominous harbinger of things to come."[89] What happened to Trebinje in the Second World War and in the 1990s changed it almost beyond recognition, but I have left the task of interpreting these events in more depth to others. Although I write little here

---

86   Retrospectively he compared Trebinje with other markets in Bosnia and Hercegovina, see Josef Friedrich Perkonig, "Markt in Banjaluka," *Völkischer Beobachter*, August 7, 1943, 4.

87   Trebinje-based Captain Sandner recorded that his comrades captured by insurgents had been mutilated with their entrails wrapped around their hands. Reinhard Günste [Rifat Gozdović Pascha pseud.], "Aus einem Feldzugstagebuch," *Pilsner Tagblatt*, May 7, 1911, 3.

88   C. Wirth, "Fahrt durch Montenegro," *Neue Freie Presse*, February 11, 1916, 1.

89   Mitja Velikonja, *Religious Separation and Political Intolerance in Bosnia and Herzegovina* (College Station, TX: Texas A and M Press, 2003), 141.

about the following century of genocide, interethnic rivalry, and suspicion, these later problems were clearly stoked—if not entirely created—by the Habsburg regime, and they did not just evaporate in 1918. While an interpretation of the events of this era does not offer an excuse or justification for later violence (and every individual is responsible for their own actions), it can at least offer some explanations for what went right as well as what went wrong. Writing in the twenty-first century and in a language very different from most of the dramatis personae, there have been occasions when presentism has inevitably crept in. I have also tried to refrain from "taking sides" against one nationality or religion by concentrating on individual agency wherever possible. This is and *should be* a challenging task as Bosnia and Hercegovina remains a divided state which still struggles with the weight of a dozen years of conflict, displacement, and genocide from three major wars during the twentieth century. Although the country has produced exceptionally talented researchers, for many the past is a trauma and the writing of history still often an act of identity affirmation. And so it is for any author.

Dignitarian beliefs inevitably emerge from within the narrative, such as a rejection of torture, mutilation, the clashing cymbals of public humiliation, appropriation of land and cultural capital, national pride, the death penalty, and revenge. Moreover, there is a driving curiosity about the foundations of life upon which we all stand, as well as the often-unacknowledged debt to shepherds, farmers, laborers, women and silent spiritual leaders, doctors, and merchants. I have consciously favored the opinions of those writers whose humanity was not destroyed by the occupation, annexation, and war, such as Fritz Telmann and Richard Neutra. There is often a marked correlation between empathy and detail which also makes writers such as Jernej Andrejka, Alice Schalek, and Moritz Oransz compelling. Among the writers quoted, there were individuals who believed that Habsburg rule should be allowed to work, and that Eastern Hercegovina could flourish with Central European guards, custodians, and rulers. I have also relied on those individuals who were not quite true believers, such as Antonio Budinich, who expressed inward doubt or unease about *Zivilisationswerk* and even the war against Montenegro in 1916.

Rather predictably, modern perspectives might be deemed to be adrift from individuals living between 1878 and 1918, many of whom did see a strong moral imperative in the subjection of the people of Hercegovina, executions, public punishments, and the ideological apparatus that accompanied them. They believed in a form of honor and that they were doing the right thing, and they had their own moral logic. And we must accept that (without necessarily agreeing with it). Karl Novottny, an officer from Vienna with distant Czech roots, evidently had a range of skills, standards, and personal qualities: he was devoted to the monarchy and to the army, as well as being a talented draughtsman and artist, head of both the Trebinje garrison casino and the local military scientific committee.[90] Novottny recorded the 1914 executions of the priest Vidak Parežanin[91] and two women (Anica Vukalović and Andja Ljubibratić) in his memoirs, at pains to emphasize that the executions were "legal and justified" (*"abgeurteilt und justifiziert"*).[92] An older woman, Anica Vukalović, was so feeble by the time of her execution that she had to be carried to the gallows.[93] A career officer of long standing, Novottny would have known that the executions "operated on the margins" of the service regulations (*Dienstreglement*) which did permit the elimination of saboteurs.[94] Both older women were denounced by neighbors for careless talk and were not actively involved in physical sabotage (as far as the authorities were aware). A sense of ultimate virtue limited Novottny's capacity to atone even years later, and he remained faithful to the vanquished state that he had served so loyally and to his own vision of virtue and honor.

90 FMLt Kutzlnigg, "Festungskommandobefehl Nr. 20, Trebinje am 28. Feber 1917," NL Karl Novottny AT-OeStA/KA NL 417: 12, Kriegsarchiv, Vienna.
91 Vidak Parežanin (1867–1914) was arrested for possession of gunpowder. Initially sentenced to four months in prison, he was given the death sentence on the direct order of Rudolf Braun. See Parežanin, *Die Attentäter*, 144.
92 Karl Novottny, "Erinnerungen aus meinem Leben während der Zeit von 1868–1918," NL Karl Novottny AT-OeStA/KA NL 417: 12, Kriegsarchiv, Vienna, 21, 26.
93 Vladimir J. Popović, *Patnje i žrtve Srba sreza trebinjskoga 1914–1918* (Trebinje na Vidovdan, 1929), 23.
94 Jonathan E. Gumz, *The Resurrection and Collapse of Empire in Habsburg Serbia, 1914–1918* (Cambridge: Cambridge University Press, 2009), 40.

Mountains, Settlements, and the Trebišnjica

Landscapes, peoples, and political events are perpetually intertwined. To understand the strategic importance of the Trebinje garrison complex, one should probably first consider the land itself.[95] Hercegovina is mountainous and thinly populated with long stretches between its green urban centers. Mostar is some eighty miles by road from Trebinje (but a little nearer as the crow flies) and was a considerable journey by horse or on foot until the train line was extended in 1901. Sarajevo is about one hundred and thirty miles from Trebinje, but again the roads were largely mountainous and travel necessarily slow. The ancient city of Dubrovnik is much closer, at just over twenty miles, but had been part of a different state for many centuries by 1878 and was only connected to Trebinje by a good road ten years earlier. Despite its remoteness from regional centers of power, Trebinje was still considered important. In 1876, the French writer and explorer Charles Yriarte assessed its military significance: "taking control in Trebinje, means controlling the whole of southern Hercegovina."[96] Carniolan officer Jernej Andrejka was also struck by the strategic position of the city, describing it as being like "a rivet in wood between Montenegro and Dalmatia."[97]

Known in the early Middle Ages as Travunia, human activity can be traced back at least 25,000 years in the region:[98] in 1954, a Paleolithic site was discovered at Crvena stijena on the banks of the river Trebišnjica. Nestling in a fertile valley surrounded by limestone karst, Trebinje's climate is transitionally Mediterranean with hot, dry summers and mild winters.[99] Initially restricted to the settlement around the Ottoman-era fortress, the city expanded onto the other side of the Trebišnjica river after the arrival of the Habsburg soldiers. Trebinje's population was both Muslim and Christian, with local numbers

95 The potential of so much virgin forest with a wide range of species was very quickly realized; see, for example, "Die Wälder der Herzegowina," *Grazer Volksblatt*, November 13, 1878, 6–7.
96 Charles Yriarte, *Bosnie et Herzégovine: Souvenirs de voyage pendant l'insurrection* (Paris: Plon, 1876), 265.
97 "kakor zagvozda v lesu, med Črnogoro in Dalmacijo," Andrejka, *Slovenski fantje*, 205.
98 Ante Figurić, *Trebinje nekada i danas* (Ljubljana: Tiskarna Slovenija, 1930), 12–13.
99 Georg V. Daneš, *Bevölkerungsdichtigkeit der Herzegovina* (Prague: E. Leschinger, 1903), 24.

inevitably augmented by professional soldiers as well as small numbers of itinerant traders. Trebinje lies in the shadow of the gray mountain of Leotar: the Adriatic is visible from the mountain peak, and it formed an "imposing" backdrop to the city and river.[100] The land around had many markers of ancient settlement including paths, cottages, watermills, fields, and tombstones.

There are many descriptions before 1878 which give us an insight into life in the Trebinje citadel prior to the Habsburg occupation. In 1858, Franz von Werner had traveled to the green "oasis" of the Trebišnjica, where he found a fortified city inhabited by "three thousand Muslims." Werner was less impressed with the "rocky, dirty" outskirts of Trebinje and the non-military settlement (*palanka*).[101] In 1864, an officer who had met up with the Habsburg Consul Vuk Vrčević in his centrally located residence found plenty to comment on in Trebinje's market: "heaps of golden tobacco," decorative silver coins, as well as the severed heads of sheep around the butcher's stall and a pack of hungry stray dogs.[102] In William Stillman's vivid account of the 1875 Uprising, he described seeing Trebinje from a distance: "its grey houses shining in the sun, and the river gleaming in sudden turns here and there."[103] Accounts published around the time of the Uprising generally emphasized the dilapidated state of the garrison in these unstable years. In his somewhat reluctant "trudge" to Trebinje, published first in the *Pall Mall Gazette* in late 1875, Edward Freeman described "dark, dingy, narrow streets, the dim arches and vaults, the bazaar, with the Turk ... squatting in his shop, the gate

[100] Milena Preindlsberger-Mrazović, *Bosnisches Skizzenbuch: Landschafts und Kultur Bilder aus Bosnien und der Hercegovina* (Dresden: Pierson, 1900), 327.

[101] Franz von Werner [Murad Efendi, pseud.), *Türkische Skizzen* (Leipzig: Dürr, 1877), 149. Werner, a Habsburg subject, had converted to Islam just before this time, so also wrote as Murad Efendi.

[102] "Von Ragusa nach Trebinje," *Jagd-Zeitung*, September 30, 1867, 560. This account recalled events three years earlier. Originally from Risan on the coast, Vuk Vrčević (1811–1882) arrived in Trebinje in 1861 to take up the important post of Habsburg Consul. He is one of the most important sources and eyewitnesses of this period.

[103] William J. Stillman, *Herzegovina and the late Uprising: The Causes of the Latter and Remedies* (London: Longmans, Green and Co, 1877), 108; A. Kutschbach, "Erinnerungen eines Mitkämpfers an die Insurrektion in der Herzegowina 1875," *Allgemeiner Tiroler Anzeiger*, January 15, 1909, 4.

with its Arabic inscription, the mosques with their minarets contrasting with the church with its disused campanile."[104]

Because of Trebinje's proximity to the coast, local architectural styles had similarities with the building techniques used on the Adriatic, including distinctive floors, masonry, painted ceilings, cabinets, wooden posts, and beams. As well as utilizing the expertise of Dalmatian stonemasons, the city's Ottoman architecture was also "immersed" in the older traditions of stonemasonry in Hercegovina.[105] Ottoman official Osman-paša Resulbegović made a lasting impact on the structure of the old city (kaštel), which benefited from comprehensive urban improvements in the early eighteenth century, including the construction of a moat (known locally by its Turkish name hendek) close to the old fort (konak). A clock tower (sahat kula) was also built during the eighteenth century.[106] The Orthodox community insisted that the sahat kula had been built upon an old chapel and opposed the later extension of military buildings and facilities on consecrated ground.[107] The Osman-paša Mosque in the center of the old city became a focal point and included an adjacent school, constructed in 1726 via funding provided by Resulbegović.[108] It was from here that the muezzin with his "more or less pleasant voice" called out to the faithful in the morning, at noon, and in the evening.[109] Jernej Andrejka found the sound of the call to prayer had a positive "soothing effect on the nerves."[110] The sound of the muezzin was often remarked upon and sometimes the call to prayer was described as "melancholy."[111] The Trebinje authorities intervened when one of the voices in a play performed by a traveling theater

---

104 Edward A. Freeman, *Sketches from the Subject and Neighbour Lands of Venice* (London: Macmillan, 1881), 270.

105 Ilić, "Revitalisation of k.u.k. fortifications in Trebinje," 55; Isidora Karan, "Trebinje on the Border between East and West: Heritage and Memory of Trebinje Bosnian-Herzegovinian Town," *Revista Bitácora Urbano Territorial* 24, no. 2 (2014): 31–40.

106 Korać, *Trebinje: Istorijski pregled*, vol. 2, part 1, 412.

107 Heiner Grunert, *Glauben im Hinterland: Die Serbisch-Orthodoxen in der habsburgischen Herzegowina 1878–1918* (Göttingen: Vandenhoeck and Ruprecht, 2016), 254–55.

108 Known as the Kastell in German-language sources; Novottny, "Erinnerungen," AT-OeStA/ KA NL 417: 12, Kriegsarchiv, Vienna, 195.

109 Helene Röhrich, "Von Mostar nach Ragusa," *Salzburger Fremden-Zeitung*, February 16, 1901, 4.

110 Andrejka, *Slovenski fantje*, 315.

111 Karl J. Fromm, "Reisen in Bosnien und der Herzegowina," *Die Zeit*, September 1, 1910, 13.

group too closely resembled the muezzin's call to prayer to avoid offending local sensibilities.[112] One of the most beautiful buildings in Trebinje was the Resulbegovića kuća, the home constructed by Osman-paša Resulbegović in the early eighteenth century with family rooms and courtyard.[113] Moving from the Bay of Kotor a few generations earlier, the Resulbegović family was "proud of the brick graves of their great-grandfathers, located on the seashore" and sang "folk songs about beautiful, white-faced Turkish women who came … to Trebinje to pick grapes and walk on dark green meadows on horses decorated with gold."[114]

Water could never be taken for granted, especially in the summer, but also sometimes at other times of the year. Immersion in the river could give people a break from the summer heat.[115] A few miles from Trebinje was the karst spring Oko,[116] which later came to supply the city with drinking water. Oko water had a good reputation: local people said that whoever drank from the spring should also (be able to) consume five kilos of meat a day.[117] The contrast between gray hills and green lowlands around the precious sources of water was embedded in local folklore: "Trebinje has gray rocks, but Bileća has green."[118] In December 1918, British diplomat Harold Temperley described the Trebišnjica river as "an appearing and disappearing stream—at this time the effect was particularly fine because of it and overflowed its banks at certain points," so that it resembled "a series of deep green, pale lakes extending for miles, like a necklace of jade on a dull green string."[119] Another author remembered that the riv-

---

112 "Mahomedanisches," *Die Presse*, April 16, 1891, 3.

113 Korać, *Trebinje: Istorijski pregled*, vol. 2, part 1, 414. There was extensive damage to the Islamic heritage in the city during the early 1990s. A symbol of a powerful local family which had housed an ethnographic collection in the Communist period, the Resulbegovića kuća was destroyed in 1993.

114 Andrejka, *Slovenski fantje*, 317. Like many other Muslim families from Herceg Novi and Risan, the Resulbegović family relocated to Staro Slano and then to Trebinje after 1687.

115 Pichler, "Quer durch Montenegro: Trebinje-Draga Obrenov Han," 17.

116 In the local language, the name of the spring means "eye."

117 Franz Ivanetič, "Allerlei aus Trebinje," *Grazer Volksblatt*, November 25, 1879, 6. Ivanetič (1849–1921) was an army cleric from Carinthia.

118 "Der Volksmund bemerkt ganz richtig 'Trebinje hat graue Felsen, Bilek grüne,'" in Preindlsberger-Mrazović, *Bosnisches Skizzenbuch*, 314.

119 Thomas G. Otte, ed., *An Historian in Peace and War: The Diaries of Harold Temperley* (London: Routledge, 2014), 352.

er's "emerald waves shot out as fast as an arrow."[120] The gray or white color of rocks was due to the limestone element, a predominant feature of the landscape from Istria to Dalmatia, Hercegovina, and Montenegro. Although limestone is a soft, porous rock, its presence delivers a dramatic landscape. Generally referred to as karst by the late nineteenth century, limestone is eroded slowly by water, which creates characteristically craggy, almost jagged moonscapes, caves, subterranean streams, and small sinkholes. Human settlement involved shaping the gray boulders into drystone walls, pathways, cottages, and gravestones. Local people believed in the healing power of the rocks that surrounded them: in Trebinje, the sick were transported through hollow rocks to fortify them.[121]

The Trebišnjica river flows for many miles: its source is found in the mountains at Čemerno and it flows across Hercegovina surfacing with a small tributary called the Ombla, one of the shortest rivers in the world that jets out of the foot of a high cliff close to Gruž. If the Trebišnjica created a natural community of kinship, language, and trade along its banks, it also became a political border which helped to make the area into a rimland. The frontier between Montenegro and Hercegovina was established in Article 28 of the Treaty of Berlin in 1878: "starting at Ilino-brdo to the north of Klobuk, the line descends to the Trebinjcica [sic] towards Grančarevo, which remains to Hercegovina, then ascends the course of that river up to a point one kilometer below its confluence with the Čepelica, and from thence passes by the most direct line to the heights which border the River Trebinjcica [sic]."[122] Although this decision reinforced the importance of a "wet border,"[123] it cut through Hercegovina and

---

120 C. W., "Trebinje: Cultur nach Osten tragen," *Militär-Zeitung*, April 24, 1885, 246.
121 Emilian Lilek, "Familien- und Volksleben in Bosnien und in der Herzegowina," *Österreichische Zeitschrift* für *Volkskunde* 6 (1900): 168. Emilian (or Emilijan) Lilek (1851–1940) came originally from the Slovene speaking village of Zgornja Voličina. He taught in high schools in Sarajevo and Tuzla while carrying outs intricate local historic and ethnographic fieldwork.
122 *The Annual Register: A Review of Public Events at Home and Abroad for the Year 1878* (London: Rivingtons, 1879), 227. In the original quotation, it is spelled Herzegovina. I have added diacritic marks for consistency with the rest of the book.
123 Alice Schalek, "An der montenegrinischen Grenze: Von Bilek nach Lastva," *Neue Freie Presse*, December 15, 1915, 2.

therefore across centuries of overlapping and shared practices.[124] After 1878, some shepherds who had once driven their herds into Montenegro were compensated with new pastures, although many were left with no new land.[125] Furthermore, the Trebišnjica was so easily traversed that it always posed a security issue on both sides. However, local cooperation could work well: the spring at Begovo Korito near Visoka glavica was used by both Montenegrin and Hercegovinian shepherds.[126] Despite gaining recognition for its statehood, the Montenegrin authorities resented some of the stipulations of the Treaty of Berlin which limited their territory and authority.[127]

Weather conditions shaped and sometimes limited life: in 1910, a soldier patrolling near Dubovac fell to his death after being caught in the wind and snow.[128] In the flat basin of Popovo polje, especially close to Zavala, people were very exposed to lightning strikes.[129] In 1886, Blaž Hribar had been killed by lightning close to Lastva.[130] On March 25, 1882, there was a minor earthquake in Trebinje that lasted for five seconds but no serious damage was recorded.[131] Water could also be a hazard. France Žagar, a soldier, drowned in the *hendek* in 1886.[132] Insurgent leader Osman Beg Tanović was reported to have drowned in the Trebišnjica in 1882.[133] When there was a hailstorm, the villagers in Gacko called upon the soul of the last person who drowned to direct the hailstone water into the sea and they each left a gift of bread, salt, and a spoon for the deceased.[134] Jiří Daneš observed that Muslim communities (*Džematen*) in Hercegovina never lacked water as they were concentrated in urban spaces.[135] While

---

124 On the development of the Montenegrin-Hercegovina border, see Grandits, *Herrschaft und Loyalität*, 568–82.
125 Wayne Vucinich, *A Study in Social Survival: The Katun in Bileća Rudine* (Denver, CO: University of Denver, 1975), 69–70.
126 "Heinz," "Das Lager auf der Visoka Glavica," *Militär-Zeitung*, September 18, 1885, 2–5.
127 John D. Treadway, *The Falcon and the Eagle: Montenegro and Austria-Hungary 1908-1914* (West Lafayette, IN: Purdue University Press, 1998), 10.
128 "Soldatentod im Frieden," *Znaimer Wochenblatt*, March 23, 1910, 8.
129 "Tod durch Blitzschlag," *Deutsches Volksblatt*, February 15, 1909, 4.
130 Andrejka, *Slovenski fantje*, 338.
131 "Erdbeben in der Herzegowina," *Innsbrucker Nachrichten*, March 29, 1882, 1092.
132 Andrejka, *Slovenski fantje*, 310.
133 "Vom Insurrektions-Schauplatze: Trebinje 31. Jänner," *Tages-Post*, February 4, 1882, 2.
134 Lilek, "Familien- und Volksleben," 168.
135 "nie an Wasser mangelt," Daneš, *Bevölkerungsdichtigkeit der Hercegovina*, 60.

this may have been true by the time Daneš was conducting his field-work, in July 1876, the "Muslim village" of Plana was set on fire by combined Montenegrin-Hercegovinian forces (without resistance as the villagers were absent because they were procuring water from Bileća).[136] Water management in Hercegovina was particularly important because the summers could bring sixty days without rain.[137] Although water was always in short supply, the garrison network itself required a lot of extra resources.[138] Lack of water remained a real challenge for the new occupiers who immediately built cisterns, one of which was appropriately named after the Emperor Franz Joseph.[139] This problem was exacerbated after 1914 in a war that was defined by water shortages across all fronts. In wartime Bileća, one soldier noted that he habitually went to bed without washing because water was so scarce.[140] Soldiers seemed to have expected privation: Antonio Budinich thought that *despite* the lack of resources, the Habsburg Army was still "first rate."[141]

A harsh wind, known as the *bura* (or *bora* in Habsburg-era sources), whipped though the hills and valleys. Windstorms could last several days and be quite violent, bringing sleet with them.[142] Unpopular with the military, an anonymous officer complained to a newspaper about the "woes of the occupation," namely the *bura*, the illness of his comrades, and his dread of the winter.[143] Another remembered that the *bura* had been so violent at the end of September 1878 that he had clung onto a boulder to avoid being swept away.[144] Weather conditions challenged the imposition of Habsburg struc-

---

136 Vrčević used the term "Turkish" village, the commonplace term for Bosniaks at that time; see "Izvještaji austrijskog Vicekonzula iz Trebinja Vuka Vrčevića 1875-1878. godine," in Arnautović, *Prilozi za istoriju Trebinja*, 56.
137 Ernst Dombrowski, "Ein verlorenes Jagdparadies," *Neues Wiener Tagblatt*, April 5, 1914, 45.
138 Werner Schachinger, *Die Bosniaken kommen: Elitetruppe in der k.u.k. Armee, 1879-1918* (Graz: Stocker, 1994), 53.
139 Eugen v. Rodiczky, "Nevesinje-Trebinje," *Wiener Landwirtschaftliche Zeitung*, September 9, 1907, 1-2.
140 "Der Entsatz bei Bilek: Skizzen aus dem Tagebuche eines Offizieres," *Fremden-Blatt*, April 23, 1915, 6.
141 Budini, *Le memorie di guerra*, 257.
142 Ivanetič, "Allerlei aus Trebinje," 5.
143 "Die Leiden der Okkupation," *Welt Blatt*, November 23, 1878, 5.
144 "Die Eroberung von Klobuk," *Morgen-Post*, October 16, 1878, 1.

tures which always remained dependent on local cooperation:[145] in March 1888, storms and freezing temperatures meant that the post was not delivered to Trebinje as usual.[146] Postal official Reinhold Oeser recalled how the telegraph lines were damaged by lightning in February 1894.[147] Winter could also bring snow which remained on Mount Orjen sometimes until May.[148] Dense fog also settled on the higher mountains for months. For Hercegovina, the normal temperature range was quite marked, from 40 degrees in the summer to –32 degrees in the winter (although it rarely went below –10 degrees in areas close to the coast).[149]

Much of Hercegovina is characterized by flat "fields" or *polja* (sing. *polje*) which often flood and have notably more fertile soil than the uplands. Gacko lies in the so-called Gatačko polje (Gacko field). The rivers Gračanica and Mušnica cross the polje subterraneously,[150] only rarely surfacing; like other parts of Hercegovina, this was a changeable landscape. In 1915, the Mušnica was swollen by "endless rain."[151] From Gacko en route to Bileća via Plana, a small settlement of wooden garrison buildings at Avtovac was established close to "uninterrupted primeval forests" that appeared to mark the end of the limestone karst.[152] It was also a whisker away from the Montenegrin border. Dalmatian officer Antonio Budinich was informed by his adjutant Mario that Plana "was a very exposed and dangerous place" and not somewhere he would want to be posted.[153] Years earlier, Daniel Salis-Soglio, a military engineer from the Swiss town of Chur, was

145 Wolfgang Göderle, "The Habsburg Anthropocene: Vipers and Mongooses in Late Habsburg Southern Dalmatia," *Südost-Forschungen* 79, no. 1 (2020): 233.
146 "Frühe Gewitter," *Steyrer Zeitung*, March 18, 1888, 4.
147 Reinhold Oeser, "Die Blitzsicherung der Militär-Telephonanlage in Trebinje," *Mitteilungen über Gegenstände des Artillerie- und Geniewesens*, 1894, 549.
148 Eduard von Kählig, "Eine Erinnerung an die Bekämpfung des Aufstandes in der Herzegowina 1882," *Danzers Armee-Zeitung*, February 21, 1907, 2.
149 H. Rebel, "Studien über die Lepidopterenfauna der Balkanländer. II. Teil. Bosnien und Herzegowina," *Annalen des Naturhistorischen Museums in Wien* 19, nos. 2-3 (1904): 103.
150 Moritz [Moriz] Hoernes, "Bosnische Gebirgsübergänge," *Zeitschrift des deutschen und österreichischen Alpenvereins* 7 (1881): 125-39.
151 Alice Schalek, "An der montenegrinischen Grenze," *Neue Freie Presse*, November 14, 1915, 2.
152 "ununterbrochene Urwälder" in "Das Barackenlager in Aftovac bei Gacko," *Neue Illustrirte Zeitung*, February 19, 1882, 327.
153 Budini, *Le memorie di guerra*, 78.

warned about the insurgents led by Stojan Kovačević and advised only traveling to Plana with a loaded gun.[154]

Bileća was already an old Ottoman trading center when the Habsburg troops arrived. After 1878, it grew as a border town with a garrison reinforced by bunkers and minor fortifications: soldiers soon outnumbered the civilian population. For military and strategic purposes, Bileća was closely linked to the Trebinje garrison complex. Described as "stony," with "poor fields and tree cover," Karl Went attributed the lack of agricultural development to its frontier position and to years of tensions between Orthodox and Muslim populations, when nobody had "the courage to cultivate the land because a harvest and a reward for hard sweat could not be counted upon."[155] Even more than a decade after the arrival of Habsburg troops, Conrad Hochbichler complained bitterly about the terrain: "From Bileća there was hardly a useable path, let alone a road. We had to be content with the Ottoman-era mule tracks.... Water was also just as unimaginable in this area as in the desert. A single cistern ... offered us a much longed-for resting place."[156] South of Bileća was the small village of Čepelica, used by the military as a rest point, which had a waterwheel and a few dwellings. Close to the Montenegrin border and the towns of Velimlje and Nikšić, Bileća increased in importance after 1878, partly because of the partial destruction of the fortress at Klobuk, which stood above the village of Aranđelovo and the Sušica river in an area known historically as Vrm or Korjenići. After the Peace of Karlowitz in 1699, when the Ottomans lost the coastal towns of Herceg Novi and Risan, some Muslims moved to the area, which was predominantly Orthodox at that time.

Moving toward the coast, the terrain became even more hilly. Orjen is a mountain range visible from Trebinje with several high peaks including Veliki kabao and Vučji zub. Despite having some of the highest rainfall in Europe, it remained dry because of the porosity of the limestone. Beyond Orjen lay the garrison towns of Kotor

---

154 Daniel Freiherr von Salis-Soglio, *Mein Leben und was ich davon erzählen will, kann und darf*, vol. 2 (Stuttgart/Leipzig: Deutsche Verlags-Anstalt, 1908), 149.

155 Karl Went von Römö, "Aus dem südöstlichen Theile des Occupationsgebietes," *Österreichisch-ungarische Revue* 17 (1894–95): 22.

156 Conrad Hochbichler, "Aus den schwarzen Bergen I," *Ischler Wochenblatt*, April 27, 1890, 2.

and Herceg Novi, which were key to the military and naval defense of Habsburg Dalmatia. A small sliver of land around Sutorina, historically part of the Ottoman Empire, extended the territory and political life of Hercegovina to the coast.[157] The Sutorina river, which ran into the sea close to Igalo, and nearby small settlements including Kruševice and Lučići were administered from Hercegovina until the end of the Habsburg Monarchy due to the retention of land which had given the Ottoman state continued access to the sea. The Sutorina valley was a key route that connected Hercegovina with the Adriatic and Dalmatia: it was described in 1876 as "a valley with a magnificent range of hills on either side. Their rugged sides and stony precipices made a sombre contrast to the bright valley ... with its olive woods and vineyards through which ran a little river running over its rocky bed..."[158] The micro-region of Krivošije, above Risan, consisting of small settlements and steep mountain paths, was described as being "without a ... tree or larger shrub."[159] Nestling within one of the finest natural fjords in the world, the bay known as Boka Kotorska had a mixed Orthodox and Catholic population: its Muslim population had largely departed for Hercegovina in the late seventeenth century. Dotted with paths, serpentines, forts, and watchtowers, it was described by one soldier as a "great citadel" on the edge of the Empire.[160] Boka Kotorska had garrisons at Herceg Novi, Kotor, and Crkvice, as well as on the island of Mamula. Many of the field exercises carried out by the Trebinje garrison officers took their men into harsh, steep rocky places but also gave them longed-for glimpses of the sea.[161]

West of Mount Orjen was a rocky area known as Zubci (sometimes spelled Zupci), where the hills were as jagged as teeth, as the name implies. Reputed to be the poorest district in Hercegovina,[162] it constituted a "sharp wedge" between Krivošije, Montenegro, and

---

157 Galib Šljivo, *Klek i Sutorina u međunarodnim odnosima 1815–1878* (Belgrade: Filozofski fakultet, 1977).
158 "A Lady Visit to the Herzegovinian Insurgents," *New York Times*, July 23, 1876, 4.
159 Pichler, "Quer durch Montenegro: Trebinje-Draga Obrenov Han," 19.
160 Hubka, *Geschichte des k. und k. Infanterie-Regiments*, 480.
161 H. H., "Der Übergang über den Orien," *Die Vedette*, May 3, 1882, 3.
162 "Durch die Zubcsi und Suttorina II," *Pester Lloyd*, March 12, 1882, 2.

FIGURE 4. A view of the Montenegrin border including Klobuk drawn by Karl Novottny. Kriegsarchiv Vienna, Austrian State Archives.

coastal Dalmatia.[163] Across Hercegovina populations moved frequently with trades or animals, but according to the Bohemian scholar Jiří Daneš,[164] the upper slopes of Orjen were only visited in summer by shepherds from the immediate locality, which may account for the even greater endurance of tradition, family loyalty, and resistance to the state among the local families. Although difficult land to farm, Bijela gora on the northern slopes of Orjen was praised for the quality and size of its potatoes, which were reputed to taste "like honey."[165] With their unusual rock formations, fauna, and narrow valleys, the regions between Hercegovina and Montenegro were of enduring interest to ethnologists, geologists, and botanists.[166]

Toward the border with Montenegro was the small, green, and fertile settlement of Lastva. After 1878, its importance increased not

---

163 "ein spitzer Keil," Preindlsberger-Mrazović, *Bosnisches Skizzenbuch*, 332. Jernej Andrejka believed that insurgency was linked to poverty and long-standing instability; see *Slovenski fantje*, 337.

164 Daneš, *Bevölkerungsdichtigkeit der Hercegovina*, 38.

165 Andrejka, *Slovenski fantje*, 337.

166 Gejza von Bukowski, "Beitrag zur Geologie der Landschaften Korjenici und Klobuk in der Hercegovina," *Jahrbuch der Kaiserlich-Königlichen Geologischen Reichsanstalt* 51 (1901): 159–69.

only as an exposed military outpost, but also as a model agricultural settlement. Turning toward Trebinje was the village of Most or Arslanagić most and the Ottoman-era bridge (*Arslanagića ćuprija*)[167] which spanned the Trebišnjica, which was relatively deep at that point. Built by artisans employed by Hajdar-beg Kusturica under the direction of Mehmed-paša Sokolović[168] and finished in 1574,[169] the bridge was staffed by local families and used to transport salt from Herceg Novi via Zubci to the rest of Hercegovina.[170] The bridge was about an hour's walk from Trebinje.[171] In 1879, Franz Ivanetič described it as a simple guardhouse built from beautiful ashlar stone (*Quadersteinen*).[172] The old guardhouse in the center of the bridge was demolished during the Habsburg occupation.[173] Frances Hutchinson found the design of the bridge both practical and elegant: "a curious round fort loop-holed for musket-fire stands at each end ... and the river twists in serpentine curves through the richly cultivated valley."[174]

In the rural areas around Trebinje there were small settlements, rarely with more than "one hundred souls"[175] and often consisting of extended families living in humble dwellings that seemed to blend into the landscape in "troglodyte settlements,"[176] or poked out "like swallows' nests" from the gray hills.[177] Multigenerational families lived in small, thatched cottages with goats, pigs, and hens within

---

167 Milan Gojković, "Arslanagića most kod Trebinja," *Zbornik zaštite spomenika*, no. 14 (1963): 21–38. The Arslanagić bridge was moved brick by brick in the 1960s, and not dynamited during the 1990s war.
168 Mehmed-paša Sokolović (1506–1579) was an Ottoman statesman who had been born to an Orthodox family in Rudo. During his time as Grand Vizier, there was extensive building in Bosnia and Hercegovina.
169 Hamdija Arslanagić and Adem Arslanagić, *Arslanagići i Arslanagića most* (Sarajevo: Maore, 1998), 18.
170 Andrejka, *Slovenski fantje*, 333.
171 Stevan R. Delić, "Ćuprija na Mostu," *Glasnik Zemaljskog muzeja u Bosni i Hercegovini*, April 1, 1891, 116. Delić (1865–1927) was a teacher and historian.
172 Ivanetič, "Allerlei aus Trebinje," 5–6.
173 Raimund Stillfried von Rathenitz photographed the bridge in 1890, and the guardhouse was still intact, although the bridge itself was rather overgrown and mossy; see his "Arslan-Agic Most," online at the Photographic Archive of the Albertina Museum, Albertinaplatz 1, 1010 Vienna.
174 Frances Kinsley Hutchinson, *Motoring in the Balkans: Along the Highways of Dalmatia, Montenegro, the Herzegovina and Bosnia* (Chicago: A. C. McClurg, 1909).
175 Daneš, *Bevölkerungsdichtigkeit der Hercegovina*, 29.
176 "Die Gährung in der Herzegovina," *Pester Lloyd*, December 18, 1881, 2.
177 "Erinnerungen au dem Wanderleben," *Wiener Salonblatt*, July 19, 1902, 17.

FIGURE 5. Arslanagić most across the Trebišnjica river, photograph from the early twentieth century. Muzej Hercegovine, Trebinje.

the homestead.[178] South of Trebinje, the settlement of Gluva Smokva was of strategic importance not least because of its proximity to the road: "the mountainous world changes into plains and a forest begins, which is mostly covered with low oaks, piles of crumbling stones, and here and there a larger tree, and along the limestone valleys carefully fenced fields planted with tobacco."[179] The fort beside Staro Slano, a settlement that was once home to the Resulbegović family,[180] was already a "poetic" ruin by 1878.[181] From the hill at Crkvina close to Trebinje there is a view of the long and flat Popovo polje.[182] The landscape and the water table have changed primarily because the Trebišnjica was dammed in the 1960s and concrete used to fill in the limestone cavities. Prior to 1967, when water drained from Popovo polje, it made a tremendous thundering noise that could

---

178 F. von M., "Auf Cordon," *Wiener Abendpost*, March 4, 1887, 3.
179 Andrejka, *Slovenski fantje*, 314.
180 Korać, *Trebinje: Istorijski pregled*, vol. 2, part 1, 221.
181 Preindlsberger-Mrazović, *Bosnisches Skizzenbuch*, 328.
182 Isidora Karan, "The Significance of the Topographic Element of Hill in the Modern Urban Context: Crkvina and Jablanica," *SPATIUM International Review* 31 (July 2014): 7–13.

be heard half an hour away. There were no individual claims for fishing rights, so using specially woven baskets, people rushed to catch the fish before all the water was gone.[183] Popovo polje generally flooded in May and again in October, which created lush ground upon which to cultivate maize. Local people had to adapt to opportunities as best they could.[184] In the fall and spring, they would put their ear to the ground close to the karst holes and listen for the rush of the water. Warning their neighbors that the water surge was imminent, people would salvage what they could and lead their cattle to elevated ground.[185] Settlements around Popovo polje were higher up, away from the extended water table, generally positioned around the edge of the valley. Beyond Popovo polje were the ancient towns of Stolac and Ljubinje.

Although the city was under Ottoman control after 1482, Trebinje always remained close to the world of the Adriatic, via the Sutorina river valley, and coastal markets which could be reached by mule. In 1868, a new road was built which connected Trebinje to Dubrovnik,[186] commended by Ludwig Passarge in 1904 for being "dead straight."[187] There had been a frontier post at Drijen (Drieno) which was wound down after the departure of Ottoman troops. When the entomologist Maximilian Hopffgarten went there just two years later in 1880, he found that "an innkeeper and his family live in a tiny, extremely primitive stone house that can hardly be distinguished from the surrounding rocks. You can get very good coffee, wine, and something to eat there."[188] Dalmatia had large rural and unlettered populations

---

183 C. H. Waldmann, "Ein lockendes Reiseziel für Naturfreunde: Nach Erinnerungen ausgezeichnet," *Salzburger Wacht*, July 9, 1930, 7.

184 Guillaume Capus, *A travers la Bosnie et l'Herzégovine: Études et impressions de voyage* (Paris: Librairie Hachette, 1896), 342. Ivo Lučić, "Povijest poznavanja Dinarskog krša na primjeru Popova polja" (Ph.D. diss., Nova Gorica University, 2009), 395.

185 D. G., "Die Eröffnung der neuen herceg-dalmatinischen Eisenbahn," *Agramer Zeitung*, July 16, 1901, 5.

186 Planskizze von Trebinje, January 3, 1870, AT-OeStA/KA KPS GPA Inland C VII 2 Trebinje, Kriegsarchiv, Vienna.

187 "schnurgerade," in Ludwig Passarge, *Dalmatien und Montenegro: Reise- und Kulturbilder* (Leipzig: B. Elischer Nachfolger, 1904), 277.

188 M. von Hopffgarten, "Bericht über eine entomologische Reise nach Dalmatien, der Herzegowina und Montenegro im Jahre 1880," *Entomologische Nachrichten* 6 (1880): 124–25. Georg Maximilian von Hopffgarten (1825–1904) was a distinguished entomologist who traveled widely in the region after 1878.

who retained deep links to Hercegovina through market trade, pilgrimage, language, and family ties. By 1878, Dubrovnik had been under Habsburg control for decades, losing its independence after the era of the Ragusan Republic. Nevertheless, it retained much of its Renaissance-era learning and education. Often referred to still as Ragusa at this time, the small walled city was the revered "pearl" of the Adriatic,[189] a "southern garden" lauded for its climate and landscapes.[190] The botanic garden at Trsteno was one of the oldest in the world, home to an increasing number of non-domestic species. Overlooking Dubrovnik was a military fort built during the Napoleonic era in a settlement called Srdj, from which it was possible to see for miles across the region. Beside old Dubrovnik was the port of Gruž, perhaps one of the best natural ports in the Adriatic (often referred to as Gravosa), a point of arrival for Habsburg troops, famed for its festive social gatherings with local dignitaries,[191] and for the barrels of wine they consumed.[192] For the inhabitants of the hinterland, the coast was also part of their route away from home. Frederick Jackson witnessed "large numbers" of migrating villagers from Hercegovina in Gruž:

...what a strange sight the pier presented, so thickly packed with people that one wondered none were pushed off. The variety of colour and picturesqueness of costume and type among the men and women was interesting, and it was touching to think of the sundering of friends and relations, and the grief at parting which many of them showed in their strongly marked countenances.[193]

---

189 Heinrich Renner, *Durch Bosnien und die Hercegovina kreuz und quer* (Berlin: D. Reimer, 1897), 374.
190 Andreas Dillinger, "Ragusa," *Dillingers Reise- und Fremdenzeitung*, March 10, 1897, 3. See also Bojan Baskar, "Southbound, to the Austrian Riviera: The Habsburg Patronage of Tourism in the Eastern Adriatic," *Anthropological Notebooks* 16, no. 1 (2010): 9–22.
191 In May 1883, Aglae St John accompanied her husband Charles to a party at a villa with frescos beside the Ombla held by Habsburg officers, "Journal Intime d'une Femme Roumaine: Première Partie," online at University of Victoria Special Collections and University Archives, British Columbia, Canada, 17–18.
192 AT-OeStA/KA BS Fronten Montenegro, 536; Hafen, Gravosa, Kriegsarchiv, Vienna.
193 Frederick Hamilton Jackson, *The Shores of the Adriatic, the Austrian side, the Küstenlande, Istria, and Dalmatia... Fully Illustrated with Plans, Drawings, by the Author, and Photographs Taken Specially for This Work* (London: J. Murray, 1908), 334. Jackson (1848–1923) was a London-born painter and travel writer.

Despite the dry land and lack of topsoil, karst botany was varied. Thyme, sage, rosemary, and lavender grew as well as the blue karst thistles. Although deforestation had taken place, perhaps because of centuries of pasturing animals,[194] and taking wood for construction, Hercegovina still had hundred-year-old beech,[195] black pine, birch, silver fir, spruce, maple, and oak trees,[196] as well as "magnificent pomegranates."[197] Volker Pachauer and Filip Suchoń have established that the "greening" of Trebinje during the Habsburg era also included variable attempts to plant traditional hedgerow plants, which develop well in areas over four hundred meters above sea level, including wild roses, blackberries, blackthorns (sloes), and garland thorns.[198] Contemporaries also noted that "dense, tenacious" thorns offered some defensive cover.[199]

Across Hercegovina, there was a wide variety of animals, although they were often well hidden.[200] The caves around Popovo polje contained myriad species of beetles and a rare underwater vertebrate, *čovječja ribica*. Wolves (*vukovi*) were the material of legend, the component of numerous personal names, but also an everyday menace. Driven toward human settlements because of hunger, wolves sometimes hunted in packs of six or eight. Local people believed that a she-wolf brought luck to a young stallion if she lived near the stable.[201] One soldier related a tale about the isolated wooden huts in the hills of Viduša where a woman had taken shelter: "more courageously than many a man," she tackled a wolf that got into the sheep pen. She had heard the cries of the sheep and armed with an axe, killed the wolf, despite being bitten badly on the hand in the pro-

---

194 Djoko Jelić, Matjaž Jeršić, Jože Lojk, and Metod Vojvoda, "The Cadastrian Commune of Trebijovi in the Karstland of Hercegovina," *Geographia Polonica* 5 (1965): 267–84.

195 Andrejka, *Slovenski fantje*, 342.

196 Rebel, "Studien über die Lepidopterenfauna der Balkanländer," 105–7.

197 Reinhard E. Petermann, "Mit der Eisenbahn in die Bocche di Cattaro," *Neues Wiener Tagblatt*, July 16, 1901, 2.

198 Volker Pachauer and Filip Suchoń, "Typy zieleni i elementy wodne w przestrzeni dawnego miasta-twierdzy Trebinje/Types of greenery and water features in the space of the former fortress-city of Trebinje," *Środowisko Mieszkaniowe*, no. 24 (2018): 86.

199 "Die Manöver in Süddalmatien," *Danzers Armee-Zeitung*, September 20, 1906, 9.

200 Hopffgarten, "Bericht über eine entomologische Reise," 124.

201 Lilek, "Familien- und Volksleben," 169.

cess. She carried the wolf into Bileća on her shoulders the following day.[202] Both wolves and bears had died out in many parts of central Europe by 1878 and ordinary soldiers had lost any knowledge of how to deal with them. In the winter of 1881, a Muslim man who had killed a bear was given a small financial reward by the local garrison commander in Hercegovina.[203] Carniolan soldier Matija Kump decided to poison offal and killed off the wolves in Visoka glavica that dared to come close to the fort.[204] Foxes and foxholes were also numerous,[205] and while dogs were reported to be relatively rare in this part of Hercegovina, cats were plentiful.[206] The presence of so many soldiers after 1878 also increased the number of dogs who usually accompanied guards on the frontier. Guard dogs could provide companionship and security or even distraction. Conrad von Hötzendorf spent a restless night in Trebinje garrison in the room of Captain Lycskowski, together with a hunting dog and a wolf pup that his roommate was caring for.[207] Dogs could also be a secret weapon of the enemy and could pine inconsolably if their trainers were killed.[208] Jernej Andrejka related how his dog Marko made so much noise that the *"hajduks"* were able to escape back across the Montenegrin border on St. George's Eve in 1888.[209]

Sheep, mules, deer, and chamois goats were the most significant animal populations in Hercegovina, and they became a symbol of a fading bucolic age. The introduction of the motorcar just before the First World War allowed incomers and visitors to speed past local people tending their flocks.[210] Robert Michel recalled his first

202 F. von M., "Die Culturarbeit der österreichischen Armee (Hercegovina) II," *Wiener Zeitung*, June 11, 1886, 3.
203 The detailed news update was sent from Trebinje, "Aus der Herzegowina," *Neue Freie Presse (Abendblatt)*, February 9, 1882, 2.
204 Andrejka, *Slovenski fantje*, 346.
205 Conrad Hochbichler, "Aus den schwarzen Bergen II," *Ischler Wochenblatt*, May 4, 1890, 1.
206 Vera Stenzel, "In der südlichen Herzegowina: Erinnerung aus Österreich," *Arbeiter Zeitung*, August 18, 1928, 6.
207 Franz Conrad von Hötzendorf, *Mein Anfang: Kriegserinnerungen aus der Jugendzeit 1878–1882* (Berlin: Verlag für Kulturpolitik, 1925), 140.
208 A. Sch., "Vor fünfzehn Jahren: Aus dem Tagebuch eines Kriegsteilnehmers," *Danzers Armee Zeitung*, March 11, 1932, 5–6.
209 Andrejka, *Slovenski fantje*, 328.
210 Alice Schalek, "An der montenegrinischen Grenze: Ein Idyll," *Neue Freie Presse*, December 23, 1915, 1.

ever car journey overland from Nevesinje to Dubrovnik via Trebinje and the shepherdess who was quite unprepared to face traffic with her sheep on the road.[211] Horses were less useful in combat in Hercegovina than elsewhere, although their utility was also declining rapidly by 1914 as they competed with motorized vehicles. In 1878, the Habsburg forces had felt hampered by the lack of water for their horses.[212] In 1887, Jernej Andrejka lost a precious horse in a blizzard, as well as one of his men, Janez Kudlek.[213] Antonio Budinich lost a good horse from heatstroke and exhaustion during the war.[214] His account of it, retold in detail and with sadness in his memoirs, confirms Yuval Noah Harari's hypothesis that "the horse was an extension of part of his master's identity, and deserved a place both in his life story and in history."[215] Knowing the challenges, local breeders tended to prefer mules or smaller hardier varieties of horse because they needed less water.[216] In the 1880s, there was a mule breeding center in Trebinje.[217] Frederick Jackson remembered at the Dalmatian port of Ploče the "late Renaissance fountain, at which country people, most of whom are Herzegovinians, may be seen watering their mules, for the road to Trebinje comes down to this gate."[218]

With its formally Ottoman garrisons, gray or green landscapes and small settlements Hercegovina offered a challenge to any regime, but also opened up a great opportunity to apply the skills that the expanding education system had given to the population of the Habsburg Monarchy. Writing in 1878, civil engineer Andreas Knobloch recognized that Bosnia and Hercegovina was "prodigally endowed with treasures of every kind, with fertile soil, cattle, wood, minerals, waterpower as well as unparalleled scenic attractions."[219] Success often depended on adaptation or wise imitation of local peo-

---

211 Robert Michel, "Meine erste Fahr im Auto," *Der Abend*, December 13, 1930, 10.
212 László Bencze, *The Occupation of Bosnia and Herzegovina in 1878* (New York: Columbia University Press, 2005), 95. On the problems of using military horses in this region, see also "Die Schwere Feldbatterie in der Hercegovina 1878," *Die Vedette*, July 3, 1889, 3–5.
213 Andrejka, *Slovenski fantje*, 335–40.
214 Budini, *Le memorie di guerra*, 152.
215 Harari, *Renaissance Military Memoirs*, 147.
216 Jelić et al, "The Cadastrian Commune of Trebijovi," 267–84.
217 "Maulthierzucht in der Herzegowina," *Wiener Landwirtschaftliche Zeitung*, July 28, 1888, 5.
218 Jackson, *The Shores of the Adriatic*, 334.
219 Okey, *Taming Balkan Nationalism*, 17.

ple. Confident despite many setbacks, Habsburg soldiers often wrote as if they had arrived in a place they already knew. Four thousand Habsburg subjects were permanently resident in Bosnia and Hercegovina before 1878,[220] so this was not completely unknown territory for the emperor's subjects: one writer compared the landscape to the more familiar limestone karst in Istria (which had been under Habsburg control for generations).[221] And the kindred spirit between South Slavs made the new regime's position seem even more providential. Nevertheless, life in Hercegovina always depended on an intricate balance and it was not easy to just pitch up and thrive.

Catholics, Muslims, and Orthodox

Hercegovina, also known as Hum,[222] was conquered by the Ottomans in the late Middle Ages. Already on the fault line between Orthodoxy and Catholicism before the fifteenth century, many of the region's ancient churches and monasteries were converted into mosques or sometimes left deserted.[223] Local people converted to Islam especially in the early years of Ottoman rule and the new faith brought mosques, religious schools (*medresse*), courtyards, as well as fortresses (*kule*) which were built everywhere adding to medieval foundations. In Hercegovina, where the population was sparse, some were poor peasants (*kmetovi*) working on *čitluk* estates as tithe laborers.[224] Ottoman subjects were organized by religion (*millet*), reinforcing divisions between landowners (*begovi*), the army (*spahija*) and civil servants, and the common people, referred to as *rayah*.[225] Spared from

---

220 Grandits, *End of Ottoman Rule*, 65.

221 "Eine überfallene Patrouille," *Die Presse*, May 17, 1888, 1.

222 There was also a small town called Hum that was connected to Trebinje via the railway after 1901.

223 John V. A. Fine, "The Medieval and Ottoman Roots of Modern Bosnian Society," in *The Muslims of Bosnia-Herzegovina: Their Historic Development from the Middle Ages to the Dissolution of Yugoslavia*, ed. Mark Pinson (Cambridge, MA: Harvard University Press, 1996), 13.

224 From the Turkish word *çiftlik*, which is sometimes also spelled as *čitluk* in Bosnia and Hercegovina.

225 Also sometimes spelled reaya, raja, etc. On landholding after the Habsburg takeover, see Husnija Kamberović, *Begovski Zemljišni posjedi u Bosni i Hercegovini od 1878. do 1918. godine* (Zagreb: Hrvatski institut za povijest, 2003).

many taxes, Muslims became staunch defenders of the Empire, al-though many of their number remained very poor.

Despite enduring historical divisions between religions and the harsh reality of exclusion from privilege and political autonomy, local people in Hercegovina were unified in many ways, not least by a shared language.[226] Local Gurbeti or Roma are likely to have been Muslim. Christian and Muslim traditions still overlapped and coex-isted in the Habsburg era in ways that surprised and intrigued in-comers. North of Bileća and Plana, in the Gatačko polje, there were a greater number of Muslim villages than around Trebinje and prac-tices associated with the agricultural year were often shared, accord-ing to Emil Lilek writing in 1900.[227] Pilgrimage remained an inte-gral part of life in the Habsburg period for the Orthodox, Muslims, and Catholics alike. If anything, piety and public manifestations of faith may have become more popular after 1878 because the price of transport reduced as the infrastructure improved.[228] People from Hercegovina traveled down to Kotor on Shrove Tuesday (*kurent*) to attend the Corn Festival and Carnival.[229] There was "joyful singing" at Ostrog in 1882, in the monastery where the miraculous relics of St. Vasilije were housed: "people of both sexes came not only from Montenegro, but also from Boka Kotorska ... [and] Herzegovina."[230] The annual religious festivals also brought people together. Accord-ing to Jernej Andrejka, Ramadan (*Ramazan*), which he compared to Lent, was strictly observed by Muslims:

> All day long, everyone must fast, and only in the evening after prayers is eating and drinking permitted. During the day, ev-erything is dead in the cities and villages, but when the stars appear in the sky, everything comes to life in the streets. The

---

226 Damir Zorić, "Način života u istočnoj Hercegovini sredinom XIX stoljeća," *Studia ethnologi-ca Croatica*, no. 1 (1989): 99–120.
227 Lilek, "Familien- und Volksleben," 217.
228 Pieter Judson, *The Habsburg Empire: A New History* (Cambridge, MA: Harvard University Press, 2016), 283.
229 For an account of Shrove Tuesday in Kotor in 1922, see E. F. Coote Lake, "The Dance of the Spirit of the New Corn in Cattaro," *Folklore* 77, no. 1 (1966): 31–40.
230 Grunert, *Glauben im Hinterland*, 92.

festivities begin, young men shoot their weapons, sing, dance, and dress up...[231]

In 1899, celebrations at the Feast of Corpus Christi in Trebinje involved a procession led by local musicians and young men dressed in gold-embroidered costumes. Although predominantly a Catholic feast (*Tjelovo*), Muslims "enthusiastically" joined this celebration.[232] The end of Ramadan (*kičik-bajram*) "was announced by gunshots or cannon fire in larger cities. Christians would then give gifts to Muslim officials. At the other Eid festivity (*bjuk-bajram*), Muslims would give each other a lamb for roasting to remember the sacrifice of Abraham, the Biblical patriarch."[233] Centuries of acculturation had collapsed many of the visible differences between the religious groups, and there was widespread syncretism across Hercegovina. Vuk Vrčević evoked the sense of shared spiritual community via the *dernek* or festival:

Not only Orthodox people, but also sometimes Muslims and Catholics made a pilgrimage from their villages often for hours to attend celebrations.... Since only a few people can find a place within these typically tiny churches, the spaces around the church were filled with people ... most of them bareheaded.... Sometimes there is a procession (*litija*) with the priest at its head, which circles around the village, its fields and pastures with crosses, icons, and flags. The people then celebrate a festival on the church square, during which there is eating, drinking, singing, and dancing...[234]

Trebinje had an important market, as did Dubrovnik, Risan, Herceg Novi, and Kotor. Markets could also create a flashpoint, especially as historic grievances from excessive taxation and the violence that accompanied its extraction enraged Christians. The Habsburg officer who spoke to Vuk Vrčević in 1864 had been warned that there

---

231 Jernej Andrejka, *Slovenski fantje*, 377. As Andrejka was an enthusiastic meat eater, Lent in Upper Carniola might well have *seemed* like an equivalent privation to Ramadan.
232 Teschenburg, "Was schreibt man über Neu-Oesterreich?," *Das Vaterland*, October 22, 1899, 2.
233 Andrejka, *Slovenski fantje*, 377.
234 Grunert, *Glauben im Hinterland*, 90.

FIGURE 6. Zasad, a settlement close to Trebinje. Muzej Hercegovine, Trebinje.

was scarcely a market day in Trebinje on which there was not a bloody fight between Christians and Muslims.[235] Markets were also key places where resistance was organized: in 1876, as a stronghold of the insurgents led by Lazar Sočica, the market at Herceg Novi was used as a base to trade arms.[236] Local people evidently traveled some way to get to markets on the coast. At Orthodox Christmas in 1881 in Risan, the marketplace:

> thronged with Crivoscian, Montenegrin, and Herzegovinian peasants from the neighboring mountains concluding their Christmas purchases, small packets of groceries, bundles of evergreens such as flourish not on the bleak rocks above, and sundry suspicious looking bottles which peeped out of the sacks wherewith their mules were laden; apples, oranges and golden tinsel.[237]

---

235 "blutige Raufereien zwischen Türken und Christen," in "Von Ragusa nach Trebinje," *Jagd-Zeitung*, September 30, 1867, 560.

236 "A Lady Visit to the Herzegovinian Insurgents," *New York Times*, July 23, 1876, 4.

237 Arthur J. Evans, "Christmas and Ancestor Worship in the Black Mountain," *Macmillan's Magazine* 43 (1881): 219. "[T]he first roses and the first oranges" grew on the Prevlaka peninsula; see Otte, *Historian in Peace and War*, 352.

In November 1881, in anticipation of local resistance to conscription, people from Krivošije were temporarily forbidden to visit the markets in Boka Kotorska.[238]

The extent of the division between Christians and Muslims in Hercegovina was somewhat fluid, changing with every historical epoch and perennially difficult for incomers to assess. Tradition prevented exogamous relationships developing (at least officially).[239] Migration had had a strong impact on all local people who moved shorter or longer distances as necessary (such as the movement of Muslims from Risan to Korjenići after 1699).[240] In Gacko, poorer people finding themselves without food in winter moved to Posavina.[241] Small migrations encouraged political thinking, which was not just confined to the immediate vicinity.[242] In Hercegovina, villages often contained a single religious group close to another village populated by one of the other local religions. Often settlements consisted of closely related families in extended households (*zadruge*) or clusters of cottages. In 1879, Franz Ivanetič noted that Muslim families in the settlement of Arslanagić most were all called Agić.[243] Bogojević Selo in Zubci was home to the Vukalović clan.[244] Jewish descendants of the exodus from Spain in the 1490s, the Sephardim, lived on the Dalmatian coast and in Mostar and Sarajevo, but rarely settled in Trebinje. The Jews that came to the city after 1878 were usually from Ashkenazi families.

Among the Orthodox, there were clear remnants of a tribal system that went back to the medieval era. The Korjenići region was a historic *župa* (a county or group of villages led by a *župan* or count) between Mount Orjen and Bileća which enveloped Lastva, Klobuk, and Zubci, including the hamlets of Aranđelovo, Župa, Gornji Ora-

---

238 Kapidžić, *Hercegovački ustanak*, 87.
239 One of the exceptions to the tradition of endogamy was the so-called *šišano kumstvo*, where a Muslim would sponsor a Christian child; see Grandits, *Herrschaft und Loyalität*, 298.
240 Ramiza Smajić, "Migracijski tokovi, društveno-političke prilike u Bosanskom ejaletu (1683.–1718.)." (Ph.D. diss., University of Zagreb, 2019).
241 Lilek, "Familien- und Volksleben," 25.
242 Dejan Djokić, *A Concise History of Serbia* (Cambridge: Cambridge University Press, 2023), 192–93.
243 Franz Ivanetič, "Arzloin Agič Most," *Klagenfurter Zeitung*, September 28, 1879, 1. He refers to the settlement simply as "Most."
244 H. H., "Der Zug über den Orien," *Der Vaterland*, April 16, 1882, 11.

hovac, Konjsko, Bogojević Selo, and Gornje Grančarevo. Neighboring Krivošije, part of Habsburg Dalmatia, had similar traditions. The people living in Zubci, often collectively referred to as Zubčani, were a distinct group within this region. Difficult to access quickly, one of the paths leading from Zubci was known as "Sablja ljuta" (sharpened sword) because it was so rocky.[245] Very close to the garrisons at Trebinje and Herceg Novi, these small settlements produced hundreds of so-called insurgents in the nineteenth century. Extended families in the foothills of Orjen often relied upon each other rather than the state. Emil Lilek argued that communal practices had survived longer among the Ljubibratić family in Ljubovo, suggesting a link between tradition and resistance to rule from outside.[246] The Banjani, a distinct *katun* (community) recorded in the Middle Ages, lived in the region close to the source of the Trebišnjica near Bileća, and in Montenegro, in the lands toward Velimlje and Nikšić. The Banjani told stories of their own origins in Kosovo, although they had lived in the region for centuries by 1878. Their dependency on grazing animals meant that they moved between the mountains in summer and lowlands in winter. Some pastoralists had early modern Vlach ancestors who spoke a language related to modern Romanian. Few vestiges of this legacy remained except in proper names, cultural traditions, and the use of the term *vlah* and *vlaški* to mean Orthodox.

Many admired the contrast between the rugged hills and more fertile patches of land, as well as the inhabitants. Writing for *The Times* in 1875, William Stillman described the character of the "mountaineers" which he contrasted with Catholic peasants: "The whole of Zubci, Yezero, Piva, Gatschko, Baniani, Rudini and Dabra, were under arms, and they possess a population of a different temper from those of Gabela, Popovo, and others bordering on Dalmatia."[247] Jernej Andrejka feared and respected the region's "tough guys" (*korenjaki*).[248]

---

245 Preindlsberger-Mrazović, *Bosnisches Skizzenbuch*, 334.
246 Lilek, "Familien- und Volksleben," 25.
247 Stillman, *Herzegovina*, 15. Elsewhere, he includes the men of Krivošije in this category: "The mountaineers (Montenegrins, Banianici, Zubcians, Pivans, Crivoscians, &c.)," 49.
248 Andrejka, *Slovenski fantje*, 337.

Of all the people of Hercegovina, the Zubčani arguably had the most subjective value projected upon them. Milena Preindlsberger-Mrazović depicted the "poor shepherds who lived a precarious existence and maintained their traditions."[249] Journalist Francis Broemel described the well-armed "dark, lurking men" from Zubci with "shiny long mustaches."[250] Women from Zubci were reported to be the prettiest, most sturdy and buxom in Hercegovina, who oiled their hair into shape.[251]

The area around Trebinje already had one of the highest densities of Orthodox churches in the whole of Hercegovina in 1878. The church or mosque could bind remote communities together. "Traditionally, the places of worship stood in exposed natural locations—on mountains and slopes—and sacred places such as cemeteries more rarely in a central place within the villages."[252] Muslim rural settlements such as Zasad, just on the edge of Trebinje, also existed.[253] Close to Trebinje, the old Orthodox Tvrdoš Monastery was almost destroyed in 1694. During the Habsburg period it remained a picturesque ruin.[254] Like markets, monasteries were also potential meeting places for rebels. The Duži Monastery was an important base for the Hercegovina rebels led by Mićo Ljubibratić in 1875.[255] The early medieval Orthodox monastery of Dobrićevo was founded beside the banks of the Trebišnjica and, like Duži, was a rebel stronghold in the mid-1870s. The Orthodox monastery of Kosijerevo, close to Dobrićevo on the opposite bank of the Trebišnjica,[256] was significant for the Banjani and a shrine for Saint Arsenije Sremac. In 1875, the rebel leader Mićo Ljubibratić had hoped to hold a popular *skupština* in the sanctuary of Kosijerevo, but the meeting did not take place.[257]

---

249 Preindlsberger-Mrazović, *Bosnisches Skizzenbuch*, 332.
250 Francis Broemel, "Auf grünen Felsen," *Wiener Allgemeine Zeitung*, November 25, 1880, 1-2.
251 "Durch die Zubcsi und Suttorina," *Pester Lloyd*, March 11, 1882, 2.
252 Grunert, *Glauben im Hinterland*, 102.
253 Korać, *Trebinje: Istorijski pregled*, vol. 2, part 1, 135.
254 Andrejka, *Slovenski fantje*, 315.
255 Grandits, *Herrschaft und Loyalität*, 643.
256 Both monasteries were moved to new locations after the creations of Lake Bileća in the mid-1960s.
257 Grandits, *End of Ottoman Rule*, 100; "Zerstörung eines montenegrinischen Klosters," *Leitmeritzer Zeitung*, November 27, 1915, 14.

Monasteries also helped to preserve local knowledge and customs. Matija Murko attended a concert at Duži where he heard a peasant (*kmet*) singing, while his words were set down by the monks and a schoolmaster who struggled to keep up.[258] The Orthodox monastery at Zavala, built in the early medieval era, lay on the edge of Popovo polje and was close to the entrance of the Vjetrenica cave. Part of the wall of the monastery was built into the caves and there are clear views across the flat karst from the church. Inhabited by Orthodox monks, it was about seventy meters above the water level at Popovo polje. Like Ostrog in Montenegro, it overlooked the karst polje. Habsburg officer Reinhard Günste thought that "it makes an almost ghostly impression and was built this way for defense."[259] The monastery library contained old printed and written fermans, fatwas, and early modern church records. A sense of community among the Orthodox going back to the piety of the medieval Nemanjić dynasty in Serbia led to political radicalism among the priesthood.[260] The clergy usually saw all Orthodox people who spoke štokavian as part of a single political community of Serbs.[261] Karl Novottny thought that Orthodox priests and the monasteries at Duži and Kosijerevo were the main source of anti-Habsburg sentiment in the Trebinje region.[262]

The landscape in Hercegovina, comprising urban spaces with water and isolated rocky settlements, reinforced and perpetuated the divisions between communities. If pastoralists were tough and "warlike," then this was because their communities had evolved over centuries to be self-sufficient and distrustful of organized trade, Islam, and the state and its laws. Living on the margins of control by the state had become a habit of the heart for many rural people.

---

258 Matija Murko, "The Singers and their Epic Songs," *Oral Tradition* 5, no. 1 (1990): 119. Murko (1861–1952) was a Styrian ethnomusicologist and philologist who did research among the South Slav nations and taught in Prague after 1920.

259 Reinhard Günste [Rifat Eff. Gozdović pseud.], "Zavala, das herzegowinische Athoškloster und die Vjetrinicahöhle [sic]," *Deutsches Volksblatt*, December 2, 1906, 21.

260 On the link between national identity and religion, see Bojan Aleksov, "The Serbian Orthodox Church," in *Orthodox Christianity and Nationalism in Nineteenth-Century Southeastern Europe*, ed. Lucian N. Leustean (New York: Fordham University Press, 2014), 65–100.

261 Speakers of the *štokavski* version of the language which was referred to variously as Serbo-Croat, Serbian, Croatian, Bosnian and Montenegrin.

262 Novottny, "Erinnerungen," AT-OeStA/KA NL 417: 12, Kriegsarchiv, Vienna, 195.

FIGURE 7. Mosque and Islamic graveyard in Trebinje, drawn by Richard Neutra in 1915. UCLA Library, Richard and Dion Neutra Papers.

At the same time, women in the cities and in the countryside were generally illiterate, making them heavily dependent on traditional wisdom, male relatives, or authority figures such as priests or imams. The arrival of Central European soldiers, priests, administrators, engineers, artists, literate women, and even musicians after 1878 was a highly disruptive event coming just after a civil war. It augured to disturb and change almost everything.

Chapter Two

THE TURBULENT 1870s

The Collapse of Ottoman Power, 1875–1878

During the nineteenth century, the Ottoman Empire lost territory and was perceived by many of its own subjects as well as international actors as a failing and oppressive state. There was an anti-Ottoman rebellion in the Serb lands in 1804 and Greece also emerged as a new state in the 1820s. Local Muslim populations were punished and excluded, which led to a long-term phenomenon that Safet Bandžović has called "de-Ottomanization."[1] Political reorganization and the assertion of local rights within the Ottoman Empire in the early 1830s may have exacerbated the instability. There were major rebellions in Bosnia and Hercegovina from 1831–1832: Ahmed-beg Resulbegović briefly took control in the Trebinje garrison.[2] After the defeat of the rebellions in 1832, Hersek (or Hercegovina) was organized as a sanjak (province) of the Bosnian eyelet, which became a separate Hercegovinian eyelet, only to be merged with Bosnia again in 1853. In 1862, Muslims responded to persecution by moving from Belgrade, Užice, Šabac, and other Serbian settlements

---

1   Safet Bandžović, "Ratovi i demografska deosmanizacija Balkana (1912.–1941.)," *Prilozi*, no. 32 (2003): 179–229.
2   Ahmed S. Aličić, *Pokret za autonomiju Bosne od 1831. do 1832. godine* (Sarajevo: Orijentalni Institut, 1996), 295–96. See also Fatma Sel Turhan, *The Ottoman Empire and the Bosnian Uprising: Janissaries, Modernisation and Rebellion in the Nineteenth Century* (London: I. B. Tauris, 2014).

en masse before settling in towns on the other side of the Drina.[3] Most of these people stayed: five Muslim families who had come from Serbia were given the right to remain in Trebinje on July 28, 1914.[4]

In 1857, a rebellion led by Luka Vukalović, who came from the village of Bogojević Selo in the Zubci region, had at its core the right of his kinsmen to bear arms. Vukalović knew Trebinje well and had trained as a gunsmith there before moving to the Dalmatian coast. During the rebellion, the Trebinje garrison was temporarily cut off from Ottoman supply routes, as was the fortress at Klobuk. Nick-named the "Garibaldi of Hercegovina" and turned into an inspirational romantic nationalist figure in the press, Luka Vukalović was reported to have "made cannons from cherry wood, tied them with iron rings, and then fired them at the Turks."[5] Vukalović wanted Hercegovina to unite with Montenegro, a de facto state ruled by the Petrović dynasty.[6] In 1852, Danilo I Petrović-Njegoš had strengthened his state by creating the Principality of Montenegro from the bishopric ruled by his family. When Nikola I Petrović-Njegoš succeeded Danilo I in 1860, he continued to attract supporters from Southern Dalmatia and Hercegovina. The Orthodox nexus in turn drew Imperial Russia into Balkan affairs. Although the exiled Vukalović was to die in Russia in 1873 after the failed uprising, he was a moving spirit behind much of the later resistance with his extended family playing a major role.[7] The Habsburg state was also not immune from rebellion. In 1869, the men of the Krivošije region of Southern Dalmatia (in the shadow of Mount Orjen and close to Zubci, where the Vukalović clan resided) refused to join the army of Franz Joseph if it meant serving in garrisons away from their own lands.[8] They had asked if they could form a local militia, a compromise

---

3   Grandits, *End of Ottoman Rule*, 46.
4   "Serbische Staatangehörige," Memo from July 28, 1914, signed by Rudolf Braun. AT-OeStA/ KA FA NFA (Trebinje 50), Kriegsarchiv Vienna.
5   Preindlsberger-Mrazović, *Bosnisches Skizzenbuch*, 333. Giuseppe Garibaldi (1807–1882), Italian revolutionary and guerrilla leader, was inspirational for revolutionaries and nationalists across Europe.
6   "Tripko Vukalović gestorben," *Agramer Zeitung*, May 2, 1898, 5.
7   Kapidžić, *Hercegovački ustanak*, 86.
8   Slavko Mijušković, *Ustanak u Boki Kotorskoj 1869* (Kotor: Centar za kulturu, 1970).

which was rejected. Several thousand troops were sent to Boka Kotorska to deal with the insurgency, but the regime found it difficult
territory in which to fight and sustained high casualties. A peace
was negotiated by the skills of local commander Stjepan Jovanović
(Stefan von Jovanovich), born in 1828 in Pazarište in the Lika region,
and a veteran of the Italian campaigns. In 1869, he was injured in
the leg and walked with a limp for the next sixteen years.[9] The authorities suspended conscription and negotiated an amnesty for the
rebels.[10] Working with the Dalmatian Governor Gavrilo Rodić (Ga-
briel von Rodich), also from an Orthodox family, Jovanović bought
the Habsburg regime much needed time, but these rebellious ways
were not doused within the population around Mount Orjen in either 1857 or 1869.

De-Ottomanization had a direct impact on Bosnia and Hercegovina while it was still under the control of the Porte. Hercegovina
began to experience what Hannes Grandits has called the "repeated
eruption of power struggles"[11] well before the arrival of Habsburg
troops. In 1874, the harvests in Bosnia and Hercegovina failed, exacerbating local frustrations about poverty and religious inequali-
ties. The peasantry faced oppressive taxes, which created short term
grievances, further augmented by structural and ideological problems.[12] Local leaders had already started to gather at the end of the
summer in 1874 and, aided by Montenegrin ruler Nikola Petrović,
sizeable caches of weapons were amassed. The leaders escaped to
Montenegro in late 1874 when their plans became known to the
Ottoman authorities. The Habsburg authorities in neighboring Dalmatia closely monitored the situation, wishing to limit Montene-

9   W. J. Stillman, "The late Baron Jovanovich," *The Times*, December 12, 1885, 3.
10 Ferdinand Hauptmann, "General Rodić i politika austrijske vlade u krivošijskom ustanku 1869/70: (Uz dnevnike generala Gabrijela Rodića)," *Godišnjak društva istoričara Bosne i Herce-govine* 13 (1962): 53–91.
11 Hannes Grandits, "Violent Social Disintegration: A Nation-Building Strategy in Late-Otto-man Herzegovina," in *Conflicting Loyalties in the Balkans: The Great Powers, the Ottoman Empire and Nation-Building*, ed. Hannes Grandits, Nathalie Clayer, and Robert Pichler (London: I. B. Tauris, 2011), 110.
12 Milorad Ekmečić, *Ustanak u Bosni: 1875–1878* (Sarajevo: Veselin Masleša, 1973).

grin influence.[13] William Holmes, the British Consul in Sarajevo, was already aware of Habsburg aspirations in Bosnia and Hercegovina and "expressed suspicion about Montenegro in the very first report on the disturbances he sent on July 2, 1875. He claimed that everything was organized by a group of 164 refugees … who had wintered in Montenegro."[14]

Anti-Ottoman discontent may have started with the Orthodox population, but it soon spread. Catholics from Popovo polje and Gabela, anticipating a likely Habsburg takeover, joined the uprising. In August 1875, Trebinje was besieged by rebels of both denominations numbering about two thousand, led by the Catholic priest Don Ivan Musić who had been inspired to fight after witnessing the suffering of the Christian *rayah*.[15] The Habsburg Consul, Vuk Vrčević,[16] regularly updated his colleagues with news of the uprising, although in mid-July 1875, fearing for the safety of his family, he fled from Trebinje to Dubrovnik.[17] He noted the ways in which the uprising had precipitated violence between local people according to political or religious loyalty. On October 18, 1875, Vrčević reported that an armed gang from Ljubinje led by Ferik Şevket Paşa had killed several unarmed "rayah" including Jovica Tomović, Lazo Kokosar, and Sava Kolak. Ferik Şevket Paşa's gangs stole scores of oxen, sheep, and goats. The Begović family from (Staro) Slano had joined the pillage.[18] A few days later, on October 22, Vrčević reported that Muslims from

---

13 Živko M. Andrijašević and Šerbo Rastoder, *Crna Gora i velike sile* (Podgorica: Zavod za Udžbenike i Nastavna Sredstva, 2006), 110. On the Habsburg perspective in 1875, see Arnold Suppan, "Aussen- und militärpolitische Strategie Österreich-Ungarns vor Beginn des bosnischen Aufstandes 1875," in *Međunarodni naučni skup povodom 100-godišnjice ustanka u Bosni i Hercegovini, drugim balkanskim zemljama i istočnoj krizi 1875–1878. godine*, vol. 1., ed. Rade Petrović (Sarajevo: Akademija nauka i umjetnosti Bosne i Hercegovine, 1977), 159–77.

14 Miloš Ković, "The Beginning of the 1875 Serbian Uprising in Herzegovina: The British Perspective," *Balcanica* 41 (2010): 58–59.

15 Ivan Musić (1848–1880) was educated by Franciscans at Široki Brijeg. He left the priesthood after the rebellion.

16 Originally from Risan, Vuk Vrčević (1811–1882) arrived in Trebinje as Consul in 1861 and remained there for over twenty years. He worked closely with the linguist Vuk Karadžić collecting detailed and nuanced ethnographic data from many local informants, including a Muslim judge.

17 Chiffon Telegramme, Mostar, July 18, 1875, to the Habsburg Consul in Sarajevo, Zbirka Austrijski Konsulat Mostar, Arhiv Hercegovine, Mostar.

18 Vuk Vrčević to the Habsburg Vice-Consul in Mostar, October 18, 1875, Zbirka Austrijski Konsulat Mostar, Arhiv Hercegovine, Mostar.

Korjenići had burned down ten villages including Mosko, Čepelica, and Dubočani.[19] After the later months of 1875, the region around Trebinje continued to be devastated by violence, which perpetuated Christian antipathy against the Muslim urban population and the Ottoman authorities and vice versa.[20] Food supplies to the garrison at Trebinje were severely restricted and the winter of 1875–76 was harsh. Convoys on roads were attacked as the Trebinje garrison became a haven for those escaping the violence. In Popovo polje, local people left their villages and braved the elements:

> 300 were out on the mountain-side on the night of the worst storm we have had this season. One woman with a new-born babe was so exhausted in her flight that she went to sleep, sitting on a rock nursing her child, fell off in her sleep, and was found by one of the other peasants next morning still sleeping, with her babe at her bosom, in a pool of water which had fallen during the storm.[21]

The 1875 rebels had significant support from Serbia and Montenegro as well as permanent revolutionaries, including *garibaldini*[22] from Italy and the veteran rebel Mićo Ljubibratić from Ljubovo, a supporter of Luka Vukalović in 1857. There were already widespread Pan-Slav sympathies in Central Europe,[23] and Ljubibratić was especially popular among the Slavs of the Habsburg Monarchy.[24] After imprisonment in 1876 in Habsburg jails, Ljubibratić went to Serbia in 1877, where he remained for over a decade. From this stage on-

---

19 Vuk Vrčević to the Habsburg Vice-Consul in Mostar, October 22, 1875, Zbirka Austrijski Konsulat Mostar, Arhiv Hercegovine, Mostar.

20 Grandits, *Herrschaft und Loyalität*, 626–29.

21 Report in the *Times* from October 19, 1875, quoted in Arthur J. Evans, *Through Bosnia and the Herzegovina on Foot during the Insurrection, August and September 1875, with an Historical Review of Bosnia, and a Glimpse at the Croats, Slavonians, and the Ancient Republic of Ragusa* (London: Longman, Green and Co, 1876), xlv, footnote 4.

22 Radical followers of Giuseppe Garibaldi who fought for national liberation elsewhere.

23 František Šistek, "Under the Slavic Crescent: Representations of Bosnian Muslims in Czech Literature, Travelogues and Memoirs, 1878–1918," in *Imagining Bosnian Muslims in Central Europe: Representations, Transfers and Exchanges*, ed. František Šistek (Oxford: Berghahn, 2021), 124.

24 Božidar Jezernik, *Jugoslavija, zemlja snova* (Belgrade: Biblioteka XX vek, 2018), 32.

ward, the internal politics of Hercegovina was perceived to have transnational significance and received frequent media attention. News of the violence left the insurgents with an enduring reputation for both bravery and savagery. The *Illustrated London News* told its readers in December 1875 that "[t]he wild and hardy sons of Gatschko, Nevesinje, Bilec, Korjenic, and Banjani, and part of Zubci, are warlike; they care little for rain or cold and only rest when there are no Turks to be got at."[25] Carl Winter remembered being asked by a person in Dubrovnik whether he had already made a will before he set off for Trebinje in August 1875.[26]

In a world where memories of oppression mixed with literary imagination, the Montenegrins often played the part of chief avengers, and writers perpetuated the idea of unsettled business between the Orthodox and Muslims. *Gorski Vijenac* (The Mountain Wreath) was published in 1847 by Montenegrin leader Petar II Petrović Njegoš.[27] The author's younger brother Joko had been killed by Smail-aga Ćengić in 1836 in Grahovo as he led troops into a battle which was seen as a significant setback for the Petrović dynasty. Ali-paša Resulbegović from Trebinje fought alongside Ćengić in a struggle that was meant to crush pro-Montenegrin sympathies in Korjenići. Mirko Petrović Njegoš, uncle of Petar II and father of the future King Nikola, published a collection of poems in 1864 which included *Boj na Zupcima* (The Struggle for Zubci), which celebrated the heroism of the Montenegrins as well as Luka Vukalović and the people living in the foothills of Orjen at the Battle of Grahovac in 1858, a significant Montenegrin victory against the Ottomans.[28] These poems could be swiftly memorized, taken to heart, and become a strong basis for self-fashioning. They also signified the emergence of a belief in the eventual triumph of Orthodox people and their reclamation of territories that had been lost to the Ottomans for generations. The journalist William Stillman recalled that the killing of Muslims in 1875 was framed as retributive justice for historic Ottoman atroc-

25 "The War in the Herzegovina," *The Illustrated London News*, December 25, 1875, 620.
26 Carl Winter, "Das herzegowinische Paris," *Neues Wiener Tagblatt*, August 21, 1885, 1.
27 Petar Petrović Njegoš, *Gorski Vijenac* (Sarajevo: Svjetlost, 1990).
28 Mirko Petrović Njegoš, *Junački spomenik, pjesne o najnovijim Tursko-Crnogorskim bojevina* (Cetinje: U knjažeskoj štampariji, 1864).

ities: "one of the fugitives had nearly reached Trebinje when he was met in the way by a Herzegovinian, of whom he begged for quarter in the usual Turkish form, 'aman' (mercy), to which the Herzegovinian replied 'taman' (enough), and cut him down."[29]

The crisis continued into the spring of 1876. On March 5, Vuk Vrčević met Gavrilo Rodić and told him: "The province is out of funds.... Many have even started to sell off their valuables and furnishings.... The troops are sufficiently equipped with ammunition and provisions—probably for about two to three months."[30] In a conflict that would be remembered as the "Nevesinje Gun" (*Nevesinjska puška*), the region between Gacko and Bileća experienced months of rebellion as armed rebel gangs (*čete*) attacked Ottoman positions and raided settlements. Orthodox cleric Pop Bogdan Zimonjić returned to his home village of Lipnik after years of exile in Montenegro, determined to settle a long score and reclaim his home. His companions included Novica Cerović, who had decapitated the notoriously cruel Smail-aga Ćengić in 1840.[31] In nearby Samobor, they found the Church of Sveti Sava had been desecrated. Horse manure covered the nave which had been used as a stable and a buried man had been disinterred and his remains mutilated.[32] In rage, forces led by Pop Zimonjić then destroyed the *kula* (tower) that had represented the power of the Ćengić family and horses were allowed to graze freely on Gatačko polje to reinforce the transfer of power and rights.[33] German Consul Friedrich Lichtenberg in Dubrovnik reported that several Muslim villages between Trebinje and Bileća were set on fire by insurgents led by Zimonjić.[34] Reporting the contents of a telegram from Dubrovnik in 1876, the *Neues Wiener Tagblatt* reported that the Muslims in Lipnik, Avtovac, Crnica, and three other vil-

---

29 William J. Stillman, *The Autobiography of a Journalist*, vol. 2 (London: Grant, 1901).

30 Grandits, *End of Ottoman Rule*, 136.

31 The events leading up to the death were described in Ivan Mažuranić, *Smrt Smail-age Ćengijića* (Zagreb: Matica Hrvatska, 1952), first published in 1846.

32 "Montenegrinischer Kriegsbericht," *Wiener Zeitung*, July 28, 1876, 2.

33 Grandits, *End of Ottoman Rule*, 214.

34 Consul Friedrich August Freiherr von Lichtenberg (1817–1877) reported that "on 12 and 13 of this month, the insurgents led by Pop Simunić burned down the Muslim villages Bubnica, Dabica, Gljubusina, Dubrava and Jasseno between Bilekie and Trebinje." See Grandits, *End of Ottoman Rule*, 118.

lages had been attacked, despite their submission to Lazar Sočica[35] and Bogdan Zimonjić.[36]

The violence reached new extremes with a decisive and crushing victory by Orthodox combatants against local pro-Ottoman forces led by Aḥmad Mukhtār Paşa on July 18, 1876, at Vučji Do, about seven kilometers east of Bileća. Sensing the danger of their position, Muslim men from Korjenići retreated from the valley which led to a frenzied rout.[37] According to Milena Preindlsberger-Mrazović, writing a generation later: "A whole battalion of dead Anatolians lay in the great valley on the Vardar. The Turkish grenades flew 'like flocks of pigeons' and the heads of the Turks 'like boiled potatoes....' After the slaughter, a terrible storm broke out, blanketing the thousands of corpses in a dense layer of hail."[38] Only a few men managed to get back to Bileća and there was panic in the town. The market and properties were locked up and many of the local people fled to Trebinje for safety.[39] Five hundred women moved onto the battlefield to scavenge valuable clothes and weapons from the dead.[40] However, "a few thousand bodies remained unburied and were attacked by beasts of prey."[41] The remains of the battle, including military buttons, spent cartridges, broken weapons, and skulls with bullet holes, were still visible to Habsburg soldiers after 1878.[42] It is estimated that thousands of Ottoman forces based at Trebinje and led by Hüseyin Paşa had already been killed at the Battle of Grahovac in 1858. Vučji Do was also calamitous. As Hercegovina was already sparsely populated, military defeats were a significant blow to local Muslim families. Jernej Andrejka spoke to a gray-haired Montenegrin veteran named Djuro who claimed to have personally beheaded thirty-seven "Turks"

---

35 Lazar Sočica (1838–1910) was a veteran anti-Ottoman rebel from Plužine, active in the 1850s, in the 1870s, and again in 1882 against the Habsburgs. Reputed to be fierce in battle, his nickname was *munjić* (lightning bolt).

36 "Telegramme vom Kriegsschauplatze," *Neues Wiener Tagblatt*, July 26, 1876, 3.

37 "Die Niederlage Mukhtar Pascha's," *Laibacher Zeitung*, August 4, 1876, 2.

38 Preindlsberger-Mrazović, *Bosnisches Skizzenbuch*, 316.

39 Spiridion Gopčević, *Der Krieg Montenegro's gegen die Pforte im Jahre 1876* (Vienna: J. W. Seidel, 1877), 76.

40 Preindlsberger-Mrazović, *Bosnisches Skizzenbuch*, 316.

41 Went von Römö, "Aus dem südöstlichen Theile," 23.

42 F. von M., "Die Culturarbeit der österreichischen Armee (Hercegovina)," *Wiener Zeitung*, June 10, 1886, 3.

at Vučji Do, Krstac, Ljubinje, and Foča. One of his compatriots then asked him if he was not afraid that God would punish him for so many crimes [*tolike zločine*]? Djuro answered that God had already punished him by giving him twenty-three children living in a small pine hut with only three acres of land.[43]

Orthodox combatants took Bileća in September 1877 and "cleansed" the Muslim population around the town.[44] Writing over a decade later in 1889, Hermann Iser thought that this region had been "the most dangerous for Muslims" and that "today one still finds skeletons in the bushes between the stones or in old cisterns."[45] The long-term demographic impact of the violence and insecurity of 1853–1878 was a sharp decline in the overall number of Muslims in the countryside in Hercegovina. Conflict forced Muslims in villages to flee to larger towns, leading to what Esad Arnautović called a "psychosis" of fear of the Montenegrin-led forces in Trebinje.[46] All denominations had also fled to the safety of Dalmatia, which had a sizeable homeless and distressed community by 1876. As late as January 1878, a ship took refugees, many of whom were Muslim, from Dubrovnik to Korčula where they were housed by the local authorities.[47] Within the remaining Ottoman garrisons there was a shortage of fresh food and scurvy had broken out in Trebinje by May 1878. Those people who did remain in their villages were effectively cut off from medical supplies and food.[48] Diplomatic action persuaded the Montenegrins that they would not be allowed to retain territory in Hercegovina, at least in the short term, but the damage was done. By 1879, it has been estimated that the Muslim population of Hercegovina had declined to only 24 percent overall from a much higher percentage before the loss of Ottoman power.[49] Many settle-

---

43 Andrejka, *Slovenski fantje*, 344. In the original text, it is spelled Gjuro.
44 Grandits, *Herrschaft und Loyalität*, 646, footnote 133. See also the term used in the press, "O Črnogorcih in njih delih: Cetinjski 'Glas Crnogorca' piše," *Slovenski Narod*, October 6, 1877, 2.
45 Hermann Iser, "Aus der Herzegowina," *Vorarlberger Volksblatt*, November 26, 1889, 1.
46 Arnautović, "Austrougarska okupacija Trebinja," 11.
47 Charles St John to Earl of Derby, Dubrovnik, January 4, 1878, FO 219, National Archives, London.
48 Harry Cooper to Charles St John, May 19, 1878, FO7 / 940, National Archives, London.
49 Justin McCarthy, "Archival Sources concerning Serb Rebellions in Bosnia 1875–76," in *Ottoman Bosnia: A History in Peril*, ed. Markus Koller and Kemal H. Karpat (Madison: University of Wisconsin Press, 2004), 145; Muhamed Hadžijahić, "Emigracije muslimana Bosne i Her-

ments remained destroyed or deserted: in 1895, there were 177 un-inhabited dwellings in Trebinje municipality (which included empty former homes in the settlements of Gorica, Gradina, Hrupjela, Mostaći, Podgljiva, Donje Police, Gornje Police, and Zasad).[50] There is no doubt that Hercegovina was utterly devastated by the years of conflict that immediately preceded the Habsburg arrival; many had died, others had been internally relocated, and some had simply left the region altogether.

Any real political victories against the Ottomans by local rebels were short-lived and disrupted by international actors. By July of 1878, the Habsburg Monarchy was poised to occupy Bosnia and Hercegovina, obliging the Ottoman authorities to leave. Nominal sovereignty remained with the Ottomans according to the terms of the Treaty of Berlin, in an odd compromise that was intended to lead to relative peace and stability and to save face. In the meantime, despite international machinations, Hercegovina was still unstable. In early 1878, insurgents started returning to Trebinje effectively encircling the city, which was cut off from other Muslim garrisons for several weeks, but still protected by its walls. By May 1878, the rebels held all of the land to the west and east of Trebinje around Popovo polje and Bileća. The road between Trebinje and Dubrovnik was reported to be deserted; the only remaining people were "the soldiers in the blockhouses [as] the villages were destroyed three years ago, and the fields have since been so overgrown that their recultivation will be hard work."[51]

The Arrival of Habsburg Troops

In the last days of June 1878, while the Congress of Berlin was still meeting, Habsburg troops prepared for a two-pronged entrance into Bosnia and Hercegovina. Existing garrisons were used as staging posts and men mobilized from across the monarchy. On hearing of the

---

cegovine u Tursku u doba austro-ugarske vladavine 1878.–1918. god.," *Historijski zbornik* 3 (1950): 70–75.

50 Božo Madžar, "Istorijat Gradskog Vodovoda u Trebinju," *Tribunia: Prilozi za istoriju, arheologiju, etnologiju, umjetnost i kulturu*, nos. 7–8 (1984): 51–64.

51 Harry Cooper to Charles St John, May 19, 1878, FO7 / 940, National Archives, London.

campaign, Jernej Andrejka "was delighted at the prospect of a swift victory: 'his heart leapt with joy thinking how a bullet was going to kill two to three hundred Turks in one strike.'"[52] The invasion, launched on July 29, was an enormous undertaking which numerically overwhelmed the local population, but the Habsburg soldiers still encountered unexpectedly fierce resistance.[53] Troops led by veteran commander Josip Filipović crossed the Sava from Slavonia and gathered in Banja Luka, before taking Sarajevo on August 19. Here they were shocked by the street-by-street fighting. Local leader Hadži Loja led resistance by the Ottoman soldiers and there were serious clashes at Maglaj and Jajce.[54] The campaign in Hercegovina was led by Stjepan Jovanović, a veteran of the Italian campaigns under General Josef Radetzky as well as the 1869 conflict in Southern Dalmatia. Troops moved north along the Neretva River and entered Mostar without significant struggle on August 5.[55] Jovanović arrived in the city the next day. The seizure of these two strategically crucial cities did not quash resistance, which swiftly moved to the mountains; only on October 20, 1878, did the fortress at Velika Kladuša finally capitulate. Jovanović anticipated insurgency around the Montenegrin border so concentrated his strategy on the Neretva valley before moving toward Trebinje and the Montenegrin border.[56] Filipović had been appointed nominal Bosnian Governor on July 13, a post he retained until November 18, 1878. Both Filipović and Jovanović were from families from the region on the old military border with the Ottoman Empire, spoke the local Slavonic language, and had distinguished themselves in other theaters of war. They also understood the chal-

---

52 Alenka Bartulović, "'We Have an Old Debt with the Turk, and It Best Be Settled': Ottoman Incursions through the Discursive Optics of Slovenian Historiography and Literature and Their Applicability in the Twenty-First Century," in *Imagining "the Turk"*, ed. Božidar Jezernik (Newcastle-upon-Tyne: Cambridge Scholars, 2010), 122.

53 Robert J. Donia, *Islam under the Double Eagle: The Muslims of Bosnia and Hercegovina 1871-1914* (New York: Eastern European Monographs, 1981), 42-43.

54 Mehmedalija Bojić, "Svrgavanje turske vlasti i odbrambeni rat Bosne i Hercegovine protiv austrougarske invazije 1878. godine," in *Naučni skup Otpor austrougarskoj okupaciji 1878. godine u Bosni i Hercegovini*, ed. Milorad Ekmečić (Sarajevo: Akademija nauka i umjetnosti Bosne i Hercegovine, 1979), 71-94.

55 "Die Besetzung von Mostar," *Grazer Volksblatt*, August 17, 1878, 6-7; Jasmin Branković, *Mostar 1833-1918: Upravni i politički položaj grada* (Sarajevo: University Press Magistrat, 2009), 80-83.

56 Andrejka, *Slovenski fantje*, 205-6.

lenges of the dry terrain, the importance of Ottoman fortifications, river valleys, mountain eyries, and the likely opposition they would face from what they referred to as "insurgents."[57] Jovanović believed that guerrilla combat was lost by underestimating the opponent.[58] At this stage, the insurgents were both Muslim and Orthodox. There were Muslim insurgents in the area around Trebinje and Korjenići led by Hadži Ali Fetahagić and Omer Šehović.[59]

Observing events in Hercegovina from only a short distance and with excellent intelligence from Vuk Vrčević, the Habsburg authorities knew what they would face when their troops crossed the borders. The conquest of the region around Trebinje was swift, but not without incident. Wilhelm Popp von Poppenheim moved with his battalion to the Dalmatian-Hercegovinian frontier at Drijen on September 2, 1878.[60] This border post was guarded by men described as "heavily tanned, strong, and bearded, looking as if they had been waiting in vain for Ottoman power to be restored."[61] Poppenheim sensed the mood for cooperation and felt that he could now move on to the strategically important Ottoman garrison of Trebinje, just a few miles away. Daniş Efendi, the Ottoman Consul in Dubrovnik, warned him that the insurgents had camped at Gluva Smokva, and that there were too many men there to avoid violence completely.[62]

On the march from Dubrovnik to Drijen, the battalion had lost "three men from sunstroke, one from suicide and one who was run through by an officer for refusing to march any further."[63] One officer recalled that on the route between Drijen and Duži, the troops had seen completely deserted settlements and "only the sky for a roof"

---

57 Clemens Ruthner, "Die Invasoren und Insurgenten des Okkupationsfeldzugs 1878 im kulturellen Gedächtnis," in *Bosnien-Herzegowina und Österreich-Ungarn, 1878–1918: Annäherungen an eine Kolonie*, ed. Clemens Ruthner and Tamara Scheer (Tübingen: Narr Francke Attempto, 2018), 134.

58 C. M., "Jovanovic Armeebefehl," *Neue Freie Presse (Abendblatt)*, February 23, 1882, 2.

59 Arnautović, "Austrougarska okupacija Trebinja," 14.

60 "Der Ausgang des Occupations-Feldzuges," *Beilage zur Weiner Abendpost*, May 13, 1880, 433–34.

61 "Aus Bosnien," *Linzer Volksblatt*, October 1, 1878, 2.

62 "Von der Okkupations-Armee. Ragusa," *Epoche*, September 4, 1878, 5. In contemporary sources, the settlement was also usually known as Gluha Smokva.

63 Charles St John to the Marquis of Salisbury, Dubrovnik, September 4, 1878. FO7 940, National Archives, London.

on the cottages.[64] At noon on Saturday, September 8, Habsburg troops took Trebinje. The Czech-speaking soldiers in the regiment celebrated the peaceful handover with cries of "živio" and "slava."[65] Some of the local forts on higher ground had already been secured by the departing Ottoman troops,[66] which meant that the battle for Trebinje itself was much less violent and intense than in Sarajevo. Article 25 of the Treaty of Berlin had stipulated that "the provinces of Bosnia and Herzegovina shall be occupied and administered by Austria-Hungary" which included the right to maintain garrisons. Habsburg soldiers were stepping almost directly into the structures left behind by the Ottomans and had a ready base from which to control the surrounding countryside.[67]

Ottoman troops were required to vacate their posts and the Trebinje garrison force led by Süleyman Paşa departed by boat from Gruž having left the city on the evening of September 8, just a few hours after their surrender. Despite the graceful concession of defeat, Habsburg troops still faced fierce opposition from outside the garrison from insurgents. Although Süleyman Paşa "had not made an allegiance with the insurgents ... he was in a very desperate position that made him want to leave Hercegovina as soon as possible."[68] The response of surrounding villages to the Habsburg occupation force was mixed, and these lines of division were perpetuated until at least 1914. Zasad, close to the city, indefensible and populated predominantly by Muslims, immediately supported the new occupiers and, in revenge, its inhabitants were attacked by insurgents.[69] Bridges were also flashpoints for conflict. In the settlement of Poljice, evidently an insurgent stronghold, the Graf Nobili regiment lost several men.[70] Half of the regiment

64   "Aus Bosnien," *Linzer Volksblatt*, October 1, 1878. 2.
65   "Von der Okkupations-Armee: Über die letzten Ereignisse auf dem Insurrektions-Schauplatze," *Epoche*, September 9, 1878, 1.
66   "Die Einnahme von Trebinje," *Die Presse (Abendblatt)*, September 20, 1878, 2–3.
67   *The Annual Register: A Review of Public Events at Home and Abroad for the Year 1878* (London: Rivingtons, 1879), 226–27.
68   Bencze, *Occupation of Bosnia and Herzegovina*, 274.
69   Abtheilung für Kriegsgeschichte des K. K. Kriegs-Archivs, *Die Occupation Bosniens und der Hercegovina durch K. K. Truppen im Jahre 1878* (Vienna: Verlag des K.K. Generalstabes/Seidel und Sohns, 1879), 752.
70   Albert August Ludwig Ritter von Plönnies, "Die Einnahme von Trebinje und Beschreibung von Klobuk," AT-OeStA/KA NL 383 (B,C), Kriegsarchiv, Vienna.

were left outside the city guarding the bridge and fought for an hour beside the Trebišnjica before successfully holding their ground. Commanded by Captain Lenk, who had just arrived, over a dozen men were either killed or declared missing. Poppenheim returned to Dubrovnik on September 8 and ordered the brigade commander László Nagy to disarm the local population and sent out troops to punish those villages that had sheltered the insurgents, many of whom fled to Klobuk or over the Montenegrin border.[71]

Within two days of arriving in Trebinje, the new authorities had set up a postal service using pack animals to connect with Dubrovnik. A telegraph connection was established by October 1.[72] Habsburg troops took Bileća, important as a road junction and surrounded by fortified sentry houses, without resistance on September 11.[73] A group of the main insurgents, including Tripko Vukalović and Bogdan Zimonjić, gathered expecting to resist the imposition of Habsburg power in Bileća on September 17, but instead decided to surrender en masse to Jovanović at Trebinje, breaking up their weapons.[74] The initial occupation of Gacko on September 18 took place without resistance, but this was followed by an ambush: a soldier was shot, and twenty to thirty insurgents fled and retreated in the direction of Foča. The local people then handed over rifles, equipment, sugar, and salt to the Habsburg troops. A telegraph connection was established between Nevesinje and Gacko, guarded by the 12th Company of the 69th Infantry Regiment. The weather conditions continued to be challenging. At the bridge at Sušica, attempts to cross the river by oxen using ropes were foiled because of the high water levels and the ropes were torn. It was only when good weather returned on October 1 that the troops could operate properly.[75]

Toward the Montenegrin frontier, some villagers had already departed. As they approached Gornje Grančarevo, the troops found

71 Bencze, *Occupation of Bosnia and Herzegovina*, 276-77.
72 "Aus Bosnien," *Grazer Volksblatt*, October 23, 1878, 1-2.
73 "Die bosnisch-herzegowinische Okkupazion," *Prager Abendblatt*, September 21, 1878, 1.
74 Jovan Jovanović, "Izvještaj Atanasija Vasiljevića Vasiljeva o završetku Hercegovačkog Ustanka 1875-1878. godine," *Prilozi*, no. 13 (1977): 328-33.
75 Abtheilung für Kriegsgeschichte, *Die Occupation Bosniens und der Hercegovina*, 773; Andrejka, *Slovenski fantje*, 203.

the village eerily deserted.[76] They expected more resistance as the settlement had been the site of heavy fighting just a few years earlier. One soldier recalled:

> All submitted without a fight; only the wild tribe of the Korjenići—relatives of the people from Krivošije—stood at Gorica, northwest of Trebinje, fighting the 74th Infantry Regiment which had advanced from Trebinje to join the 18th Troop Division. The Korjenići retreated toward the Montenegrin frontier, believing that no soldier would penetrate the stone fortress of their residences ... the isolated people of Korjenići lurked on the walls of the ravine, while most of them awaited the call to battle at Grančarevo.[77]

At the fortress at Klobuk, local men withstood the Habsburg occupation forces for three days.[78] Considered to be almost insurmountable,[79] Klobuk was described as a "Hercegovinian Gibraltar."[80] After the Montenegrin victory against the Ottoman forces based at Trebinje led by Hüseyin Paşa at the Battle of Grahovac in 1858, the Muslim combatants had retreated to the safety of Klobuk. The fortress had been a stronghold of the Uprising in 1875, a base from which Stojan Kovačević had operated with two thousand Montenegrins under his command.[81] In 1878, Jovanović led the campaign against Klobuk with deep personal conviction and he was familiar with its strategic significance.[82] As a young officer in the late 1850s, he had been involved in Habsburg diplomatic missions that took him to Montenegro. The assault on Klobuk was a difficult mil-

---

76 Dr. Alfred Ebenhoch, "Aus meinem Tagebuche in der Herzegowina," *Mühlviertler Nachrichten*, September 5, 1889, 1.
77 "Eine schwere Feldbatterie in der Hercegovina 1878," *Die Vedette*, June 26, 1889, 420. See also, Franz Heller, "Vor Dreißig Jahren," *Salzburger Volksblatt*, August 14, 1908, 3–4.
78 Plönnies, "Die Einnahme von Trebinje," AT-OeStA/KA NL 383 (B,C), Kriegsarchiv, Vienna.
79 Albert August Ludwig Ritter von Plönnies, "Beschreibung von Klobuk," handgeschriebene Berichte aus dem Okkupationsfeldzug 1878, AT-OeStA/KA NL 383 (B,C), Kriegsarchiv, Vienna.
80 "Jovanović Pacificator," *Militär-Zeitung*, December 10, 1885, 1.
81 Communiqué No. 179, Vice-consulate in Mostar, September 2, 1875, Austrijski Konsulat Mostar, Arhiv Hercegovine, Mostar.
82 Tado Oršolić, "Sudjelovanje dalmatinskih postrojbi u zaposjedanju Bosne i Hercegovine 1878," *Radovi Zavoda za povijesne znanosti HAZU u Zadru*, no. 42 (2000): 303.

itary operation as the fortress was inaccessible on three sides due to very steep terrain.[83] Furthermore, there was very heavy rain and the troops had left Trebinje with only light provisions.[84] Jovanović demanded every day that the defenders of the fortress surrender,[85] but Klobuk withstood artillery bombardment. The siege ended because the insurgents slipped across the Montenegrin border early one morning before dawn. As Jernej Andrejka's comrade Juri Mišir put it, all the "birds escaped from the cage": Mišir then climbed onto the ramparts and waved a white banner and Jovanović gave three cheers for the emperor.[86] Letting the insurgents escape may have been a deliberate tactic by Jovanović and would have certainly saved lives on both sides.[87] The soldiers from the Graf Nobili regiment watched the explosion of the old building (which had been earmarked for destruction by Jovanović) as if it were a fireworks display: cigars had just arrived with the reinforcements, and they sang and drank beside their campfires as their tattered uniforms dried out in the sun.[88] In an official account of the campaign published in 1879, the symbolic value of destroying the medieval fortress was spelled out:

> The Klobuk mountain fortress had been attacked repeatedly during earlier wars by both the Russians and the Montenegrins, but always in vain. The local people considered it to be impenetrable and so it became a traditional symbol of unbroken resistance. Its suppression and destruction were therefore a political and military necessity. This made the deepest impression on the population and was profoundly consequential for the pacification of Hercegovina.[89]

During the campaign to subdue Hercegovina, the weather had been extremely inclement; initially very hot, then stormy and

---

83 "Die bosnisch-herzegowinische Okkupazion," *Prager Abendblatt*, September 30, 1878, 1.
84 "Die Eroberung von Klobuk," *Morgen-Post*, October 16, 1878, 1.
85 Arnautović, "Austrougarska okupacija Trebinja," 19.
86 "že vsi ptički ušli iz ptičnice," Andrejka, *Slovenski fantje*, 206.
87 Jovanović was described as a "humane leader" by one of his men during this campaign; see H. H., "Der Übergang über den Orien," *Die Vedette*, April 30, 1882, 3.
88 "Die Eroberung von Klobuk," *Morgen-Post*, October 16, 1878, 1-2.
89 Abtheilung für Kriegsgeschichte, *Die Occupation Bosniens und der Hercegovina*, 791.

wet.[90] Rudolph von Wartburg remembered how his exhausted men sheltered from the rain once they reached Trebinje.[91] One soldier reported that the small number of people left in the city were "mistrustful,"[92] although another found them to be "friendly."[93] On September 28, the sun came out again, and the occupying troops were reportedly "elated."[94] Trade soon resumed. Enterprising Dalmatians and Italians soon appeared in Trebinje to sell draft beer directly from the barrel to soldiers who queued to buy the local tobacco.[95] Stjepan Jovanović had first arrived in Trebinje on September 18 and on October 4, after the fall of Klobuk, he held a large victory celebration in front of the former Habsburg vice-consulate, home to Vuk Vrčević who had first been posted to Trebinje in 1861. There was cannon fire, music, and dancing, and a group of local people gathered to watch the "good humored" soldiers who shared their food and wine.[96] Popular with his men and in the patriotic press, Jovanović was known as "our old, trustworthy Jovo."[97] He was described as "a great, fat man, very simple and kindly looking" by Margaret Freeman.[98] Inevitably her husband Arthur Evans was less enamored with Jovanović, who he described as a "court Janissary, a renegade Slav with Germanising proclivities and an eye to decoration."[99] The implicit comparison between Habsburg occupation and Ottoman power had also been made by the insurgents.

---

90 "Während wir uns früher des prächtigsten Wetters zu erfreuen hatten, waren wir jetzt reichlich von Regen überströmt," Dr. Alfred Ebenhoch, "Aus meinem Tagebuche in der Herzegowina," *Mühlviertler Nachrichten*, September 28, 1889, 2.

91 Dr. I. Rudolph von Wartburg, "Meine Erinnerungen an die Kämpfe um Trebinje 7. bis 29. September 1878," *Salzburger Volksblatt*, September 23, 1908, 3.

92 "Aus einem Feldpostbriefe," 2.

93 "Aus Bosnien," *Linzer Volksblatt*, October 1, 1878, 2.

94 "The Austrian Occupation: Capture of Livno and Klobuk," *The Daily Telegraph*, September 30, 1878, 3.

95 "Aus Bosnien," *Grazer Volksblatt (Beilage)*, October 10, 1878, 5.

96 "Die Namensfeier des Kaisers in Trebinje," *Welt-Blatt*, October 20, 1878, 4.

97 He was described in his obituary as a father figure ("Soldatenvater"). "Dem Andenken des Feldmarschall-Lieutenants Baron Jovanović," *Kremser Volksblatt*, December 19, 1885, 3.

98 Joan Evans, *Time and Chance: The Story of Arthur Evans and His Forebears* (London: Longmans, Green and Company, 1943), 218.

99 Our Ragusa Correspondent [Arthur J. Evans], "Austria on the East Adriatic Shores," *Manchester Guardian*, May 18, 1883, 5. The term "janissary" here referred to a male child taken from its Christian South Slav family and brought up as a Muslim in Istanbul.

On October 5, several hundred fugitives and former rebels returned to Trebinje, some of whom had been in exile for three years, and were met in person by Stjepan Jovanović.[100] Although the regimental band of the Graf Nobili regiment welcomed the fugitives, Jovanović asked them to disarm immediately. Allowed to stay in the military encampment overnight, they were given three days' worth of food and twenty Kronen.[101] Jovanović quickly sought recognition and legitimacy from the local population;[102] for example, he made the former anti-Ottoman insurgent Luka Petković captain of the police in Trebinje. His usual practice was to find compromise wherever possible, though he was extremely tough toward those who had opposed the Habsburg takeover. Nine men, eight of them Muslim, were executed almost immediately.[103] In the spring of 1879, more refugees from the earlier conflict returned to Hercegovina. They faced destroyed buildings, damaged wells, and untended fields,[104] but also a shortage of basic crops and food due to the disruption in the agricultural cycles and transhumance.[105]

Over the following years, many soldiers would write about their participation in the 1878 campaign. Jernej Andrejka described his own experience in the 17th Regiment: he decided to publish his notes that had been in a dusty trunk for twenty-five years, in part to glorify the role that Slovene-speaking soldiers had played in the occupation of the new "pearls" of the Monarchy.[106] Habsburg soldiers had imagined themselves as liberators from the Ottoman yoke, not

---

100 "Aus Bosnien," *Grazer Volksblatt*, October 20, 1878, 9.

101 "Rückkehr von Herzegowinern aus Montenegro," *Welt-Blatt*, October 20, 1878, 2. The Krone or crown (known as kruna in Hercegovina) was a unit of currency introduced in the Habsburg Monarchy after 1867.

102 Robert J. Donia, "The Habsburg Imperial Army in the Occupation of Bosnia and Hercegovina," in *Insurrections, Wars, and the Eastern Crisis in the 1870s*, ed. Bela K. Kiraly and Gale Stokes (Boulder, CO: Social Science Monographs, 1985), 386–88.

103 The executed men were Ahmet-efendi Saradžić, Hamid Domuščić, Šuljo Misirlić, Hasan Misirlić, Šaćir Begović, Hašum Begović, Omer Čajić, Imš Babović (orthography unclear), and a Serb called "Grkavac or Glogovac." Arnautović, "Austrougarska okupacija Trebinja," 22–23.

104 F. von M., "Die Culturarbeit," June 10, 2.

105 "Repatriirung," *Grazer Volksblatt*, May 31, 1879, 5.

106 "Predgovor," Andrejka, *Slovenski fantje*, 1–2. On the significance of the writings of Andrejka, see Rok Stergar, *Slovenci in vojska, 1867–1914: Slovenski odnos do vojaških vprašanj od uvedbe dualizma do začetka 1. Svetovne vojne* (Ljubljana: Oddelek za zgodovino Filozofske fakultete, 2004), 137.

as new oppressors, but as Jernej Andrejka recalled: "the inhabitants, who were seeing Austrian soldiers for the first time in this deserted place, were very frightened by our arrival."[107] Memoirs often recalled the violence against their fellow soldiers, which was far more extreme than they had expected. Triestine soldier Ivan Mankoč recalled that one of his comrades was so tired that he could no longer walk. After the comrade was captured, he had his head chopped off by the "Turks."[108] A lieutenant named Schmidt was reported to have been decapitated in September 1878, close to Bileća.[109] One soldier thought this kind of atrocity was carried out to prevent their souls entering paradise.[110] In Grančarevo in September 1878, soldiers found the blood-soaked uniform of their missing comrade named Marx, from a Prague regiment, as well as a cartridge case filled with severed noses and ears.[111] They had entered a theater of war in which the combatants used guerrilla tactics to defend their own lands. They also used battle cries which scared Habsburg soldiers. Many years later, Julius Beranek recalled the fearful cry of "Allah il Allah" as they were ambushed by a thousand insurgents on the march from Mostar.[112] This bitter encounter with more archaic forms of combat coincided with the gradual codification of new rules of war after the 1859 Battle of Solferino between Habsburg and Italian forces, a catastrophic event which led directly to the formation of the Red Cross in 1863 in Geneva by Henri Dunant and his business partners. As a result of the transition toward different rules of war and a paradigm shift against direct brutality, the Habsburg press often dwelt

---

107 Andrejka, *Slovenski fantje*, 110.

108 Ivan Vogrič, "Zasedba Bosne in Hercegovine leta 1878 pismih Ivana Mankoča," *Zgodovinski časopis* 70, nos. 3-4 (2016): 314-36.

109 "Die Expedition gegen Bilek," *Die Presse (Abendblatt)*, September 23, 1878, 2-3.

110 Wartburg, "Meine Erinnerungen an die Kämpfe um Trebinje," 2.

111 "So fand man eine Patrontasche, gefüllt, mit abgeschnittenen Nasen und Ohren, mehrere abgeschnittene Köpfe und auch die über und über mit Blut bedeckte Uniform des am 15. September gefallenen Lieutenants Marx (eines Prägers)," in "Die Eroberung von Klobuk," *Morgen-Post*, October 16, 1878, 1; See also, Božidar Jezernik, *Wild Europe: The Balkans in the Gaze of Western Travellers* (London: Saqi, 2004), 121-46.

112 Julius B[eranek], "Ein Todessprung: Erinnerungen an die Occupation der Herzegowina," *Reichspost*, December 19, 1896, 1. The language of this feuilleton by Beranek may have been influenced by Karl May's 1892 novel *Durch die Wüste*.

upon the dissonance of violent mutilation:[113] "just action" was juxtaposed against "unjust violence" as a rationale for occupation.

The conquest of Bosnia and Hercegovina in 1878 had left the occupying forces with a good idea of the new challenges they would face: namely environmental extremes, local lines of division, and antipathy from a population who had been largely sidelined by international diplomacy. Casualties in 1878 on the Habsburg side involved a loss of 2 percent of their mobilized troops, which, according to John Dredger, "attests to the overall accomplishment of the Austro-Hungarian army, especially considering not only the low numbers of dead and wounded rates, 946 and 3980 respectively, and only 272 men missing."[114] These men were not forgotten. Jernej Andrejka thought that his comrade Maks Švajger went missing in the fight to take Trebinje: "insurgents probably threw him into a cave or a river."[115] Some missing bodies were only found years later, and their discovery made the local press. In 1912, a Trebinje postmaster Leo Weirather found a skeleton of a Tyrolean soldier from one of the Kaiserjäger battalions clutching a bayonet in a forty-five-meter deep shaft in Sovica jama near Mostar. He also found there a small stash of rifles and daggers, three skeletons of local men (assumed by the press to be Orthodox), and a set of handcuffs.[116]

Soldiers arriving in Bileća saw the ruins of the old Ottoman town. By February 1879, the devastation from the recent conflicts was still in evidence: some residents were living under cloth tarpaulins, temporary barracks were very rudimentary, ancient fruit trees had been burned down, but official gatherings could still be held at the century-old oak tree in the town center that had survived the conflict.[117] Arriving in and shortly after 1878, Habsburg soldiers were very aware that Hercegovina had already been unstable and conflict-ridden for some time:[118] they had read about it in detail in the press and now

---

113 A. Sch., "Zum fünfzigjährigen Gedenke," *Danzers Armee Zeitung*, March 4, 1932, 2.
114 John A. Dredger, *Tactics and Procurement in the Habsburg Military, 1866–1918: Offensive Spending* (Cham: Palgrave Macmillan, 2017), 105.
115 Andrejka, *Slovenski fantje*, 327.
116 "Ein Aussehen erregender Höhlenfund," *Volksblatt für Stadt und Land*, December 29, 1912, 7.
117 "Von der Okkupationsarmee," *Epoche*, February 28, 1879, 5.
118 "Heroic blood had already been shed in Popovo polje … in 1876," Andrejka, *Slovenski fantje*, 310.

they could speak directly to the survivors.[119] Many remarked on the ruins after years of insurrection. One soldier described the large number of recently dug graves around the "miserable" city of Trebinje,[120] while another remarked upon the burned-out and deserted villages across Hercegovina as he moved from Stolac to Bileća.[121] In 1879, garrison priest Franz Ivanetič took a two-hour mule journey to Arslanagić most, where he found the chapel beside the bridge was a ruin.[122] Risto Mitrov, a seventy-three-year-old from Jasen, told a reporter that fifteen homes in his village had been burned.[123] He had fled to the safety of Dalmatia with his family, but his younger son had fought with the insurgents to avenge his brother, whose severed head had been found stuck on a pole on the haystack outside his home. Returning to their devastated settlement, the Mitrov family badly needed seeds to reestablish their farmstead.[124]

The new Habsburg authorities believed that they were providentially harnessing the potential of Bosnia and Hercegovina and bringing much-needed calm to a conflict zone. Many believed they were helping to expel the Ottomans from Europe and bringing a better kind of order. They could see the ruins of the old regime all around them in destroyed farmsteads, uncultivated fields, and damaged buildings. They could also see the human suffering that had been endured. Jovanović's victory celebrations in Trebinje and Klobuk communicated to local people and ordinary soldiers that a transfer of power had taken place. The celebrations also rewarded and recognized soldiers who were a long way from home. Although they were aware that challenges lay ahead, the Habsburg military commanders believed that they could now begin to build a new order.

---

119 See, for example, "Die bosnisch-herzegowinische Okkupation," *Prager Abendblatt*, October 1, 1878, 1.
120 "Aus einem Feldpostbriefe," 2.
121 "Soldatenleben in der Herzegowina," *Freie Stimmen*, June 17, 1887, 6.
122 Ivanetič, "Arzloin Agič Most," 1. Without the help of guidebooks (which started to appear only slowly after 1878), he recorded things as he heard them as a native speaker of Slovene, including rendering the name of the bridge as "Arzloin Agič Most."
123 German Consul Lichtenberg reported that the settlement of "Jasseno" (likely to have been Jasen) had been burned down in 1876; see Grandits, *End of Ottoman Rule*, 118.
124 "Zur Stimmung in der Herzegowina," *Welt-Blatt*, December 7, 1878, 5. In the original text, the name is spelled Mitrow.

Chapter Three

CREATING THE TREBINJE GARRISON COMPLEX

The Vision and Drive of Djuro Babić and Anton Galgóczy

Habsburg soldiers quickly stamped their mark on the city of Trebinje. A white memorial pyramid for the fallen of the 74th Graf Nobili Regiment was built in 1880.[1] Just fifteen minutes from the city center, on a path lined with pines and cypresses, the limestone was quarried in Čičevo and a cross was chiseled into it "by an expert hand."[2] In November 1879, just a year into the occupation, Franz Ivanetič reported that the city had transformed: there was now a café (*kafana*) as well as two places to purchase tobacco, guesthouses, and a bookshop whose owner had moved up from Dubrovnik.[3] The urban modernization of Trebinje was shaped by the "paternal rule" of Djuro Babić, who had commanded the 74th Infantry Regiment of Graf Nobili since November 1878.[4] Babić personified the style of leader-

---

1 "Friedhofweihe in Trebinje," *Das Vaterland*, May 8, 1880, 5. The expansion of the Habsburg Monarchy into Bosnia and Hercegovina increased the number of Dalmatian stonecutters from Brač and Korčula.
2 The source did not distinguish between the current settlements of Gornje, Dornje, or Poljice Čičevo. "Trebinje," *Grazer Volksblatt*, April 8, 1880, 2. In 1880, the population of both settlements was far more numerous.
3 Ivanetič, "Allerlei aus Trebinje," 5. Other bookshops selling newspapers and postcards opened after 1878, including businesses run by Stefan Winckelhofer, Anton Peričević, Hamdija Repčić, and Todor Perivić.
4 "The Austrians in Herzegovina," *The Times*, October 6, 1883, 7. Djuro Babić (1826–1890), born in Sveti Rok close to the Velebit Mountains, was a career officer in the Habsburg army.

ship already present in Dalmatia under Gavrilo Rodić and Stjepan Jovanović, in which direct and fluent communication with local people was a vital strategy to build up trust.[5] Like Jovanović, Babić had been seriously injured, in his case by a gunshot wound to the chest in 1859: he slowly recovered his full strength and was described as "dashing and heroic."[6] A veteran of the 1878 campaign, who had fought at Stolac and Klobuk, Babić was tall, well-built with rosy cheeks, silver hair, and a cheerful, friendly voice. Nevertheless, he had strong and firm ideas about the changes he wanted to see, or as he put it: "In Trebinje, I command."[7] Babić became synonymous with the creation of a new urban space.[8]

Trebinje was quickly transformed from a "filthy nest" still damaged by years of rebellion into a "fine European city."[9] Babić ordered buildings destined for demolition to be marked up with chalk and advised local families to move beyond the old city walls.[10] Quite a lot of the houses in Trebinje and Bileća in 1878 were spacious, designed to accommodate extended Muslim families and their visitors. One reporter found nowhere to stay in Trebinje in early 1882, and considered sleeping outside, but was offered a room by a Muslim host in his home as long as he vowed not to visit the women's quarters.[11] The new authorities encouraged small-scale horticulture:[12] it served several purposes in that it was inexpensive, nutritionally beneficial, and gave the men a purposeful physical task. Rank and file soldiers contributed to the greening of the city by growing vegetables just to supplement their rations.[13] In 1881, Charles St John returned to Trebinje after almost two and a half years, recalling that the city had been "dirty" and "dilapidated" when he had last been

---

5   Salis-Soglio, *Mein Leben*, 173.
6   Hubka, *Geschichte des k. und k. Infanterie-Regiments*, 383–84.
7   Carl Winter, "Das herzegowinische Paris," *Neues Wiener Tagblatt*, August 21, 1885, 2.
8   "Von Ragusa nach Trebinje," *Neue Freie Presse (Abendblatt)*, February 6, 1882, 2; Novottny, "Erinnerungen," AT-OeStA/KA NL 417: 12, Kriegsarchiv, Vienna, 195.
9   "Aus der südlichen Herzegowina," *Wiener Bilder*, March 4, 1900, 6.
10 Andrejka, *Slovenski fantje*, 320.
11 "Aus der Herzegowina," *Wiener Allgemeine Zeitung (Mittagblatt)*, February 17, 1882, 2. Larger Muslim homes in Trebinje, such as the Resulbegovića kuća, did have separate quarters for men and women.
12 C. W., "Trebinje: Cultur nach Osten tragen," 246.
13 "Trebinje," *Militär-Zeitung*, April 24, 1885, 245–47.

there. On this return visit, he noted the general cleanliness and new villas with gardens: "the houses have been painted and numbered; the streets repaired and named."[14] Babić apparently felt under pressure to assure the central authorities that he had the region under control.[15] The French traveler Léon Hugonnet (1842–1910) offered a sketch of the military commander:

> [Babić] offered us excellent cigars and gave us some insight into his ways of thinking and acting. This distinguished officer, who speaks Italian well, was struck by the general misery of the local people. He recognizes the goodness and honesty of the Muslim people, while deploring the negligence of poor Ottoman government. In order to teach the people of the country how to cultivate, he created a garden, where the soldiers plant vegetables in a vast field located at the gates of the citadel. It is near the cemetery, and where many Ottoman soldiers were laid to rest during the uprising. In this way the Austrians now feed themselves with produce grown from decomposition of cadavers, which has made the ground very fertile. This innovation is considered by some natives as profane, and they think that Babić is a tyrant.[16]

The military administration of Bosnia and Hercegovina officially ended on January 1, 1880, but in practice garrison towns and cities were still tightly controlled by the military.[17] Although Charles St John was impressed by the changes to the city, he thought that Babić had "exerted considerable military pressure and ... treated ... [Trebinje] as he would have treated a barrack yard."[18] The new regime found other ways to make their mark. A primary school was established

---

14 Charles St John to Earl Granville, Dubrovnik, March 24, 1881, FO 7/1023, National Archives, London.
15 Andrejka, *Slovenski fantje*, 331.
16 Léon Hugonnet, *La Turquie Inconnue: Roumanie, Bulgarie, Macédoine, Albanie* (Paris: L. Frinzine, 1886), 186.
17 For insight into the way in which the Habsburg military presence could alter a town and its local politics (in this case Pula), see Frank Wiggermann, *K.u.K. Kriegsmarine und Politik: Ein Beitrag zur Geschichte der italienischen Nationalbewegung in Istrien* (Vienna: Österreichische Akademie der Wissenschaften, 2004), 19–25.
18 Charles St John to Earl Granville, Dubrovnik, March 24, 1881. FO 7/1023, National Archives, London.

FIGURE 8. Shady center of Trebinje. Nachlass Hans Wagner-Schönkirch, Österreichische Nationalbibliothek, Vienna, Austrian State Archives.

in 1879, despite concerns from both Muslim and Orthodox notables that education would be in German.[19] There is some evidence that the Orthodox population did not always enroll their children in school, but the new regime certainly wanted them to attend.[20] Babić had to face opposition to change,[21] but the extensive planting of chestnut, mulberry, and plane (*platani*) trees that he pioneered gave the city a new character and welcome areas of shade. The new trees made Trebinje visually similar to Habsburg cities such as Zagreb, where there was extensive plantation of planes:[22] similar trees already prospered on the Dalmatian coast in Trsteno, where people

---

19 Mitar Papić, "Prve Škole u Trebinju," *Tribunia: Prilozi za istoriju, arheologiju, etnologiju, umjetnost i kulturu*, no. 2 (1976): 97.

20 "An example of the efforts of the local administration to attract Orthodox students is the request of the district office of Trebinje … in 1882 to campaign for more Orthodox children to enroll in the municipal elementary school as this would be 'in the general interests of the Orthodox,' since their number would otherwise be disproportionately low compared with their overall population within the district." See Grunert, *Glauben im Hinterland*, 370.

21 Kreisbehörde Mostar no. 5137. "An das Obergericht für Bosnien und die Hercegovina in Sarajevo," Mostar, April 26, 1885, Arhiv Bosne i Hercegovine, Sarajevo.

22 Zrinjevac Park in Zagreb was planted with over 200 *platani* imported from the coast and opened to the public in 1873.

danced the *kolo* in their shade.[23] Like the importation of red roof tiles, the planting of imported tree saplings from villages closer to the sea extended the reach of Dalmatian styles into Hercegovina.[24] The shade of the trees protected the city center from flies and allowed market traders to set up stalls in more open spaces than before.

As was the case with other military leaders, pithy maxims by Babić were repeated in memoirs and newspaper stories. Apparently, he valued artisanal skills above trading: "anyone who has ten forints and then purchases cigarette paper and tobacco, calls themselves a merchant."[25] A generation of men who came from fiercely loyal *Grenzer* communities were certain that they understood the landscapes and the people.[26] They were confident that they could include Orthodox communities into the Habsburg "mission."[27] Stjepan Sarkotić, the future Governor of Bosnia, recalled that not only was Babić respected by all the religious denominations, he was also a trusted leader. When he sat down and drank black coffee with his guests, then he expected that he had earned their trust and was disappointed when it was not returned.[28]

Djuro Babić worked closely with Anton Galgóczy,[29] the officer in charge in Bileća, who was highly rated as a good army man by Daniel Salis-Soglio (and other contemporaries).[30] Transferred to the region to lead the 6th Mountain Brigade in 1881, Galgóczy was given credit for the rapid defeat of the insurgency in 1882. In Bileća, new barracks were constructed beside the old Ottoman fort and at Neu-

---

23 Igo Kasch, "Skizzen aus Süddalmatien," *Badener Zeitung*, October 3, 1906, 4. Igo Kaš (1853–1910) was a prolific Styrian travel writer and former soldier; see Jaroš Krivec, "Pogled na drugega: Podobe Bosne in Hercegovine in njenih prebivalcev med 1878 in 1918" (MA thesis, University of Ljubljana, 2021).

24 Plane trees in Trsteno (often known by their Italian name Cannosa) were admired for their size and general appearance, see for example, R. A., "Cannosa," *Prager Tagblatt*, February 12, 1898, 1–4.

25 Papić, "Prve Škole u Trebinju," 97.

26 The Military Border (*Militärgrenze*) was formally dissolved in 1881, three years after the occupation of Bosnia and Hercegovina and the same year that conscription was extended there.

27 Andrejka, *Slovenski fantje*, 320.

28 Stefan Freiherr von Sarkotić, "Aus meinen Erinnerungen," *Danzers Armee-Zeitung*, April 8, 1927, 2–3.

29 His surname was sometimes also Germanized to Galgotzy.

30 "ein Soldat von echtem Schrot und Korn," Salis-Soglio, *Mein Leben*, 148.

Bilek, about a fifteen minute walk from the old town and close to the new border.[31] Originally from a Szekler family from Sfântu Gheorghe, Galgóczy often went to see Babić in Trebinje—seventeen kilometers away—on foot, even in storms or scorching summer heat, "preferring to walk than sit in the saddle."[32] Both were working with limited budgets.[33] Abundant local resources such as wood and stone were an obvious starting point. Augmenting the existing fortress system was a vital part of Habsburg military strategy. As John Dredger has argued, "[e]ven while engaged in a guerrilla war, fortresses continued to occupy the minds of Austro-Hungarian military thinkers."[34] Galgóczy was given credit for a much firmer material demarcation of the border between Hercegovina and Montenegro "with wood, willow, and water."[35] While regional building materials were inventively used, older buildings were sacrificed along the way. In 1882, Daniel Salis-Soglio had enjoyed a meal in Čepelica beside the old bridge, as well as a "wonderful coffee" served by a beautiful Orthodox woman in colorful local dress. When he returned just four years later after the suppression of the rebellion, the inn was gone, as was the old bridge (replaced by a new one), and there was no sign of the woman who had served him.[36]

The occupation of Hercegovina was observed at a short but critical distance by the English archaeologist Arthur Evans, who had traveled in the region since 1875 and only recently settled in Dubrovnik. He and many of his contemporaries felt that they had the right to judge the performance of the Habsburg state in relation to their Berlin Treaty commitments. Always implicitly critical of the occupation (because he believed that the South Slav lands should be self-governing), he published articles in the *Manchester Guardian* under the thin veil of their "Ragusa correspondent." While exploring the Ombla river without his passport in March 1881, Evans was marched for four hours to Trebinje, where he was held under arrest until he

---

31 "Zum Tode des Feldzeugmeisters Galgoczy," *Tagblatt*, November 8, 1929, 3–4.
32 P. L., "Ein Mann der Zukunft," *Mährisches Tagblatt*, April 7, 1887, 1.
33 Salis-Soglio, *Mein Leben*, 176.
34 Dredger, *Tactics and Procurement*, 112.
35 "Generalmajor Anton Galgotzy," *Die Presse*, March 4, 1887, 9.
36 "Kaffeehaus, Serbin und alte Brücke waren verschwunden," Salis-Soglio, *Mein Leben*, 148, 187.

was recognized and released.[37] At this stage, his critical journalism was still tolerated.

Perhaps more than anything else, the poor roads symbolized poor government and past tribulations. The roads that did exist were few in number.[38] Paths seemed to lead nowhere and were pitted with rubble or rocks the size of a human head.[39] Many observers remarked about the drift of rocks onto existing roads. In 1857, more than twenty years before the Habsburg arrival, the Sarajevo-based Russian Consul Alexander Hilferding noted just how bad the roads were at Dražin Do: "we crossed the Trebišnjica River in a primitive wide boat; we were transferred first and then the horses. The road was in poor condition here as well ... it was inexplicable to me why heaps of stones were deliberately scattered in several places along this path so that one could stumble."[40] Edward Freeman's journey to Trebinje in 1875 also involved crossing the Trebišnjica in a "primitive punt" and he too complained about the state of the roads.[41] Like Babić, Galgóczy was preoccupied by roadbuilding in part because the unevenness of the roads constituted a very visible lack of order. The emphasis on manual labor was also intended to instill a kind of toughness (*tvrdost/Zähigkeit*) in the troops.[42] Galgóczy insisted that in the absence of tools, gravel should be made for the roads by a hundred soldiers crushing the stones with a larger rock.[43] Soldiers were commanded to undertake heavy duties, thus supplying one of the most important factors of production in creating the garrison complex, namely manual labor. Djuro Babić also expected his men to be pro-

---

37 Evans, *Time and Chance*, 234.
38 "Das ganze Land war 1878 straßenarm." Conrad, *Mein Anfang*, 11.
39 "Durch die Zubcsi und Suttorina II," *Pester Lloyd*, March 12, 1882, 2.
40 Gligor Samardžić and Goran Popović, "The Importance of the Ottoman-era Travelogues for the Reconstruction of the Roman Road Network in Bosnia and Herzegovina," in *Voyages and Travel Accounts in Historiography and Literature*, vol. 2, ed. Boris Stojkovski, online at https://trivent-publishing.eu/, accessed July 1, 2021. His name is sometimes spelled Gilferding.
41 Freeman, *Sketches from the Subject*, 268.
42 Hämmerle, *Ganze Männer?*, 235–36. Richard Neutra thought that "exercises dominated by harsh commanders" led directly to logistical difficulties; see Volker M. Welter, "From the Landscape of War to the Open Order of the Kaufmann House: Richard Neutra and the Experience of the Great War," in *The Good Gardener? Nature, Humanity, and the Garden*, ed. Annette Giesecke and Naomi Jacobs (London: Black Dog, 2014), 219.
43 P. L., "Ein Mann der Zukunft," 2–3.

active: "roads are important to us soldiers. When you walk home and see a large rock lying on your path, kick it aside!"[44] The military leadership's strategy was evidently successful. By the mid-1890s, when Harry Craufuird Thomson visited Hercegovina, the road infrastructure was good enough for him to remark that "like all the roads built by the Austrian, [it] is the perfection of a mountain road, the gradient never being steep enough to be dangerous or even inconvenient."[45] Other observers agreed that the roads had improved: "the mere presence of a company or two of Austrian soldiers brings into existence, as if by magic, military roads, bridges and a European quarter."[46] Franz von Werner had suggested that "bad roads" preserved autonomy in Hercegovina and that the population had valued their freedom more than transport or accessibility.[47] Good roads that could accommodate multiple columns of troops or vehicles meant that local people could be controlled.

For the historian Esad Arnautović, the Habsburg takeover in Trebinje, although rapid, was very harsh in terms of retribution, in part because local men were forced to repair the damaged roads.[48] Many appreciated better roads and clearer authority. One reporter noticed the busy Muslim stonemasons when he arrived in Trebinje in 1886, which demonstrated that "the population of Hercegovina had become accustomed to honest work."[49] Writing to his father-in-law Edward Freeman, Arthur Evans associated road construction with a kind of new tyranny:

There can be no doubt that Trebinje has gained in some material ways from its new drill-masters; its trading Begs and bugs have alike diminished; it certainly is cleaner. But I should say the present administration was quite intolerable in all other respects. The people are treated not as a liberated, but as a conquered and inferior race; their sense of Right—which they do possess in a re-

44 Andrejka, *Slovenski fantje*, 313.
45 Harry Craufuird Thomson, *The Outgoing Turk: Impressions of a Journey through the Western Balkans* (New York: D. Appleton, 1897), 196.
46 Robert J. Kennedy, *Montenegro and its Borderlands* (London: Hatchards, 1894), 33-34.
47 Werner, *Türkische Skizzen*, 136.
48 Arnautović, "Austrougarska okupacija Trebinja," 22.
49 "B," "Der Kronprinz in der Herzegowina," *Neues Wiener Tagblatt*, April 4, 1886, 3.

markable degree—is simply trodden underfoot. It is military law plus bureaucratic vexation. I saw gangs of men and boys forced to work on the roads without receiving any pay—simply the old Corvée—one of the familiar oppressions of Turkish rule, reintroduced into districts which had succeeded in putting a stop to it by armed resistance.[50]

Legends were created around Babić and Galgóczy in a kind of army personality cult encouraged and repeatedly nourished by the patriotic press. For the first seven years he was in charge in Trebinje, Babić is reported to have only left once for a swimming trip to the coast.[51] The legends endured beyond the nineteenth century. Many military records and diaries contained Galgóczy anecdotes, not least because he lived into his nineties, and worked well beyond the usual retirement age, having served in the army for fifty-nine years.[52] He was said to be brusque, with his orders like a "clip round the ear."[53] Galgóczy neither drank nor gambled, and he was reported to have often ridden out at night to the local houses to check everything was in order.[54] He was celebrated in the press as "Unser Anton" (our very own Anton) and was described as a "gaunt figure with a tough nature that defied the *bora*."[55] Once, when he asked how long it would take a cadet to learn to salute, and was told "about ten minutes," he reportedly replied that "a schoolboy could learn it in five."[56] He was reputed to have ordered a uniform for a "medium sized general" and when pressed for specific measurements, replied "I want a tailor, not a carpenter."[57]

Many accounts discussed the sheer hard labor of building forts on the cordon, as the border was referred to in Habsburg sources.

50 Evans, *Time and Chance*, 223.
51 Carl Winter, "Das herzegowinische Paris," *Neues Wiener Tagblatt*, August 21, 1885, 2.
52 F. Michael Florer, "Kriegsaufzeichnungen," AT-OeStA/KA NL 654 (B), Kriegsarchiv, Vienna, 257.
53 "wie eine Ohrfeige," "Feldz[e]ugmeister Galgotzy gestorben: Ein populärer General des alten Oesterreich Ungarn," *Neue Freie Presse*, November 6, 1929, 2.
54 Alexander Günthersen, "Erinnerungen an Feldzeugmeister Galgotzy," *Reichspost*, November 7, 1929, 7.
55 Emil Seeliger, "General Galgotzy—der eisener General," *Wiener Sonn- und Montags-Zeitung*, August 20, 1923, 5.
56 "Zum Tode des Feldzeugmeisters Galgoczy," *Tagblatt*, November 8, 1929, 3.
57 "Austria: Unser Anton," *Time*, December 9, 1929, 28.

FIGURE 9. Marble tombstones (*stećci*) close to the village of Radmilovića Dubrava. Photo by Jovan Vidaković, Wikimedia Commons.

Water supplies were often so limited that they had to be brought by donkey.[58] Officer Karl Hanke was ordered to establish a border post at Radmilovića Dubrava in driving rain in December 1882. When he arrived, he discovered only foundation stones and rubble, the remnants of a settlement that was probably destroyed in 1876. The work to construct the frontier post began immediately: "everyone with hands used them."[59]

Close to Vardar and almost directly on the border, ancient marble tombstones or *stećci* were used to construct the fort of Vrbica where Reinhold Oeser was eventually posted in 1914. As János Asbóth explained:

Unfortunately the inexorable demands of war used a large number of these tombstones, when the 20th Battalion of Rangers built this station, upon the occasion of the last insurrection. Almost the whole of the strong stone fencing is formed of these enor-

---

[58] Andrejka, *Slovenski fantje*, 338.
[59] "Die Arbeit begann sogleich. Alles, was Hände hatte, arbeitete." Karl Hanke von Hankenstein, "Weihnachten am Kordon," *Teplitz-Schönauer Anzeiger*, December 25, 1909, 1.

mous blocks and squares, which were so near and so easy to get whilst building materials would otherwise have only been attainable by great expenditure of labor, time, and money.[60]

Military resources could replace missing factors of production, especially enterprise and labor, although capital remained in short supply and local commanders always worked within limited budgets.

Service in Bosnia and Hercegovina gave young conscripts experience in harsh, demanding terrain. The opportunities arising from the occupation allowed a large and well-organized army to fulfil its potential and create a new order very rapidly. Businesses opened up alongside the military installations and professionals moved into the region. Strategically placed former Ottoman garrisons were expanded to suit the needs of the Habsburg Monarchy. Leadership from experienced officers, many of whom already spoke Serbian or Croatian, helped to smooth over differences of opinion. In many respects, the rapid transfer of power to the Habsburg state in 1878 looked successful, or, at the very least, decisive. As both Charles St John and Arthur Evans noted at the time, peace and reconstruction was imposed upon Hercegovina by army leaders lacking confidence in local people, who already had a strong sense of their own rights, to transform themselves. While some acquiesced or capitulated to the new normal, others thought better of it. Some weighed up their options before giving their qualified support to the Habsburg military.[61] Bogdan Zimonjić, who was "as tall as a tree and had pistols, daggers, and swords on his belt," is reported to have laid aside his weapons because Anton Galgóczy stared directly at him and asked him to do so (even though this was regarded as an insult in Hercegovina).[62] His son Stevan reported that his father was in Mostar in late 1878 when Stjepan Jovanović asked him to remove the Montenegrin coat of arms from his uniform. Zimonjić replied that

---

60 János Asbóth, *An Official Tour through Bosnia and Herzegovina with an Account of the History, Antiquities, Agrarian Conditions, Religion, Ethnology, Folk Lore, and Social Life of the People* (London: Swan Sonnenschein, 1890), 348. Asbóth (1845-1911) was a Hungarian political scientist and constitutional expert.

61 Kapidžić, *Hercegovački ustanak*, 122.

62 "Galgoczy-Legenden," *Wiener Allgemeine Zeitung (Samstag Mittagblatt)*, March 5, 1887, 2; "Anton Galgóczy," *Pester Lloyd*, March 5, 1887, 5.

Jovanović should first get him a new one from Vienna and then he would decide which one he thought was better.[63] Decisive Habsburg rule did not necessarily transform into instant or universal approval from the people of Hercegovina.

Reluctant Soldiers: Uprisings against Conscription in 1881–1882

As a response to a surge of popular revolutionary nationalism in 1848 in Prague, Budapest, Milan, Zagreb, and in the capital Vienna, the Habsburg Monarchy became even more dependent upon its army to remain unified. Everyday life became increasingly militaristic: as Mark Twain observed in the 1890s, the army was "everywhere ... as pervasive as the atmosphere."[64] Emperor Franz Joseph cultivated a warm relationship with the rank and file as well as the officer command, seeing himself as a leader above class and nationality. During his sixty-eight years on the throne, the loyalty of the multinational conscript army became one of the state's "strongest centripetal forces."[65] Like the Apache braves imagined in popular fiction, acquired names could honor youth and courage, representing a heroic form of self-fashioning: Field Marshal Adam Brandner von Wolfszahn had led the defeat of insurgents at Vučji zub in early May 1882, when he spotted their location on Mount Orjen.[66] His noble title, conferred years later, celebrated his bold decision-making and the name of the peak (Vučji zub translates as "wolfstooth"). Likewise, Captain Valentin Kasperl from Carinthia was thereafter known as "the old wolf" by his men for his daring military strategy during the 1882 Uprising.[67]

---

63 Grunert, *Glauben im Hinterland*, 316f.

64 Laurence Cole, *Military Culture and Popular Patriotism in Late Imperial Austria* (Oxford: Oxford University Press, 2014), 3. On the culture of the army, see Hämmerle, *Ganze Männer?*; Richard Bassett, *For God and Kaiser: The Imperial Austrian Army 1619–1918* (New Haven, CT: Yale University Press, 2015).

65 Gunther Rothenberg, *The Army of Francis Joseph* (West Lafayette, IN: Purdue University Press, 1976), ix.

66 "Lieutenant Adam Brandner (des 16. Infanterie-Regimentes)," *Militär-Zeitung*, March 11, 1884, 5. Brandner (1857–1940) was born in Vojvodina (Banat) and had a long career in the Habsburg army, retiring in 1918.

67 "Stadt und Land," *Klagenfurter Zeitung*, May 29, 1912, 1255.

After 1867, and the *Ausgleich* or compromise between Austria and Hungary, a national army was recruited from both halves of the monarchy, supported by the Cisleithanian Landwehr as well as the Hungarian Honvéd. This army functioned because of compulsory conscription for young men, introduced in 1868. Three years of active service (with breaks to return home for the harvest) and a further nine years in the reserve service and home reserve militia (*Landsturm*) shaped the men of the Empire into loyalists who toughened up along "a *via crucis* that had to be overcome."[68] Writing in 1927, Stjepan Sarkotić looked back to his military service in Trebinje under Djuro Babić in the 1880s as "hard, but beautiful times."[69] Conscription created a new class of educated, cosmopolitan, and *kaisertreu* officers, whose service would span the territories of the monarchy, and almost all of their battalions were multilingual. Each individual regiment had its heroes, standard, uniforms, embroidered insignia, marching music, and its store of anecdotes, many of which were retold in the press. If Franz Joseph remained close to this army, then the admiration was reciprocated. His picture was stuck into diaries and notebooks, and in Trebinje, it graced the officers' dining room.[70] The emperor's pre-dawn breakfasts, long hours at his desk, stoicism, tragic personal history, penchant for dress uniforms, as well as his genuine interest in the detail of military affairs, all made him a revered leader, even when he was in his eighties.[71] Conversely, resistance to the rigors of armed service defined a particular form of delinquency and a rejection of the emperor's paternalism. In 1904, when

---

68 "Stations of the cross," Cole, *Military Culture*, 119. The mixed experience of conscripted Slovene soldiers is discussed in Stergar, *Slovenci in vojska, 1867–1914*, 32–39. An English student spent the summer cycling with his friend X who "only knew twelve words of the language": "At home he is a respectable young manufacturer, in Bosnia he had been doing his annual four weeks military service with a mountain battery," in "A Summer Holiday," *The Caian* 18 (1908): 147–48.

69 Sarkotić, "Aus meinen Erinnerungen," 2–3. On the early years of his service in the hospital at Trebinje, see Ernest Bauer, *Der letzte Paladin des Reiches: Generaloberst Stefan Freiherr Sarkotić von Lovćen* (Graz: Styria, 1988), 11.

70 Novottny "Erinnerungen," AT-OeStA/KA NL 417: 12, Kriegsarchiv, Vienna, 195.

71 On the politics of popular patriotism, see the essays in Laurence Cole and Daniel L. Unowsky, eds., *The Limits of Loyalty: Imperial Symbolism, Popular Allegiances, and State Patriotism in the Late Habsburg Monarchy* (New York: Berghahn, 2007).

FIGURE 10. New recruits in Trebinje, 1909. Muzej Hercegovine, Trebinje.

disappointed soldiers rioted in Bileća and Trebinje, they got drunk and tore up pictures of Franz Joseph.[72]

Compulsory military service drove young men to carry out elaborate forms of malingering that became even more prevalent during the First World War. Mile Popović, an Orthodox cadet from Čitluk, was reported to have cried himself to sleep and wandered off from the barracks. Mile was put in a punishment cell where he stopped eating, before finally escaping from the barrack's hospital after the garrison doctor had recommended that he be put there. He was clothed only in his bed shirt.[73] Mile's story was retold with the intention of humiliating him, although he did then disappear, which might be judged a good outcome for him. For men from remote homes, unused to the company of people other than their closest relatives, conscription was a wrench.[74] The choices that young men faced sometimes seemed arbitrary and predetermined. Antonio Budinich recorded how he felt about his allotted garrison: "I received

---

72 "Die Soldatenrevolte in Bilek," *Neues Wiener Journal*, January 4, 1904, 4.
73 Robert Michel, "Der Deserteur," *Pilsner Tagblatt*, December 13, 1914, 2-6.
74 On the question of national identity and desertion, see Siniša Malešević, "Forging the Nation-Centric World: Imperial Rule and the Homogenisation of Discontent in Bosnia and Herzegovina (1878-1918)," *Journal of Historical Sociology* 34, no. 4 (2021): 665-87.

the order about my posting from Mostar. I opened the envelope silently with a trembling hand."[75]

Trebinje came under Habsburg rule at a time when the army was the monarchy's most powerful administrative institution. Compulsory military service was extended to Bosnia and Hercegovina in November 1881, to commence the following spring.[76] It also included the men of Krivošije in Southern Dalmatia, who had resisted the imposition of military service in 1869. The introduction of conscription challenged the terms of the Berlin Treaty of 1878 and led to an immediate negative reaction across the newly occupied lands. A government report in December 1881 indicated that the atmosphere in Eastern Hercegovina was "tense and explosive."[77] In the three years between the fall of 1878 and the winter of 1881, former anti-Ottoman insurgents had developed an ambivalent relationship with the new authorities.

If there were signs of hostility to the draft in 1881, then signs of general disorder were also reemerging. Some "bold" men had already retreated into the forests close to the Montenegrin border as early as 1879.[78] The postal service was sabotaged in August 1881 close to Avtovac and men were killed by the assailants, who were all reported to be Orthodox.[79] Commenting on support for Stojan Kovačević in September 1881, the British Consul in Sarajevo, Edward Freeman, noted that bonds were strong within the rural population: "the peasants will not betray them ... because *hajduks* are regarded in this country not as mere brigands, but as heroes and patriots."[80] The security situation in the Trebinje region, already dangerous, deteriorated rapidly. An unnamed reporter for *Pester Lloyd* sent an article on Decem-

---

75 Budini, *Le memorie di guerra*, 71.
76 Dahlen's proclamation was printed in German and Bosnian (both in the Latin and Cyrillic scripts) in the *Sarajevski list* on November 4/October 23, 1881, 1–13.
77 Dževada Šuško, "Bosniaks and Loyalty: Responses to the Conscription Law in Bosnia and Hercegovina 1881/82," *Hungarian Historical Review*, no. 3 (2014): 537.
78 Kapidžić, *Hercegovački ustanak*, 88. On the interplay between local "agency" and Habsburg control, see Iva Lučić, "Law of the Forest: Early Legal Governance in Bosnia-Herzegovina during the Inter-Imperial Transition between Ottoman and Austro-Hungarian Rule 1878–1901," *Slavic Review* 81, no. 3 (2022): 595–99.
79 "Ein Badener in der Herzegowina," *Badener Bezirks-Blatt*, August 20, 1881, 6.
80 Edward Freeman to the Secretary of State for Foreign Affairs, September 6, 1881, FO 7/1023, National Archives, London. The original is spelled Haiduk.

ber 10, published just over a week later, which noted that while most of the insurgents had dispersed after 1878, Stojan Kovačević and his followers were still active. The reporter also noted the performative outward obedience of the local population; while affirming their loyalty to the regime, they actually supported the insurgents.[81] In late December 1881, the wife of a caterer in Trebinje garrison was attacked and gagged while her husband served food and wine to soldiers. Their possessions were taken from their humble stone house not sixty paces from the military buildings by two armed men, one from Korenjići and the other a Montenegrin.[82] Outside the garrison complex, security was even more precarious. Men from the 16th Varaždin regiment marched toward the woods in Gornje Grančarevo. They had wanted to build a hall (*Turnplatz*) in Trebinje and because there were no reported insurgents in the area, they went out unarmed. They were fired upon by local men who then vanished, apparently into thin air.

> A detachment, consisting of a non-commissioned officer and eighteen men, went to a forest … about ten kilometers from Trebinje on Saturday 26th to cut down the necessary wood there. Since nothing suspicious had ever appeared so close to the fortress, the road leading to Župa is patrolled day and night, and a gendarmerie post has been established in Grančarevo itself, the detachment … did not take rifles, but only the tools necessary for felling wood. It was about 4 o'clock in the afternoon when the soldiers, having finished their work, went away with the felled tree trunks on their shoulders, singing and marching back. The route back went through a bottleneck…. Two men then fell to the ground badly wounded; two others had minor injuries. As firing continued from the heights, the soldiers had no choice but to flee. Given the nature of the bottleneck, the soldiers could not have done anything else even if they had had rifles with them, for it was downright impossible to fight from low ground with Hercegovinians lying hidden behind boulders on the heights of the embankment.[83]

---

81 "Die Gährung in der Herzegovina," 2.
82 "Der Überfall von Grancarevo," *Tages-Post*, December 28, 1881, 2.
83 "Der Überfall von Grancarevo," 1.

In Zubci in 1882, the estimated 350 rebels were all Orthodox and probably from extended families.[84] The new occupiers were also aware that the strong family ties still extant in Hercegovina would not easily be broken, even by years of chaos and fighting. Bogojević Selo was described by one soldier in 1882 as:

> a group of thatched cottages in an idyllic location, embedded in mighty mountains, surrounded by green meadows and lush trees, [it] seemed destined to be a place of comforting stillness, of peaceful tranquility. But this was the home village to the Vukalović family, who provided generations of leaders for every insurgent movement. All the able-bodied men were already in the high mountains and only old men, women, and children inhabited the poor huts.[85]

In early 1882, civilians were forbidden to carry arms, especially in the border region.[86] The army reinforced its military presence in Kruševice and Zubci, wary of the close connection with Krivošije; the gendarmerie in Lastva was also reinforced.[87]

The insurgency spread across Bosnia and Hercegovina with significant regional pockets of resistance. The barracks at Ulog-Obrnja were surrounded on the evening of January 10, 1882, and on January 17, a supply column was attacked on the way to Bileća. Six Habsburg soldiers were killed immediately, and the two missing men were later found dead and mutilated, one with his nose cut off.[88] Muslim families fled from small settlements to Bileća to escape the wrath of the insurgents.[89] The Grančarevo incident coincided with an insurrection led by Stojan Kovačević, once a comrade of Luka Vukalović, but also a veteran of the 1875 Uprising.[90] Sutorina had been a frequent meet-

---

84   Kapidžić, *Hercegovački ustanak*, 202.
85   H. H., "Der Zug über den Orien," *Der Vaterland*, April 16, 1882, 11.
86   "Aus der Herzegowina," *Wiener Allgemeine Zeitung (Mittagblatt)*, February 17, 1882, 2.
87   Kapidžić, *Hercegovački ustanak*, 120–21.
88   Josef Morokutti, "Der Aufstand im Süden des Okkupationsgebietes im Jahre 1882," *Kärntner Zeitung*, October 5, 1907, 2.
89   "Aus dem Tagebuch eines Reservemannes," *Marburger Zeitung*, February 12, 1882, 2.
90   "Die Kämpfe unserer Truppen 1881–1882," *Militär-Zeitung*, May 3, 1893, 272–74. Stojan Kovačević (1821–1911) was originally from Srdjevići, near Gacko, but moved to Montenegro after the 1882 rebellion. Because of his long life and evasion of Habsburg justice, he remained the archetypal insurgent in the monarchy's press.

ing place for the rebel leaders, including Lazar Sočica, Tripko Vukalović and Tomo Tomašević. In 1858, Luka Vukalović had temporarily taken over the Ottoman garrison there and raised the red flag with a white cross of Montenegro.[91] In April 1876, these leaders (excluding Luka Vukalović who had died in exile in 1873) had met the Dalmatian Governor Gavrilo Rodić there,[92] and continued to view the settlement as a strategic asset. In December 1881, having traveled through the Sutorina valley, Kovačević raided Herceg Novi, taking a hundred sheep and five oxen.[93] Despite military reinforcements at key forts, his armed followers had apparently moved through the region with ease.[94] The flat terrain in the valley favored rapid advancement, but there was also the option to retreat to the surrounding hills and caves where the paths were move difficult to move along with speed. In January 1882, an officer was robbed by a man from the Kovačević gang, and his watch and silver chain were taken. His assailant was reported to be "armed to the teeth." After this time, officers were not allowed to walk alone for leisure.[95] The postal service in the region was accompanied by a military guard for several weeks.[96] Kovačević's men emboldened others to follow, and the insurgents began to destroy the school and rectory houses; guard houses and coastal towns were no longer safe from these raids.[97] Throughout the campaign, Stojan Kovačević was regarded as the most important insurgent leader.[98] Hamdija Kapidžić argued that the insurgent gang led by Kovačević attracted young men who were determined to avoid conscription and were not necessarily all Orthodox by religion.[99]

---

91 James Zohrab to Henry Bulwer, Mostar, September 26, 1858, FO 195/578, National Archives, London.

92 Grandits, *End of Ottoman Rule*, 158.

93 Our Ragusa Correspondent [Arthur J. Evans], "With the Bocchese Insurgents," *Manchester Guardian*, December 12, 1881, 5.

94 Kapidžić, *Hercegovački ustanak*, 121.

95 "Vom Insurrektions-Schauplätze," *Tages-Post*, January 18, 1882, 2.

96 "Aus Dalmatien," *Pester Lloyd*, March 13, 1882, 1.

97 Hubka, *Geschichte des k. und k. Infanterie-Regiments*, 480.

98 Daniel Salis-Soglio to Hans Salis-Soglio, Dubrovnik, April 6, 1882, Staatsarchiv Graubünden, Chur. Johann Salis-Soglio (1854–1916), also an officer in the Habsburg army, was based in Sarajevo during the 1882 Insurgency.

99 Kapidžić, *Hercegovački ustanak*, 102. On the question of Muslim-Christian relations after 1878, see also Nada Tomović, "Saradnja muslimanskog i pravoslavnog stanovništva u toku

From January 1882, reinforcements were sent from the garrison at Dubrovnik to Trebinje.[100]

[A] unified command structure was created on 17th January with the establishment of the Southern Dalmatia and Hercegovina Command; by early March this corps level command, headquartered in Dubrovnik, would possess the 18th Division at Mostar, the 44th Division at Trebinje ... and the 47th Division at Castelnuovo ... six mountain and two infantry brigades in all, a total of 40 infantry battalions ... supported by eight mountain batteries.[101]

Charles St John reported that the public in Dubrovnik were "completely in the dark" about the insurgency, despite being so close to the theater of conflict.[102] Days later he picked up more information observing that "rifle guns (were) being mounted intended to command the Trebinje road ... that some fighting has been going on in the vicinity of Trebinje there can be no doubt as wounded have arrived and wreaths of flowers have been sent from here for the dead."[103] Stjepan Jovanović had requested 40,000 extra soldiers to be sent to the region, so Habsburg soldiers should have had an overwhelming advantage. A priest named Jovan Vasiljević told the military authorities that the insurgent leader (Tripko) Vukalović from Zubci had four hundred men under his control.[104] On January 28, Habsburg troops encountered five hundred insurgents at Necvijeće and fought around the stone bridge and in the water. The rebels found themselves trapped by a bayonet charge and many were killed.[105]

---

austrougarske okupacije Bosne i Hercegovine 1878–1882. godine," *Almanah*, nos. 81–82 (2019): 65–74.

100 Charles St John to Earl Granville, Dubrovnik, January 16, 1882, FO7 1041, National Archives, London.

101 John R. Schindler, "Defeating Balkan Insurgency: The Austro-Hungarian Army in Bosnia-Hercegovina, 1878–82," *Journal of Strategic Studies* 27, no. 3 (2004): 543.

102 Charles St John to Earl Granville, Dubrovnik, January 24, 1882, FO7 1041, National Archives, London.

103 Charles St John to Earl Granville, Dubrovnik, January 28, 1882, FO7 1041, National Archives, London.

104 Ivan Pederin, "Vojne operacije domaršala baruna Stjepana Jovanovića u Hercegovini 1878. i u Krivošijama 1882," *Bosna Franciscana*, no. 35 (2011): 130.

105 In the original text the village was named as Nedzvecje. "Vom Insurrektionsschauplatze," *Teplitz-Schönauer Anzeiger*, February 8, 1882, 1.

Trebinje was crucial to the coordination of the military and therefore in the suppression of the uprising, and the garrison was soon filled to capacity.[106] Troops had set off from Gruž at half past one in the afternoon on foot on January 14, only reaching Trebinje at ten in the evening. They were warmly welcomed by Djuro Babić, who told them that some would be accommodated in the city, while a portion of the troops would be billeted in villages nearby.[107] While the welcome may have been warm, one soldier remembered the bitterly cold wind on the march to Trebinje, his fingers too cold to cut his bread, men who stumbled from fatigue in the dark, as well as the dank walls of the very basic accommodation they were offered.[108]

The insurgents were dealt a significant blow in late February when a Habsburg soldier wandered into a cave at Orahovac and found a stash of smoked meat, a hundred hams, and five hundred pounds of potatoes. As with the later fighting at Vučji zub, the soldiers had been watching the rebels for some time and knew that they had a hiding place.[109] In Lučići and other nearby settlements in 1882, Habsburg officials found 927 different sorts of weapons as well as a cannon, all concealed in ordinary homesteads.[110] This was to be a struggle of attrition. There were very icy conditions on Mount Orjen in March 1882.[111] Tactical improvements favored the Habsburg troops, and they abandoned the "the black trousers, caps, sashes, and swords that differentiated them as leaders from the enlisted men and gave the enemy obvious targets."[112] On February 8, Conrad von Hötzendorf from the division headquarters distributed military equipment to the troops in the coastal stations.[113]

The 1882 rebels operated in small numbers, attacking key strategic positions and using their superior knowledge of the mountains and valleys. They also used guerrilla tactics and avoided direct bat-

---

106 Kapidžić, *Hercegovački ustanak*, 106.
107 Rudolf Pfeffer, *Geschichte des k. u. k. Infanterieregiments Freiherr Kray Nr. 67: Erster Band 1860–1910* (Vienna: Im Selbstverlage des Regiments, 1912), 136.
108 "Tagebuch eines Mobilisirten," *Pester Lloyd*, January 25, 1882, 3.
109 "Zur Tagesgeschichte," *Innsbrucker Nachrichten*, February 27, 1882, 2.
110 "Vom Insurrectionsschauplatze," *Mährisches Tagblatt*, April 3, 1882, 6.
111 "Der Aufstand," *Neue Freie Presse*, March 12, 1882, 4.
112 Dredger, *Tactics and Procurement*, 116.
113 Hubka, *Geschichte des k. und k. Infanterie-Regiments*, 478–79.

tles: the small garrison in Avtovac had its telegraph line cut by the rebels.[114] A "depressed" Stjepan Jovanović had little time for the tactics of the insurgents: he told Charles St John that these men were "(expletive) rebellious brigands whose mode of warfare was to shoot down the military from behind rocks."[115] Jovanović had preferred to wait until warmer weather to deal with the insurgency, but the Bosnian Governor Hermann Dahlen wanted the immediate suppression of any anti-regime forces.[116] The Habsburg authorities used local auxiliaries or the *Streif-Corps* (*štrafuni*) and a hundred were sent to Hercegovina.[117] Margaret Freeman described the febrile atmosphere to her mother: "[Dubrovnik] swarms with soldiers drilling, parading, marching about, washing, idling, smoking, road-making. Detachments pass going up to Trebinje with mountain guns. Loads of provisions are always going by and sometimes an ambulance wagon returns laden with sick soldiers."[118]

The insurgents fought with the weapons that they had. People around Trebinje who did not want to join the rebellion were reportedly told by insurgents that their houses would be set on fire as punishment.[119] As John Schindler puts it, "particularly unnerving was the bandits' predilection for hiding in the hills and singing taunting songs at nearby Austro-Hungarian units while they tried to sleep."[120] "Come up here, Austrian billy goats" was one taunt.[121] One soldier recalled "the monotonous howling of the insurgents by night,"[122] although sometimes wolves came near the encampments and their howl was mistaken for the voices of humans. The war cries (*Indianergeheul*) of the insurgents led by Tripko Vukalović in 1882

114 "Vom Insurrections-Schauplatze," *Militär-Zeitung*, April 4, 1882, 211.
115 Charles St John to Earl Granville, Dubrovnik, January 23, 1882. FO7 1041, National Archives, London. We can only guess what the expletive word was that Jovanović used. See also Andrejka, *Slovenski fantje*, 314.
116 Hermann Dahlen von Orlaburg (1828–1887), originally from Košice, was the third Bosnian Governor. He retired due to poor health after the insurrection.
117 Schachinger, *Die Bosniaken kommen*, 23.
118 Evans, *Time and Chance*, 256–57.
119 "Inland," *Neue Freie Presse (Morgenblatt)*, January 18, 1882, 3.
120 Schindler, "Defeating Balkan Insurgency," 544.
121 "Kommt herauf, ihr österreichischen Geißböcke!" Morokutti, "Der Aufstand im Süden," 3.
122 "Lilienstengel," "Meine Erinnerungen an die Kämpfe in Süddalmatien im Jahre 1882," *Danzers Armee-Zeitung*, March 14, 1907, 2.

were compared to those of native
Americans.[123] The steep, harsh terrain
was also feared. A Habsburg soldier
explained their predicament: "The
outside world does not know a hundredth part of what we have to un-
dergo. It is impossible to close with
these Herzegovinians. Our troops
think to surround them, and when
the operation is complete and our
men are worn out with scrambling
over the rocks, we find no one and
are suddenly attacked in the rear."[124]

Outside of Trebinje and other
urban spaces, the loyalty of local people was always suspect: it was feared
that a man from Hercegovina would
"hide his weapon in a stone crevice,
calmly walk past and greet the gendarmerie meekly before going back

FIGURE 11. Stojan Kovačević around 1900.
Muzej Hercegovine, Trebinje.

to his stash."[125] One reporter complained: "many a wild fellow who
scowled at us as we crossed the Trebinje bridge may well have made
the acquaintance of our soldiers already, out there in the mountains."[126]
In an official report submitted from Mostar on February 12, Stjepan
Jovanović assessed that the Orthodox population in Central and
Eastern Hercegovina supported the insurgency, that they still had
a sense of their own independence due to the separate church traditions, and furthermore, they were inclined to be bellicose. He also
suggested that apparently loyal Orthodox people going about their
business had sympathy with the insurgency. Jovanović noted only
small pockets of resistance by Muslims and assumed the loyalty of

---

123 "Vom Insurrektions-Schauplatze," *Tages-Post*, March 15, 1882, 1.
124 Our Ragusa Correspondent [Arthur J. Evans], "The Military Position of Austria in the Insurgent Provinces," *Manchester Guardian*, March 8, 1882, 8.
125 "Der Überfall von Grancarevo," *Tages-Post*, December 28, 1881, 2.
126 "Von Ragusa nach Trebinje," *Neue Freie Presse (Abendblatt)*, February 6, 1882, 2.

Catholics to the Habsburg regime.[127] When Jovanović arrived in Trebinje to inspect the troops on February 16, he was met with cheers by the urban population who apparently wanted military protection from the insurgency.[128]

Following the example of Vuk Vrčević, who had written intricate reports of the 1875 Uprising from his position as Habsburg Consul in Trebinje, many local people thought that their struggles were over and that they could live with the new monarchy and emperor. Luka Petković, once a close comrade of Mićo Ljubibratić, Bogdan Zimonjić, and Luka Vukalović, became an invaluable supporter of the Habsburg regime after 1878.[129] Tripko Vukalović had led an insurgent battalion with Tomo Tomašević which was recruited from combatants from Zubci, Kruševice, and Sutorina, who had surrendered their authority to Jovanović in September 1878.[130] Babić had wanted to build upon that legacy of capitulation from 1878 and deal with the local Orthodox people through dialogue and trust, so the participation of the Vukalović clan in the rebellion was seen as a personal affront; Babić was reported to be angry.[131] Tripko had received permission to carry a revolver from the authorities in Trebinje in January 1882 and had sworn his loyalty to the regime over numerous glasses of rakija.[132] He had then traveled to Grahovo in Montenegro to collect the gun and connected with other insurgents there.[133] Tripko Vukalović's transfer of loyalties was regarded as a personal betrayal of trust by the whole officer command, including the junior officer Stjepan Sarkotić, who became Governor of Bosnia in 1914.[134]

---

127 Kapidžić, *Hercegovački ustanak*, 176.
128 "Vom Insurrektions-Schauplatze: Armeebefehl des FML. Jovanovic. Ragusa, 18. Februar," *Neuigkeits Welt Blatt*, February 25, 1882, 6.
129 Luka Petković to Mićo Ljubibratić, Grahovo, January 15, 1869, Fond Mićo Ljubibratić, MLj 1601, Arhiv Hercegovine, Mostar.
130 Jovanović, "Izvještaj Atanasija Vasiljevića," 330.
131 Sarkotić, "Aus meinen Erinnerungen," 2–3.
132 "Vom Aufstande in Dalmatien, Bosnien und der Herzegowina," *Welt-Blatt*, April 26, 1882, 1–2. In the original text, it was "Schnaps." Sarkotić remembered these negotiations taking place over "black coffee," in "Aus meinen Erinnerungen," 2–3.
133 "Von den Insurgenten-Führern," *Neuigkeits Welt Blatt*, April 26, 1882, 2.
134 Sarkotić, "Aus meinen Erinnerungen," 2–3. Sarkotić remembered this as the duplicity of the son of the dead rebel Luka Vukalović, whom he also called "Luka," but it is likely that it was his nephew Tripko who actually spoke to Babić.

Even more problematic for the Habsburg military was the sympathy of some soldiers toward the insurgency. As early as February 1882, it was reported that some soldiers "had gone over to the enemy."[135] En route from Trebinje to Dubrovnik in mid-February 1882, Jovanović met the Archimandrite from the Duži Monastery, who pressed him to grant an amnesty for those insurgents who wanted to return quietly to their homes. Jovanović replied firmly that an amnesty would only be granted if they submitted unconditionally.[136] Continued defiance of Habsburg power came at a heavy price. Insurgents or their supporters were brought to the fortress and paraded in front of the urban population:

> Before too long a wait, an eerie procession appeared. Gendarmes, frontier guards [*Panduren*],[137] and some infantrymen bring four locals, who let their dark, unsteady eyes wander with contempt over the crowd watching them. With their hands tied to their backs and manacled with iron, the prisoners walk forward with bold steps. One immediately recognizes them to be most dangerous types: these are the individuals who have maintained contact with the insurgents.[138]

According to Arthur Evans, there had been public humiliations of Orthodox men in Trebinje before. In March 1880, he reported the public beating of "a Serb, Okitza by name, a man held in general esteem by his compatriots, (who) was unfortunately found to be in possession of a sword and pistol. The wretched man had his hands bound behind him and was marched off to Trebinje. On the way, he was most cruelly maltreated by his captors, who beat him, bound as he was with the butt end of their guns and dug the barrel into his back."[139]

---

135 Charles St John to Earl Granville, Dubrovnik, January 23, 1882, FO7 1041, National Archives, London.

136 "eine unbedingte Unterwerfung auf Gnade und Ungnade," in "Die Situation auf dem Insurrektionsgebiete," *Pester Lloyd*, March 2, 1882, 2.

137 Adapted from the Croatian word *pudar*, these troops had been used as frontier guards in the Habsburg Monarchy since the eighteenth century.

138 C. M., "Aus Trebinje," *Neue Freie Presse* (*Abendblatt*), February 24, 1882, 2.

139 From our Ragusa correspondent [Arthur J. Evans], "Austria's Difficulties in Bosnia and Herzegovina," *Manchester Guardian*, March 27, 1880, 7.

Whether they intended to or not, this kind of retribution reinforced the view of a dangerous countryside and safe garrison, with Trebinje returning to its role during earlier conflicts. Popovo polje, an insurgent stronghold in 1875, was peaceful in 1882, which left the border region with Montenegro strategically more isolated.[140] Bileća was much more acutely threatened by the insurgency than Trebinje and Jovanović congratulated its "heroic" defenders by telegram.[141] The proximity to the Montenegrin border also meant that insurgents could again retreat more effectively.[142] The 1882 Uprising started to die out by mid-March,[143] amid intense repression. The battles around Mount Orjen between March 7 and 10 took place in one of the most difficult theaters of war, where the absence of roads and harsh limestone terrain held the Habsburg forces back. Both guns and pack animals sank into the high snowdrifts and although the soldiers tried to move the ammunition forward, they struggled because of the glacier surfaces on the impacted ice.[144]

In March 1882, local people fled from the foothills of Mount Orjen, leaving their stoves still warm, and the soldiers helped themselves to their potatoes. Poljice was reported to have been burned down by the insurgents.[145] Interpreting the news differently, British Consul Charles St John believed that the grain of suspected insurgents in the border area was burned by Habsburg troops. St John thought that the people who lost their crops were not insurgents but were being punished as if they were.[146] The Dalmatian coast with its coves and boats offered a plausible escape route for rebels and, like the mountains, it was also difficult to defend or police without special measures. As a result of the insurgency, martial law was declared in Dubrovnik on March 8, 1882, accompanied by a general crackdown. Arthur Evans had started to provoke the authorities.

---

140 "Aus der südlichen Herzegovina," *Pester Lloyd*, April 4, 1882, 2.
141 "Die Gefechte um Bilek am 17., 18., 19., und 20. Jänner," *Pester Lloyd (Abendblatt)*, February 25, 1882, 1.
142 C. M., "Das Gefecht auf der Kobila-Glava," *Neue Freie Presse (Abendblatt)*, February 23, 1882, 2.
143 Daniel Salis-Soglio to Hans Salis-Soglio, Vienna, March 15, 1882, Staatsarchiv Graubünden, Chur.
144 Hubka, *Geschichte des k. und k. Infanterie-Regiments*, 482.
145 "Vom Insurrections Schauplatze," *Die Presse*, March 13, 1882, 7–8.
146 Charles St John to Earl Granville, March 3, 1882, F07 1041, National Archives, London.

A December 12, 1881 article on the "Bocchese Insurgents" had reportedly been "translated and circulated in the occupied provinces"; furthermore, to travel around Risan, Evans was reported to have "evaded the military watch."[147] In the press, Evans "and his comrades" were credited with exaggerating the extent of the uprising by spreading "tendentious lies."[148] Just prior to his arrest, he had sent another report to the *Manchester Guardian* in which he relayed the news that a hangman had been dispatched from Trieste and court-martials were sitting in Trebinje, Kotor, and Mostar.[149]

On March 7, 1882, at the height of the counteroffensive around Mount Orjen, Evans was arrested, and he spent six weeks in solitary confinement.[150] He was implicated for "harboring" a deserter from the 16th regiment.[151] On March 2, his wife Margaret had expressed concern that the deserter was hanging around their house and asking for women's clothes; she thought that he might have been sent to trap Evans.[152] In his statement made under arrest, Evans admitted that a young man "from the Weber Regiment" had come to his home looking for "la roba per tranestirsi" (a dress to help him change his appearance).[153] While Evans admitted going to Risan, he claimed he was only interested in antiquities. He was also adamant that he did not know an insurgent named Luka from the settlement of Gluva Smokva.[154] Also arrested was Spiridion Gopčević, a jour-

---

147 Charles St John to Earl Granville, Dubrovnik, January 16, 1882, FO7 1041, National Archives, London.
148 "tendenziöse Lügen ... durch Evans und seine Genossen systematisch verbreitet wurden." C. M., "Der Aufstand," *Neue Freie Presse (Morgenblatt)*, March 7, 1882, 2.
149 Our Ragusa Correspondent [Arthur J. Evans], "The Military Position of Austria in the Insurgent Provinces," *Manchester Guardian*, March 8, 1882, 8.
150 Branko Kirigin, *Arthur Evans in Dubrovnik and Split (1875–1882)* (Oxford: Archeaopress, 2015), 7.
151 Arthur J. Evans, "The Austrian War Against Publicity," *Contemporary Review* 42 (September 1882): 397.
152 Brigitta Mader, "Zu Arthur J. Evans' Ausweisung und Verhaftung in Ragusa aus den Geheimakten der k. k. Statthalterei für Dalmatien in Zara 1880 und 1882," *Eteokriti: Verein zur wissenschaftlichen Erforschung Kretas und der Ägäis*, no. 3 (2013): 16.
153 Nell' Ufficio delle Carceri Criminali Ragusa di 4. Aprile 1882: Estratto dagli arreste Arturo Evans, HL IV. 40/e, Hadtörténeti Intézet és Múzeum, Budapest. In modern Italian, "la roba" does not mean a dress, but rather "things" or "stuff." However, in this case, Evans did mean a dress.
154 A shadowy insurgent figure, this Luka is likely to have been Luka Sjenić.

nalist who had family roots in the village of Podi, near Herceg Novi.[155] The Dubrovnik home of Evans, where Gopčević also frequently stayed, was reachable by boat and was reported to have been a meeting point for "Slavonic agitation."[156] Margaret knew that there were also rumors about her involvement in the uprising: "best of all was … that I went more than once after midnight on horseback to Trebinje with secret despatches!"[157] Evans was released on April 23 amid continuing accusations of funding the rebels.[158] He was probably lucky not to have been executed. His friend Isabel Burton had warned him even before his incarceration:[159] "I know that the Austrians attribute their misfortunes in Herzegovina to you and such as you [i.e., other regime critics] and that they will, as sure as you live, hang you up to the first tree if they can catch you out of bounds. Many of them had told me so."[160] Although the prosecutor thought that there were insufficient grounds for a charge of treason, his behavior was not deemed suitable for a foreigner who lived as a guest in the Habsburg Monarchy and Evans was expelled.[161] Nevertheless, his criticism of Habsburg rule continued *in absentia*. By early April, the army were sure that they were on top of the situation, especially as the weather had warmed up and Mount Orjen was more accessible. Habsburg soldiers celebrated the end of hostilities with patriotic zeal. An amnesty was announced on April 22, 1882, by Emperor Franz Joseph for all but the top two hundred and forty leaders.[162] Konstantin Varičak's court-martial in Trebinje in May had given the military authorities valuable insight into the networks of the insurgents, including Stojan Kovačević.[163] Most of the rebels ac-

---

155 Insinuations were made in the press about the "notoriously intimate relationship" between Gopčević and Evans; see, for example, "Zur Affaire Gopcević," *Wiener Allgemeine Zeitung* (*Abendblatt*), May 27, 1882, 1.
156 "Inland: Ragusa," *Neue Freie Presse*, March 5, 1882, 3.
157 Evans, *Time and Chance*, 244.
158 "Inland: Ragusa," *Wiener Zeitung*, April 26, 1882, 2.
159 Isabel Burton (1831–1896) was married to the English Orientalist and translator Richard Burton (1821–1890) and lived in Trieste, where he was British Consul.
160 Mader, "Zu Arthur J. Evans' Ausweisung," 16.
161 "Zur Verhaftung Evans," *Prager Abendblatt*, April 26, 1882, 1.
162 Grunert, *Glauben im Hinterland*, 290.
163 "Garnisons Gericht in Trebinje," Protokolle, May 4, 1882, Hadtörténeti Intézet és Múzeum, Budapest.

cepted the offer or left for Montenegro, but tensions simmered until November of that year.[164]

The defeat of 1882 was a turning point for Habsburg rule, which now looked unassailable. A whole generation had grown up with instability in their daily lives or, as British Consul Edward Freeman put it in January 1882, "the people of Herzegovina may be said to have been in a state of chronic rebellion for the last thirty years."[165] Peace at least looked possible, but many officers including Alfred Schenk, Stjepan Sarkotić, and Daniel Salis-Soglio would carry their experience of the campaign and dislike of insurgents in their hearts for the rest of their careers.[166] Jovanović was so impressed with Conrad von Hötzendorf's 1882 work on local military tactics and how to defeat guerrilla tactics,[167] that he purchased offprints of his work to distribute to his officers.[168] One response to the 1882 crisis was to build even more fortifications, intended primarily to protect the regime from its own subjects. Many former insurgents moved to nearby Nikšić, and the border region suffered from stark decline and depopulation.[169] A new series of imposing fortifications to guard the southern flank of the empire were built around Crkvice. Like Trebinje and Bileća, this garrison complex had the dual purpose of defending the coastline against both its external enemies and its own people. A train line to the coast at Zelenika was completed in 1901, which speeded up military communication and the region's accessibility.[170]

---

164 Ekmečić, "Ustanak u Hercegovini 1882.," 55. The British Consul in Sarajevo thought that about 500 insurgents were still operating around Bileća; Edward Freeman to Secretary of State for Foreign Affairs, Sarajevo, October 21, 1882, F07 1041, National Archives, London.

165 Edward Freeman to Secretary of State for Foreign Affairs, Sarajevo, January 27, 1882, F07 1041, National Archive, London.

166 See for example, A. Sch., "Vor fünfzehn Jahren: Aus dem Tagebuch eines Kriegsteilnehmers," *Danzers Armee Zeitung*, March 11, 1932, 5–6.

167 Franz Conrad von Hötzendorf, "Einiges über den südherzegowinischen Karst in militärischer Hinsicht," *Organ der militär-wissenschaftlichen Vereine* 24, no. 1 (1882): 1–46.

168 Lawrence Sondhaus, *Franz Conrad von Hötzendorf: Architect of the Apocalypse* (Leiden: Brill, 2000), 26.

169 Deserted dwellings were noted near Vrbanje (Kruševice), "Drei elende Strohhütten, verlassen von ihren Bewohnern...," in H. H., "Der Übergang über den Orien," April 30, 1882, 3.

170 The link between the effectiveness of the occupation and the provision of trains was made by Aristides von Arensdorff, "Erinnerungen," AT-OeStA/KA NL 782 (B,C), Kriegsarchiv, Vienna.

Opposition to the Habsburg occupation had clearly waned among the Muslims in just a few short years: in Trebinje in 1882, they were unwilling to get involved thanks to the "direct influence" of the Ottoman Consul General Daniş Efendi in Dubrovnik.[171] This was also the case for many Orthodox who adapted to the new normal. Veteran rebel Bogdan Zimonjić had refused to take part and as a result his debts were written off personally by the emperor; he was honored with the Order of Franz Joseph and was "given the right to wear an Ottoman saber."[172] Many former Orthodox rebels just returned quietly to the land after the uprising was defeated. Charles St John noted that insurgents had "hidden their arms and taken to the plough."[173] Hercegovina's Muslims had effectively lost their direct political links to the Ottoman Empire, but the existence of Montenegro and Serbia kept Orthodox hopes for a different kind of politics alive. Habsburg diplomats had also done their best to keep Montenegrins directly out of the insurrection, concerned about their influence on the rebels. Stojan Kovačević and Lazar Sočica lived for several more decades in exile in Nikšić, and Tripko Vukalović was buried with honors in Montenegro after his death in 1898. Collective defiance did not completely subside after 1882 and nor had the taste for retribution. In Prince Nikola, many of the Orthodox saw a ruler who had emerged through a tribal system that they regarded as legitimate onto the international stage. Agrarian reform was much more extensive in Montenegro.[174] Montenegrins could also "bear arms" in the form of guns and knives, whereas by law, men from Hercegovina could only carry knives.

Disturbances continued in the border area. While hardly threatening the bases of Habsburg power, unrest did prevent trust from developing. Clothes and jewelry were taken by armed robbers close

---

171 "Vom Insurrektions-Schauplatze," *Tages-Post*, February 7, 1882, 1–2. Daniş Efendi had himself been taken prisoner by insurgents in August 1878; see Charles St John to Salisbury, Dubrovnik, August 27, 1878, FO7 1041, National Archives, London.

172 Grunert, *Glauben im Hinterland*, 316.

173 Charles St John to Earl Granville, Dubrovnik, April 8, 1882, FO7 1041, National Archives, London.

174 Charles Jelavich, "The Revolt in Bosnia-Hercegovina, 1881–2," *The Slavonic and East European Review* 31, no. 77 (1953): 422.

to Arslanagić most in 1884.[175] In June 1885, the former insurgent and robber Ivo Gogorović was hanged at the garrison at Bileća. Gogorović had denied committing murder. Before the execution, he was allowed to send his farewells to his family, receive prayers from an Orthodox priest, and drink a bottle of rum. After his burial, a witness who had testified at his trial was killed in revenge.[176] Another insurgent, Luka Sjenić from Korjenići, escaped to Montenegro. It was reported that he was wanted dead or alive for a reward of a thousand florins. When he was eventually caught, badly wounded, he was hanged behind the barracks and buried close to a dung pit in Bileća.[177] In the settlement of Begović Kula, close to Trebinje, there were persistent concerns about security.[178] More retributive killings occurred. A year after Sjenić was executed, a patrol was targeted in the very same place that he fell, and soldiers were killed. Local people insisted that this was in revenge for the insurgent leader.[179] As late as 1895 in Vrbanje, three military officials were attacked, robbed, and left to die of their wounds. Only one man, Simon Ribarić, survived the attack and was taken to the military hospital in Trebinje to recover.[180] To deal with the rebellious population, the government considered resettlement of the region with people from the Tyrol, who would understand the challenges of living in the mountains but would be more loyal to the Habsburg regime. The areas around Nevesinjsko polje, Dabarska ravnica, and the route from Bileća to Korita along the Montenegrin border were deemed most suitable for resettlement, although this plan never materialized.[181]

The church, which had enjoyed some independence under the Ottoman millet system, also continued to nourish a sense of injustice among its community of the faithful, especially at the local level and

175 "Räuberunwesen in der Herzegowina," *Welt Blatt*, June 28, 1884, 5.
176 "Bosnisches Recht," *Militär-Zeitung*, June 2, 1885, 327–28. "Gogorović" is the given name in this German-language source, but it is probable that the name was different in the local language.
177 Andrejka, *Slovenski fantje*, 331.
178 "Gendarmerie-Corps-Commando für Bosnien und die Hercegovina," No. 918. "An die Landesregierung Sarajevo," December 31, 1899, Arhiv Bosne i Hercegovine, Sarajevo.
179 "Von nah und fern," *Wiener Allgemeine Zeitung (Mittsgblatt)*, June 17, 1887, 2.
180 "Gendarmenmord in der Krivoscie," *Tages-Post*, September 1, 1895, 4.
181 Tomislav Kraljačić, *Kalajev režim u Bosni i Hercegovini (1882–1903)* (Sarajevo: Izdavačko Veselin Masleša, 1987), 106.

among the less high-positioned clergy. It was often difficult to disentangle the compliance or hostility of people from the attitudes of their religious leaders and priests:

> In 1907 ... a customs patrol picked up a gang of smugglers east of Lastva, right on the border with Montenegro. When one of the delinquents was mortally wounded during the arrest, a crowd of angry villagers quickly gathered. The priest Vidak Parežanin and the village leader Deretić repeatedly insulted the officials with profane words.... The village leader also threatened to emigrate tomorrow.[182]

Parežanin was prosecuted at the time (and only later hanged in 1914).[183] In late June, on St Vitus' Day (*Vidovdan*), Orthodox people remembered the defeat of the Serbian Prince Lazar in 1389 by the Ottomans on Kosovo polje. This brought them together as a national and religious community and strengthened the link to Serbia and Montenegro. On the five hundredth anniversary of the battle in 1889, the state government banned the usual commemorations in public spaces, which were often accompanied by bonfires. In some cities *Vidovdan* events took place in parish halls rather than outdoors. In 1891, it was reported that Muslims in Livno and Trebinje were planning "a kind of victory celebration" for the Battle of Kosovo, but were persuaded not to demonstrate in public by the Habsburg authorities.[184] At other times, Muslims exercised claims to hegemony: Safvet-beg Bašagić's 1891 poem "Bošnjaku" envisaged a Bosniak community "from Trebinje to the gates of Brod" ("*Od Trebinja do Brodskijeh vrata*") and so the city retained a symbolic importance.[185]

"Paternal rule"[186] had changed the dynamic of the relationship between the Orthodox and Muslims (or rather reinforced an Ottoman pattern of town and country divisions with new rules).

---

182 Grunert, *Glauben im Hinterland*, 241.
183 Parežanin, *Die Attentäter*, 144.
184 Grunert, *Glauben im Hinterland*, 308–10.
185 Vahidin Preljević, "'Zauberhafte Mischung' und 'Reine Volksseele': Literatur, Kultur und Widersprüche der imperialen Konstellation im habsburgischen Bosnien-Herzegowina um 1900," in Ruthner and Scheer, *Bosnien-Herzegowina und Österreich-Ungarn, 1878–1918*, 384.
186 "The Austrians in Herzegovina," 7.

The Habsburg military created firm urban bases in
which Muslims could congre-
gate, which strengthened
their collective relationship
with the Habsburg Monar-
chy. At the same time, the
growth of neighboring Serbia and Montenegro encouraged hopes for a pan-Serb political community. Habsburg
soldiers were aware that they
were still an occupying force
that needed to find an effec-
tive *modus vivendi* with the
local population. An officer
in Sarajevo told James Cotton
Minchin in 1882: "we must

FIGURE 12. Stjepan Jovanović wrestles with Stojan
Kovačević, as Prince Nikola looks on; cartoon from the
newspaper Humoristische Blätter, n.d. 1882.

educate these men as well as drill them.... At present ... they would
shoot us at the first opportunity."[187]

Undoubtedly a pragmatic military leader who sought to instill
fear and respect for the regime, Jovanović acted firmly to avoid violent conflict whenever possible. With the defeat of the insurgency
and the exodus from rebel villages, it looked as if fear and respect
had indeed been instilled, at least in the urban spaces. The countryside, especially close to the border with Montenegro, remained a dangerous space. When a soldier called France Novak was killed and mutilated on the route to Lastva in 1886, his body was carried back to
Trebinje by his comrades, and the entire battalion, as well as a large
crowd of civilians, attended his funeral.[188] Approaching Bileća from
Plana, Antonio Budinich had to pass a place which he was told was
called the "Galgóczy Oaks": in 1882, local rebel leaders had been

---

187 James George Cotton Minchin, *The Growth of Freedom in the Balkan Peninsula: Notes of a Traveller in Montenegro, Bosnia, Servia, Bulgaria, and Greece, with Historical and Descriptive Sketches of the
People* (London: John Murray, 1886), 53.

188 Andrejka, *Slovenski fantje*, 331.

hanged from these strong trees.[189] While the insurgency had not unseated the Habsburg authorities, it had left them rattled and distrustful of insurgent settlements. The insurgency had a formative effect on younger soldiers who felt that they knew the Trebinje region and understood the enemy. Rudolf Braun, Stjepan Sarkotić, and Conrad von Hötzendorf were all young soldiers at the time, eager to advance the cause of the emperor. The defeat of the insurgency in 1882 was a turning point for Habsburg rule. Stjepan Jovanović had delivered a swift victory and, had he waited until spring as he actually wished to, there would have been fewer casualties. There was a saying in Hercegovina that may have dated back several centuries: "the Turks are masters in this land, but they are not masters in the mountains."[190] By introducing universal male conscription rather than the selective conscription that had existed before 1868, the Habsburg military knew that they had to break the spirit of resistance to their rule in Southern Dalmatia, in Bosnia, and in Hercegovina: in other words, they had to succeed where the Ottoman Empire had failed. From 1882 onward, the division between supporters of the monarchy and their opponents hardened round the garrisons:[191] in effect, the Habsburg authorities had made the same pragmatic compromise that the Ottomans had made over control of the land, and neither side forgot the hard realities of division despite the decades of subsequent peace.[192] After 1882, soldiers recruited from Bosnia and Hercegovina were sent to different parts of the Monarchy. Initially they were sent to Vienna in order to dilute any rebellious tendencies within the big city, but later they were also sent to garrisons in Graz, Wiener Neustadt, Bruck an der Leitha, Trieste, and Budapest.[193]

---

189 Budini, *Le memorie di guerra*, 89.

190 "Dem Andenken des Feldmarschall-Lieutenants Baron Jovanović," *Kremser Volksblatt*, December 19, 1885, 1.

191 Petko Luković, "Slovenci i hercegovački ustanak protiv Austro-Ugarske 1882. godine," *Zgodovinski časopis* 36, nos. 1–2 (1982): 45–83, 72.

192 Slaviša M. Vulić, "Austrougarska okupacija Bosne i Hercegovine i prve godine uprave (1878–1882)" (Ph.D. diss., University of Belgrade, 2021), 209–19.

193 Alexander Baumann, "Das 2. Bosnisch-hercegovinische Infanterieregiment in Graz Die öffentliche Wahrnehmung der Bosniaken" (BA thesis, Karl-Franzens-Universität Graz, 2017), 18.

Chapter Four

LIFE IN THE CITADEL, 1882-1914

Urban Infrastructure

The defeat of the 1882 rebellion was followed by a transformative period in Trebinje, involving ever greater military construction as well as solid economic growth.[1] Most towns in Bosnia and Herce-govina expanded dramatically in size after 1878: Trebinje and Bileća grew even more rapidly than the average.[2] A new complex of build-ings had started to emerge in Trebinje with "spacious" barracks.[3] Fortifications were designed to protect the Trebišnjica as well as the Dubrovnik and Bileća gates. Writers commented on the favorable mix of architecture in the "colorful" town.[4] Notable was "the enor-mous military work which the Austrians have accomplished here. There is a whole quarter of huge barracks, in their bold rigid outline and their red-tiled roofs ... and as all of these tiles have been brought here by sea ... some notion may be formed of the labour ... which ha[s] been expensed on the new constructions."[5] The domination

1   Marijan Sivrić, "Radnički pokret u Trebinju od konca 19. stoljeća do 1918. godine," *Tribu-nia: Prilozi za istoriju, arheologiju, etnologiju, umjetnost i kulturu*, no. 6 (1982): 95.
2   Iljas Hadžibegović, *Bosanskohercegovački gradovi na razmeđu 19. i 20. stoljeća* (Sarajevo: Institut za istoriju, 2004), 34.
3   H. H., "Der Übergang über den Orien," April 30, 2.
4   Kurt Hassert, *Reise durch Montenegro, nebst Bemerkungen über Land und Leute* (Vienna: Hartle-ben, 1893), 110.
5   "The Austrians in Herzegovina," 7.

FIGURE 13. Trebinje garrison with barracks, 1910. Wikimedia Commons.

of the military can be deduced from population numbers in garrisons across the border regions.[6] The census of 1895 indicated that there were 2966 individuals living in Trebinje; 1291 were civilians and 1674 were military. A further 318 military personnel were based outside the main garrison in the Trebinje district, which had a population of 21,951 civilians.[7] In Eastern Hercegovina by 1878, Muslims primarily lived in the urban settlements, where some had sought safety, while many Orthodox and Catholic people still lived in the countryside. In 1912, according to the officer Karl Novottny, within the city of Trebinje itself there were 1500 Muslims, 900 Orthodox, 600 Catholics and "c. 12 Jews."[8]

Daniel von Salis-Soglio was tasked with strengthening local fortifications around the garrison. His family had a long tradition of service to the Habsburg dynasty. Like Babić and Galgóczy, he also became a legendary figure within the army, the subject of affection and pride especially because of his work on the Przemyśl fortress

---

6   Hadžibegović, *Bosanskohercegovački gradovi*, 50.

7   Madžar, "Istorijat Gradskog Vodovoda, 51–64.

8   Novottny "Erinnerungen," AT-OeStA/KA NL 417: 12, Kriegsarchiv, Vienna, 195.

complex.[9] The new defensive military installations also had the useful role of policing local people. Salis-Soglio believed that the visibility of the fortress at Gliva, which had proved very difficult to construct, would impose the reality of military power.[10] Gliva had been an important stronghold of the Orthodox insurgents in 1877 and was therefore significant to them.[11] The garrison complex became the main way in which a potentially insurgent rural community was monitored, suppressed, and controlled, as well as defending the state's borders. Montenegrins were not building fortifications along the border to the same level of intensity, which puts the emerging narrative about their propensity toward violence into some context.[12] The Trebinje garrison complex dominated the landscape, which "bristle(d) with forts old and new."[13] An American author described the scene leaving Trebinje in 1908: "we have the novel sensation of riding between ranks of armed men! There are soldiers everywhere and forts on all the heights."[14] One traveler in 1890 left a puzzled note in his diary:

> Bilek, September 21…. Hot: about 85 degrees in shade. Lodged with a Dalmatian merchant, and fed at a little inn crowded with officers. Forts everywhere. Ragusa, September 22. Arrived here, via Trebinje, where I spent several hours. Country, if possible, more uninviting. Trebinje, one of the old Turkish fortresses, a rather more prosperous-looking place than Stolatz and Bilek, equally surrounded by forts on every hill. It seemed extraordinary that all these elaborate defences should be considered necessary to protect Austria from Montenegro, a country with a population of under half a million.[15]

---

9   John E. Fahey, *Przemyśl, Poland: A Multiethnic City During and After a Fortress, 1867–1939* (West Lafayette, IN: Purdue University Press, 2023), 27–31.

10 Volker Konstantin Pachauer, "Austro-Hungarian Fortification in Bosnia-Herzegovina and Montenegro: Cultural Heritage between Value, Touristic Potential and Extinction." *International Journal of Heritage Architecture* 2, no. 1 (2018): 151.

11 Arnautović, "Austrougarska okupacija Trebinja," 11.

12 Velimir Terzić, Dragić Vujošević, Ilija Jovanović, and Uroš Kostić, *Operacije crnogorske vojske u prvom svetskom ratu* (Belgrade: Vojno Delo, 1954), 89–90.

13 Maude Holbach, *Dalmatia: The Land Where East Meets West* (London: J. Lane, 1910), 160.

14 Hutchinson, *Motoring in the Balkans*, 225.

15 Thomas Wodehouse Legh Newton, *Retrospection* (London: J. Murray, 1941), 58.

In practice, the border region might have been porous, and soldiers sometimes slipped across the state frontier without telling their officers.[16] Nevertheless, Montenegrins often remained wary of their Habsburg neighbors. In 1892, Alfred Schenk, based at the Trebinje garrison but interested in geological research, stayed in Montenegro so that he could undertake fieldwork. By chance, his Montenegrin host had fought at Jankov vrh ten years earlier with the insurgents. When his host refused to return his passport until he had contacted the authorities in Cetinje, Schenk left undetected and returned to the frontier post at Visoka glavica at night, gaining admittance back into the Habsburg realm by means of a password. Writing in 1932 and with the benefit of hindsight, he saw the incident as a harbinger of the conflict to come between the two states.[17] Jernej Andrejka recorded breaking up a row between his regiment and Montenegrin border guards at Begovo Korito about who the better marksmen were, which was settled amicably by a shooting competition when the Carniolan soldier Varšek hit the target. Andrejka took a coin from his pocket and stuck it down on the tree trunk with pitch. He exhorted the Montenegrin falcons (*sokoli*), with their keen eyesight, to choose their best marksman:

[A Montenegrin then] took aim and shot; the buck did not move, just some bark from the trunk flew off. The conduct of our boys after this shot was exemplary; not one uttered a word, laughed, or even jeered; everyone was serious and quiet.... To the honor of the Montenegrins, I must admit that they behaved quite decently on this occasion. Initially, they were a little surprised, but soon that stupor passed; they warmly saluted the victor [Varšek] at his brilliant success, and henceforth they always spoke with great respect of our soldiers and Austrian military prowess...[18]

This incident was in the mid-1880s, when the Habsburg authorities thought they had quelled most local resistance. It also relied on

16   "Unsere Soldaten an der Grenze," *Der Bezirksbote für den politischen Bezirk Bruck an der Leitha*, March 14, 1909, 2.
17   Sch. "Vor fünfzehn Jahren," 5–6.
18   Andrejka, *Slovenski fantje*, 338–39.

the linguistic skills of Andrejka, who was a great admirer of firm, direct negotiating in the style of Stjepan Jovanović and Djuro Babić, whom he directly praised. Universal conscription in 1868 eventually thinned out the predominance of officers from the old military border who had consistently dealt with all denominations by speaking to them in their own language and assuming their loyalty to the crown. Stjepan Sarkotić remembered that, in his youth in the Lika region, both Orthodox and Catholics were equally dependable.[19]

Other threats to military life existed apart from insurgents, inclement weather, and a perennial shortage of water. Brigitte Fuchs has argued that "Austro-Hungarian public health officers noted a state of general 'degeneration' in the Bosnian population" and therefore demanded that modern healthcare services be provided.[20] Small hospitals were constructed in Bosnia and Hercegovina in the 1880s, adding to the emergency care facilities (*Notsspittaler*) used by the garrisons. In Trebinje, the new hospital had twenty-seven beds.[21] Dr. Alois Pick served in the Trebinje garrison and used his time there to undertake work on endemic sandfly fever (*papatačijeva groznica*),[22] a debilitating illness in high summer.[23] Sandfly fever poses a particular problem to military garrisons because although death is virtually unheard of, the patient is almost completely debilitated for several days after being bitten by the insect. Sufferers complained of a high fever, conjunctivitis, neck pains, and headache. Once the fever abated, the patients felt nausea and lassitude which often lasted for several weeks.[24] Michael Ludwig Edler von Appel, Director of the Bosnian

19 "eine Stütze des Thrones," "Berechtigte scharfe Worte des unseren Landeschefs Bosniens über unsere Serben," *Österreichische Volkszeitung*, February 23, 1915, 5.

20 Brigitte Fuchs, "Orientalizing Disease: Austro-Hungarian Policies of 'Race,' Gender and Hygiene in Bosnia and Herzegovina, 1874–1914," in *Health, Hygiene and Eugenics in Southeastern Europe to 1945*, ed. Christian Promitzer, Sevasti Trubeta, and Marius Turda (Budapest-New York: Central European University Press, 2011), 58.

21 Izet Mašić, "One Hundred Fifty Years of Organized Health Care Services in Bosnia and Herzegovina," *Medical Archives* 72, no. 5 (2018): 374–88.

22 Alois Pick, "Zur Pathologie und Therapie einer eigenthümlichen endemischen Krankheitsform," *Wiener Medizinische Wochenschrift*, no. 33 (1886): 1141–45. Heinz Flamm, "Aufklärung des Pappataci-Fiebers durch österreichische Militärärzte," *Wiener Klinische Wochenschrift*, no. 120 (2008): 198–208.

23 "Pappatacifieber," *Arbeiter Zeitung*, August 22, 1909, 7.

24 Robert Doerr, *Das Pappatacifieber: Ein endemisches Drei-Tage-Fieber im adriatischen Küstengebiete Österreich-Ungarns* (Vienna: Deuticke, 1909), 28.

Gendarmerie between 1903 and 1907, who came to Trebinje for troop inspections,[25] received over eighty sandfly bites in one night and fell ill a week later.[26] Pick and his colleague Dr. Robert Doerr were the first medical professionals to identify the insect as the source, but here they relied on local knowledge.[27] It was known locally as "dog's disease" and the soldiers adopted this term to describe the debilitating impact of the illness in high summer.[28] The discussion of sandfly fever in professional journals with strategic recommendations from medical staff for the military illustrates how intertwined different elements of the Habsburg state were.[29]

Soldiers contracted malaria which could hit them quite suddenly. Reinhard Günste collapsed while he was hunting and, lying immobilized, believed he would die undiscovered as carrion circled above. Local people found him and took him semi-conscious on the back of a horse to the train station wrapped in their own shirts.[30] Günste was also aware of the threat of typhus-infested water to soldiers.[31] Typhus spread amongst the troops in 1882 during the insurrection.[32] In 1899, there was an outbreak of typhus in the Trebinje garrison, which was also recorded in other garrisons in Eastern Hercegovina the previous year.[33] The frequent arrival of new regiments left the incoming soldiers vulnerable to disease.[34] Garrison doctors vaccinated against typhus during the First World War.[35] As well as caring for military personnel, doctors were expected to inspect brothels and meat processing plants and care for the railway construction

25 Felix Hetz, "'Ronde': Bilder aus Österreich-Ungarns Vergangenheit," *Der Österreichischer Kamerad (Neues Wiener Journal)*, January 6, 1937, 15.
26 Doerr, *Das Pappatacifieber*, 147.
27 Mirsada Hukić and Irma Salimović-Besić, "Sandfly-Pappataci fever in Bosnia and Herzegovina: The New-Old Disease," *Bosnian Journal of Basic Medical Sciences* 9, no. 1 (2009): 39–43.
28 "Pappatacifieber," *Arbeiter Zeitung*, August 22, 1909, 7.
29 "Pappatacifieber," *Der Militärarzt*, August 20, 1909, 256.
30 Reinhard Günste [Rifaat Gozdović Pascha pseud.], "Aus den Erinnerungen eines Pilsner Kindl's," *Pilsner Tagblatt*, July 24, 1910, 4.
31 Reinhard Günste [Rifat Gozdović Pascha pseud.], "Bosnische Kuriosa," *Pilsner Tagblatt*, October 26, 1913, 1.
32 "Trebinje," *Pester Lloyd*, April 14, 1882, 2.
33 Madžar, "Istorijat Gradskog Vodovoda," 51–64.
34 Doerr, *Das Pappatacifieber*, 140.
35 "Arbeiterapport," March 21, 1925, K. u. K. Geniedirektion in Bileća, AT-OeStA/KA FA NFA (Bileća 1309), Kriegsarchiv, Vienna.

workers.[36] The old city of Trebinje had been surrounded by an Ottoman-era moat (*hendek*), first dug in the eighteenth century by engineers brought in from Dubrovnik.[37] Guided by Dr. Rudolf Löwy, the moat was partially filled in 1910 and then again in 1932 to prevent malaria. Polders located at the lower course of the Trebišnjica were used for defensive purposes. The embankment was reinforced by concrete and steel: its "final section ... was enclosed by the Bregovi shelter built around 1912, which was armed with machine gun emplacements."[38]

A cast-iron water fountain commemorating the time Djuro Babić had spent in Trebinje was built in 1890, depicting a woman with her arms raised and the water gushing out of a lion's mouth.[39] It became one the most important sources of water in the city. In 1900, Rudolf Löwy sent water samples from the Babić fountain to a Sarajevo hospital for testing; the water was deemed to be very pure. In 1898, investigations had begun concerning the possibility of supplying Trebinje with water from the karst spring Oko, and construction of the aqueduct commenced in 1902 with assistance from the army.[40] The Oko spring supplied Trebinje with decent quality drinking water after 1903.[41] Wooden rafts and barges, made by local artisans, crisscrossed the river and the so-called Pioneer Bridge increased accessibility. Picturesque irrigation wheels were captured on postcards and the system that kept the fields so well-watered was widely admired.[42]

In 1882, during the insurgency, the *kule* or "block houses left by the Turks [were] repaired and fortified."[43] By the end of the 1880s, a generation of Habsburg military men inspired by Field Marshal Josef Radetzky von Radetz had transformed Trebinje and the sur-

36 Ivan Tepavčević, "Boka Kotorska at the Beginning of the 20th Century," *Montenegrin Journal for Social Sciences* 3, no. 1 (2019): 110.
37 Korać, *Trebinje: Istorijski pregled*, vol. 2, part 1, 214.
38 Pachauer and Suchoń, "Typy zieleni i elementy wodne," 84.
39 Maria Zuccaci, "Markttag in Trebinje: Ein Stück Orient in Jugoslawien," *Neues Wiener Journal*, September 6, 1930, 8.
40 Madžar, "Istorijat Gradskog Vodovoda," 51–64.
41 Andrejka, *Slovenski fantje*, 317.
42 C. W., "Trebinje: Cultur nach Osten tragen," 246.
43 Charles St John to Earl Granville, Dubrovnik, January 28, 1882, FO7 1041, National Archives, London.

FIGURE 14. Rudolf Braun (end right) seated next to Karl Novottny in 1915. Austrian State Archives.

rounding garrisons into a fortified region comparable in concept with the Quadrilateral around northern Italian fortresses at Verona, Mantua, Peschiera del Garda, and Legnano.[44] The construction of a narrow-gauge railway line to Trebinje in 1901 speeded up the provision of supplies to the garrison complex. In the space of just over three decades, this wider region was transformed. At Crkvice on the coast, a vast fort was built and the quay of the old city of Dubrovnik was extended, which made landing even easier. Troops were sent up from the coast and many soldiers wistfully watched the blue Adriatic disappear as they traveled up from Gruž to forts in the hinterland.[45] Edith Durham remembered "the great grey warships (that) lay off the coast ... the army arriving, disembarking and marching up to Trebinje."[46]

---

[44] Pachauer, "Austro-Hungarian Fortification," 151.
[45] Andrejka, *Slovenski fantje*, 308.
[46] Mary Edith Durham, *Twenty Years of Balkan Tangle* (London: George Allen Unwin, 1920), 150.

Challenges and Catastrophe

The "African" heat in Hercegovina stunned many incomers.[47] On the border, Conrad Hochbichler complained about "stones and yet more stones, it seemed like the Sahara Desert where the grains of sand looked like stones the size of houses."[48] Maude Holbach made colonial connections: "[t]he tropical summer is so trying that, as with us in India, the officers' wives are all sent away during the hot months—indeed, there are many points of resemblance between the Austrian officers' lot in Herzegovina and that of the British officer in India."[49] Attempts to "tame" nature may have started to destroy a delicate natural ecological balance even before 1878 and contributed to both the dry heat and floods. American geographer William Morris Davis visited Trebinje in May 1899 and asserted that "artificial deforestation ... woodcutting and unrestricted grazing are the only and sufficient means of explaining the failure of natural reforestation."[50] Trees had been taken from the Trebišnjica banks after the Habsburg arrival,[51] and from alongside the newly built and designed roads between the garrisons and forts. For a couple of days in early December 1903, the city was inundated with water when the banks of the Trebišnjica broke.[52]

The unshaded roads that Babić and Galgóczy had created in Hercegovina were the site of a disaster in July 1903 and when the soldiers rioted in January of the following year, this disaster was still fresh in their minds. Men had been marching over dry terrain from Trebinje to Bileća with heavy backpacks laden with a spare pair of boots and full parade uniform in temperatures of more than 40 degrees:[53] their eventual destination was Nevesinje. The route march

47 "Der Entsatz bei Bilek: Skizzen aus dem Tagebuche eines Offizieres," *Fremden-Blatt*, April 23, 1915, 6.
48 Hochbichler, "Aus den schwarzen Bergen I," 2.
49 Maude Holbach, *Bosnia and Herzegovina: Some Wayside Wanderings* (London: J. Lane, 1910), 228. British writer Holbach (1868/9–1934) was the author of popular travel books accompanied by photographs by her German-born husband Otto Holbach.
50 W. M. Davis, "An Excursion in Bosnia, Hercegovina and Dalmatia," *Bulletin of the Geographical Club of Philadelphia*, no. 2 (1901): 29.
51 F. von M., "Die Culturarbeit," June 10, 4.
52 "Überschwemmung in der Herzegowina," *Grazer Volksblatt*, December 4, 1903, 3.
53 "Die Manöveropfer von Bilek," *Reichspost*, July 29, 190, 1–2.

between two garrisons normally took six hours with a rest scheduled at Mosko, which was approximately halfway. The march started from Trebinje in the early morning. By July 20, it had not rained for several weeks and the water in the shallow cisterns beside the road was very hot and insufficiently thirst-quenching. The troops started to flag about two kilometers from Bileća and nine soldiers died immediately of heatstroke, with another six dying soon after they reached their destination. The victims were buried hastily in a common grave. Only five military musicians were available to play at the funeral because so many had died of heat exposure.[54] News of the extent of the disaster started to seep out as letters home from soldiers revealed some of the terrible detail.[55] The officers in Bileća were in the mess listening to Roma music (*Zigeunermusik*) while the tragedy unfolded. The inference was that they had neglected their men for the sake of idle pleasure. The headquarters of an officer in Trebinje were burned down on July 31, presumably as a protest against the forced march.[56] The details of the debacle were discussed at length in the Hungarian Parliament.[57] Trials followed in the spring of 1904, and two officers, Albert Grünzweig and Stefan (István) Török, were found guilty of neglect and given short custodial sentences.[58]

The year 1903 was emphatically not the first time that Habsburg soldiers had died of extreme conditions in Bosnia and Hercegovina: "[t]he 6th Division lost 11 dead to heat exhaustion" in 1878,[59] while others collapsed due to illness and physical abuse.[60] Men stationed in Hercegovina had complained of thirst or hunger for years before the 1903 catastrophe.[61] Indeed, it formed an important part of their recollection of military service, perhaps a reflection on how the gar-

54 "Eine Hitzschlagübung in der Herzegowina," *Villacher Zeitung*, July 30, 1903, 2–3.
55 "Der Todesmarsch in Bosnien," *Mährisch-Schlesische Presse*, August 1, 1903, 2.
56 "Der verhängnisvolle Uebungsmarsch nach Bilek," *Leitmeritzer Zeitung*, August 1, 1903, 2.
57 "Ungarisches Abgeordnetenhaus," *Wiener Zeitung*, July 28, 1003, 1.
58 "Ein militärgerichtliches Urteil," *Militär-Zeitung*, March 27, 1904, 1; "Das Urteil von Bilek," *Österreichische Land-Zeitung*, April 2, 1904, 2–3.
59 Schindler, "Defeating Balkan Insurgency," 538.
60 Klara Volarić, "Under a Gun: Eugen Kumičić on the Austria-Hungary Occupation of Bosnia and Herzegovina," in *European Revolutions and the Ottoman Balkans: Nationalism, Violence and Empire in the Long Nineteenth Century*, ed. Dimitris Stamatopoulos (London: Bloomsbury, 2019), 191.
61 "Aus dem Tagebuch eines Reservemannes," *Marburger Zeitung*, February 12, 1882, 2.

rison complex was built and staffed with very few resources.[62] Jernej Andrejka recalled how his brigade ran out of bread in Jezero in early August 1878, but still had enough coffee and water to keep themselves going.[63] Alfred Schenk went without water and food for forty hours in 1882, so much so that his dry tongue stuck to his mouth.[64] Troops arriving in Trebinje after its capture in 1878 were parched and were offered an already limited supply of water by the people left in the city: "The inhabitants ... brought as much water as they could—and truly, the best champagne did not taste so good as the first drop of water that wet my thirsty tongue in Trebinje."[65] Even during the First World War, troops suffered from privation. Alfred Möser went to Bileća and then Trebinje "dead tired" after fierce fighting and two days without bread or water in late August 1914.[66]

Cisterns were built by the occupying troops whenever they constructed a new set of fortifications, in contrast with local shepherds who found cool places and took in water as they rested.[67] Furthermore, in abandoning and destroying the fortress at Klobuk, the Habsburg military authorities had also lost one of the deepest and coolest cisterns in the region.[68] Jernej Andrejka observed careful water management at Visoka glavica because local people knew that there was not enough water readily available for consumption in rural areas. Ice from a perpetually frozen cave was melted for animals and a trough had been cut in the trunk of a beech tree which allowed cattle to drink.[69] In extreme necessity, people chewed on dewy grass just for the water content, spitting it out afterwards.

---

62 "Rekruteneinrückungen in der Vorkriegszeit: Von Freistadt nach Bilek," *Tages-Post*, September 20, 1937, 10–11.

63 Andrejka, *Slovenski fantje*, 104.

64 Sch., "Vor fünfzehn Jahren," 5–6.

65 "Aus Bosnien," *Linzer Volksblatt*, October 1, 1878, 2.

66 Alfred Möser, "Feldpostbriefe," *Leitmeritzer Zeitung*, October 14, 1914, 10.

67 Jevto Dedijer, "La transhumance dans les pays dinariques," *Annales de Geographie* 25, no. 137 (1916): 351; Wayne Vucinich, "Transhumance," in *Yugoslavia and Its Historians: Understanding the Balkan Wars of the 1990s*, ed. Norman M. Naimark and Holly Case (Stanford, CA: Stanford University Press, 2003), 73–75.

68 "Die Eroberung von Klobuk," *Morgen-Post*, October 16, 1878, 1; Hivzija Hasandedić, *Muslimanska baština u Istočnoj Hercegovini* (Sarajevo: El-Kalem, 1990), 300.

69 Andrejka, *Slovenski fantje*, 338.

Through this course of action, they demonstrated their physical autonomy, resilience, and sense of their own rights.[70]

Geographer John Walter Gregory visited Trebinje in 1911 and published his photographs in 1915 in the widely available *Geographical Journal*, published in London. By this time, the British Empire and the Habsburg Monarchy were at war and these pictures could have been of direct military use.[71] The constant recitation of news about their technological progress in books and newspapers, as well as other pronouncements, may have left the Habsburg Monarchy more vulnerable. The frequent publication of details about Trebinje's water supply at Oko presented a source of information about the garrison's potential vulnerability even before the outbreak of war. In 1908, for example, the *Manchester Guardian* announced that mines had been laid "in all the passes and all the water springs in all the places where the Montenegrin troops would be likely to encamp" close to Trebinje.[72] A dependency on print culture, as opposed to the word of mouth favored among rural people, potentially slowed the garrison operations down. Governor Johann von Appel had voiced his concern regarding photographs and articles about military installations in the popular press as early as 1894.[73] It was as if, in an almost David and Goliath contest, the giant advertised his hardware, tactics, and movements in advance. Habsburg policy around Trebinje was intended to overwhelm a thinly populated region and induce the local population to adopt their culture through education and the draft. Granted, it was difficult terrain in both respects, but the size of the population gave the authorities the firm but incorrect notion that technological knowledge was power. Aware of their insurgency issue from the outset in 1878, they continued to

---

70   This may have only happened in an emergency; see "Die Bileker Räuberbande," *Grazer Volksblatt*, June 12, 1888, 5.

71   John Walter Gregory, "Pseudo-Glacial Features in Dalmatia." *The Geographical Journal* 46, no. 2 (1915): 105–17. See also Douglas W. Freshfield, "The Southern Frontiers of Austria," *The Geographical Journal* 46, no. 6 (December 1915): 414–33.

72   "Anxiety in Vienna: Triple 'Entente' and Triple Alliance the Troops in Bosnia," *Manchester Guardian*, December 8, 1908, 7.

73   "Landesregierung für Bosnien und die Hercegovina, 702/1, January 7, 1895, Der Chef der Landereierung Appel," in Risto Besarović, *Kultura i umjetnost u Bosni i Hercegovini pod Austrougarskom upravom*, vol. 4 (Sarajevo: Arhiv BiH, 1968), 127.

underestimate alternative sources of loyalty, technologies, and communication systems.

The authorities were sensitive about photography and much of Bosnia, Hercegovina, and even Dalmatia was off limits without prior permission.[74] William Stillman recalled asking Stjepan Jovanović for permission to photograph the old city walls in Dubrovnik, and he replied: "I cannot give you permission to photograph or draw any fortification, but if you wish to photograph the piazza or anything near the city and the walls happen to come into the view, you will not be disturbed."[75] The spread of speedy Kodak camera technology in the 1880s made it more difficult to suppress photography entirely:

FIGURE 15. Flocks of sheep and shepherdesses in 1913. Photo by Marie Marvánková, Moravské zemské muzeum, Brno.

74 Pierre Marge, *Voyage en Dalmatie, Bosnie-Herzégovine et Monténégro* (Paris: Plon-Nourrit, 1912), 265.
75 William J. Stillman, "The late Baron Jovanovich," *The Times*, December 12, 1885, 3. Hermann Bahr faced police interrogation for taking pictures (of seagulls) in Dubrovnik with his Kodak; see Roísín Healy, "From Travel to Mobility: Perspectives on Journeys in the Russian, Central and East European Past," in *Mobility in the Russian, Central and East European Past*, ed. Roísín Healy (London: Routledge, 2019), 2.

nevertheless, the tourist Adolf Kabrhel was arrested in 1902 for taking photographs in Trebinje and the original plates were confiscated.[76] Some subjects were perhaps less controversial because they both captured and idealized the country. Marie Marvánková took photographs that captured everyday life in the Hercegovina karst, but she tended to focus on sheep and their herders or handicraft workers rather than military installations (moreover, her husband Karel Absolon was friendly with the military authorities).[77]

By the early twentieth century, Trebinje bore many of the hallmarks of a Habsburg city: one visitor in 1906 called the city "half Italian and half Turkish" in style. They also found the pleasant greenery of the Kállay-Park constructed around an old Islamic graveyard to be a "splendid contribution" to the city which helped to break up the summer heat.[78] From 1882 until his death in 1903, Benjamin von Kállay was Imperial Minister of Finance and Chief Secretary for Bosnia and Hercegovina. His concept of *bošnjaštvo* (Bosnian identity) was a challenge to Serbian and Croatian national ambitions and may have served to strengthen Muslim identity. Kállay had visited Trebinje in August 1895. The park named after him was "where the little fashionable world of Trebinje, consisting of the officers and their wives, saunter[ed] under the trees, and discusse[d] the gossip of the garrison."[79] When Kállay returned in 1901, he told the assembled crowd that he was always pleased to visit Trebinje, "a small but important city," and a thousand voices shouted "živio!"[80]

The new railway link from Hum to Trebinje meant that the city was increasingly accessible.[81] Kállay had been instrumental in the decision to include a branch line to Trebinje.[82] In February 1901,

---

76 "Spionage," *Pilsner Tagblatt*, March 29, 1902, 4.
77 Petr Kostrhun and Martin Oliva, *K. Absolon: Fotografie z evropských jeskyní a krasů* (Brno: Moravské zemské muzeum, 2010).
78 "Die Reise des Kaisers an der Hercegovina," *Wiener Montags-Post*, August 13, 1906, 7.
79 Holbach, *Dalmatia*, 161.
80 D. G., "Die Eröffnung der neuen herceg-dalmatinischen Eisenbahn," *Agramer Zeitung*, July 16, 1901, 6. In Hungarian sources, the Bosnian governor was known as Béni Kállay de Nagy-Kálló.
81 Helga Berdan, "Die Machtpolitik Österreich-Ungarns und der Eisenbahnbau in Bosnien Herzegowina" (master's thesis, University of Vienna, 2008).
82 Dževad Juzbašić, "Austrougarski planovi gradnje strateških željeznica na Balkanu uoči kretske krize i izgradnja željezničke pruge prema Boki Kotorskoj, Trebinju i Dubrovniku," *Prilozi*, no. 8 (1972): 11–32.

Helene Röhrich described the hive of activity that accompanied the construction, as she saw "hundreds of people working diligently."[83] An enormous feat of engineering, the railway construction took its toll on workers, many of whom contracted malaria or died in accidents. An unnamed twenty-seven-year-old bricklayer from Udine worked on the railway: according to his medical notes, he slept in "wooden barracks on the bare earth" with ninety other construction workers and was gripped with a "violent fever" that lasted twelve days.[84] Antonio Budinich noticed that midges (*moscerini*) were a problem for the railway along the flat Popovo polje: "swarms … attached themselves to the trains and followed them … and the train proceeded as if in a cloud."[85] With the building of the railway, the city was home to temporary workers with progressive views on rights. Some 110 workers left their railway jobs due to poor pay and conditions, having been radicalized by construction workers from Sutorina.[86] Other building projects proved fatal: the aqueduct from the Oko spring to Trebinje used large quantities of dynamite which caused the death of construction worker Tomo Sač.[87]

The Trebinje station, just beside the Trebišnjica, was admired for its location and its elegant two-story building.[88] It had six civilian tracks and blinds, while the seventh and eighth tracks were for strategic and military use. The rapid construction of a railway network was a reminder that military needs were prioritized.[89] Short train journeys increased the capacity of soldiers to take time off, visit their comrades, and become tourists, if only for a few hours. Alfred Jansa (1884–1963), later notable as an Austrian general who resigned in 1938, remembered the pleasure of traveling on the new railway line: "going to Herceg Novi or Trebinje is just as beautiful as the southern railway line to Trieste. [I visited] Captain Kuk, commander of a bat-

---

83 Röhrich, "Von Mostar nach Ragusa," 5.
84 Alfred Brunner, "Über Maltafieber," *Wiener Klinische Wochenschrift*, February 15, 1900, 149–50.
85 Budini, *Le memorie di guerra*, 50.
86 Sivrić, "Radnički pokret u Trebinju," 98.
87 Madžar, "Istorijat Gradskog Vodovoda," 51–64.
88 "Trebinje," *Wiener Zeitung*, April 21, 1900, 5–6.
89 Hadžibegović, *Bosanskohercegovački gradovi*, 50.

FIGURE 16. The Railway Station in Trebinje, 1916. Österreichische Nationalbibliothek, AKON – Ansichtskarten Online, AKO26_221.

talion of Plzeň's Infantry Regiment no. 35, stationed east of Mostar on the Ulok Obrija[90] plateau. Kuk placed immense value on good food … (and) Pilsner Urquell at the temperature that a brewery would serve it. His vegetable garden was a sight to behold."[91] Marian Cruger Coffin described traveling through Hercegovina from Dubrovnik, encountering local people on the train:

> Soon the tropical vegetation of the coast had been left behind.… We made several stops, when wild women from the hills of Herzegovina, in white linen trousers and tunics, their legs encased in top boots, peered shyly at us, afraid to meet our eyes, much less face the camera. We passed several trainloads of peasants traveling fourth class in vans marked "12 horses or 30 people."[92]

---

90 Ulog-Obrnja, where there was a small garrison.
91 Peter Broucek, ed., *Feldmarschalleutnant Alfred Jansa: Ein österreichischer General gegen Hitler; Erinnerungen* (Vienna: Böhlau: 2011).
92 Marian Cruger Coffin, "Where East Meets West: A Visit to Picturesque Dalmatia, Montenegro and Herzegovina," *National Geographic*, May 1908, 309–44.

The role of the railway platform as a greeting place is now largely lost or submerged in rules designed to safeguard passenger safety, but platforms had much more ceremonial importance in the late Habsburg era. The new station opened in Trebinje with great local jubilation on a very hot day on July 17, 1901.[93] There was "national" dancing, houses were festooned with imperial, regional, and green flags,[94] lamb was roasted, champagne and beer were consumed, and the military band played *O Du mein Österreich.*[95] People climbed onto the rooftops to see the arrival of the first locomotive.[96] Von Appel toasted the emperor as the 83rd Infantry Regiment formed a guard of honor. Parallel exuberant celebrations were held at all the newly launched stations on the route which echoed the *dernek* described by Vuk Vrčević back in 1882, bringing locals of all faiths together in their best clothes. The new train, decked with flowers, was welcomed by music, including a stringed *gusle* and a kind of bagpipe (*gajde*, or *Dudelsacks*).[97] There were three new stops between Hum and Trebinje at Taleža, Ljubovo-Duži, and Volujac. In Trebinje, a choir sang "Gott erhalte Franz den Kaiser" (which also had a version with words in Bosnian) to welcome the new railway.[98] This tune had taken a curious journey there. Adapted by Joseph Haydn in 1787 from a Burgenland Croat folk song, "Stal se jesem v jutro rano,"[99] it had become the anthem that transported soldiers back to their own regions and reminded them of their reverence for another Franz, namely his grandson, Franz Joseph.

In some respects, the new railway station amplified the division of Trebinje as it lay on the opposite riverbank to the *kaštel*, but was

---

93 The old station is still visible in Trebinje, but the last train left the city in the Communist era.

94 D. G., "Die Eröffnung der neuen herceg-dalmatinischen Eisenbahn," *Agramer Zeitung*, July 16, 1901, 6.

95 A popular patriotic song composed by Split-born musician Franz von Suppé in 1849.

96 X[aver] von Gayersperg, "Neue Eisenpfade," *Welt Blatt*, August 9, 1901, 8.

97 "Bosnisch-dalmatinische Eisenbahnen," *Pester Lloyd*, July 16, 1901, 9.

98 Theodor Friedrich, "Bosnische Eindrücke II," *Pester Lloyd*, July 21, 1901, 3. Friedrich also heard the tune again on the journey, this time sung by a children's choir.

99 The title in the *kajkavski* dialect of Croatian translates as "I got up early in the morning." The tune became the German national anthem only after 1922 with the new words "Deutschland über alles," and without reference to the Kaiser, Franz I (1768–1835), for whom it was composed.

only a few minutes' walk over the nearby bridge.[100] In 1909, the evening train arrived at 19:00, which allowed new troops to get a sense of both the fortress and the surrounding mountains if they traveled in the summer.[101] Although the new railway significantly boosted the Trebinje garrison's military function, the borders of Bosnia and Hercegovina remained difficult to supply and defend. Railway lines to Uvac and Vardište, both close to the border with Serbia, were opened in 1906, but as a rule, the borders with both Montenegro and Serbia remained difficult to reach quickly. For seventeen years, Trebinje became one of the best-connected places in Hercegovina, which may account for the myriad descriptions of life there from both soldiers and visitors. Changing trains at Hum, some seventeen kilometers from Trebinje, meant that soldiers could easily go to Cavtat or Zelenika on the Dalmatian coast.[102] While the railway created the preconditions for much greater regional unity and cultural uniformity,[103] it often went at a "snail's pace."[104] Bileća and the eastern part of Hercegovina was relatively remote, remaining without a railway connection until 1931. In 1910, the post chaise left Trebinje at 06:00 and only arrived in Bileća three and a half hours later.[105] During the war, soldiers were still being transported slowly from Trebinje to Bileća in horse-drawn omnibuses.[106]

Many accounts testify that Trebinje became a cosmopolitan city after 1878, especially in terms of the languages spoken there. For much of this period, loyalty to the state and the emperor was a higher principle than nation in the ethnic sense. Officers tended to Germanize their names, and local garrison commander Djuro Babić (often known as Georg von Babich) wanted school instruction in Trebinje

---

100 "Eine Reise durch Dalmatien und das Okkupationsgebiet," *Österreichische Illustrierte Zeitung*, July 1, 1906, 904.
101 "Die Zweiundvierziger in Bosnien," *Pilsner Tagblatt*, January 15, 1909, 3-4.
102 As Johann Cvitković put it, these new lines met the state's real "thirst" for railways; see "Eine Adriareise," *Neue Freie Presse*, May 28, 1914, 25.
103 "Eisenbahn von Gabela in die Bocche di Cattaro mit Abzweigungen nach Trebinje und gegen Gravosa," *Verkehrs-Zeitung*, May 1, 1898, 97-100.
104 Budini, *Le memorie di guerra*, 75.
105 Hugo Schulz, "Bosnische Geschichte," *Glühlichter*, June 4, 1910, 3.
106 Edmund Glaise von Horstenau, *Ein General im Zwielicht: die Erinnerungen Edmund Glaise von Horstenau K. u. K. Generalstabsoffizier und Historiker*, vol. 1, ed. Peter Broucek (Vienna: Böhlau, 1980), 202.

to be in German.[107] Many individuals were functionally bi- or trilingual and came from linguistically intermediate places like Sopron, Klagenfurt, or Brno. Describing Trebinje in 1886, one visitor noticed "some very good shops and several inns, mostly with German signs."[108] Just before the First World War, Trebinje had an organization of speleologists (*Verein für Höhlenkunde*) and its daily language of communication was German (which was not the case for equivalent societies in Split, Zadar, Rakovica, and Zagreb).[109] Although officers were compelled to learn the language of their men and given instruction booklets to teach themselves, the army was perhaps more German-speaking than other milieus in the Habsburg Monarchy and it remained the language of command. Correspondence and conversations among officers were often in German, although there were important concentrations of other languages such as Czech and Slovene in the Trebinje garrison complex depending on the composition of a given regiment. Carl Winter arrived in the city in the summer of 1885:

> A valiant Carniolan armed with bayonets ... asked me in the idiom of his homeland what I wanted. Slovene may be a beautiful language, but I confess that it is as foreign to me as the language of the Zulu Kaffirs. I therefore asked the son of the Karavanke: "Is the Herr General [i.e., Djuro Babić] at home?"[110]

Being in the army and not speaking even basic German was considered noteworthy.[111] It is therefore likely that after 1878, Trebinje was an almost bilingual city with German spoken among officers and their associates. This is not to suggest that all soldiers spoke German fluently. Historian Wayne Vucinich, born in 1913, remembered

---

107 Papić, "Prve Škole u Trebinju," 97.
108 F. v. M, "Über Ragusa nach Trebinje III," *Wiener Zeitung*, March 20, 1886, 3.
109 Johannes Mattes, *Reisen ins Unterirdische: Eine Kulturgeschichte der Höhlenforschung in Österreich bis in die Zwischenkriegszeit* (Vienna: Böhlau, 2015), 234, 259. See also "Bosniens Höhlen," *Bosnische Post*, September 1, 1913, 1.
110 Carl Winter, "Das herzegowinische Paris," *Neues Wiener Tagblatt*, August 21, 1885, 2.
111 The sentry at the small frontier garrison at Plana in 1908 was a "Croatian" who spoke no German; see "A Summer Holiday," 149. Antonio Budinich also found that most soldiers stationed in Plana during the war only spoke "Croatian"; see Budini, *Le memorie di guerra*, 197.

his cousin Tripo could speak "pidgin German" and would amuse the family with stories of his military adventures during the First World War: "vigorous applause would encourage Tripo to start another barrage of stories ... inserting a German word now and then to impress his eager audience."[112] Knowing a few words could speed up military communication. Army Slavonic (*Armeeslawisch*), consisting of several dozen rudimentary words,[113] was used among the Habsburg military for basic tasks and its equivalent, *Armeedeutsch*, was the lingua franca for basic commands.[114] It is therefore likely that a lot of communication was less than optimal. One English traveler thought it hard to gauge the legitimacy of Habsburg rule in 1908: "conversation with the natives is impossible, while from soldiers and officials one hears only the official side, but one is led to understand that outward appearances are very deceptive."[115] Lack of a common language could make military service even more miserable and lonely, "exacerbating bizarre communication problems."[116] Viennese soldier Richard Neutra complained that one of the men in his regiment, Kulschetzkij, could almost only speak Polish.[117]

Long stretches of military service with time for study or contemplation made many officers quite accomplished linguists. Conrad von Hötzendorf preferred officers to acquire international languages, "especially French,"[118] so we can assume many had basic knowledge. Linguistic fluency might have accelerated promotion. Alfred Schenk, born in Ljubljana, but also fluent in Czech and German, was quickly elevated to higher rank at a young age.[119] Among Habsburg soldiers and officials, language acquisition was always a question of individ-

---

112 Vucinich, "Transhumance," 70.
113 Anna-Maria Meyer, "Was ist Armeeslavisch?" in *Linguistische Beiträge zur Slavistik*, ed. Ivana Lederer, Anna-Maria Meyer, and Katrin Schlund (Berlin: Peter Lang, 2020): 63–88.
114 Tamara Scheer, *Von Friedensfurien und dalmatinischen Küstenrehen: Vergessene Worte aus der Habsburgermonarchie* (Vienna: Amalthea Signum, 2019), 39, 35.
115 "A Summer Holiday," 156.
116 Hutečka, *Men Under Fire*, 160.
117 R. J. Neutra, Diary, 1915–16, BOX 335. Richard and Dion Neutra Papers, UCLA Library Special Collections, Charles E. Young Research Library, vol. 4, 4.
118 Tamara Scheer, *Die Sprachenvielfalt in der österreichisch-ungarischen Armee (1867–1918)* (Vienna: Heeresgeschichtliches Museum, 2022), 151.
119 Alfred von Schenk (1863–1952) was an Austrian general who served on the Isonzo and Russian fronts in the First World War.

FIGURE 17. The Orthodox Church of the Transfiguration (1908) designed by Josef Ceipek. Photo by Janko Samoukovic, Wikimedia Commons.

ual ability and inclination. When Leo Weirather was still learning to get by, his friends would write translations of phrases (such as "is there a cave here?") on pieces of paper for him.[120] Language acquisition could also become a statement of political sympathies.[121] Knowledge of other Slavonic languages was usually helpful: Alois Pick and Reinhard Günste (both originally from Bohemia) spoke the local language in Hercegovina fluently.[122] Richard Neutra spent a lot of time speaking to women and country people, which increased both his language proficiency and sense of empathy.[123] Even during the

---

120 Bernd Hauser, "Ein autobiographisches Fragment von Leo Weirather (1887–1965), dem Tiroler Pionier der biospeläologischen Erforschung des Balkans," *Contributions to Natural History: Scientific Papers from the Natural History Museum Bern*, no. 12 (2009): 609.

121 F. Michael Florer thought that the use of the term "naschki" separated locals from Italian speakers in the Bay of Kotor; see "Kriegsaufzeichnungen," AT-OeStA/KA NL 654 (B), Kriegsarchiv, Vienna, 290.

122 "Generaloberstabarzt Professor Alois Pick," *Neues Wiener Journal*, March 2, 1919, 7.

123 Neutra, *Life and Shape*, 107–8. Neutra expressed his preference for learning languages by ear. His beautiful memoir, written without a translator, is full of characteristically unidiomatic phrases.

war, Antonio Budinich received presents as a sign of affection and respect from the people he interacted with: "like them, I sat on the ground, legs crossed, spitting in the fire, talking about sheep, goats, pigs, oxen, potatoes, turnips. They offered me milk, honey, and very often ... they greeted me, and put four or five eggs as a gift in the pockets of the saddle of the horse."[124]

Through the entire period from the 1870s until 1918 and beyond, much of the urban population of Trebinje was Muslim. The presence of garrison troops, professionals, and tradespeople, many of whom were baptized Catholics, significantly increased the non-Muslim population in Trebinje after 1878.[125] Writing about Trebinje's mosques and churches in 1889, Hermann Iser noted that "this is a border area between cultures."[126] The construction of "two large new churches put the rise of the mosque minaret out of joint," according to Edith Durham in 1900.[127] There were also a number of Jews among the soldiers, but the nearest synagogue remained in Dubrovnik. A new Catholic cathedral dedicated to Mary, Mother of God (*Katedrala Male Gospe*) was constructed between 1880 and 1884.[128] The local Catholic bishops Paškal Buconjić and Alojzije Mišić were both born in Ottoman Bosnia and Hercegovina, unlike Mato Vodopić who was from Dubrovnik. The former were also Franciscans, which allowed some sort of continuity and knowledge with the Ottoman period.[129] The historic Orthodox diocese of Zahumlje, Hercegovina, and the Littoral included Trebinje. Their clergy were close to the local people in terms of influence and ways of thinking. A beautiful new Orthodox Church of the Transfiguration (*Saborna Crkva Preobraženja Gospodnjeg*) was completed in 1908 in the center, close to the Kállay-Park. It was

---

124 Budini, *Le memorie di guerra*, 142.
125 Hadžibegović, *Bosanskohercegovački gradovi*, 60–61.
126 Hermann Iser, "Aus der Herzegowina," *Vorarlberger Volksblatt*, November 22, 1889, 3.
127 Mary Edith Durham, *Diary from 1900*, RAI MS 42, vol. 1, Royal Anthropological Institute, London.
128 It was the seat of Bishop Mato Vodopić (1816–1893) from 1882 to 1890 in the newly constructed diocese of Trebinje-Mrkan. He was succeeded by Paškal Buconjić (1834–1910) who led the diocese until 1910 and then by Alojzije Mišić (1859–1942) from 1912 until 1942.
129 The Franciscans were the only Catholic order that had been tolerated by the Ottomans before 1878.

FIGURE 18. Celebrations of twenty years of civil administration at the entrance to Trebinje's old city in 1900. Muzej Hercegovine, Trebinje.

designed by Josef Ceipek,[130] who also restored religious buildings.[131] In Bileća, a mosque named after Franz Joseph (Carska or Careva džamija) was finished in 1895.[132] The Chapel of Our Lady of the Visitation, built in the 1890s in Gradina, was built around the *stećci* as well as a bronze age fort.[133] At its most confident, the Habsburg project looked multi-confessional and dynamic.

Trebinje offered something of the "romance" of the Orient, with its "slender minarets emerging from a tangle of roofs."[134] Dora Münch also visited Trebinje on a Friday and was told by her red fez-wearing guide that "if she was lucky, she might see the Turks in prayer."[135] The Ottoman legacy was perceived to be scenic and worth a detour. Readers of the *Grazer Volksblatt* were informed: "this place was under the Crescent for five hundred years and this oriental character has

---

130 Josef Ceipek (1844–1940) was a military architect originally from Brașov.
131 Novottny, "Erinnerungen," AT-OeStA/KA NL 417: 12, Kriegsarchiv, Vienna, 195.
132 "Telegramme des Correspondenz-Bureau. Bilek," *Neue Freie Presse*, August 28, 1895, 20.
133 Domagoj Vidović, "Toponimija sela Zavala, Golubinac, Belenići i Kijev Do u Popovu," *Folia onomastica croatica*, no. 20 (2011): 219.
134 "Von Ragusa nach Trebinje," *Neue Freie Presse (Abendblatt)*, February 6, 1882, 2.
135 Dora Münch, "Ein Erlebnis in Trebinje," *Bukowinaer Post*, July 7, 1912, 1.

131

not quite yet been shaken up (*gerüttelt*) by European culture."[136] Often this trope juxtaposed order and disorder. An anonymous Habsburg soldier who arrived in September 1878 (after years of conflict, low food stocks, and a siege) noted that the streets were narrow and that there was trash piled up.[137] In 1910, Maude Holbach observed that "Turkish Trebinje has gained in cleanliness by coming into touch with European standards, but its picturesqueness remains. Our visit was on a Friday, and as we sauntered down the main street all the male population were engaged in ablutions preparatory to visiting the mosques. The feet-washing was a wonderfully simple performance."[138] Negative views of Islam did not disappear entirely after 1878 and festered through the perpetuation of contradictory stereotypes.[139] As one visitor remarked: "the Bosniaks, I discovered, exist on black coffee, cigarettes and a very limited amount of work."[140] As well as an acceptance of *kismet*, Muslims were regarded as colorful dressers, lazy, superstitious, sensuous—this included frequent references to the harem—but they also had great cuisine served in generous portions, expert artisanal products, and beautiful domestic interiors. In 1890, Conrad Hochbichler wrote down what he ironically termed a "humane saying" which he claimed was told by a Muslim: "killing a Serb is as simple as drinking a glass of water."[141] Charles St John expressed pessimism about the perpetuity of poor relations between the faiths when he visited Trebinje in 1881. He thought that a Muslim could not live "on terms of equality with those who for centuries he has been accustomed to look down upon and despise."[142]

Preparing and serving coffee was bound up with local identity in Trebinje,[143] but enjoyed tremendously by incomers. Oskar Teuber en-

---

136 "Ragusa-Trebinje," *Grazer Volksblatt*, April 21, 1912, 19.
137 "Die Gassen, wenn man sie so nennen darf, sind nur Gänge, von Pflaster keine Spur. Unrath und Koth in Masse," "Aus Bosnien," *Linzer Volksblatt*, October 1, 1878, 2.
138 Holbach, *Dalmatia*, 162.
139 Emily Greble, *Muslims and the Making of Modern Europe* (Oxford: Oxford University Press, 2021), 90.
140 "A Summer Holiday," 148.
141 Conrad Hochbichler, "Aus den schwarzen Bergen III," *Ischler Wochenblatt*, May 11, 1890, 1.
142 Charles St John to Earl Granville, Dubrovnik, March 24, 1881, FO 7/1023, National Archives, London.
143 Bosnian Muslim immigrants to Chicago set up coffee shops when they emigrated circa 1900; see Samira Puskar, *Bosnian Americans of Chicagoland* (Charleston, SC: Arcadia, 2007), 12.

joyed "an authentic, thick mocha" for just five Kronen in 1896.[144] In 1912, Dora Münch was persuaded that she could not leave Trebinje without having a "real Turkish coffee."[145] A coffeehouse, *Die Stadt Wien* (*Kod grada Beča*), opened very quickly after the occupation.[146] In 1882, it was smoky and packed with up to fifty officers in the morning, even though there were only three tables.[147] A new *Café Šuljak*, owned by the eponymous Hasan Šuljak from nearby Zasad, often filled with soldiers still wearing their uniforms. *Café Luft* opened in Bileća, run by Sajmi Muzdović, who had returned from a pilgrimage to Mecca. He served black coffee with figs from Gorica and grapes from Lastva to his military clientele while they played chess.[148] Light bentwood chairs manufactured by Thonet and brought in from the Moravian town of Koryčany allowed aspiring café owners to expand their seating quickly and comfortably. One visitor to Trebinje in 1883 noted that locals ate "in orthodox Mahomedan style with their fingers; one or two of them helping themselves a little with a pocket-knife; but they washed down their repast with no inconsiderable draught of wine and raki."[149] Lemonade[150] and tamarind-flavored drinks were often served, as well as rose or quince jam[151] and filo pastry (*pita*), stuffed with almonds during Bajram.[152] Rice dishes sweetened with raisin or almond and flatbreads (*Sultanbrot*) were often culinary novelties for soldiers stationed in Bosnia and Hercegovina. A breakfast consisting of fruit followed by a cigarette was considered typically Muslim.[153] Arriving in 1878 in Trebinje, Rudolph von Wartburg commented that meat, vegetables, and rice were cooked in the same pot, perhaps not a common dish in Central Europe at that time.[154]

---

144 Oskar Teuber, "Eine Ungarn-Kolonie in der Herzegovina," *Pester Lloyd*, November 4, 1896, 3–4.
145 Münch, "Ein Erlebnis in Trebinje," 4.
146 Ivanetič, "Allerlei aus Trebinje," 5.
147 "Tagebuch eines Mobilisirten," 5.
148 Alexander Stern, "Aus B. H. D.," *Donauland*, 1917, 1125.
149 "The Austrians in Herzegovina," 7.
150 Reinhold Oeser, "Ein Ausflug zu Rad von Ragusa nach Trebinje," *Club-Organ des Oester-reichischen Touring-Club*, no. 10 (1899): 5.
151 Reinhard Günste [Rifat Gozdović Pascha pseud.], "Die Pekingenten," *Pilsner Tagblatt*, May 23, 1915, 5.
152 "Erinnerungen aus dem Wanderleben," *Wiener Salonblatt*, July 26, 1902, 18.
153 Sepp Heimfelsen, "Reisebriefe aus Bosnien, Herzegovina und Dalmatien," *Der Fremden-verkehr*, April 19, 1914, 7.
154 Wartburg, "Meine Erinnerungen an die Kämpfe um Trebinje," 2–3.

FIGURE 19. Hotel Naglić in 1915. Kriegsarchiv Vienna, Austrian State Archives.

The Hotel Naglić was important to Trebinje's garrison in several ways. It had first opened in 1887 on the main Kaiserstrasse, providing a location where visitors could enjoy reassuringly familiar "German cooking," a shady garden with a music pavilion, and the company of the likeminded.[155] By this time, a distinctive cuisine had evolved in the Habsburg Monarchy which included breaded schnitzels, hams, goulash, pancakes, cake, dumplings, fruit strudels, and the emperor's favorite, beef brisket with root vegetables (*Tafelspitz*). Officers arriving on their first night might be billeted at the Naglić before settling into their quarters.[156] The hotel's Catholic owners were conspicuously *kaisertreu* and celebrated the emperor's birthday with fireworks and music.[157] Some were skeptical about the claims of the "Grand Hotel Naglić,"[158] viewing it as rather provincial. The Naglić also had a few competitors. The "veritable hovel" of a hotel in Bileća got a very poor review in 1911 from Lionel Franceys, who

---

155 Röhrich, "Von Mostar nach Ragusa," 5. Local doctor Rudolf Löwy and his friend, the watchmaker Boris Dubelier, both Jewish, would regularly meet at the Naglić for Sunday lunch.

156 Novottny, "Erinnerungen," AT-OeStA/KA NL 417: 12, Kriegsarchiv, Vienna, 194–95.

157 "Tagesneuigkeiten," *Deutsches Volksblatt*, August 24, 1904, 2.

158 Eugen von Radiczky, "Nevisinje-Trebinje," *Wiener Landwirtschaftliche Zeitung*, February 9, 1907, 2.

claimed to have left with bedbugs.[159] In Trebinje, Jovo Andrić ran the eponymous Hotel Andrić, which advertised "elegant rooms at reasonable prices."[160] In his "brilliantly decorated" restaurant, officers celebrated carnival in 1888 with their wives, danced until after midnight, and listened to the piano.[161] There was also a small hotel, run by former soldier Ivan Müller from the Bohemian town of Cheb and his wife Terezija Žagar from Črnuče in Carniola. Their coffee bar was known as "Therese's" by the soldiers.[162] Ivan had saved his wages from the army to establish the hotel, which was more modestly priced than the Naglić. A busy social hub, the hotel also took in laundry from the garrison.[163]

Hotels played a direct role in supporting the defense of the realm. Archduke Leopold Salvator (1863–1931) stayed in the apartment of the Hotel Naglić while inspecting the troops in 1912.[164] Military visitors could be accommodated temporarily in comfortable quarters with a good bath and "the only modern water closet in the city,"[165] which contrasted with the more rudimentary facilities in military buildings. During the war, the hotel was a convenient place to meet quietly. In 1915, Captain Endlicher had breakfast at the hotel with his colleague Ritter after arriving very early from Dubrovnik.[166] Other businesses offered emergency dining or accommodation. With the military influx in 1882, Hotel Müller in Trebinje was ready to serve soldiers a supper of meat consommé on top of the "so-called salami," bread, and wine they had had at lunch.[167] Forty-eight soldiers were billeted in *Café Sarajevo* in Bileća in 1915.[168]

In peacetime, garrisons in Bosnia and Hercegovina could offer limited but clean accommodation; this was especially useful close

---

159 "On Adria's Shores," *The Fleetwood Chronicle*, February 14, 1911, 8.
160 *Neues Wiener Journal*, May 1, 1904, 20.
161 "Unsere Truppen in der Herzegowina," *Bogen des Neuigkeits Welt-Blatt*, February 25, 1888, 5.
162 Hopffgarten, "Bericht über eine entomologische Reise," 125.
163 Miklobušec, "Od Trebinja do stratišta," 194.
164 "Erzherzog Leopold Salvator in Trebinje," *Das interessante Blatt*, August 8, 1912, 11.
165 "das einzige englische Klosett," in Alexander Stern, "Aus aller Welt," *Tagblatt*, August 30, 1930, 3.
166 Neutra, Diary, 1915–16, Richard and Dion Neutra Papers, vol. 4, 8.
167 "Tagebuch eines Mobilisirten," 5.
168 Untitled memo dated March 7, 1915, K. u. K. Geniedirektion in Bileća, AT-OeStA/KA FA NFA (Bileća 1309), Kriegsarchiv, Vienna.

to the borders with Serbia and Montenegro where there were generally fewer hotels and indeed, fewer buildings. Kurt Hassert stayed in the barracks at Plana and noted that most of the *Wachthäuser* had guest rooms.[169] Officers seemed to enjoy the chance to act as hosts to visitors in the new domains. William Morris Davis recalled that "we rose at Gacko at 4.30am and had a brisk walk of about three miles to see a new reservoir for irrigation; after breakfast we drove all day long, and did not reach Trebinje until two o'clock at night—but officers of the garrison were even then waiting to welcome us; there we slept two hours, rising at daybreak for an all-day trip over Mt. Orjen."[170] Maude Holbach recalled a pleasant lunch with the officer Godwin von Lilienhoff-Adelstein, and afterwards his wife took her for a visit to a "Turkish harem."[171]

Railway stations provided places to eat and freshen up at interchanges or a point of departure. Antonio Budinich ate lunch at Hum, partly because eating in the restaurant filled the time between the scheduled trains.[172] Cycling enthusiast Vjekoslav Novotni took his bike on the train as far as Trebinje and then cycled to Orjen.[173] The new network brought *Sokol* members to Trebinje on *Kaisertag* in August in large numbers and in holiday mood.[174] From 1910, soldiers and travelers could use the new tram system from Gruž into the old city of Dubrovnik. Soldiers traveled to the coast on the weekend to swim in the sea or meet women or fellow soldiers and could still make it back to Trebinje in the evening.[175] The allure of the coast, with its lush vegetation and Adriatic traditions, served as a welcome contrast to the harsh limestone of Mount Leotar. Soldiers and their guests could stay at the Hotel Petka in Gruž,[176] which first opened

169 Hassert, *Reise durch Montenegro*, 110.
170 W. M. Davis, "An Excursion in Bosnia, Hercegovina and Dalmatia," *Bulletin of the Geographical Club of Philadelphia*, no. 2 (1901): 23-24.
171 Holbach, *Dalmatia*, 162 and viii. Godwin von Lilienhoff-Adelstein (1862-1929) spoke fluent English.
172 Budini, *Le memorie di guerra*, 36.
173 Vjekoslav Novotni, "Iz Zagreba preko Orjena do Kotora," *Hrvatski Planinar* 7, nos. 3-4 (1904): 20-27.
174 H. K., "Ein Kaisertag in der Heimat des Bombenwerfers: Eindrücke aus Trebinje," *Reichspost*, July 10, 1914, 7.
175 Hetz, "'Ronde': Bilder aus Österreich-Ungarns Vergangenheit," 15.
176 Eduard Kriechbaum, "Dalmatien," *Neue Warte am Inn*, March 4, 1927, 8-9.

in 1867. In 1912, one visitor remarked on returning to Gruž in the moonlight: "There is still a lot of life here. A cruiser squadron with a torpedo flotilla is anchored ... [and] our elegant naval officers and brave blue jackets are spending the Easter holidays here."[177] Visitors to the coast could also stay in Hotel Plaža in Zelenika which opened in 1902, or alternatively in Dubrovnik's impressive Hotel Imperial, completed in 1897, which offered a "comfortable place in this corner of paradise."[178]

By the early twentieth century, obligatory military service had become a way of life and was accepted by many. The first day might be even marked by celebration. Robert Michel described recruits arriving from the villages in the Neretva valley to the garrison in Mostar: the men's names were read out, there was singing, a *kolo* was formed and local girls joined in the dance, and sellers arrived with cornbread, cheese, black coffee, cooked lamb, and "oriental refreshments."[179] While there may have been similar celebrations in Trebinje, it would be fair to say that for many, the festive feeling was very short-lived, if it existed at all. Although flogging for soldiers was abolished in 1867, life remained lean, strict, and harsh. Every garrison had a prison block, suitable for both local miscreants and errant recruits. On October 24, 1879, after an enquiry into the incident,[180] a sub-lieutenant named Zahradnik was arrested and "punished severely" in Trebinje after he reportedly manhandled Alice Evans and repeatedly flourished his sword in front of her.[181] Soldiers found many ways of protesting against their posting, both in peacetime and during the war. In 1902, Ernst Ratkowsky of the sixth artillery regiment deserted and used the railway at Trebinje to make

177 Z.-A. Michel Humpelstetter, "Osterreise 1912 des Österreichischen Toüristen-Klubs nach Bosnien, der Herzegowina und Dalmatien," *Österreichische Touristenzeitung*, June 1, 1912, 137.

178 Andreas Dillinger, "Ragusa," *Dillingers Reise- und Fremdenzeitung*, March 10, 1897, 4. This hotel was favored by Karl Novottny; see "Erinnerungen," AT-OeStA/KA NL 417: 13, Kriegsarchiv, Vienna, 194.

179 Robert Michel, "Der Deserteur," *Pilsner Tagblatt*, December 13, 1914, 2. Born in the Bohemian town of Chabeřice, Michel (1876–1953) first came to Hercegovina in the 1890s.

180 Arthur J. Evans to Consul M. E de Sainte-Marie in Ragusa (Acting Consul of Her Britannic Majesty), November 2, 1879, National Archive, London.

181 Lettre de General Klimburg à Consul M. E de Sainte-Marie (Acting Consul of Her Britannic Majesty in Ragusa), November 21, 1879, National Archive, London.

his getaway.[182] Christmas was a symbol of family time and not an occasion to be cooped up with other men. Antonio Budinich recalled that Catholic Christmas Eve in 1915 was so sad that none of his comrades had the courage to talk about it.[183] To cheer up the men stationed on the border post at Radmilovića Dubrava, Karl Hanke found a fir tree and put candles on it so that it was lit up at night.[184] One soldier recorded his joy when Christmas presents including sweets, apples, and nuts were sent by a firm in Vienna.[185]

Reluctance to serve in the army created anti-Habsburg diaspora communities. Although life was often very tough for migrants, young men took the chance to leave the continent altogether rather than do military service. The American writer John Marich recalled his journey as a fourteen-year-old from the small village on the banks of the Trebišnjica to Dubrovnik in 1895, from whence he set off for a new life in the United States: "[f]or centuries the people of my homeland knew the well-worn paths over the peaks and summits from Trebinje to the Adriatic Sea. It is better to say that they were forced by the enemy to know these paths of escape."[186] Janko Milošević was born in 1892 in Kruševice and arrived in Chile in 1916,[187] thus escaping the fate of much of his extended family.[188] Alongside the fear of the draft, economic factors also precipitated migration. Actor Karl Malden's father, Petar Sekulovich, left Bileća in 1906 to go to the United States: "the promise of work (as well as an escape from obligatory service in the Austro-Hungarian army) motivated Petar and

---

182 Possibly Raikowsky, not Ratkowsky as the newspaper spelled it; "Ein flüchtiger Lieutenant," *Neues Wiener Tagblatt*, August 27, 1902, 4.

183 Budini, *Le memorie di guerra*, 197.

184 Karl Hanke von Hankenstein, "Weihnachten am Kordon," *Teplitz-Schönauer Anzeiger*, December 25, 1909, 3. See also Andrejka, *Slovenski fantje*, 270.

185 N. N., "Brief eines Grenzsoldaten," 3.

186 John T. Marich, *Memoirs of John T. Marich, 1881–1965* (Gary, IN: n.p., 1968), 8. John came from Bijograd and his wife Goša came from nearby Zasad, traveling to the United States at the age of eighteen.

187 "Molba za pasoš, 720/31," 1931, Pasoš ka arhiva, AJ-428-4 – Počasni konzulat KJ u Antofagasti (Nesređena građa), Arhiv Jugoslavije, Belgrade. Many thanks to Richard Mills for finding this source.

188 Kruševice was regarded as a security risk by the Habsburg authorities in the late summer of 1914 after the outbreak of war. Although the Milošević family came mostly from Turani, Janko's mother was called Krunoslava Vavić and her relatives Božo, Mijo, Pero and Petar Vavić, and Nikola Vavić-Golub, were all interned in 1914.

two of his friends to come to this alien world."[189] After the declaration of war in 1914, some Hercegovinians returned to fight against the hated oppressor.[190] In Boka Kotorska, men joined the Montenegrin army as volunteers rather than serve in the army of Franz Joseph.[191] In the other direction, some men returned from the Americas to serve the Habsburg Monarchy. Poor crop yields and the phylloxera blight had also precipitated migration to the Americas. Migrants were often from the countryside and in Trebinje, the population became more heavily dependent on the garrison trade.[192] Muslims from Trebinje emigrated to Chicago, where they established the benevolent society *Džemijetul Hajrije* in 1906.[193]

Poor mental health and self-harm were not unknown among soldiers even in peacetime.[194] In 1905, Udo Bracher, an officer on leave from Trebinje, checked himself into a Viennese hotel and shot himself through the heart.[195] Agon Trost was reportedly so depressed by the monotony of the border post that he shot himself in 1886.[196] Even the usually upbeat Richard Neutra found military service hard to bear at times. According to his wife Dione, he "didn't talk much about the war. He talked about some of the people he met there and about the meanness of people, you know: to be shut up in a fort for months and with people with whom you are not in agreement, and how the mannerisms of each person started to grate on his nerves."[197]

---

189 Karl Malden with Carla Malden, *When Do I Start? A Memoir* (New York: Proscenium, 1997), 18–19.
190 James B. Lane, *City of the Century: A History of Gary, Indiana* (Bloomington: Indiana University Press, 1978), 76–77.
191 Milan Šćekić, "Crnogorski dobrovoljci u prvom svjetskom ratu (1914–1916)," *Matica crnogorska*, no. 66 (2016): 223–56.
192 As Nicola Fontana has demonstrated, a large number of soldiers could alter the culture of a Habsburg town or city; "Trient als Festungs- und Garnisonsstadt: Militär und Zivilbevölkerung in einer k. u. k. Festungsstadt, 1880–1914," in *Glanz—Gewalt—Gehorsam: Militär und Gesellschaft in der Habsburgermonarchie (1800 bis 1918)*, ed. Laurence Cole, Christa Hämmerle, and Martin Scheutz (Essen: Klartext, 2011), 177–98.
193 Puskar, *Bosnian Americans of Chicagoland*, 9.
194 Hannes Leidinger, "Suizid und Militär: Debatten—Ursachenforschung—Reichsratsinterpellationen, 1907–1914," in Cole, Hämmerle, and Scheutz, *Glanz—Gewalt—Gehorsam*, 337–58.
195 "Selbstmord eines Offiziers," *Die Zeit*, August 31, 1905, 6.
196 Andrejka, *Slovenski fantje*, 250.
197 "To tell the truth: oral history transcript," Dione Neutra (1901–1990), interviewed by Lawrence Weschler in 1978, BANC MSS 84/85 c, online at University of California, Berkeley, The Bancroft Library, 33.

Habsburg newspapers often focused on the brighter side of service: "wherever there are Imperial [k. u. k.] soldiers, there is always a cheerful life and [they] spice up the place with a fresh, happy soldier's spirit."[198] The regional press also let quite a few critical letters through, especially if they came from locals sent far away from their home regions. Many complained about heat or cold. One soldier who signed himself H. H. traveled with a monkey that he had brought back from India. He reported that the monkey was cross about the cold weather on Orjen in March 1882 and warmed himself on the campfire. They had come up via Trebinje and then Bileća, where the weather had been much milder.[199] One soldier, returning to Trebinje in the summer after the campaign around Orjen in 1882, remembered that "it was scorching hot there, the water was bad, military service was terribly monotonous, and our free time was unspeakably boring."[200] Space was often limited, rations arrived in tins, and the summer heat was harder to bear in uniform in a city with no brewery. Some local people reputedly raised prices on the unwritten principle that "Švabe have money and ought to pay."[201] One soldier described how his brigade was asked to sleep squashed together on rat-infested straw after an exhausting march in the heat and was woken before dawn by the bugle call.[202]

Conditions in the cash-strapped outlying forts could be quite tough and the struggle to meet need from existing resources is a striking theme throughout this period.[203] In the late summer of 1882, soldiers found two dead insurgents as well as their supplies of ham and red wine. After burying the men, the soldiers consumed the booty.[204] One visitor arrived in a fort close to Orjen and found the men were using a "large potato" as a candlestick.[205] The bunker in

198 Sepp Heimfelsen, "Reisebriefe aus Bosnien, Herzegovina und Dalmatien," *Der Fremdenverkehr*, April 19, 1914, 8.
199 H. H., "Der Zug über den Orien," *Der Vaterland*, April 16, 1882, 9–11.
200 Hubka, *Geschichte des k. und k. Infanterie-Regiments*, 496.
201 Went von Römö, "Aus dem südöstlichen Theile," 34.
202 "Soldatenleben in der Herzegowina," *Freie Stimmen*, June 17, 1887, 6.
203 "Die Befestigungen in der Herzegowina," *Pester Lloyd*, March 23, 1883, 2.
204 "Die letzten Kämpfe in der Herzegowina," *Welt Blatt*, September 10, 1882, 2.
205 F. von M., "Auf Cordon," *Wiener Abendpost*, March 4, 1887, 2. The local potatoes were reputed to be extremely large.

Lastva, in which the men were completely underground, was nick-named "Hotel Bück dich" (Stooping down hotel).[206] The drystone forts in Zubci were described as unventilated, full of smoke, and so cramped that it was impossible to distinguish between officers and regular servicemen.[207] On the way to Avtovac in 1908, the Czech Jungbunzlau Regiment no. 36 demonstrated at conditions in their railway carriage, where they had been cooped up "like cattle," and they even shouted "down with Austria."[208] In the fall of 1914, men from the 9th Landsturmer infantry regiment "often slept outside at night like gypsies" while they were on field guard.[209] Felix Hetz re-membered how tough military service was in 1899: "building roads for a whole year in Risan, despite the scorching heat and icy bora, cinema and radio were still unknown, then the boat to Herceg Novi and a route march to Trebinje for cadet exercises": when his brigade arrived in Trebinje, they were inspected by von Appel, but to get there, they had endured frequent shouting, uphill marches, and the inevitable sunburn.[210]

Privation made men tougher: indeed, it was seen to make them "resourceful, independent, and capable of facing the enemy on diffi-cult terrain."[211] Nevertheless, shouting and dark sarcasm forced a wedge between officers and men. In January 1904, soldiers in Bileća and Trebinje rioted because their leave was delayed.[212] The discon-tented soldiers sang a version of the 1848 revolutionary Kossuth song (*Kossuth-nóta*) in the barracks in Bileća "all day long."[213] The men were reported to be so upset that they wept together, and in Trebinje they also started to subvert orders. They responded to an order to

206 Schalek "An der montenegrinischen Grenze," December 15, 1915, 4.
207 "Garnisonsleben in der Herzegowina," *Linzer Volksblatt*, March 16, 1882, 1.
208 "Meuternde tschechische Infanterie," *Österreichische Land-Zeitung*, December 25, 1908, 3.
209 Josef Worm, "Auf Feldwache vor der Festung Trebinje," *Österreichische Volkszeitung*, Novem-ber 3, 1914, 5.
210 Hetz, "'Ronde': Bilder aus Österreich-Ungarns Vergangenheit," 15.
211 Went von Römö, "Aus dem südöstlichen Theile," 40.
212 "Die Soldatenrevolte in Bilek," *Neues Wiener Journal*, January 4, 1904, 4.
213 "Angebliche Unruhen in der Bileker Garnison," *Pester Lloyd* (*Abendblatt*), January 2, 1904, 1. Lajos Kossuth was perhaps the most famous Hungarian nationalist of the Franz Joseph era, who left the Habsburg Monarchy in late 1849 and lived in exile until his death in 1894. In 1903, composer Béla Bartók wrote his symphonic poem *Kossuth*.

look right by looking left with "scornful laughter."[214] On December 28, a soldier asked his officer Zier when they would be allowed to go on leave and received the reply "when the double-headed eagle [i.e., the regiment's standard] flies away."[215] A soldier then pulled down the eagle and threw it into the gutter to wild applause from the other men. When it became clear that they would still not get the leave they had been promised, the soldiers got drunk, shouted their way through the streets, destroyed guesthouses, and tore up pictures of Franz Joseph. In the aftermath, so many were arrested that the garrison at Bileća had insufficient prison rooms for the rioters who were taken to Trebinje, which functioned as the "iron heart" of the regime as it had done in 1882.[216]

Larger garrisons were designed to be very similar to each other, with official blueprints in which the number of bedrooms, officer quarters, pharmacies, bakeries, tailors, munitions depots, sickbays, surgeries, and bathrooms would all be included.[217] The Trebišnjica had a swimming school and Habsburg officers enjoyed parties beside the river. Garrisons also had a casino and reading rooms intended to foster comradely interactions.[218] In Bileća, the comfortably furnished casino was called Galgóczy's "finest legacy."[219] There was also time for luxury, but even that was necessarily limited, and tedium soon set in. This was the case for both peace and wartime. Soldiers sometimes quarreled. In 1901, two officers from Trebinje were involved in a twenty-five-step one shot pistol duel which resulted in fatal injury for Lieutenant Kramer, who died several hours after the event.[220]

---

214 "Die Aufregung in Bilek," *Arbeiter Zeitung*, January 6, 1904, 3.

215 "Die Meuterei in Bilek und Trebinje," *Villacher Zeitung*, January 10, 1904, 3.

216 "Meuterei bei den ungarischen Truppen in Bosnien," *Innsbrucker Nachrichten*, January 5, 1904, 7–8.

217 See for example, "Belag- und Ubikationsübersichten der Geniedirektion Bilek unterstehenden Stationen: Bilek, Avtovac, Cemerno, Deleuse, Gat, Mosko und Vardar," 1903, AT-OeStA/KA KPS LB K VII m, 46-24 E, Kriegsarchiv, Vienna. On the importance of internal garrison design, see Michael Viktořík, *Hinter den Wällen der Festungsstadt: Ein Beitrag zu Alltagsleben, Organisation und Einrichtung der Festungsstadt im 19. Jahrhundert (am Beispiel der Festung Olmütz)* (České Budějovice: Bohumír Němec-Veduta, 2018), 123–39.

218 "Ein Militär-Casino in der Herzegowina," *Militär-Zeitung*, December 28, 1878, 827; Scheer, *Die Sprachenvielfalt*, 246.

219 P. L., "Ein Mann der Zukunft," 2.

220 "Zweikämpfe mit tödtlichem Ausgang," *Steirische Alpenpost*, October 12, 1901, 3.

Antonio Budinich found the life of the garrison "boring and unbearable."[221] In 1915, Alice Schalek noted the same ennui: "the officers walk two kilometers from the barracks in Bileća to drink the same coffee in smoky bars, read the same newspapers, and gamble in the casino."[222] Lack of entertainment could also be productive, at least in the longer term: although Richard Neutra came to dislike the stone forts which he was sent to, historian Volker Welter has argued that he carried forward the rugged landscapes of the limestone Hercegovina karst into his architectural career and Californian villa designs.[223] Reading became an important pastime and a way of testing local knowledge against the national.[224] Men stationed on the border were happy to receive newspapers even if they were ten days old.[225] The *Bosnische Post*, a German-language daily founded in Sarajevo in 1884, offered regional perspectives which were remediated via newspapers in other parts of the monarchy.[226] At the end of October 1918 in Trebinje, Fritz Telmann remembered that he had not seen a copy of the *Bosnische Post* for three weeks and that he felt completely cut off from the world.[227] Antonio Budinich found it to be a mixed blessing:

> I subscribed to … the *Bosnische Post*, which came twice a week, and yet it was by no means an enjoyable read. It reported the news of the war, but with such partiality that many times I threw it away angrily. Over time I learned to read between the lines by guessing what was not said, thereby following the vicissitudes of foreign policy and, in particular, the attitude of the Italians. I had brought the *Count of Monte Cristo* with me from Trieste: I read it

221 "La vita nella guarnigione diventava sempre più noiosa e insopportabile," Budini, *Le memorie di guerra*, 160.
222 Schalek, "An der montenegrinischen Grenze," December 15, 1915, 1.
223 Welter, "From the Landscape of War," 216–33.
224 Holly Furneaux has highlighted the importance of British soldiers following events via newspapers and the parallel to their own experiences; see *Military Men of Feeling: Emotion, Touch and Masculinity in the Crimean War* (Oxford: Oxford University Press, 2016), 155.
225 Andrejka, *Slovenski fantje*, 330.
226 A Bosnian-language version of the newspaper *Bosanska pošta* was also launched in 1896, but did not achieve the circulation numbers necessary to endure; see Mary Sparks, *The Development of Austro-Hungarian Sarajevo, 1878–1918: An Urban History* (London: Bloomsbury, 2015), 153.
227 Fritz Telmann, "Die letzen Tage von Trebinje," *Die Zeit*, May 30, 1919, 1.

twice; I did not have the courage to read it a third time.[228]

Cheap fixes for frustration could be found from pornography. One of the best known and popular publications of this type was Gottfried Sieben's *Balkangreuel*, issued in Vienna in 1909,[229] which depicted mass rapes of physically perfect Christian women by men in uniforms and fezzes (probably meant to represent a bashi-bazook [*başıbozuk*] or irregular Turkish soldier). In many of the lithographs, the rapists are already assumed to have killed the local men, whose lifeless bodies (stabbed or hanged) are included in the pictures. There was evidently a market for vicarious sadism in a Balkan context: pirate editions in English and Czech followed the German edition and the original book was then reprinted as a series of postcards.

FIGURE 20. Jernej Andrejka in 1878, by Karl Pippich. Wikimedia Commons.

Although a soldier's life was dominated by the barracks, by routine and rigor, sexual contact inevitably did take place. The relationship between the military occupation and erotic conquest was sometimes quite explicit. Large numbers of young unmarried men conscripted for several years brought prostitution to the region. Alexander Stern remembered that time slots were allotted by regiment for visits to the Trebinje bordellos "for every day of the week."[230]

---

228 Budini, *Le memorie di guerra*, 39.
229 Irvin Çemıl Schick, "Christian Maidens, Turkish Ravishers: The Sexualization of National Conflict in the Late Ottoman Period," in *Women in the Ottoman Balkans: Gender, Culture, and History*, ed. Amila Buturović and Irvin Çemıl Schick (London: I. B. Tauris, 2007), 273.
230 "Der Bordellbesuch hat in folgender Reihenfolge zu erfolgen: Montag: K. u. k. Infanterieregiment Erzherzog Karl Stephan Nr. 8. Dienstag: K. u. k. -Infanterieregiment General von Waldstätten Nr. 81. Mittwoch: K. u. k. Infanterieregiment Georg, König der Hellenen, Nr. 99... und so weiter, für jeden Tag der Woche," in Alexander Stern, "B. H. D," *Der*

One conscript confessed that seeing a "pretty creature" in the café *Die Stadt Wien* was the only "ray of light" during his posting in Trebinje.[231] Soldiers could also travel to Dalmatia to meet "friendly" women.[232] Special *Feldbordellen* were set up during the war to limit the spread of venereal disease and distribute prophylactics.[233] Richard Neutra described the bordello in Trebinje in July 1914 "with the girls after a long night and as yet without renewed hairdo, already up and looking out the open windows." He talked freely to a woman who had been impregnated by an officer during the war and mentioned a captain who "visited" his landlord's daughter.[234] Olmütz Pascha (so-called because he had served time in prison in the Moravian city of Olomouc as punishment for his resistance in 1878) offered a service: "his Turkish coffeehouse was a popular destination, and he was a friend and confidant of the Sarajevo rakes (*Lebemänner*). For a high price, he could deliver a 'real' Muslim woman, freshly shaved, colored with henna and heavily veiled, to his coffeehouse."[235] The war may have made local women more open to exploitation. Writing in 1918 in a style intended to be provocative, Dževad beg Sulejmanpašić suggested that not only were rural Muslim women resorting to prostitution, but that non-Muslim women were also wearing the veil to seduce Habsburg soldiers and retain anonymity.[236]

Hercegovinian Muslim women tended to be veiled in public.[237] One former soldier recalled "many veiled women with a black mask over their face, but fiery eyes."[238] Carniolan soldier Josip Wester wondered:

Kuckuck, July 31, 1932, 12. Stern (1886–1949) was a journalist who often revisited Trebinje in his articles.

231 "Tagebuch eines Mobilisirten," 5.

232 Moonlight trysts took place on the coast; see "-burg," "Ragusa," *Danzers Armee-Zeitung*, April 15, 1909, 9.

233 Nancy Wingfield, "The Enemy Within: Regulating Prostitution and Controlling Venereal Disease in Cisleithanian Austria during the Great War," *Central European History* 46, no. 3 (2013): 576.

234 Neutra, *Life and Shape*, 106–8.

235 Scheer, *Von Friedensfurien*, 183–84.

236 Dževad beg Sulejmanpašić, *Jedan prilog rješenju našeg muslimanskog ženskog pitanja* (Sarajevo: Daniel and A. Kajon, 1918), quoted in Fabio Giomi, *Making Muslim Women European: Voluntary Associations, Gender, and Islam in Post-Ottoman Bosnia and Yugoslavia (1878–1941)* (Budapest-New York: Central European University Press, 2021), 119.

237 Budini, *Le memorie di guerra*, 89.

238 Perkonig, "Zwischen Abend und Morgen," 2.

"do Turkish women blush and do they even need to?"[239] In Sarajevo, William Bailey recalled "a couple of *beaux sabreurs* of the Austrian garrison, big and swaggering, ogling some veiled ladies in a cool, persevering manner. Naturally these veiled females are interesting; the undiscovered is always attractive."[240] If the veil made Muslim women more alluring, their domestic confinement also implicitly sexualized them in the eyes of soldiers. It was also suspected that clothing could conceal more than the female body. In 1880, the soldiers stationed in Trebinje were so worried about secret stashes of weapons that they searched the clothes bags of women.[241] By 1914, there was probably more respect for Muslim customs. Antonio Budinich worried that the traditional dress of Muslim women could easily be used by infiltrators in Plana, right on the frontier with Montenegro. Civilians traveled in great numbers along an exposed road, and he found that it was easy to search the men. His colleague, Lieutenant Muftić, made a stand and refused to let the military search the women by asking them to remove their veils.[242] There were countless descriptions written by incomers of the fine physical appearance of the people of Bosnia and Hercegovina, both male and female, which combined desire and aesthetics. Noting the "artistic dress" of Hercegovinians in the market in Dubrovnik, William Miller suggested that "the emancipated Oriental too often seeks to disguise his splendid physique."[243] Jernej Andrejka admired the complexion of a Bosnian woman he encountered: "She was probably about twenty-eight years old; she had black eyes, black hair, a regular nose, beautifully cut lips, with white straight teeth: her elongated face was tanned."[244] In Mostar, Bernard Wieman spotted "nice-looking Orthodox girls in *dimije* ... Habsburg officers sitting for coffee, slim country women from Hercegovina entirely dressed in white.... I am struck by the beauty of the people."[245]

---

239 Josip Wester, "Tri pisma o Bosni," *Ljubljanski Zvon* 30, no. 11 (1910): 655.
240 William Frederick Bailey, *The Slavs of the War Zone* (New York: E. P. Dutton, 1916).
241 From our Ragusa Correspondent [Arthur J. Evans], "Austria's Difficulties in Bosnia and Herzegovina," *Manchester Guardian*, March 27, 1880, 7.
242 Budini, *Le memorie di guerra*, 89–90.
243 William Miller, *Travels and Politics in the Near East* (London: T. F. Unwin, 1898), 28.
244 Andrejka, *Slovenski fantje*, 110.
245 Bernard Wieman, *Bosnisches Tagebuch* (Kempten: Kösel'schen Buchhandlung, 1908), 215–16. *Dimije* could be translated as baggy or harem trousers in English; Wieman used the word *Pumphosen*.

A few soldiers found domestic security and comfort. In 1909, a Hercegovinian Orthodox woman, Ana Prhal, married Vincenc Lakić, a Catholic sergeant who guarded the ammunitions store in Trebinje. Kata(rina) Zokanović was the illegitimate daughter of an Hercegovinian Orthodox mother and Catholic father stationed in Trebinje.[246] Married officers were permitted to bring their wives with them. Karl Novottny's wife Elsa worked as a nurse in the garrison hospital alongside other military spouses.[247] Other men were so dedicated to their careers that they skipped marriage or left it very late.[248] Anton Galgóczy served for six decades in the army, retiring well after the usual age. Famously unmarried, he once told a friend that the only woman he could tolerate was his wife and then promptly married her himself at the age of sixty after the friend had passed away.[249] Homosexuality was not unknown in the Habsburg army, though nor was it openly acknowledged or permitted.[250] Georg Veith was labelled an "eccentric who avoided women" (*"absolut frauenfeindlicher Sonderling"*).[251] It was rumored that Oskar Potiorek and his adjutant Eric von Merizzi were lovers.[252] He was labelled a *Weiberfeind* (enemy of women), an unsympathetic term used for gay men or "confirmed bachelors" at that time.[253] Unmarried men lived in the barracks, where they created a home from home in which they repaired their uniforms, practiced musical instruments, read novels, and cultivated allotments in their spare time.[254] In these circumstances and with the luxury of local excursions, a love for Hercegovina and its people could flourish.

---

246 Grunert, *Glauben im Hinterland*, 211–12.
247 Novottny "Erinnerungen," AT-OeStA/KA NL 417: 12, 195.
248 On the marital status of Habsburg officers and its impact on their lives, see István Deák, *Beyond Nationalism: A Social and Political History of the Habsburg Officer Corps 1848–1918* (Oxford: Oxford University Press, 1990), 139–53.
249 "Austria: Unser Anton," *Time*, December 9, 1929, 28.
250 Alfred Redl (1864–1913) was a high-ranking Habsburg officer, originally from Lvov, who was blackmailed by the Russian Secret Services because he was homosexual. After he was exposed as a spy, he committed suicide to avoid espionage charges.
251 Vinette Wucherer to Carl Patsch, Gleinstätten, November 6, 1925, Briefe an Carl Patsch 1888–1944, Südost-Institut, Munich.
252 Rudolf Jeřábek found this idea speculative; see his *Potiorek: General im Schatten von Sarajevo* (Graz: Styria, 1991), 218.
253 Geoffrey Wawro, *A Mad Catastrophe: The Outbreak of World War I and the Collapse of the Habsburg Empire* (New York: Basic Books, 2014), 141.
254 Andrejka, *Slovenski fantje*, 316. For parallels with the British Army, see Furneaux, *Military Men*, 89.

Chapter Five

CITADEL AND COUNTRYSIDE

The Bounty of the Land

For the incomer missing domestic comfort, the Hercegovinian countryside must have seemed timeless, a place that used the same wooden
equipment as it had in the time of Alexander of Macedon.[1] Heavy
types of plough (*ralo* and *crtalo*) were remarked upon.[2] Josef Perkonig contrasted urban life with the surrounding countryside. For
him, time passed much slower outside the city: "around Trebinje
there are small villages.... The farmers are poor, but they feed on
small portions of timeless contentment prepared for the frugal. They
sow tobacco and plant the olive tree, they harvest corn and press
tart wine, and they weave the wool of their own sheep."[3] The high
quality of local food in Hercegovina was often commended.[4] In
the fields near Trebinje, potatoes, buckwheat, wheat, corn, beans
(probably a local variety, *poljak*), rye, millet, and barley were already
grown at the time of the Habsburg takeover.[5] The existing cultiva-
tion of tobacco, indigo, hemp, flax, olives, wine, apples, figs, mulber-
ries, rowan, pomegranate, medlars, and "ancient nut and cherry trees"

---

1   Kornel Abel, "Im Auto durch den Karst," *Neue Freie Presse*, March 13, 1938, 2–3.
2   "Repatriirung," *Grazer Volksblatt*, May 31, 1879, 5.
3   Perkonig, "Zwischen Abend und Morgen," 2.
4   Salis-Soglio, *Mein Leben*, 152.
5   Ivanetič, "Arzloin Agič Most," 1.

was further developed after 1878,[6] as regional links were built and artisan goods produced in workshops in Trebinje.

After the mid-nineteenth century, new cheese-making techniques were adopted: hard Alpine-style cheeses were made in Livno, and Trappist cheese was made by Cistercians after the establishment of their abbey in Banja Luka in 1869.[7] Trebinje's Hotel Naglić was serving Trappist with figs to their customers by 1907.[8] New techniques did not entirely displace traditional methods of making softer cheeses which had developed over centuries, especially amongst the Herce-govinian and Montenegrin Orthodox communities. Rural house-holds usually contained a *škip* or wooden trough for making the tra-ditional cream cheese of *skorup*, or *kajmak*.[9] The excellence of soft cheese was remarked upon.[10] *Sir iz mješine* was made by keeping the milk in the gut of the sheep. Among country people, cooking was generally done in a large (but portable) pot called a *sač*. These rural communities also made a hard salty cheese called *torotan*, which they rarely sold at market.[11] Vuk Vrčević wrote about the importance of cheese, as well as other gifts: "pious people flock from remote places, mostly to make vows in the church. They bring donations according to their means: on the coast ... in the form of money, and in the vil-lages usually by bringing wool, wax, cheese, and incense."[12]

Another highly prized local product was honey, which was usu-ally gathered from a *dubovina* or empty (oak) tree trunk, but there were occasional inventive variations. One man asked Jernej Andrejka whether he would like to buy honey and then offered him a horse skeleton which had been populated by bees after the animal had died. Andrejka learned that the ants devoured the remains of the horse, bees then flew in via the eye cavities, and finally the whole skeleton was placed over a fire to smoke out the remaining bees.[13]

6   Günste, "Aus den Erinnerungen," 1.
7   "Die Wunder Bosniens und der Herzegowina," *Bregenzer Tagblatt*, June 5, 1910, 1–2.
8   Eugen von Radiczky, "Nevisinje-Trebinje," *Wiener Landwirtschaftliche Zeitung*, February 9, 1907, 2.
9   Vucinich, *A Study in Social Survival*, 137.
10   "Reisebriefe aus Bosnien," part 4, *Das Vaterland*, September 4, 1881, 9.
11   Vucinich, "Transhumance," 79.
12   Grunert, *Glauben im Hinterland*, 90, footnote 106.
13   Andrejka, *Slovenski fantje*, 342–43.

Other than the tinned sardines eaten by William Stillman in Trebinje in 1875,[14] fish was highly prized.[15] Crab arrived in Visoka glavica from Dalmatia,[16] while eels, bass, and flatfish were caught in Popovo polje.[17] Reinhard Günste enjoyed mussel risotto washed down with plentiful wine.[18] The Hotel Naglić served trout and *gaovica*, an indigenous species found in Popovo polje,[19] which was eaten "salted and preserved,"[20] and "esteemed by the natives as a great delicacy."[21] Varying in size from anchovies to larger plumper fish, the *gaovice* were caught in specially constructed baskets held at the opening of the *ponor* (sink hole) or in silk nets.[22] Geologist Albrecht Penck compared Popovo polje to Lake Cerknica in Carniola, which was famous for its myriad species of fish.[23] Like hunting, fishing in the Trebišnijca was viewed a great opportunity for leisure travelers.[24] Rafts (*catare*), as well as larger flat-bottomed barges constructed by local carpenters, were used to get across the river in Trebinje. One officer remembered that the air was filled with the shouts of fishermen and the sound of the oars as the fish were driven into nets.[25]

Reinhard Petermann appreciated the landscape between Zavala and Trebinje, with its oak groves, tobacco fields, and red pomegranate bushes interspersed.[26] Tobacco was one of many crops that came

14 Stillman, *Herzegovina*, 38.

15 On the rich variety of local fish, see Vejsil Ćurčić, *Narodno ribarstvo u Bosni i Hercegovini* (Sarajevo: Zemaljska štamparija, 1910). Ćurčić (1868–1959) wrote in depth about other natural resources in Hercegovina.

16 Andrejka, *Slovenski fantje*, 343.

17 Günste, "Aus den Erinnerungen," 5.

18 Reinhard Günste [Rifat Gozdović Pasha pseud.], "Paschastreiche," *Pilsner Tagblatt*, August 11, 1912, 1.

19 Trout is known locally as *merdžanka*. On Popovo polje, see Ivo Lučić, "Shafts of Life and Shafts of Death in Dinaric Karst, Popovo Polje Case (Bosnia and Herzegovina)," *Acta Carsologica* 36, no. 2 (2007): 321–30.

20 X[aver] von Gayersperg, "Neue Eisenpfade," *Welt Blatt*, August 9, 1901, 7.

21 Holbach, *Bosnia and Herzegovina*, 230.

22 Oransz, "Die Gesellschafts-Radreise," October 15, 1903, 4; Andrejka, *Slovenski fantje*, 310.

23 Albrecht Penck, "Geomorphologische Studien aus der Herzegowina," *Zeitschrift des deutschen und österreichischen Alpenvereins*, no. 31 (1900): 25–41.

24 See, for example, Camillo Morgan, *Das Jagdwild unserer Adrialänder: Gedenkbuch zur Erinnerung an die Jagdgruppe der Oesterreichyischen Adria-Ausstellung* (Vienna: Druck von W. Philipp, 1913).

25 Günste, "Aus den Erinnerungen," 6.

26 Reinhard E. Petermann, "Mit der Eisenbahn in die Bocche di Cattaro," *Neues Wiener Tagblatt*, July 16, 1901, 2.

from the Americas and was cultivated in the Ottoman lands: toma-
toes and potatoes were also popular. The tobacco grown around
Trebinje was highly valued, described as "exquisite,"[27] and was already established as a crop before 1878.[28] Indeed, Edward Freeman
thought that "mighty little grows save backy" close to the city.[29] Tobacco production was encouraged after the Habsburg arrival, with
investment in new administrative buildings in the city.[30] In 1883,
one visitor described the "long garlands of tobacco leaves hung up
in front of the houses to dry, and some still in a half-grown state."[31]
According to contemporary sources, smoking was enjoyed by men,
women, and children.[32] One writer recalled a roast lamb supper,
after which fortunes were predicted and then the long pipe (čibuk)
was passed around with black coffee, while the ninety-year-old guslar Djuro Raić sang about Prince Marko and the 1389 Battle of Kosovo.[33] Cigarettes from Bosnia and Hercegovina were famous for their
flavor and their "slender conical instead of cylindrical shape."[34] "Drin-
azigaretten," produced in Sarajevo after 1878, were popular with soldiers.[35] Local people did without matches, preferring to light their
long pipe directly from the fireplace.[36]

Wine drinking was a central aspect of Habsburg life, especially
among soldiers who regularly praised the quality and depth of color
of the "black" local wines.[37] There were "huge casks of wine ranged

27 "Am Cordon," *Neues Wiener Journal*, August 25, 1901, 4.
28 On the continuing importance of the tobacco trade, see Marija Naletilić, "O povijesti duha-
    na u Hercegovini do kraja Prvoga svjetskoga rata," *Godišnjak Centra za balkanološka ispitivan-
    ja* 39 (2010): 189–97; Rachel Trode, "The Sarajevo Tobacco Factory Strike of 1906: Empire
    and the Nature of Late Habsburg Rule in Bosnia and Herzegovina," *Central European History*
    55, no. 4 (2022): 493–509.
29 W. R. W. Stephens, *The Life and Letters of Edward A. Freeman* (London: Macmillan, 1895), 127.
    Backy is an affectionate English slang term for tobacco.
30 Sivrić, "Radnički pokret u Trebinju," 96.
31 "The Austrians in Herzegovina," 7.
32 "Unsere Soldaten an der Grenze," 2.
33 S. N., "Eine hercegovinische Idylle," *Agramer Zeitung*, 1908, 4. In the original text, it is
    spelled Gjuro.
34 Neutra, *Life and Shape*, 115.
35 Reinhard Günste [Rifat Gozdović Pascha pseud.], "Huflattich," *Pilsner Tagblatt*, March 12,
    1916, 18.
36 Hochbichler, "Aus den schwarzen Bergen II," 2.
37 "Die Expedition in die Herzegowina," *Welt Blatt*, May 4, 1882, 32.

along the wall" in Drijen in 1883.[38] Other accounts suggest that "heavy Dalmatian wine" was favored in the garrisons;[39] according to one memoir, Habsburg soldiers could drink two liters of "good Dalmatian wine" each per day.[40] Other sources also suggest that army rations of wine and meat were topped up by individuals, which meant that soldiers could often drink with their lunch and dinner.[41] A soldier stationed in Sarajevo remembered the officer's mess, where "an extraordinarily high amount of wine was drunk."[42] It is possible that for beer-drinking Central Europeans, local wine was simply a readily available substitute, but with far greater potency. Unlike wine, beer was rather expensive for soldiers.[43] There were already breweries in Sarajevo, Banja Luka, and Tuzla by the 1880s (though there was no brewery in Trebinje) and many soldiers came from places such as Jihlava or Brno where the production of beer was part of the fabric of the city, always fresh and readily available. The technology for transporting beer improved in the 1870s, fortunately just preceding the Habsburg takeover in Bosnia and Hercegovina.[44] Although neither Trebinje nor Bileća had a brewery in situ, decent draft beers could still be enjoyed.[45]

Wine consumption was still reliably high during the First World War. Richard Neutra recorded the prodigious amount of wine drunk by troops during the invasion of Montenegro.[46] On March 12, 1916, Neutra purchased 714 liters of wine and two liters of olive oil for his

---

38 "The Austrians in Herzegovina," 7.
39 "Eine Episode aus dem Garnisonsleben im Okkupationsgebiet," *Welt Blatt*, September 28, 1911, 14. The article discusses events from twenty years earlier.
40 Wartburg, "Meine Erinnerungen an die Kämpfe um Trebinje," 2. This wine consumption was on top of the ratio supplied by the army, where two liters of wine per man was recorded as a *weekly* ration; see Bencze, *Occupation of Bosnia and Herzegovina*, 336, footnote 15.
41 "Mittags und Abends haben wir sehr kräftige Kost, zweimal Fleischspeisen und vielen, guten und starken Wein (Etappenwein oder eingekauften)." "Aus der Herzegowina," *Prager Tagblatt*, April 30, 1880, 1.
42 "...in die Offiziersmesse wo viel Wein, sehr viel Wein, außerordentlich viel Wein getruncken wurde." Reinhard Günste [Rifat Gozdović Pascha pseud.], "Die Pekingenten," *Pilsner Tagblatt*, May 23, 1915, 2.
43 "Unsere Soldaten an der Grenze," 2; N. N. "Brief eines Grenzsoldaten," 3.
44 Catherine Horel, "Franz Joseph's Tafelspitz: Austro–Hungarian Cooking as an Imperial Project," in *Food Heritage and Nationalism in Europe*, ed. Ilaria Porciani (London: Routledge, 2019), 138–54.
45 "Die Stadt und das Militärlager Bilek," *Welt Blatt*, September 5, 1914, 7.
46 Welter, "From the Landscape of War," 216-33.

battalion in Kotor and returned on April 1, to buy a further 240 liters of red wine.[47] Fine wines were cultivated in the Lastva valley,
which were subsequently exported across Europe. An agricultural
training school was established.[48] Viticulture remained commercially
underdeveloped during the Ottoman period but flourished after 1878.
The nearby coast had grape varieties such as *vranac* and *kratošija*,[49]
grown at the Bay of Kotor and in Budva, and both the *žilavka* and *bla-
tina* grape varieties had been grown in limited quantities in Hercegovina for hundreds of years before the Habsburg period.[50] Comparing it to a white burgundy, Adolf Ružička found *žilavka* "exquisite."[51]
Reported also to be Franz Joseph's favorite wine, *žilavka* won a prize
in Paris for its excellence. The department of agriculture in Sarajevo
was commended for its vigorous attempts to combat phylloxera,
which had been a scourge in Dalmatia, by grafting local grape varieties with resistant American strains. Visitors to Lastva could drink
the local wine at guesthouses run by Četko or by Bogdan Ćelović.[52]
Winzer (wine growing) families from Hungary brought tried and
trusted methods with them when they arrived in Lastva and Jazina.[53]
Incentivized to cultivate vines through a land ownership scheme,
most families settled.[54] Hungarian wine growers in Lastva taught new
techniques to produce wines similar to *Tokaji*.[55]

People in Hercegovina ate many of the natural foods available.
Foraging is often associated with privation and crisis rather than
being quotidian practice, but knowledge about wild plants was pre-

47 Neutra, Diary, 1915-16, Richard and Dion Neutra Papers, vol. 4, 73-75.
48 The *žilavka* grape had been grown in Hercegovina for hundreds of years, but its commer-
    cial potential was realized only after 1878.
49 A red grape variety, close to Zinfandel.
50 Jernej Andrejka believed that local viticulture dated back to Roman times; *Slovenski fantje*,
    332.
51 Adolf Ružička, "Bosnien-Herzegowina-Cettinje: Ein Ausflug dahin." *Kaufmännische
    Zeitschrift*, July 1, 1901, 107-9.
52 Oeser, "Ein Ausflug zu Rad," 5.
53 "Landwirthschaftliche Bilder aus der Hercegovina," *Wiener Landwirthschaftliche Zeitung*, Sep-
    tember 26, 1896, 1-2.
54 One *Winzer* settler, Elisabeth (Erzsike) Szántó, wished to convert to Orthodoxy to marry
    Milan Tomić. After her marriage, she took the name Anđelina, and her son was baptized
    as Orthodox in 1907. See Grunert, *Glauben im Hinterland*, 202-3.
55 Oskar Teuber, "Eine Ungarn-Kolonie in der Herzegovina," *Pester Lloyd*, November 4, 1896,
    3-4.

served from one generation to the next. There is bountiful evidence for the consumption of stinging nettle (*žara, žigorica,* or *koprive*), dandelion (*maslačak*), as well as wild chard (*blitva*), comfrey and its root (*gavez*), mint (*menta*), rosemary (*ruzmarin*), thyme (*timijan*), and sage (*žalfija*). These abundant food sources offered reliable sustenance for poorer people. Botanist Sulejman Redžić contrasted the foraging habits of coastal and inland communities, arguing that the former were less conservative about the use of wild plants.[56] In Hercegovina, wild fruit was also plentiful. Blackthorn (*crni trn*) and rosehip (*šipak*) were gathered, elderberry juice (*bazga*) was consumed, and bitter wormwood (*gorki pelin*) and St John's Wort (*kantarion*) were used to make *pelinkovac*, an alcoholic drink. In Gatačko polje, close to the Čemerno mountain source of the Trebišnjica, a kind of casserole called *pirjan* was prepared with beans, meat, potatoes, and nettles.[57] Vejsil Ćurčić recorded the wild vegetables that were gathered and consumed in Hercegovina,[58] including fennel (*morač*) and the distinctive black bryony (*kuka*).[59] Trees that grow in Hercegovina also have edible components and their leaves were used to decorate interiors in festive seasons. Poppy seeds (*kukurijek*) were used in baking. Maple (*javor*) was traditionally used for flour, while horse chestnuts (*kesten*) provided starch. Other native species including beech (*bukva*), birch (*breza*), and oak (*hrast*) had edible components in the inner bark known as cambium which could be eaten by country people all year round, allowing them to survive (and even thrive) in times of hardship and isolation.[60] In times of exceptional hardship, not only bark cambium but also the tuber from lords-and-ladies (*kozlac*) were consumed.[61] Trees

---

56 Sulejman Redžić, "Wild Edible Plants and their Traditional Use in the Human Nutrition in Bosnia–Herzegovina," *Ecology of Food and Nutrition* 45, no. 3 (2006): 191.
57 HadžiMuhamedović, *Waiting for Elijah*, 102.
58 Łukasz Łuczaj and Katija Dolina, "A hundred years of change in wild vegetable use in southern Herzegovina," *Journal of Ethnopharmacology* 166 (2015): 297–304.
59 *Kuka* is toxic, except for the shoots, and therefore must be prepared by an individual with experience. It is still often eaten with pasta in southern Europe, usually by people of Croatian descent, and is sometimes referred to as "wild asparagus."
60 Older members of the family of Vladimir Gaćinović "could still remember the times when they had to make bread from the bark of the mapletree." Misha Glenny, *The Balkans, 1804–2012: Nationalism, War and the Great Powers* (London: Granta, 2020), 293.
61 Georg Veith was surprised to find that *kozlac* tasted like paprika; see Veith, *Der Feldzug von Dyrrhachium zwischen Caesar und Pompejus* (Vienna: L. W. Seidel 1920), 254–56. Only the root is edible; the berries are quite toxic.

had special qualities: the walnut (*orah*) was the "tree of life and fate," the horse chestnut offered relief from rheumatism, and the linden tree (*lipa*) brought protection and should therefore never be chopped down.[62]

Game was evidently plentiful and taken plentifully. Jernej Andrejka remembered that "once a month, the battalion commander went to inspect the cordon posts. He always announced his arrival a few days in advance and on these occasions, dining at Visoka glavica was no less delicious than at a hotel in Vienna, including rabbit, partridge, and fried dormice."[63] The Slovenes are not the only people in Europe who regularly cook dormice, but their consumption and the use of their fur was already known in Slovene culture in the seventeenth century (and was also a story that they told about themselves).[64] In Visoka glavica, Carniolan soldiers would climb beech trees, "no matter how high," to catch the dormice and even made hats from the fur.[65] Many other sources mention the excellence of the hunt, which was regarded as an "El Dorado."[66] Habsburg battalions were always strapped for cash, so hunting, fishing, and tending allotments supplemented quite meagre rations, as well as teaching the soldiers to love the land even more. Railway Commissioner Reinhard Günste (writing under his pseudonym, Rifat Gozdović) went duck hunting with the Trebinje-based teacher Lucijan Matulić.[67] He remembered the autumn glory, flowers and hovering dragonflies.[68] Hunting was a way in which officers from different garrisons could meet up, sometimes by chance, and share the "splendid tart local wine" in country inns.[69] Not only was game free (and local people were available to row boats, carry bags, or serve

---

62 Lilek, "Familien- und Volksleben," 170.

63 Andrejka, *Slovenski fantje*, 341–43.

64 C. Carmichael, "'Za filozofa preveč romantičnega pridiha': Nekaj zapazanj o Valvasorjevi etnografiji," *Traditiones* 24 (1995): 95–107.

65 Andrejka, *Slovenski fantje*, 344–45.

66 Ernst Dombrowski, "Ein verlorenes Jagdparadies," *Neues Wiener Tagblatt*, April 5, 1914, 45.

67 Reinhard Günste [Rifat Gozdović Pascha pseud.], "Als ich das zweitemal einen Vortrag hielt," *Pilsner Tagblatt*, September 6, 1914, 2; Reinhard Günste [Rifat Gozdović Pascha pseud.], *Pilsner Tagblatt*, December 25, 1914, 2.

68 Günste, "Huflattich," 18.

69 Alexander Günthersen, "Erinnerungen an Feldzeugmeister Galgotzy," *Reichspost*, November 7, 1929, 7.

breakfast in situ), but army officers also found that many places had not been disturbed by hunters before. Habsburg family members were keen hunters. When Franz Ferdinand traveled to Japan by steamship, he stopped off in the Raj to hunt. His party waited for him in Mumbai for several days as he added to the tally of thousands of animals he had already killed in Central Europe.[70] Crown Prince Rudolf was also an enthusiastic hunter. Regarded as light and nimble on his feet, he wore a woolen cloak while hunting close to Gluva Smokva, as well as a red waistcoat, in the style worn in Zadar.[71]

Food in Bosnia and Hercegovina was not always lean and wild; it could also be calorie-laden and rich. In 1858, Franz von Werner had described the diet in Hercegovina as consisting of "Vlach corn (*walachischen Mamaliga*), onion, sheep's cheese, and milk, with rice and roast lamb on feast days."[72] In Drijen, a reporter recalled a man in a red fez serving cheese and the "rows of brown hams hang[ing] from the ceiling."[73] A "frugal" local diet of milk, cheese, lamb, *pogača*, plum brandy, and wine was seen to have kept Hercegovinian Orthodox people strong and hardy.[74] Modern kilns were introduced to dry plums and plum brandy (*šljivovica* or *rakija*) was exported.[75] In popular culture and especially among soldiers, the consumption of plums and plum brandy became associated with all South Slavs.[76] Agricultural products from Bosnia and Hercegovina were highly valued in the Habsburg Monarchy and it proved an excellent place to grow apples, chestnuts, and grapes, as well as the ubiquitous plums.[77]

The reaction to the delicious food served in Bosnia and Hercegovina was heartfelt, with real appreciation for the quality and cleanli-

---

70 Sigismund Ritter von Pozzi, "Marine Erlebnisse eines Blinden," AT-OeStA/KA NL 183 (A,B), KA, 35–6.

71 "Die Opanken des Kronprinzen," *Wiener Allgemeine Zeitung*, April 17, 1886, 5.

72 Werner, *Türkische Skizzen*, 138. On the history of corn in the Balkans, see Alex Drace-Francis, *The Making of Mămăligă: Transimperial Recipes for a Romanian National Dish* (Budapest–New York: Central European University Press, 2022).

73 "The Austrians in Herzegovina," 7.

74 "das landesübliche Fladenbrod," K. H. "Das Hajdukenthum," *Die Presse*, July 28, 1891, 3.

75 Peter F. Sugar, *Industrialization of Bosnia-Hercegovina, 1878–1918* (Seattle: University of Washington Press, 1963), 164.

76 Scheer, *Von Friedensfurien*, 213–14.

77 Moriz Hoernes, *Dinarische Wanderungen: Cultur- und Landschaftsbilder aus Bosnien und der Hercegovina* (Vienna: C. Graeser, 1894), 71.

ness of the presentation. Peasants and pastoralists ate more filling meals, especially meat and vegetable stew (*čorba*) and polenta (*pura*) with a thick sauce made with cheese (*cicvara*), but also occasionally ate the roast meat and potatoes that were habitually served to visitors.[78] Roasted lamb was inexpensive to buy.[79] In the years just before the First World War, a whole roasted lamb could cost just two Kronen.[80] Moritz Oransz remembered an idyllic lunch of lamb (*Hammelbraten*) in Lastva under the shade of the trees in 1902.[81] As with almost everything else, dietary practice was a marker of religious identity. Jernej Andrejka left this description of mealtimes among Muslims:

> All participants of the meal sit ... on the floor. Each guest has their own ladle, with which they scoop the first broth or soup from the bowl, just like our [i.e., Carniolan] peasants do.... Finely chopped mutton is brought for the soup, then a strong dish and rice or pilaf, which must not be omitted ... this is followed by sweet milk, hazelnuts, walnuts, and honey. The Muslims pay special attention to the fact that there should be sweets at every meal, which they are very fond of. The unleavened bread, only a few centimeters thick, is not cut but broken by hand. Fruit and water are always available.[82]

Cyclist Moritz Oransz had watched the meat for his roast lunch in Lastva being prepared by a Hercegovinian Muslim cook over an open fire and remarked on the raw onions that accompanied the meal.[83] Cheese, garlic, onions, dried or fresh goat, and lamb were among the food sold in the market at Trebinje.[84] The Bohemian doctor Anna Bayerová recorded the love of onion and garlic among Muslims in Hercegovina.[85] Edmund Schneeweiß noted the "extraor-

---

78 "Bosnien und die Herzegowina," *Morgen-Post*, July 19, 1878, 1–2.
79 "Unsere Soldaten an der Grenze," 2.
80 Hauser, "Ein autobiographisches Fragment von Leo Weirather," 610.
81 Oransz, "Die Gesellschafts-Radreise," September 15, 1903, 5.
82 Andrejka, *Slovenski fantje*, 370.
83 Oransz, "Die Gesellschafts-Radreise," September 15, 1903, 5.
84 F. v. M, "Über Ragusa nach Trebinje," *Wiener Zeitung*, March 20, 1886, 3.
85 Jitka Malečková, *"The Turk" in the Czech Imagination (1870s–1923)* (Leiden: Brill, 2020), 130–31.

dinarily high" consumption of onions and garlic in the Pliva valley,[86] a culinary preference that Daniel Salis-Soglio had also noticed in Hercegovina.[87] A high consumption of beans was associated with Orthodox people and Muslims reportedly "mocked" them for this.[88] In Orthodox culture, plum brandy was associated with religious festivals and the *slava* or *krsna slava*, the celebration of the patron saint of an extended family. This custom is usually found only among the Orthodox and accordingly became a symbol of Serbian identity. Among the Banjani, the family saint was usually Saint John (*Sveti Jovan*). At the time of the *slava* or at funerals, Orthodox families in Hercegovina, Montenegro, Dalmatia, and Serbia consumed ritual wine (*pune/punje*) and *koljivo* (overnight soaked wheat with nuts, sugar, and spices). Like seasonal Easter cakes elsewhere, *koljivo* was often decorated with a cross.[89]

Agricultural output in Bosnia and Hercegovina took off rapidly after 1878, and the fertile settlement of Lastva was presented as a Habsburg success story with its neat white houses and college buildings. Soldiers posted to forts on the frontier were expected to cook their own food and were given basic rations of army bread (*Kommiß-brot*), or alternatively rice or potatoes.[90] Green vegetables such as asparagus were grown by soldiers to supplement their vitamin-deficient rations.[91] Soldiers also bought local food, which they often liked, but they also inevitably grumbled. One soldier complained that the bread rolls in Trebinje were as "small as a child's fist."[92] Another remarked that the "coarse ground" bread in Hercegovina was thrown straight onto the fire and consumed with real gusto, even though it carried the taste of the embers.[93] This might have been freshly baked cornbread. Flour, lard (or oil), beef, coffee, wine, sugar,

---

86 Edmund Schneeweiß, "Volksnahrung im Plivatal (Bosnien)," *Österreichische Zeitschrift für Volkskunde* 24, no. 4 (1918): 93.
87 Salis-Soglio, *Mein Leben*, 152.
88 Schneeweiß, "Volksnahrung im Plivatal (Bosnien)," 85.
89 Grunert, *Glauben im Hinterland*, 70–71.
90 "das selige Kommißbrot der österreichisch-ungarischen Monarchie," Francis, "Wir war'n beim k. u. k. Infanterie-regiment: Der letzte Traum der Reservisten," *Neues Wiener Journal*, November 9, 1930, 7.
91 C. W., "Trebinje: Cultur nach Osten tragen," 246.
92 "Unsere Soldaten an der Grenze," 2.
93 Hochbichler, "Aus den schwarzen Bergen III," 1.

black or red pepper, and salt were included in the rations in 1878.[94] As a result of local traditions in Hercegovina, butter was not generally available.[95] During the battle against the insurgents at Vučji zub in 1882, officers ate a "frugal risotto" cooked with melted snow. During the same campaign, Major Gatti went without food for two days, having had a bread roll in Trebinje before he marched to Orjen.[96] Other accounts of that campaign mention that food supplies ran out. Soldiers could not sleep because they did not want to be caught unaware, so they crouched around the campfires and listened to the howling wind. Deprived of resources, the men were bound closer together.[97] Throwing caution to that wind, officers decided to share their dwindling reserve of bacon, schnapps, and wine with their men.[98] "Iron rations"[99] of tins and blocks of chocolate could serve as supper and breakfast combined for soldiers on duty in the border areas.[100] As food on the march could be very basic, ranging from "rock hard ship's biscuits"[101] to tinned goulash[102] for soldiers and hardier travelers in this region, the allure of freshly cooked food eaten at leisure was even more keenly felt. Sandor Barković wrote to his friend Felix in 1917 to complain that "everything was much better for soldiers in Hungary than in Bosnia and Hercegovina," not least because it was very expensive in Trebinje.[103] During the war, salt became a precious commodity as stocks often ran low.[104]

Local people mastered the land by walking upon it. Traveling on foot for long distances remained tremendously important for both

94 Bencze, *Occupation of Bosnia and Herzegovina*, 336, footnote 15.
95 "Butter ist gar nie," Went von Römö, "Aus dem südöstlichen Theile," 37.
96 Major R. Gatti, "Der Übergang der Mittelcolonne über die Orjenska lokva, 9. bis 11. März 1882: Aus meinem Tagebuch," *Danzers Armee-Zeitung*, May 1, 1902, 5.
97 Michael Roper, *The Secret Battle: Emotional Survival in the Great War* (Manchester and New York: Manchester University Press, 2009).
98 Hubka, *Geschichte des k. und k. Infanterie-Regiments*, 483.
99 Bencze, *Occupation of Bosnia and Herzegovina*, 106.
100 H. H., "Der Übergang über den Orien," April 30, 3.
101 "Lilienstengel," "Meine Erinnerungen an die Kämpfe in Süddalmatien im Jahre 1882," *Danzers Armee-Zeitung*, March 14, 1907, 1–3.
102 Reinhard E. Petermann, "Auf den Orjen," *Österreichische Touristenzeitung*, October 16, 1901, 230.
103 Sandor Barković (Trebinje Feldpost) to Felix Grill Schultz, Ključ, January 6, 1917, Collection of the Muzej Hercegovine, Trebinje.
104 Budini, *Le memorie di guerra*, 142.

men and women: in 1876, it was reported that Hercegovinians "think
nothing of walking fifteen miles for a glass of water, and back again."[105]
In 1889, the Orthodox priest Špiro Lučić wrote that many families
walked up to an hour and a half to get to their church in Sutorina.[106]
Edith Durham, who was at the monastery at Ostrog some twenty
years after Vuk Vrčević, described the pilgrims who had flocked
"thither in thousands tramping on foot from Bosnia, the Herzegovina.... Not Christians alone but also Mohammedans."[107] Trebinje's
marketplace was a meeting place between the town and country and
women would set out with baskets to walk very early, like the basket women (*šavrinke*) of Istria who broke the dawn to walk to Trieste,[108]
a practice often found among subsistence farmers.[109] In Drijen, at
the old border, one visitor recalled women arriving with fruit in
baskets.[110] Charles St John remembered the market as a female space
in 1881: "It was a market day, and [Trebinje] was crowded with country people in their national dresses, chiefly women, who towards
evening were seen leaving for their mountain homes—laughing and
singing as they left."[111]

When shepherds moved their flocks, they went into the cooler
high hills, often traversing an official state border.[112] Shepherds
walked along the ancient routes from Čemerno via Gacko, Avtovac,
Bileća, and Trebinje to Dubrovnik and the market.[113] In Trebinje,
the market brought local Hercegovinian Muslim, Catholic, and Orthodox traders together, but Orthodox women were more visible
there because Muslim women were supposed to confine themselves

105 "A Lady Visit to the Herzegovinian Insurgents," *New York Times*, July 23, 1876, 4.
106 Grunert, *Glauben im Hinterland*, 486. Sometimes, riders were forced to dismount from their
    horses because the roads could only be covered on foot; see, for example, Harry Cooper to
    Charles St John, May 19, 1878, FO7 / 940, National Archives, London.
107 Durham, *Through the Lands of the Serb*, 26.
108 On the "basket women" of Istria, see Špela Ledinek and Nataša Rogelja, *Potepanja po poteh
    Šavrinke Marije* (Ljubljana: Slovensko etnološko društvo, 2000).
109 Marta Verginella, "La mobilità femminile tra confini politici e nazionali nell'area alto-adri-
    atica tra Ottocento e Novecento," *DEP*, no. 38 (2018): 69–82.
110 "The Austrians in Herzegovina," 7.
111 Charles St John to Earl Granville, Dubrovnik, March 24, 1881, FO 7/1023, National Ar-
    chives, London.
112 Dedijer, "La transhumance," 359.
113 Hildebert Isnard, "Notes sur la transhumance pastorale en Herzégovine," *Méditerranée* 2, no.
    2 (1961): 40.

to the home.[114] Franz Ivanetič described the bustle of the market: "the busiest times there are on Friday, the Turkish holy days, Sundays and other feast days of the Greeks [i.e., Hercegovinian Orthodox]. On days like this, people come from the surrounding areas on business in their often very colorful clothes."[115]

Candles, Clothing, and Sounds

Although not sent to Hercegovina to study the local people, soldiers and officials inevitably commented on local customs, clothes, melodies, and voices while they were stationed in the "Volksmuseum of Europe."[116] On a more personal level, officials and soldiers left impressions of their time in service, often captured in drawings and watercolors. Edmund Misera was an artillery officer from Brno based in Mostar from 1879 to 1883. In 1881, he sketched the new barracks in Trebinje, capturing the lime white or gray of Mount Leotar.[117] For incomers in Hercegovina, the dress and appearance of the local people was a constant source of curiosity.[118] Elaborate layers, garments that were wrapped around the wearer, and color codes of red, black, and white were carefully noted as if they were describing very distant people rather than near neighbors. These were not the clothes of subalterns, but of appearance-conscious people with a proud gait whose "eyes flashed with self-confidence."[119] Writing in 1911, the botanist Emilia Noel thought "the Herzegovinians are said to be very poor, but they are so beautifully dressed that they are a great sight."[120] Irish writer Emile J. Dillon (1854–1933, writing under the pseudonym E. B. Lanin) made a similar observation in 1894:

---

114 Münch, "Ein Erlebnis in Trebinje," 2.
115 Franz Ivanetič, "Aus Trebinje," *Klagenfurter Zeitung*, August 23, 1879, 1.
116 Maria Todorova, *Imagining the Balkans* (Oxford: Oxford University Press, 1997), 63.
117 Vefik Hadžismailović, "Edmund Misera," *Behar* 109 (2013): 65–66, 74.
118 Baron C. May, "Krivoscie," *Dillingers Reise- und Fremdenzeitung*, April 10, 1893, 2–3.
119 Friedrich, "Bosnische Eindrücke I," 3.
120 "Greece and Bosnia, 1911," The Notebooks of Emilia Noel, Royal Geographical Society, London, GB 0402 EFN -27, 25. Noel (1868–1950) was a botanist and illustrator.

FIGURE 21. "Trebinje" drawn in 1915 by Richard Neutra. UCLA Library, Richard and Dion Neutra Papers.

The women are often beasts of burden who labour in the fields, cultivate the kitchen garden, tend cattle, build walls and houses, rear a number of children and yet withal manage to keep alive a passionate love of flowers with which they dress their hair, deck their clothing and sweeten the air of their homes.... [T]he women place their ideal of happiness not in better food or more comfortable dwellings but in costly holiday raiment.... The Sunday costume of a peasant woman is often a masterpiece of rich embroidery set off with a necklace of golden coloured glass beads which always last a lifetime...[121]

One of the ways that difference between the army and the people of Hercegovina was most discernible was through garments, shoes, and headwear. Incomers frequently noticed how well-armed

---

[121] Lanin, "Bosnia and Herzegovina," 756–57. Reinhard Günste made very similar observations about exuberant flowers as decoration; see Reinhard Günste [Rifât Effendija Gozdović pseud.], "Bosniens römische Katholiken," *Reichspost*, October 27, 1906, 1–2.

Hercegovinians were:[122] "the feared, two-foot-long curved *handžar* ... made a strong impression on Habsburg troops."[123] Every shepherd in Hercegovina "would tuck a knife in his belt" so that a lamb could be killed and roasted on the spot.[124] Hermann Iser observed that Muslim and Orthodox men dressed very similarly, the former being distinguishable by a green silk belt and a fez or turban: "No Serb man or woman enters the room with shoes on, but only in stocking feet. Shoes were removed at the threshold and only put back on to go home."[125] Shopping for clothes could also form part of the fantasy of Orient and leave the incomer thinking that they had joined a "theatre set."[126] Recalling her trip to the market in Trebinje before the war, Vera Stenzel remarked upon the "gossamer lace, flowers embroidered on headscarves, brightly colored saddlebags, and leather *opanci*."[127] Noting the range of colors, turbans, and baggy trousers, Pierre Marge thought that Ottoman-style traditional clothes had been even better preserved in Hercegovina than in Turkey.[128] Traditional goods made by "blacksmiths, cobblers, bakers, saddlers, traditional attire and costume makers" were found in the Krš suburb of Trebinje.[129] Tobacco boxes with carved patterns similar to folk embroidery were produced locally. "[O]rnamental pistols, daggers, and small sabers were an obligatory purchase for the soldiers who rotated through Bosnia until 1918."[130] Aglae St John received her "oriental luggage" at the Dubrovnik consulate in 1883, which included textiles and carpets collected over the previous years of service and

---

122 "Aus der Herzegowina," *Wiener Allgemeine Zeitung (Mittagblatt)*, February 17, 1882, 1.
123 Schindler, "Defeating Balkan Insurgency," 543.
124 "The Hercegovinian might have preferred a gun as well as a knife, but these were outlawed." See Dr. J. B., "Eine Fahrt durch die Suttorina," *Wiener Landwirtschaftliche Zeitung*, October 21, 1885, 1.
125 Hermann Iser, "Aus der Herzegowina," *Vorarlberger Volksblatt*, November 29, 1889, 3.
126 Mary Edith Durham, *Diary from 1900*, RAI MS 42, vol. 1, Royal Anthropological Institute, London.
127 Stenzel, "In der südlichen Herzegowina," 6.
128 Marge, *Voyage en Dalmatie*, 265.
129 Siniša Cvijić and Jasna Guzijan, "Urban Regeneration as an Instrument of Identity Preservation: A Case Study of Trebinje's Krš District," *Arhiv za Tehničke Nauke/Archives for Technical Sciences*, no. 14 (2016): 19–27.
130 Diana Reynolds Cordileone, "Swords into Souvenirs: Bosnian Arts and Crafts under Habsburg Administration," in Johler, Marchetti, and Scheer, *Doing Anthropology in Wartime*, 185.

her husband's visits to Hercegovina.[131] Arthur Evans "bought a complete Turkish outfit and donned it in triumph and spent all his remaining money in a bazaar" in Kostajnica.[132] Evans later purchased "magnificent flint locks of antique form, with stocks richly inlaid with mother of pearl and golden arabesque."[133] When he died in 1940, his bequest to the School of Slavonic and East European Studies in London included "my specimens of old needlework from Herzegovina and other East Adriatic regions principally collected by me from 1875 to 1882."[134] Edith Durham donated her collection of textiles and jewelry to the Bankfield Museum in Halifax in 1935, almost a decade before her death in 1944. No doubt this material was legitimately purchased, but valuable commodities were likely whisked away for a song during the Habsburg years.[135] Despite the availability of such careful and intricately produced artisanal products, standard orientalist tropes about indolence were used to describe people on the border,[136] as well as men in Trebinje "lolling in their shops."[137] One soldier in 1878 commented on the (relative) lack of furniture, as well as characteristic squatting by local men.[138] Another former soldier remembered the serene men "sunk in Ottoman times" in baggy trousers and *opanci*, "whose job it was not to have a job."[139] Jernej Andrejka observed that Muslims actually had very few holidays and would close up businesses on Fridays in the morning only.[140]

Dwellings in the countryside were often described as humble, sparsely decorated, and smoky. Traveling in Hercegovina, Conrad Hochbichler remembered "little furniture, a mud floor, just a kettle on the fire, blankets, and dried goatskins for warmth."[141] In the hills

131 Aglae St John, "Journal Intime d'une Femme Roumaine: Première Partie," online at University of Victoria Special Collections and University Archives, British Columbia, Canada, 15.
132 Evans, *Time and Chance*, 166.
133 Evans, *Through Bosnia and the Herzegovina*, 272.
134 Ivan Lupić, "Arthur Evans and the Illyrian Parnassus," *Dubrovnik Annals* 25 (2021): 149–50.
135 Ibrahim Defterdarović expressed concern that Ottoman-era material culture was rapidly disappearing: see "Stare listine porodice Resulbegović," *Glasnik Zemaljskog muzeja u Bosni i Hercegovini*, April 1, 1897, 193–226.
136 Kählig, "Eine Erinnerung," 1.
137 W. R. W. Stephens, *The Life and Letters of Edward A. Freeman* (London: Macmillan, 1895), 127.
138 "Aus Bosnien," *Linzer Volksblatt*, October 1, 1878, 2.
139 Perkonig, "Zwischen Abend und Morgen," 2.
140 Andrejka, *Slovenski fantje*, 377.
141 Hochbichler, "Aus den schwarzen Bergen III," 1.

close to Popovo polje, the houses were also described as poor: "Not a house ... in Grebci had a chimney. The two or three hovels into which we ventured were so filled with smoke from the fires on the hearth that we were compelled to retreat. The furniture was of the simplest description. There were no beds, but low stone couches like those one sees in houses in Pompeii; on these straw and blankets were spread. Chairs, tables, and such luxuries evidently had never been heard of."[142] At a time when many Europeans had adopted prêt-à-porter garments which changed with seasonal fashions, people in Hercegovina dressed in styles of garments which were known centuries earlier. In July 1878, the Viennese daily *Morgen-Post* gave its readers a detailed description of what to expect in Bosnia and Hercegovina, comparing local people to the Vlachs (*Morlaken*) in Dalmatia and Krajina.

Red is the favorite color,[143] especially among the Muslims, and after that blue. Christian women wear their hair in long braids over the shoulder with a broad silk tassel, which is often made from small coins.... The folds of their wide, dark blue trousers reach to the ankles, and they wear red shoes.... The men wear wide trousers that fasten below the knee ... a long shawl serves as a belt.... In the country, *opanci* or shoes with straps [*Riemenschuhe*] are universally worn.[144]

While the comparison with peoples already in the Habsburg Monarchy familiarized the subjects of Franz Joseph to their new lands, the idea of an exotic journey into a new land would remain an enduring part of the Habsburg curiosity about Bosnia and Hercegovina. Incomers had found their Orient in Trebinje, or as Reinhold Oeser put

---

142 Edward King, *Descriptive Portraiture of Europe in Storm and Calm: Twenty Years' Experiences and Reminiscences of an American Journalist* (Springfield, MA: C. A. Nichols and Co, 1888), 685. In the original text, it was written as Grebzi.
143 Red garments were often worn and the Orthodox sometimes claimed that this was to remember the blood shed by their ancestors at the Battle of Kosovo in 1389. Green had been reserved for Muslims during the Ottoman years and does not seem to have been a popular color choice after 1878.
144 "Bosnien und die Herzegowina," *Morgen-Post*, July 19, 1878, 1–2.

FIGURE 22. "Young Muslim Women," by Richard Neutra, Trebinje, 1915.
UCLA Library, Richard and Dion Neutra Papers.

it, "the wonderful shine of the ethereal, clear southern sky."[145] In the hills, they discovered the tough, heroic types with rugged clothes that they imagined from popular fiction.[146] Some writers were negative about the position of Muslim women, with frequent comments on the gaudiness of clothes.[147] The silk trousers (*dimije*) that women wore could be red, gold, light blue, but were "primarily orange."[148] Maude Holbach described a Muslim bride who had arrived by special train from Sarajevo to Trebinje: "The bride … was a girl of perhaps sixteen, gorgeous in yellow flowered satin, made with the traditional full trousers…. She wore a quantity of jewelry, including a necklace of heavy gold coins, which must have been uncomfortably weighty, and similar coins were suspended from her tiny cap, sewn all over with seed

---

145 Oeser, "Die Kriegsmassige Sprengung des Kordonspostens Vardar," AT-OeStA/KA FA NFA (Bileća 309) Kriegsarchiv, Vienna.

146 "Vom Insurrektions-Schauplatze," *Tages-Post*, March 15, 1882, 1.

147 Münch, "Ein Erlebnis in Trebinje," 2.

148 "Erinnerungen aus dem Wanderleben," *Wiener Salonblatt*, July 26, 1902, 18.

pearls.... She may have been happy, but her sad little painted face and lack-luster eyes did not bespeak it."[149] Other writers projected positivity onto the appearance of Orthodox as compared to Muslim women: "The former have a very fair eye for colour and the latter, the crudest," opined Edith Durham in Trebinje in 1900.[150]

Ernst Neweklowsky left very precise descriptions of the clothing worn in Trebinje, Bileća, Ljubinje, and Western Montenegro and paid attention to detail about the difference between these areas. An engineer by profession, he was sent on an official wartime mission to Montenegro, but also included research on Hercegovina. His findings were published in 1917, by which time Montenegro was also being reshaped in the Habsburg manner. Younger men were described as wearing a kapa or *zavrata*, "a round flat cap with a black rim, red top, and golden embroidery." Older men around Trebinje and Bileća wore a red fez and wrapped a woolen cloth around themselves in winter, along with a black woolen cap, a *janjetina* or *subara*.[151] Neweklowsky's ethnographic data seemed academic given that after the declaration of war with Serbia in July 1914, men in Hercegovina were forbidden to wear caps with Serbian or Montenegrin coats of arms or caps with embellishments in the colors of those states.[152] Overgarments were made from wool and undergarments from cotton, linen, or hemp. In Trebinje, Bileća, and Montenegro, the white undershirt (*halina*) was so long that it reached to the knees.[153] Spinning was usually quite sedentary elsewhere in Europe, but local women in Hercegovina took spinning frames with them on the move.[154] Even though they walked along

149 Holbach, *Dalmatia*, 163.
150 Mary Edith Durham, *Diary from 1900*, RAI MS 42, vol. 1, Royal Anthropological Institute, London.
151 Ernst Neweklowsky, "Volkskundliches aus Westmontenegro," *Österreichische Zeitschrift für Volkskunde* 23 (1917): 59–69.
152 "Kopfbedeckungen mit serbischen oder montenegrischen Wappeninsignien," Landesregierung für Bosnien und die Hercegovina, July 31, 1914, AT-OeStA/KA FA NFA (Trebinje 50), Kriegsarchiv Vienna.
153 Neweklowsky, "Volkskundliches aus Westmontenegro," 59–69.
154 "da man nicht selten serbischen Weibern begegnet, die auf irgend einem Geschäftsgänge oder dgl. begriffen, emsig spinnend einherwandeln." Hochbichler, "Aus den schwarzen Bergen II," 2.

in pairs while spinning, they did not talk among themselves.[155] Many contemporaries commented upon homespun woolen clothes, including the heavy mantles worn by women in the Trebinje market all year round.[156] Franz Xaver von Gayersperg expressed some surprise that "the local [*autochtone*] people do not feel the heat. Despite loden wool skirts and coats and thick embroidered waistcoats and jackets, the women ... jump up in their colorful dances."[157] Warm weather dressing and physical stamina was also noticed by William Miller in Dubrovnik: "women from Hercegovina in long dark coats, scarlet fezzes with a flower behind the ear and white veils streaming down their backs may be seen here buying vegetables and then trudging off in their thick felt leggings, despite the summer heat."[158]

Neweklowsky noted that the Christian men wore wide knee-length trousers (*gaće* or *sarvale*), usually in a blue shade (or white in Bileća) and fastened with a *svitnjak*. Their trousers differed quite considerably in shape from the Muslims.[159] The white thick wool socks (*bijeove*) and the *čarape* worn by older men were embroidered with bright colors. The heads of Hercegovinian Orthodox women were lightly covered by woolen scarves rather than a veil. Men also wore a woolen shawl (*struka*) over their shoulders, which allowed them to adapt very quickly to the "violent" cold of the *bura*.[160] Insurgents on Mount Orjen in 1882 slept in karst sinkholes at night and kept warm under their *struke* while living off frugal supplies in their bags (*torbice*).[161] Neweklowsky was careful to compare the dress of Hercegovina and Montenegro in detail, pointing out differences where they existed and using local words: this was research produced with respect.

Footwear was perhaps the most commented upon aspect of dress, typically consisting of leather shoes (*opanci*) or leather sandals (*kundure*). Pigskin was used by the Hercegovinian Orthodox and Catho-

---

155 F. v. M, "Über Ragusa nach Trebinje II," *Wiener Zeitung*, March 19, 1886, 3.
156 "Erinnerungen aus dem Wanderleben," *Wiener Salonblatt*, July 26, 1902, 17.
157 X[aver] von Gayersperg, "Neue Eisenpfade," part IV, *Welt Blatt*, August 18, 1901, 8.
158 Miller, *Travels and Politics*, 28.
159 Neweklowsky, "Volkskundliches aus Westmontenegro," 59–69.
160 Ivanetič, "Allerlei aus Trebinje," 5.
161 Hubka, *Geschichte des k. und k. Infanterie-Regiments*, 476.

lics, but calf and goat leather was used by local Muslims. Neweklowsky thought that *opanci* were "excellent for the limestone cliffs of the karst; they alone enable the population to walk quickly on the rugged terrain."[162] *Opanci* were made by hand in the countryside: they featured a large piece of leather for the sole with holes pierced around the sides, which was then wrapped around the foot and tied together by a thin leather thong. They were sold in the market in Trebinje and worn by vendors. Different regions had distinctive designs so they could also make their wearers stand out according to origin; in this way, *opanci* marked the ethnic differences between boot-wearing conscript soldiers and local men.[163] From the outset of the occupation of Hercegovina, soldiers had felt deep anxiety about the inadequacy of army-issue boots, and one man recounted how he had gladly replaced his damaged boots with sheepskin in 1878.[164] Military sources commented on the superiority of the texture and grip of *opanci* for the terrain in Hercegovina,[165] which allowed the wearer to move silently. On January 2, 1882, it was reported that a young officer from one of the Jäger battalions was walking near the canal at Sutorina in order to take in the "splendid view" when he was taken by surprise, attacked by an insurgent from a band led by Stojan Kovačević. Because the ground was damp, the assailant was able to sneak up silently in his *opanci*.[166] The tactile nature of the leather shoes became important in the imagination of soldiers and civilians alike.[167] Crown Prince Rudolf had *opanci* specially made for him in Dubrovnik for the hunt.[168] Alice Schalek thought that *opanci* gave the wearer an ability to move safely from rock to rock, gripping them with their feet "almost like an ape."[169] The preoccupation with the power of shoes may not have been entirely new:

---

162 Neweklowsky, "Volkskundliches aus Westmontenegro," 59–69.
163 Hugo von Martiny, "Wie Mihalčić es erzählte," *Die Quelle: Sonntag- Beiblatt der Reichspost*, May 1, 1932, 17.
164 "Die Eroberung von Klobuk," *Morgen-Post*, October 16, 1878, 1–2.
165 Hauptmann Himmel, "Opanken: Keine Militär-Beschuhung," *Die Vedette*, March 4, 1883, 134–35.
166 "Vom Insurrektions-Schauplätze," *Tages-Post*, January 18, 1882, 2.
167 Furneaux, *Military Men of Feeling*, 217.
168 "Die Opanken des Kronprinzen," *Wiener Allgemeine Zeitung*, April 17, 1886, 5.
169 Schalek, "An der montenegrinischen Grenze," November 14, 1915, 2.

opanci were prepared in readiness for rebellion in 1875, when the local authorities had been surprised to find a stash of seven thousand pairs in the villages near Trebinje.[170]

There are references to sounds and music in many sources, perhaps because Central Europeans brought different music and dance with them to Bosnia and Hercegovina, which had its traditional rhythms of *sevdalinka*[171] and the *gusle*. *Stećci* (old tombstones) reveal evidence of older soundscapes: one of the figures found at Kolac was a man holding a drum and sticks.[172] During the years of occupation and annexation, musical culture in Hercegovina remained exuberant and distinctive. Styrian ethnomusicologist Matija Murko met Archimandrite Nićifor Šimonović at Kosijerevo and heard a *gusle* being played there: "one cannot believe that such beautiful sounds could emanate from such a primitive instrument."[173] Like Pierre Marge, who thought that traditional clothing was better preserved in Bosnia and Hercegovina, Murko asserted that the local music heritage was "exceptionally rich."[174] Music gave scholars plenty to work with. For instance, the folklorist Franjo Kuhac worked on rich local material in Trebinje. In 1888–89, Kosta Hörmann published collections of Muslim folk poetry and songs.[175] Although the *gusle* was temporarily banned in 1880, the authorities became more relaxed about local music over time, and there was a *tamburica* concert at Hotel Naglić in 1902.[176] Popular new cafés sprung up with instruments placed for decoration on the wall.[177] Rizvan Kadrović, originally from Trebinje, was the first known *guslar* from Hercegovina to be

---

170 Hajdarpašić, *Whose Bosnia?*, 111.
171 *Sevdalinke* are traditional love songs; the old Turkish word *sevdah* could be translated as "the melancholy of being in love."
172 Jasmina Talam, *Folk Musical Instruments in Bosnia and Herzegovina* (Newcastle-upon-Tyne: Cambridge Scholars, 2013), 4.
173 Murko, "The Singers and their Epic Songs," 121.
174 Jasmina Talam and Tamara Karača Beljak, "Matija Murko and His Researches in Bosnia and Herzegovina," in *"Music in Society": The Collection of Papers* (Sarajevo: Musicological Society of the Federation of Bosnia and Herzegovina Academy of Music, University of Sarajevo, 2016), 552.
175 Kosta Hörmann, *Narodne pjesne Muhamedovaca u Bosni i Hercegovini* (Sarajevo: Zemaljska štamparija, 1888–89).
176 Oransz, "Die Gesellschafts-Radreise," September 15, 1903, 6.
177 Vlado Milošević, "Tambura i harmonika u bosanskom varoškom pjevanju," *Zbornik Krajiških muzeja* 1 (1962): 132–35.

recorded in 1907 and again in 1913.[178] The portability of the *gusle* kept performers busy, even if the performance was lacking.[179] According to Murko, who did fieldwork in Hercegovina in 1909, 1912, and again in 1913, people would sing at night on horseback, in the marketplace, in coffeehouses, and outside churches, but the *gusle* was not played at night.[180] Different voices and instruments often enchanted listeners. Ernst Dombrowski described an encounter with an elderly shepherd who sat on a rock playing a flute "in a melancholy way."[181]

The air in Hercegovina was filled with local voices. In Popovo polje and the valley of the Trebišnjica, William Stillman remembered that "here and there we could catch the cries of the shepherds and goatherds to their flocks."[182] Traditional voices were suppressed or supplanted by regimental bands, traffic, and industrial projects. Remembering back to September 1913, Kornel Abel sped through the countryside by car: he rarely saw shepherds, but he could hear their pipes.[183] Shepherds made instruments out of goat horns, called *rozine* or *rogulja*, which could be used with or without a mouthpiece. Their sound traveled for miles.[184] While stationed at Visoka glavica, Jernej Andrejka would ask the shepherd to convey menu orders to the nearby villagers and swift footed *opanci* wearers would bring the soldiers what they needed very quickly.[185] During the 1882 Uprising, long calls from mountain to mountain proved a very reliable means of communication that worked for hundreds of miles. On March 21, 1882, several battalions marched toward Bijela gora on the northern slopes of Orjen:

---

178 Risto Pekka Pennanen, "Immortalised on Wax—Professional Folk Musicians and their Gramophone Recordings Made in Sarajevo, 1907 and 1908," in *Europe and its Others: Notes on the Balkans*, ed. Božidar Jezernik, Rajko Muršič and Alenka Bartulović (Ljubljana: Filozofska fakulteta, 2007), 121.

179 Hochbichler, "Aus den schwarzen Bergen II," 2.

180 Murko, "The Singers and their Epic Songs," 111, 116.

181 Ernst Dombrowski, "Auf heißem Boden," *Neues Wiener Tagblatt*, February 22, 1914, 40. The word "melancholy" was often used for local music in Hercegovina, perhaps alluding to the frequent use of the pentatonic rather than the heptatonic scale.

182 Stillman, *Herzegovina*, 108.

183 Kornel Abel, "Im Auto durch den Karst," *Neue Freie Presse*, March 13, 1938, 2-3.

184 In Trebinje in the 1870s, the folklorist Franjo Kuhač (1834-1911) noted that the goat horns were intricately carved with scenes from epic battles; see Talam, *Folk Musical Instruments*, 192.

185 Andrejka, *Slovenski fantje*, 343.

The march began in the morning mist; there was no trace of the insurgents, but long, drawn-out shouts came through the fog: "*O Jovo, hoj Djuro bježte, bježte evo Švaba, mnogo Švaba!*"[186] You could also hear the fuzzy tones of distant horn signals, apparently from the Montenegrin border guards, who shouted to their friends and brothers that caution was the better part of valor.[187]

In 1882, calling out to the next village from a high point was temporarily forbidden in an effort to stem resistance to the regime. Friedrich Funder explained that local people could communicate long distances through calling out because the air was very pure and the lack of vegetation meant that sound traveled further.[188] Just as leather shoes or *opanci* were seen as superior to boots because they were light on the karst terrain, so the human voice was seen as superior to modern forms of communication and a reminder that the local population would defy the *Švabe*: "The clear still mountain air carries the sound of the human voice from one herd to the other, and these calls from the shepherds are their newspapers and telephones, betraying war secrets and setting ambushes."[189]

At the same time, occupying soldiers put their own musical stamp on the region. Songs bound soldiers together in deep faith. Close to Bileća at the Catholic Christmas of 1882, the soldiers in the border post at Radmilovića Dubrava blasted out songs including the national anthem, "Gott erhalte Franz den Kaiser."[190] Patriotism was often expressed though music: the troops that arrived in Trebinje in September 1878 joked and sang songs before they sat to rest.[191] The garrisons were equipped for Viennese-style entertainment. An upbeat regimental march, "Gruss an Trebinje," was composed by Moravian musician Franz Sommer. In the officers' mess in Bileća, Rudolf

---

186 "Look out Jovo and Djuro, get out quickly, there are loads of Austrians, so many of them!" In the original text, it is spelled Gjuro.
187 Hubka, *Geschichte des k. und k. Infanterie-Regiments*, 486.
188 Friedrich Funder, "Im Kampf mit den Räubern," *Reichspost*, July 17, 1903, 1.
189 Stenzel, "In der südlichen Herzegowina," 6.
190 "God save Franz the Emperor." Karl Hanke von Hankenstein, "Weihnachten am Kordon," *Teplitz-Schönauer Anzeiger*, December 25, 1909, 3.
191 Julius Beranek, "Der neue Compagnie-Commandant: Erinnerung eines Veteranen," *Reichspost*, December 25, 1900, 23–25.

Sieczyński's 1914 patriotic song "Wien, du Stadt meiner Träume" was sung, evoking an Austria surrounded by enemies.[192] There were regional additions to the musical repertoire and signs that the music of the two worlds had come together: in 1901, the "national kolo" was played by a military band in Crkvice.[193] Hugo Riedel composed "Der Stürmer-Marsch," a stirring piece which he published in Trebinje in 1915. Riedel was also responsible for the garrison's homing pigeons.[194] As Daniel Salis-Soglio observed, wherever there were enough Habsburg soldiers, music bound the men together and entertained them during bad weather.[195] Antonio Budinich thought that Christmas was the time during military service that men felt most nostalgic and "national," but that the music of other peoples could be "magnificent."[196] Richard Neutra confirmed that diverse music helped morale during the war: "I listened to the unison of Hungarians, the six-part harmonizing of Slovene voices, Romanian clarinets doing pirouettes ... Italian *canzones*, Swabian-German sentimental songs, Czech and Polish songs.... I became a cosmopolitan in the army of a far-flung empire, marching and camping in strange lands."[197]

There was a long tradition for lighting summer bonfires in Hercegovina.[198] Vidovdan, which falls in late June, was also marked by lighting fires, at a time very close to the summer solstice. In 1884, the emperor's August birthday (*Kaisertag*) was celebrated in Bileća with music, light, and an enormous bonfire that could be seen in nearby Montenegro.[199] Bonfires were lit in the military fort at Crkvice to celebrate the emperor's birthday in 1901, illuminating the whole of the Bay of Kotor.[200] In Trebinje, *Kaisertag* was celebrated with a colorful pyrotech-

---

192 "Vienna, City of My Dreams," Budini, *Le memorie di guerra*, 85.
193 "Eine patriotische Feier in der Krivosije," *Pester Lloyd*, August 23, 1901, 5.
194 Memo dated August 3, 1914, signed by Rudolf Braun. AT-OeStA/KA FA NFA (Trebinje 50), Kriegsarchiv, Vienna.
195 Salis-Soglio, *Mein Leben*, 175. On the role of music in garrison culture, see Eugen Brixel, "Es rauscht Musik, der Trommelwirbel hallet Versuch einer Militärmusikgeschichte der Garnison Graz," in *Graz als Garnison: Beiträge zur Militärgeschichte der steirischen Landeshauptstadt*, ed. Wilhelm Steinböck (Graz: Leykam, 1982), 194–209.
196 Budini, *Le memorie di guerra*, 197.
197 Neutra, *Life and Shape*, 113–14, spelled "Rumanian" in the original.
198 Grunert, *Glauben im Hinterland*, 119.
199 "Patriotisches aus der Herzegowina," *Welt Blatt*, August 28, 1884, 5.
200 "Eine patriotische Feier in der Krivosije," *Pester Lloyd*, August 23, 1901, 5.

nic display (*bengalische Lichte*) from the hill at Crkvina and drinks at the Hotel Naglić.[201] There were other reminders of the power of the monarchy. Pierre Marge thought that the first act of the Habsburg authorities in Bosnia and Hercegovina had been to paint black and yellow everywhere and to engrave the imperial initials on almost everything.[202] Signs of occupation were found around Trebinje. By 1886, the "good bridge" over the Trebišnjica had a signpost painted in black and yellow.[203] To remind the locals and the Montenegrins nearby of Habsburg power in Neu-Bilek: "the striking imperial initials 'F. J. I.' some ten feet long [were] outlined in white stones upon the mountain slope."[204] F. J. I. was also shone onto the bare rock face of Crkvina, visible to people below.[205] In Kruševice in 1900, the church festival included speeches, toasts for the emperor, gun salutes, and *kolo* dancing, bringing in people from Dalmatia.[206] Richard Neutra remembered *Kaisertag* in Trebinje on August 18, 1914: "a milling crowd of soldiers on furlough, Serbian peasants and lots of girls had got together for the celebration and preparations had been started for the fireworks in the evening."[207]

The authorities in Trebinje and in nearby garrisons put on a good show to welcome royal visitors. Crown Prince Rudolf was taken around the *Ciganska mahala* or gypsy quarter by Djuro Babić in April 1886. Local men placed their hands to their fez in greeting and the Crown Prince expressed interest in the old buildings and their inhabitants:[208]

> ...under a beautifully displayed triumphal gate, the crown prince was greeted with great respect and enthusiasm by the community council, the clergy, officials, school pupils, and a population of thousands who had flocked from all parts of the district. The

---

201 H. K., "Ein Kaisertag," 7.
202 Marge, *Voyage en Dalmatie*, 265.
203 B., "Der Kronprinz in der Herzegowina," *Neues Wiener Tagblatt*, April 4, 1886, 3.
204 Hutchinson, *Motoring in the Balkans*, 227.
205 H. K., "Ein Kaisertag," 7.
206 Grunert, *Glauben im Hinterland*, 355, footnote 340. Other observers remarked that the *kolo* united Catholic and Orthodox people; O. H., "Briefe aus der Krivosije," *Linzer Volksblatt*, April 24, 1913, 2.
207 Neutra, *Life and Shape*, 109.
208 B., "Der Kronprinz in der Herzegowina," *Neues Wiener Tagblatt*, April 4, 1886, 3.

mayor gave a short speech, which the crown prince graciously answered. The crown prince was accompanied by the population from the triumphal gate to his quarters, and vividly applauded by cries of "živio!"[209]

Archduke Albrecht visited Trebinje in May 1886 in his role as the army's Inspector General. He marched through the arch into the *kaštel* and was greeted by Djuro Babić, mayor Stevan Cerović, Bishop Mato Vodopić from Dubrovik, and Archimandrite Prović, as well as clergy from all denominations.[210] When he got to Bileća, Albrecht stepped through a newly erected triumphal arch.[211] Franz Ferdinand traveled to Trebinje in September 1906 and thanked the large crowd for its loyalty, telling them he was glad to be on Hercegovinian soil and to meet its "heroic" population, if only for a short time.[212] He was greeted by Abdulrahman Resulbegović, and then walked on foot toward the city center. There he was shown a selection of local crafts, including rugs. Infantry Regiment no. 12 played marching tunes, school children were lined up to cheer, local notables appeared in "splendid" national costume, and a banner with "*dobro došao*" (welcome) in the "Latin, Cyrillic, and Turkish" scripts was erected on the bridge.[213] With the rotation of regiments, such a repetitive style of ceremony was unlikely to have been a problem, but even Franz Joseph seemed to tire of the same imperial formulas, always laconically remarking that "it was nice. We enjoyed it."[214] While these festivities were undoubtedly fun and an opportunity for the religious communities to mingle and wear their best clothes, we might also note that patriotism sometimes coincided with state funding (and the prospect of free food).[215]

---

209 "Trebinje," *Neues Wiener Tagblatt*, June 26, 1888, 6; "Zahlreiche Hercegoviner ... lagerten in malerischen Gruppen längs des Strassenzuges," in "Der Kronprinz in der Herzegowina," *Südsteirische Post*, April 7, 1886, 5–6.

210 "Telegramme des Telegraphen-Correspondenz-Bureau," *Wiener Zeitung*, May 10, 1886, 2.

211 "Die Reise des Erzherzogs Albrecht," *Das Vaterland*, May 13, 1886, 5.

212 "Erzherzog Franz Ferdinand in Trebinje," *Neue Freie Presse*, September 14, 1906, 9.

213 "Die Manöver in Dalmatien: Erzherzog Franz Ferdinand in Trebinje," *Agramer Zeitung*, September 15, 1906, 1–3.

214 Martyn Rady, *The Habsburgs: The Rise and Fall of a World Power* (London: Allen Lane, 2020), 288.

215 Vladimir Dedijer recorded a story, perhaps passed through his family, that in 1906 the authorities had paid the crowd to cheer the arrival of Franz Ferdinand in Trebinje; see *The Road to Sarajevo* (New York: Simon and Schuster, 1966), 133.

The Accumulation of Scientific Knowledge

Highly educated people posted to a new place often immersed themselves in studying the land and people around the Trebinje garrison complex, but they also engaged their friends, visitors, and acquaintances in scientific pursuits. The special role that the postal services and garrison hospitals had in Bosnia and Hercegovina (both directly under military control) also meant that the role of officials was much closer to the army than it would have been elsewhere in the Habsburg state. The growth of Serbia and Montenegro also meant an increase in significant empirical contributions to understanding the people and land in Hercegovina. Belgrade flourished as a center for culture and learning from the nineteenth century onwards, promoting the study of all the people it defined as Serbs. In 1903, the Serbian Academy published a study of Zubci by Obren Đurić-Kozić in its series on the ethnography of the Serbian people, as well as Jevto Dedijer's work on the Rudine vicinity of Bileća.[216] The geographer Jovan Cvijić (1861–1928), perhaps the most significant and influential academician in Serbia, was a fluent speaker of German and deeply connected within its academic discourses.[217] In 1896, he published a comprehensive study of Serbian Orthodox villages outside Serbia.[218] His research was viewed as disruptive in some circles, and in 1908, Cvijić had his right to travel in the Habsburg Monarchy temporarily revoked.[219]

While Sarajevo could not rival Belgrade in terms of scale or ambitions, it dramatically expanded in size, with its population more than doubling to 51,919 by 1910.[220] The growth of this garden city with its "white, dice-shaped houses, towering needle-slender minarets, and green orchards"[221] also signaled a shift toward its intellec-

---

216 Obren Đurić-Kozić, *Šuma, Površ i Zupci u Hercegovini* (Belgrade, Srpska kraljevska akademija, 1903); Jevto Dedijer, "Bilećke Rudine," *Srpski etnografski zbornik* 5 (1903): 669–899.
217 Vedran Duančić, *Geography and Nationalist Visions of Interwar Yugoslavia: Modernity, Memory and Identity in South-East Europe* (Cham: Palgrave Macmillan, 2020), 49–94.
218 Jovan Cvijić, *Upustva za proučavanje sela u Srbiji i ostalim srpskim zemljama* (Belgrade: Srpska kraljevska akademija, 1896).
219 Besarović, *Kultura i umjetnost u Bosni i Hercegovini*, 386–87.
220 Hadžibegović, *Bosanskohercegovački gradovi*, 34.
221 Reinhard Günste [Rifat Effendija Gozdović pseud.], "Die bosnische Ostbahn," *Reichspost*, March 27, 1906, 1.

tual and administrative importance, especially after 1908. Sarajevo's urban center was distinctively reshaped by the architect Josip Vancaš, a Croat from Sopron, who designed the Sacred Heart Cathedral in Sarajevo as well as adopting environmental and historic causes.[222] In 1911, Vancaš pushed through a law protecting caves and the karst environment.[223] A fervent circle around Sarajevo's provincial museum (*Landesmuseum/Zemaljski muzej*)[224] gathered as much information as possible about Hercegovina:[225] its curators often became the first point of contact for academic researchers in the army.[226] Carl Patsch set up an *Institut für Balkanforschung* in 1908 which promoted scientific cooperation across the region.[227] In 1901, the Director of the *Landesmuseum*, Konstantin (Kosta) Hörmann, traveled on the first ever train to Trebinje, where he gave a lecture to the passengers on the historical significance of the route.[228] The pioneering and "amply subsidized" publication *Glasnik Zemaljskog muzeja u Bosni i Hercegovini* also promoted local knowledge.[229] Ćiro Truhelka followed Hörmann, serving as Director of the *Landesmuseum* from 1906 to 1922, and added a distinctly political element to the role.[230] Truhelka was influenced by new ideas about race and physiognomy. In 1913, an expedition to the Prača valley led by Hermann Bock found human bones in a cave, which were promptly sent to the *Landesmuseum* for analysis.[231] Bock was sure that the bones could not be the remains

222 "Eine Ehrung des Baurates Josef v. Vancaš in Sarajevo," *Agramer Zeitung*, December 9, 1908, 5.
223 Anton Kapel, "First Legal Acts on Cave Protection in Bosnia and Herzegovina," *Slovenský kras* 37 (1999): 109–14.
224 The museum was housed in a grand new building after 1913, designed by Bohemian architect Karel Pařík (1857–1942). On its impact, see Maximilian Hartmuth, "The Habsburg Landesmuseum in Sarajevo in its ideological and architectural contexts: a reinterpretation," *Centropa* 12, no. 2 (2012): 194–205.
225 "Cultur-Arbeit in Bosnien," *Grazer Volksblatt*, April 21, 1891, 5.
226 Dr. M[ichael] Haberlandt, "Aus Bosnien," *Wiener Zeitung*, June 25, 1895, 5–7.
227 Daniel Baric, "Archéologie classique et politique scientifique en Bosnie-Herzégovine habsbourgoise: Carl Patsch à Sarajevo (1891–1918)," *Revue germanique internationale* 16 (2012): 73–89; Carl Patsch, *Historische Wanderungen im Karst und an der Adria*, vol. 1, *Die Herzegowina einst und jetzt* (Vienna: Forschungsinstitut für Osten und Orient, 1922).
228 X[aver] von Gayersperg, "Neue Eisenpfade," *Welt Blatt*, August 9, 1901, 7.
229 Hajdarpašić, *Whose Bosnia?*, 182.
230 Originally from Osijek in Slavonia, of mixed Czech-German heritage, Truhelka (1865–1942) was a founder of modern Croatian nationalism.
231 Hermann Bock (1882–1969) was a prominent cave explorer who was born in Brno and academically active in Graz.

of "insurgents" (as Truhelka hypothesized) because these skulls did not have a "high and steep Serb forehead"; as such, he concluded that they must be Neolithic remains, not least because there were no artefacts found with the bodies.[232]

The completion of the railway line led to an almost exponential growth in accounts about Eastern Hercegovina, demonstrating how interlocked military technology and local knowledge were.[233] For incomers, scientific research was imperative because they believed that so little had been undertaken in the Ottoman era.[234] Moravian botanist Karel Vandas accompanied troops on maneuvers between Trebinje and Bileća, during which time he found opportunities to gather plant species; these specimens are still in Brno.[235] Trebinje had limited secondary schooling in the Habsburg period,[236] but it did have a profusion of educated people, a hospital, a library, and a training college in Lastva. The maintenance of a kind of *Kultur* was a vital part of the civilizing mission, in which soldiers were willing participants. Edvard Formánek, a high school teacher from Brno, spent July through to mid-September every summer in Hercegovina collecting specimens—40,000 of which are still in the Moravian Museum—and soldiers were called upon to assist him.[237] Officials could approach the tasks in hand with curiosity as well as the vigor and élan of youth. Creating small gardens could expend a lot of energy in the very rocky landscape, but it could also create a break from routine.[238] Daniel Salis-Soglio recalled seeing a *Jägermajor* in Bileća tending his large allotment. He asked the major what he was staring at so intently; he replied that he was trying to read the Latin

---

232 "hohe und steile serbishe Stern," in Hermann Bock, "Die Knöchenhöhle im Pratschaltale und die neuentdeckte Tropfsteingrotte," *Pester Lloyd*, September 25, 1913, 2.

233 See for example, Reinhard Günste [Rifât Effendija Gozdović pseud.], "Die bosnische Ostbahn," *Reichspost*, March 27, 1906, 1–3.

234 "Bosnien war noch türkisch und ebenso unbekannt," in "Die Gründung des bos.herc. Landesverbandes des Vereins für Hohlenkunde in Oesterreich-Ungarn," typed report, no author (possibly written by Augusta Birgmeier, the Verein secretary), Collections Leo Weirather, Muséum d'histoire naturelle de Genève.

235 K[arel] Vandas, "Beiträge zur Kenntniss der Flora von Süd-Hercegovina," *Österreichische Botanische Zeitschrift* 39 (1889): 266–69.

236 Hadžibegović, *Bosanskohercegovački gradovi*, 82.

237 Edvard Formánek, "Beitrag zur Flora von Bosnien und der Hercegovina," *Österreichische Botanische Zeitschrift* 39, no. 4 (April 1889): 145–47.

238 Andrejka, *Slovenski fantje*, 341.

names on the seed packets in order to label the vegetables properly.[239] Botanist Carl Bäenitz asked soldiers to help him collect roses.[240]

The Trebinje garrison doctor Alois Pick hosted Sigmund Freud in 1898 as part of a medical delegation.[241] The brief visit seems to have had a discernible effect on him and it was at this time that Freud began to think about his first essay on the mechanics of the unconscious.[242] The visit also gives us a snapshot of the life of a garrison doctor and some of his patients in 1898. In Trebinje, he observed that "these Muslims [*Türken*] value the sexual drive above all else and if their drive fails, they fall into a despondency which makes a striking contrast to their resignation in the face of death." According to Freud's notes, one local patient had told his doctor "when that no longer works, life has no worth."[243] This idea of Muslim fatalism became a common trope among Habsburg officials: military judge Michael Florer also noticed it.[244] Dr. Josef Schorr, a senior doctor based in Priboj in Sandžak, found his Muslim patients to be both "stoic" and "fatalist."[245] In Trebinje, Freud recounted that the carers of a mortally sick person would answer: "Sir, what is there to be said? I know that if he could have been saved, then you would have done so."[246] It is likely that Freud began to see sexual drive differently at this time, making a personal decision to seize the day ("carpe diem") as life is short and death imminent.[247]

In the summers before the First World War, enthusiasts and scientists explored the hills, caves, and Popovo polje. Societies and clubs

---

239 Salis-Soglio, *Mein Leben*, 152.

240 "Der Commandant der Forts überliess mir die nach Rosen duftenden Blüten, welche seine Soldaten für ihn gestern abgepflückt hatten," Carl Bäenitz, "Botanische Reisen," *Österreichische Botanische Zeitschrift* 47, no. 7 (1897): 270.

241 Šarić, Salko "Sigmund Freud u Trebinju 1898. godine," *Most*, no. 175 [85] (2004), online at https://www.most.ba/085/095.aspx, accessed May 5, 2024.

242 Dušan I. Bjelić, *Normalizing the Balkans: Geopolitics of Psychoanalysis and Psychiatry* (Farnham: Ashgate, 2011), 38. Peter Swales argued that this excursion saw the development of Freud's notion of *Signorelli parapraxis* (often referred to as the "Freudian slip"); see "Freud, Death and Sexual Pleasures: On the Psychical Mechanism of Dr. Sigmund Freud," *Arc de Cercle*, no. 1 (2003): 4-74.

243 Sigmund Freud, *Zur Psychopathologie des Alltagslebens (Über Vergessen, Versprechen, Vergreifen, Aberglaube und Irrtum)* (Berlin: S. Karger, 1904), 5-6.

244 Florer, "Kriegsaufzeichnungen," AT-OeStA/KA NL 654 (B), Kriegsarchiv Vienna, 122.

245 Scheer, "Minimale Kosten, absolut kein Blut!," 134-35.

246 Freud, *Zur Psychopathologie*, 5.

247 Sigmund Freud, *Die Traumdeutung* (Leipzig/Vienna: Franz Deuticke, 1914), 156-57.

proliferated in Bosnia and Hercegovina. One leading researcher was the agronomy teacher Lucijan Matulić, who was originally from Pučišća on Brač in Dalmatia, an island renowned for stonemasonry and viticulture. He had been encouraged to collect specimens by Viktor Apfelbeck,[248] a curator from the *Landesmuseum* in Sarajevo who walked the length and breadth of Bosnia and Hercegovina on foot to record all the local species.[249] Matulić was an avuncular, sociable person,[250] and part of an expedition that got lost in a cave in October 1913. The story of the rescue captured an excitement about cave research, which was growing in popularity across the Monarchy.[251] Like Matulić, Trebinje-based postmaster Leo Weirather was an enthusiastic member of the *Verein für Höhlenkunde*, while his wife Augusta Birgmeier was the club secretary.[252] Like Marie Marvánková, Augusta was also an active part of the research expeditions.[253] Other *Verein* members included officers from the garrisons in Mostar and Trebinje.[254]

Finding pre-Ottoman historical artefacts motivated many Habsburg officials. Christian Marchetti has argued that the occupation of Bosnia and Hercegovina gave keen historians, archaeologists, and ethnologists a new location to study. Moriz Hoernes was "engaged by the Ministry of Education to travel through Bosnia and Herzegovina cataloging Roman archaeological sites."[255] Felix von Luschan was responsible for collecting a lot of data about *stećci*, which began to draw in tourists.[256] The white and gray *stećak* (plural *stećci*)

248 Marinko Gjivoje, "Prilog historijatu speleologije u Hrvatskoj," *Speleolog: Časopis za Speleologiju* 2, no. 2 (1954): 49.
249 Viktor Apfelbeck, *Die Käferfauna der Balkanhalbinsel mit berücksichtigung Klein-Asiens und der insel Kreta*, vol. 1 (Berlin: Friedländer, 1904).
250 Bäenitz, "Botanische Reisen," 270.
251 "Abenteuer einer Höhlenexpedition," *Grazer Volksblatt*, October 14, 1913, 7.
252 Leo Weirather to Carl Patsch, February 21, 1914, Briefe an Carl Patsch 1888–1944, Südost-Institut, Munich, Germany.
253 Leo Weirather to Karel Absolon, Trebinje, December 29, 1913, Sbirka Karla Absolona, Brno.
254 "The study of the subterranean world [*Schachtforschung*] was initiated by military personnel," in anon, "Die Gründung des bos. herc. Landesverbandes," Collections Leo Weirather, Muséum d'histoire naturelle de Genève.
255 Christian Marchetti, "Austro-Hungarian Volkskunde at War: Scientists on Ethnographic Mission in World War I," in Johler, Marchetti, and Scheer, *Doing Anthropology in Wartime*, 211.
256 Heinz Kurz-Schiltern, "Radwanderziele in Österreich-Ungarn," *Club-Organ des Oesterreichischen Touring-Club*, no. 3 (1910): 2–4.

tombstones, carved in the Middle Ages, preserve ancient patterns and words. Other researchers focused on burial places and the culture that surrounded them. Emil Lilek was fascinated by elements of culture that predated the religious conversions of the sixteenth century and those customs that tied Muslims and Christians together by tradition. In Trebinje, Lilek noted that a candle or lamp was kept in the house of the deceased for forty days because it was believed that his or her soul flew around their grave for this length of time before departing to the next world.[257] Authors versed in the classics looked for antiquity in local practices. In Trebinje, a shepherd would drive his cattle into the cattle yard between burning candles.[258] It was believed that a similar Christmas Eve ceremony in Risan, where family members waited in their courtyard to receive the sheep and shepherd, could be traced back to antiquity and the Roman Saturnalia.[259] Lilek recorded that small stones were rolled onto graves in Trebinje and the tombs of the Hercegovinian Orthodox had a different appearance from those of the local Muslims. Country people in Hercegovina did not want to be buried in coffins but taken to graves on palls, where they would be buried facing from east to west.[260]

Although Trebinje lay in a fertile river valley, the new authorities had an uphill struggle to tame the dry limestone environment, irrigate the land for new crops, and introduce machinery. An engineer and meteorologist from Graz, Philipp Ballif used local people as his informants in Gacko when studying its crops, pastures, and meadows.[261] Popovo polje is a horizontal longitudinal karst plain, surrounded by hills, with small settlements on higher ground on its periphery. The valley has some unique ethnographic heritage: corn was dried in the *salaš*, the *ponor mlinica* was a watermill, the *poljarica* was a stone hut used for shelter, and the *estavela* was a watermill that

257 Lilek, "Familien- und Volksleben," 210.
258 Lilek, "Familien- und Volksleben," 214.
259 Arthur Evans, "Christmas and Ancestor Worship in the Black Mountain," *Macmillan's Magazine* 43 (1881): 222. Saturnalia were exuberant festivities held in Rome in December in the pre-Christian era.
260 Lilek, "Familien- und Volksleben," 63–65.
261 Philipp Ballif, *Wasserbauten in Bosnien und der Hercegovina*, vol. 1, *Meliorationsarbeiten und Cisternen im Karstgebiete* (Vienna: A. Holzhausen, 1896–1899).

rotated in both directions.[262] Before the dam project of 1967, the Trebišnjica was a sinking river which flowed into Popovo polje and its cave system. One of these caves, Vjetrenica, has a good view of Popovo polje from its entrance; its name derives from the word in the local language for wind (*vjeter*). Skeletal remains of a distinct species of cave bear were discovered,[263] as well as numerous species of stygobites and troglobites. Hristofor Mihajlović, an Orthodox monk also revered by Catholics and based in the Zavala monastery, published a plan of Vjetrenica including the entrance to the cave drawn by Ewald Arndt.[264] This was followed by further technical details from Josip Vavrović, a former Habsburg soldier, also published in *Glasnik*.[265] The cave system proved to be quite an attraction, bringing in travelers from the wider region. In contrast, local people might have been less enthusiastic about subterranean caverns. Ernst Dombrowski described how an "old shepherd" implored him not to descend into a cave and made the sign of the cross to protect him, but then asked him curiously what he had actually seen once he reemerged safely.[266] Locals apparently believed that fairies or spirits danced the ring dance (*kolo*) at the entrances of caves. When no fairy drumbeat could be heard, it was said that years of bloodshed would follow.[267]

Leo Weirather, originally from Bressanone, was a great enthusiast for cave science and unlikely to let politics get too much in the way of his pursuits. In September 1913, he wrote to Carl Patsch to say that he had taken advantage of the good weather to do as much research as possible, documenting new discoveries around the un-

---

262 Borut Juvanec, "Popovo polje, a different view," *Acta Carsologica* 45, no. 3 (2016): 276.

263 "Tages-Neuigkeiten," *Bogen des Neuigkeits Welt Blatt*, November 24, 1896, 9.

264 Hristifor Mihajlović, "Manastir Zavala i Vjetrenica pećina," *Glasnik Zemaljskog muzeja u Bosni i Hercegovini* 2, no. 2 (1890): 130–143; Jasminko Mulaomerović, "Caves as Illustrations in Popular and Scientific Articles," in *Proceedings of the International Symposium on History of Speleology and Karstology in Alps, Carpathians and Dinarides, ALCADI 2018* (Sarajevo: Center for Karst and Speleology, 2019), 50–61.

265 Josip Vavrović, "Nešto o Vjetrenici pećini," *Glasnik Zemaljskog muzeja u Bosni i Hercegovini* 5, no. 2 (1893): 709–15.

266 "Herr, geh' nicht da hinunter, ich rate dir gut!," in Ernst Dombrowski, "Auf heißem Boden," *Neues Wiener Tagblatt*, February 22, 1914, 40. Dombrowski (1862–1917) was a hunter and writer from Bohemia.

267 Reinhard Günste [Rifaat Gozdović Pascha pseud.], "Das Popovo Polje," *Pilsner Tagblatt*, July 27, 1910, 4–5.

derground river of Mušnica in Gatačko polje.[268] In the deep sink-hole of Jasovica, he found that the mist from the water was so intense that the flame from a gas lamp could not be seen some thirty meters away.[269] This discovery established Weirather's reputation as a researcher.[270] Like Apfelbeck, he also often traveled on foot and extended the knowledge of the region established by other scientists such as the geologist Albrecht Penck.[271] Weirather's *Verein* collaborated with Karel Absolon, an eminent young scientist from Brno, during his frequent visits to Hercegovina. Perhaps best known for leading the team that discovered the stone Venus of Dolní Věstonice (*Věstonická venuše*) in 1925, Absolon's enthusiasm for the karst in Moravia also extended to the limestone in Hercegovina.[272] He visited several times before and after the First World War and was particularly smitten by Popovo polje.[273] In 1913, he spent a month doing field-work in Popovo polje before heading to the Dalmatian island of Brač.[274] Absolon was the first individual known to have entered the channel which starts six hundred meters from the entrance of Vje-trenica (which is now appropriately known as *Absolonov Kanal*).[275] By placing dye in the Trebišnjica, scientists established that the colored water would eventually flow out near the coast at the mouth of the Ombla. Absolon found the soldiers in Trebinje garrison exceptionally helpful to him as he attempted to chart and describe karst phenomena. No doubt, he noted, this work was also a "welcome refreshment after the tedium of a Balkan garrison."[276] A boat was brought

---

[268] Leo Weirather to Carl Patsch, September 20, 1913, Briefe an Carl Patsch 1888–1944, Südost-Institut, Munich, Germany.

[269] "Interessantes Ergebnis der Höhlenforschung in Bosnien und Herzegowina," *Das interessante Blatt*, October 30, 1913, 39.

[270] The significance of the work was recalled almost a decade later; Karel Absolon to Leo Weirather, Brno, October 1, 1922, Collections Leo Weirather, Muséum d'histoire naturelle de Genève.

[271] Albrecht Penck, "Geomorphologische Studien aus der Herzegowina," *Zeitschrift des deutschen und österreichischen Alpenvereins*, no. 31 (1900): 25–41.

[272] Petr Kostrhun, "Prehistorie v období Československé republiky: Rozvoj moravské paleolitické archeologie mezi léty 1918–1938" (Ph.D. diss., Institute of Archeology and Museology, Masaryk University, Brno, 2013).

[273] Karel Absolon to Johann (Ivan) Čadek, Brno, March 25, 1930, Sbirka Karla Absolona, Brno.

[274] Karel Absolon, "Výsledky výzkumných cest po Balkáně: Část třetí," *Časopis moravského musea zemského*, 1914, 216.

[275] Lučić, "Povijest poznavanja Dinarskog krša," 27–28.

[276] Absolon, "Z výzkumných cest po krasech Balkánu," 622–24.

FIGURE 23. Karel Absolon (lower center) and Lucijan Matulić (sitting beside him smoking) on a caving expedition in 1912. Moravské zemské muzeum, Brno.

into Vjetrenica for the first time in 1913 with the help of the army;[277] when the boat capsized, the cavers were forced to swim to safety in very cold water.[278] They found the skeleton of a diluvial great cat and very thick mud, which impeded their movement. Georg Lahner, whose miner's lamp had blown out underground, recorded that he and his party of speleologists from the *Verein* were stranded; six officers and twenty-five cadets came out to Vjetrenica to help them. Afterwards, they all enjoyed an evening of hospitality at the Trebinje garrison with Lucijan Matulić, who had telegraphed for help.[279] Lahner recalled years later that in 1913, he was hampered by the fact that he had to use the lamp and row simultaneously, highlighting the precarious dangers of these expeditions.[280]

Like the dangers that men in the garrison faced after 1914 (and from 1878–1882), the sense of risk also enhanced a genuine scientific

---

277 Anton Kapel, "Contribution to the History of the Explorations of the Cave Vjetrenica in Zavala to 1914," *Acta Carsologica* 26, no. 2 (1997): 97.

278 "Abenteuer einer Höhlenexpedition," *Salzkammergut-Zeitung*, October 19, 1913, 5.

279 Georg Lahner, "Eindrücke von der Forschungsreise des Vereines für Höhlenkunde nach Bosnien und Hercegovina," *Weiner Abendpost*, March 17, 1914, 3. See also, "Bosnisch-herze-gowinische Höhlenforscherwoche," *Linzer Volksblatt*, September 12, 1913, 5.

280 Georg Lahner, "Lebend begraben: Warnende Betrachungen zum Üngluck in der Frauen-mauer-Höhle," *Linzer Volksblatt*, January 6, 1929, 5.

fraternity and may be one reason why so many of these scientists stayed in touch with each other after the collapse of the Habsburg state.[281] These men also seemed to regard national sentiment as an obstacle to research or, as Weirather reflected to Absolon in 1950, "one's own people are more hateful than those of so-called hostile nations."[282] Support from garrisons offered safer travel in the border region with Montenegro without too much risk of trouble. On a more practical level, garrison culture meant that people from around the monarchy could find conviviality and intellectual friendship within the army home from home.[283] Leo Weirather, who moved to Innsbruck after the war, felt that the garrison complex allowed researchers to initiate serious projects. As he wrote to Karel Absolon in 1958: "The two wars set us back enormously and unpredictably, preventing us from exercising the urge to explore; what we could have done in these decades of impoverishment and xenophobia if the research plans we made in Trebinje had actually been carried out."[284]

Georg Veith was known throughout the garrisons of Hercegovina as "Schlangenveith" because of his expertise in the local snakes. He spent long hours on expeditions, wore very thick leather gloves to prevent bites, and carried a camera with him. For some of the war years he was based in a small fort at Mosko, about two hours' march from Trebinje.[285] Toward the end of the war, Veith's reptile specimens were given to the *Landesmuseum* in Sarajevo.[286] There was a spe-

---

281 Although Lucijan Matulić passed away in 1917, his research was not forgotten and its importance was acknowledged in later correspondence. See, for example, Leo Weirather to Karel Absolon, Innsbruck, September 16, 1942, Collections Leo Weirather, Muséum d'histoire naturelle de Genève.

282 Leo Weirather to Karel Absolon, Innsbruck, December 14, 1950, Collections Leo Weirather, Muséum d'histoire naturelle de Genève.

283 Edmund Glaise von Horstenau (1882-1946) was pleased to meet an old acquaintance from St Pölten in Bileća, as well as getting a snapshot of life in the town; see Glaise von Horstenau, *Ein General im Zwielicht*, 202.

284 Leo Weirather to Karel Absolon, Innsbruck, November 28, 1958, Collections Leo Weirather, Muséum d'histoire naturelle de Genève.

285 Veith was primarily based in Kordonposten Mosko, but inevitably spent time in the officers' mess both in Trebinje and Bileća; see Georg Veith to Carl Patsch, Bileća, April 9, 1916, Briefe an Carl Patsch 1888-1944, Südost-Institut, Munich, Germany. See also Gernot Sattler, "Vorwart," *Herpetozoa* 3, nos. 3-4 (1991): 99-102.

286 Otto Wettstein, "Oberst Veith, der Schlangensammler," *Neues Wiener Tagblatt*, November 1, 1925, 6-7; Helga Happ and Paul Mildner, "Georg Veith—Herpetologe, Altertumsforscher und Soldat," *Rudolfinum: Jahrbuch des Landesmuseums für Kärnten* (2003): 435-43.

cies of harmless land lizard, known as *blavor* in the local language and *Panzerschleie* in German.[287] Veith took local knowledge very seriously: "The native population knows the '*blavor*' quite well, at least where it is common, and knows how to distinguish it from other snakes and generally spares it; in general, the incoming intelligentsia is less well oriented in this respect, and mostly regards the *blavor* as an Aesopian serpent."[288] Alfred Jansa remembered Veith's intelligent company in garrison society:

> There was the commander of a mountain artillery detachment in Trebinje, Captain (soon to be Major) Veith, a skilled snake researcher and ... a historian of ancient Rome and its grandiose road constructions across the Balkans to Asia Minor. Each of Veith's vacations were spent on research trips. It was a pleasure to be able to talk to him for an evening.[289]

Veith's research struck a chord because snakebites were a persistent problem for the military in Hercegovina. In 1891, Captain Wilka was the second man from his regiment to die from a snakebite that year in Trebinje.[290] He was on a field exercise and rested beside a rock in the heat. The pain of the bite was reported to have struck him like a lightning bolt and he was driven insane by it before he died a few days later. After Wilka's death, the troops were reportedly forbidden to rest in the open air.[291] Draft animals could also perish from snakebites.[292] In 1909, another soldier, Geza Bassarits from Sopron, was killed by a poisonous viper (*viper aursinii*).[293] The contrast between the knowledge of the incomer and the imbedded and the deep knowledge of local people is a key part of this narrative in the early

---

287 Described as "friendly" by Reinhard Günste, the *blavor* was also a useful mouse-catcher: Reinhard Günste [Rifaat Gozdović Pascha pseud.], "Eine Jagd am Utovo Blato," *Pilsner Tagblatt*, July 31, 1910, 4–5.

288 Georg Veith, "Die Reptilien von Bosnien und der Herzegowina," ed. F. Tiedemann and F. Grillitsch, *Herpetozoa*. 3, nos. 3–4 (1991): 179.

289 Broucek, *Feldmarschalleutnant Alfred Jansa*.

290 (Wlcha in some sources), "Folgen eines Schlangenbisses," *Linzer Volksblatt*, August 22, 1891, 4.

291 "Tod in Folge eines Schlangenbisses," *Steirische Alpenpost*, August 23, 1891, 398.

292 "Festung Bileća 1914–1918," AT-OeStA/KA FA NFA (Bileća 309), Kriegsarchiv Vienna.

293 "Tagesneuigkeiten," *Mährisch-Schlesische Presse*, May 8, 1909, 4.

years, but Habsburg writers were learning very quickly and implementing new strategies to understand their "anthropocene."[294] Emil Lilek asserted that people in Bosnia and Hercegovina believed their life and wellbeing depended on the necessary coexistence between themselves and animals. Milk was sometimes left for snakes on the edge of dwellings to deter entrance.[295] The people built stone walls around their dwellings specifically to protect themselves from snakes, according to one memoir looking back to 1908.[296]

Over the forty years of Habsburg occupation and then annexation, far greater levels of codified scientific knowledge developed as the occupiers came to know and understand the place. The role of individuals such as Vuk Vrčević was crucial in bridging the knowledge gap. Stjepan Jovanović was familiar with the terrain around Orjen from the counterinsurgency in 1869, which may be why he ordered the destruction of the fortress at Klobuk in 1878. The army had a better knowledge of the terrain in 1882 than just thirteen years earlier: lights from the warship *Erzherzog Albrecht* were used to illuminate the slopes of Orjen to detect the insurgents who were "creeping up" along the rocks.[297] The assistance of local informants helped to break the power of the insurgency. Perhaps it is no accident either that Habsburg soldiers who served in Southern Dalmatia, Hercegovina, or Bosnia kept their maps long after their service had finished. The Central Europeans who set up the garrisons in the area around Trebinje were superb surveyors and mapmakers,[298] but their technical acumen was pitted against the local knowledge of people who had walked over the hills and through the valleys since childhood, imbibing centuries of adaptation and imparted wisdom.

---

294 On the island of Mljet, a small mongoose population was introduced into the state forest in 1910 to try and tackle the local snakes; see Göderle, "The Habsburg Anthropocene," 215–40.
295 Lilek, "Familien- und Volksleben," 169.
296 H. P., "Zehn Jahre auf der Jagd nach Vipern," *Illustrierte Kronen Zeitung*, September 3, 1940, 6.
297 "das Anschleichen der Insurgenten," "Vom Insurrekzionsschauplatz," *Prager Abendblatt*, March 6, 1882, 2.
298 Novottny "Erinnerungen," AT-OeStA/KA NL 417: 12. Conrad believed mapmaking was an essential skill for an officer: see Sondhaus, *Franz Conrad von Hötzendorf*, 14; Wolfgang Göderle, "Materializing Imperial Rule? Nature, Environment, and the Middle Class in Habsburg Central Europe," *Hungarian Historical Review* 11, no. 2 (2022): 462.

Chapter Six

CRISIS, WAR, AND A NEW ERA

The Gathering Storm, 1908–1914

After thirty expensive years of occupation, the Habsburg state con-
solidated its gains at the Berlin Congress and annexed Bosnia and
Hercegovina in 1908. The finality of the act antagonized Serbia and
Montenegro, rebounded within the international community, and
appalled pro-Serbian and Montenegrin locals in Hercegovina. In 1908,
Jevto Dedijer, originally from the village of Čepelica, left the *Landesmuseum* in Sarajevo to move to Serbia, where he continued his research on traditional life.[1] Serbia did reluctantly accept the Bosnian
annexation in 1909, at least officially. At the same time, leading in-
tellectuals Jovan Cvijić, Stojan Novaković, and Ljubomir Jovanović
called the Berlin Treaty of 1878 "unsympathetic and unjust." They
stated that it was fitting "to cede to Serbia and Montenegro the whole
of the Podrinje and the region of Trebinje."[2] This was not a new idea:
in 1877 William Stillman, a close friend of Arthur Evans and Margaret Freeman, had suggested that a "part" of Hercegovina "may be

---

1   See, for example, Dedijer, "La transhumance," 347–65.
2   Vladimir Ćorović, *The Relations between Serbia and Austria-Hungary in the 20th Century* (Bel-
    grade: Archives of Yugoslavia, 2018), 312–13. Podrinje was the Drina river basin and the
    state border; Frederik Lange, "Kooperation und Konfrontation—Der Grenzstreit in der
    habsburgisch-serbischen Kontaktzone Drina-Becken, 1878–1914," *Storia e regione* 31, no. 2
    (2022): 91–110.

wisely united to Montenegro."[3] In 1913, this position had found some sympathy abroad. An anonymous letter to *The Times* of London asked readers to consider whether it "[w]ould it be reasonable and even politic for Austria … to offer (the Montenegrin) King a rectification of frontier in the districts of Krivoshia, Trebinje, and Bilek, thus affording her an outlet on the Gulf of Cattaro at Risano?"[4]

Widespread opposition to the annexation did not prevent the Habsburg state from continuing its "civilizing mission": in 1910, when Franz Joseph had visited Bosnia and Hercegovina, he announced a new constitution which gave the region increased political rights.[5] Education at primary level had been introduced by the Habsburg authorities and only Muslim girls were exempted.[6] Education also created aspirations. A new group known as *Mlada Bosna* (Young Bosnia) were activists for freedom from the Habsburg yoke, radicalized at a young age within the state-funded school system.[7] They were almost all devotees of poetry and humanist literature and advocates of violence. It was a great paradox that central resources inspired so much anti-state sentiment. Some *Mlada Bosna* members had roots in Hercegovina and remembered their family origins: for instance, Nedeljko Čabrinović's father came from Trebinje,[8] while Vladimir Gaćinović was from Kačanj, close to Bileća, and contributed to the journal *Bosanska Vila*. This journal was edited by Dimitrije Mitrinović, who was born in Berkovići, also a day's walk from Bileća.[9] Nevertheless, many people remained unlettered, even by

---

3   Stillman, *Herzegovina*, 153.
4   "The Montenegrin Danger: A Suggestion to the Editor of the Times," *The Times*, April 10, 1913, 5.
5   Maureen Healy, "Europe on the Sava: Austrian Encounters with 'Turks' in Bosnia," *Austrian History Yearbook* 51 (2020): 73–87.
6   Fabio Giomi has argued that the new regime tried very hard to make Muslim female education a viable option; see his *Making Muslim Women European*, 44.
7   Miloš Vojinović, "Political Ideas of Young Bosnia: Between Anarchism, Socialism, and Nationalism," in *The First World War and the Balkans: Historic Event, Experience, Memory/Der Erste Weltkrieg auf dem Balkan: Ereignis, Erfahrung und Erinnerung*, Südosteuropa-Jahrbuch 42, ed. Wolfgang Höpken and Wim van Meurs (Berlin: Peter Lang, 2018), 162–96.
8   The initial reports of the assassination of Franz Ferdinand tried to make a link between the garrison city and *Mlada Bosna*, which was rather tenuous; see, for example, H. K., "Ein Kaisertag," July 10, 1914, 7–8. See also Adnan Velagić, "Atentat u Sarajevu i njegove refleksije na području Hercegovine," *Historijski pogledi*, no. 2 (2019): 174–93.
9   Djokić, *Concise History of Serbia*, 332.

the First World War: Dalmatian officer Antonio Budinich noted that the local soldiers on the border during the war were "quasi tutti analfabeti."[10]

Nascent political parties had developed and the Bosnian Diet (*Sabor*), established in 1910, promoted political participation. While political consciousness was growing, civil society was also flourishing in Trebinje: a voluntary fire brigade was formed to protect the old city.[11] In 1908, the officer Philipp Nauhs founded a sports society in Trebinje, offering football and water polo in the summer.[12] Lucijan Matulić was involved with the local Red Cross Society in 1909.[13] In August 1910, a Trebinje library and reading room was established through voluntary donations. Benefactors included a broad mix of local Orthodox, Catholic, and Muslim notables including Mićo Kebeljić, Franjo Markić, Spasoje Grković, Jovo Sekerez, Ismet Salahović, Risto Lečić, Omer Pivodić, and Huso Babović.[14] *Sokoli* or youth societies developed rapidly among enthusiasts in Trebinje.[15] The annexation of Bosnia and Hercegovina in 1908 also served to heighten local antagonisms. In November 1911, leatherworkers in Trebinje went on strike; their protest was broken up with the help of the garrison. Marijan Sivrić argued that the strategic vulnerability of Trebinje and its proximity to the Montenegrin border made the authorities even more jumpy about the threat of industrial action.[16] In 1913, an argument between Habsburg soldiers and a local Orthodox official in Trebinje rebounded. Soldiers had started singing patriotic, pro-monarchy songs and an "official exclaimed: 'Down with it,' leading to a violent confrontation that reached the pages of regional media and the ears of government officials in Sarajevo."[17] Fears of disease exacerbated the problems of security. In August 1913,

---

10 "Almost all illiterate." Budini, *Le memorie di guerra*, 87.
11 Andrejka, *Slovenski fantje*, 317.
12 "Vor 50 Jahren Länderteam-Tormann," *Murtaler Zeitung*, December 1, 1951.
13 "Die letzte Aktion des Roten Kreuzes," *Die Zeit*, March 31, 1909, 6.
14 Sivrić, "Radnički pokret u Trebinju," 103.
15 H. K., "Ein Kaisertag," 7–8.
16 Sivrić, "Radnički pokret u Trebinju," 101.
17 Amir Duranović, "The Aggressiveness of Bosnian and Herzegovinian Serbs in the Public Discourse during the Balkan Wars," in *War and Nationalism: The Balkan Wars, 1912–1913 and Their Sociopolitical Implications*, ed. M. Hakan Yavuz and Isa Blumi, foreword by Edward J. Erickson (Salt Lake City: University of Utah Press, 2013), 392.

an annual pilgrimage to Kosijerevo was forbidden due to fears of an outbreak of cholera.[18] By this time, the deteriorating situation for the Orthodox community was becoming much clearer.

A fear of the border people (and the atrocities that might be committed upon those who fell into their hands) had been circulating for decades close to Trebinje and Bileća. One of Conrad von Hötzendorf's enduring ideas after 1878, reinforced by his experiences in the fighting around Orjen in 1882, was that "hard and unruly" Orthodox men were "cruel" in combat.[19] This prejudice seemed to be quite commonplace in the army and many remembered the atrocities of conflicts on the border. Habsburg soldiers who were captured and killed on the way to Klobuk in 1878 had had their severed ears left "in rows" on the rocks for their comrades to see.[20] Jernej Andrejka recalled that his slaughtered comrade France Novak from Dolenje Jesenice had had one of his ears cut off on the narrow route to Lastva.[21] In January 1882, a carpenter from Dalmatia was captured by insurgents in Bijela Rudina and had his hands tied behind his back and a rag placed in his mouth. When his body was discovered, his chin had been tied with a rope over the head, both eyes were gouged out, and nose and ears had been cut off.[22] Soldiers remained wary of the inhabitants of this area for years afterwards. In 1887, one soldier observed that the inhabitants of Gornje Grančarevo were as "moody and unpredictable as the weather." He continued by asserting that although they "sang soft melancholy songs, they were able to immediately torture an enemy with subtle cruelty."[23]

From 1912–1913, the Habsburg reading public followed Balkan War correspondents who sent vivid first-hand reports of the fighting back home on an almost daily basis. Reports created a clear image of Balkan cruelties (*Balkangreuel*), often specifically Serbian cruelties (*Serbengreuel*).[24] It was reported that Montenegrin troops had cut

---

18 "Die Cholera," *Neue Freie Presse*, August 28, 1913, 9.
19 Conrad, *Mein Anfang*, 169.
20 Wartburg, "Meine Erinnerungen an die Kämpfe um Trebinje," 3.
21 "Tudi mu je manjkalo eno uho," Andrejka, *Slovenski fantje*, 336.
22 "Bilek," *Südsteirische Post*, January 31, 1882, 3.
23 F. von M., "Auf Cordon," *Wiener Abendpost*, March 4, 1887, 1–3.
24 "Serbengreuel," *Vorarlberger Volksfreund*, March 19, 1913, 5.

off the ears and noses of their Albanian enemies.[25] Even Richard
Neutra, who learnt the local language and consistently showed empathy toward Orthodox people, feared that "twelve men from Bosnia and a young officer aspirant [i.e., himself] were … facing the
mountains and mountaineers of Montenegro, who had knives with
which to cut our throats, pistols, guns and matches."[26] The superior hardware and numerical advantage of Habsburg troops was constantly eroded by the sense of an inscrutable and cruel enemy over
the border, as well as the real fear that the Orthodox country people in Hercegovina were sympathetic to Montenegro.

Men from Krivošije, Montenegro, and Hercegovina were seen as
authority-defying, delinquent, boastful, bloody-minded, hardy, bel-
ligerent, mercurial, deceptively cruel, tall, craggy, almost superhu-
manly strong, and the singers of ancient songs. Stories in the press
tended to emphasize archaic or savage characteristics.[27] Dr. J. B.
opined that the locals in Sutorina were "close relatives of Montenegrin 'heroes,' who would rather steal a sheep than raise it themselves."[28]
The Montenegrins lived in "a land of mutton thieves,"[29] but they
were also deemed to be frugal soldiers "who could last all day with
a piece of bread and homemade sheep's cheese," according to Ludwig Magyar in 1915.[30] The accusation of uncleanliness and theft
was levied: "the concept of what is mine and what is yours was as
unknown to … [insurgent Ivo Gogorović] as is the use of almond
soap to a Montenegrin."[31] Among Habsburg writers, there were also
some positive stereotypes of Montenegrins that acknowledged that
the small country might offer an alternative, autonomous way of or-
dering life for South Slavs. Antonio Budinich, posted near the wartime border, found a lot to admire. He realized that their collective

25 "Kriegsbriefe aus Montenegro," *Danzers Armee-Zeitung*, October 31, 1912, 4.
26 Neutra, *Life and Shape*, 107.
27 See for example, (Amand von) Schweiger-Lerchenfeld, "Aus der Herzegowina," *Die Presse*,
    September 11, 1875, 1–2.
28 There seems to be no sense here that Central Europeans might have "stolen" Hercegovi-
    na from its autochthonous population. Dr. J. B., "Eine Fahrt durch die Suttorina," *Wiener
    Landwirtschaftliche Zeitung*, October 21, 1885, 1.
29 Morokutti, "Der Aufstand im Süden," 4.
30 Ludwig Magyar, "In den Schwarzen Bergen," *Mährisches Tagblatt*, November 13, 1915, 2.
31 "Der Begriff zwischen 'Mein' und 'Dein' war ihm so unbekannt wie einem Montenegriner
    der Gebrauch der Mandelseife." "Bosnisches Recht," *Militär-Zeitung*, June 2, 1885, 327.

sense of commitment both to each other and to their homeland was total, despite their absence of recently built fortifications and far poorer munitions:

> The Montenegrins ... had the advantage of being in possession of the positions further away from the border, from which they could dominate the Austrian area below. They were also very brave soldiers, perfectly expert about their own land, very agile in the tremendous mountains which they moved through with surprising ease, without roads, and without paths. Insuperable masters of snares and ambushes, it could be said that they were also not regular soldiers. They were the men of the border villages.... Their war was a people's war, for the defense of homes and families, in which they were helped by women, old people, and children.[32]

Beyond propaganda and stories from the army and press, the appeal of Montenegro for its near neighbors of Orthodox faith looked unstoppable and this pull factor remained an unsolved political issue from the 1850s until the end of the First World War. James Cotton Minchin remembered an incident when leaving Kotor in 1882: "we had no sooner crossed the frontier than the guide ... who was an Austrian subject slipped from his horse and knelt and kissed the consecrated soil."[33] By 1910, Montenegro had become a small but confident kingdom and, like Serbia, expanded further during the Balkan Wars. It offered the Orthodox people of Hercegovina an apparently dynamic egalitarian alternative rule by one of their own. The ascendancy of the Karadjordjević dynasty also increased the allure of the Kingdom of Serbia after 1903 for Orthodox people in Hercegovina. Moreover, religious leaders clearly provoked radical sentiments and (re)built the human bridge to Orthodox Serbs in Serbia and Montenegro among their illiterate but pious congregations. In Kruševice, in the Church of Sveti Lazar in June 1913, the priest Vaso Novaković

---

32 Budini, *Le memorie di guerra*, 76.
33 Cotton Minchin, *The Growth of Freedom*, 1–2.

preached that "Kosovo is avenged" (by victory in the Balkan Wars).[34]
Another priest, Špiro Lučić, "collected 120 kilograms of shirts, trousers, shawls, towels, and 1067 Kronen, half of which was donated to
Belgrade and half to Cetinje," after delivering a rousing sermon to
his congregation in Sutorina in October 1912.[35] And this kind of
sentiment was hardly discouraged in Montenegro. Furthermore,
Montenegrin nationalist expansionism generally excluded Muslims,
which extended the problematic legacy of 1875–78.[36] King Nikola
was supported by the Karadjordjević dynasty (and vice versa). Adding further to this atmosphere of destabilization (or anticipation), it
was even rumored in the Habsburg press that Nikola had visited
Trebinje in disguise.[37]

After 1908, close to the border with Montenegro, Habsburg army
recruits already in uniform were perhaps even more tempted to quit.
Desertion represented a rebellion against the "paternal rule" of the
Habsburg state. A young Orthodox man from Avtovac, Jovo
Vukmanović, was signed up for military service by his father even
though he was still technically underage in 1910. Vukmanović left
his garrison in coastal Tivat and made it back to the state border
where he stopped in a Montenegrin monastery. Here he adopted
local clothes and was seen chatting animatedly with Montenegrins
of his own age. His anxious father traveled overland by mule and
reported his son to the Habsburg gendarme. Given a severe repri-
mand from his regiment, but allowed to return to duty, Vukmanović
absconded and hid in Cetinje, once again adopting Montenegrin
dress to blend in. His angry father then disinherited him and advised him to travel to South America with an acquaintance from
Bar.[38] Although the officer who retold the story, Michael Florer, pre-

---

34 Grunert, *Glauben im Hinterland*, 329.
35 Grunert, *Glauben im Hinterland*, 506.
36 Heiko Brendel, "'Our land is small and it's pressed on all sides. Not one of us can live here
   peacefully': Population Policy in Montenegro from the Long Nineteenth Century to the
   End of the First World War," in *The First World War as a Caesura? Demographic Concepts, Population Policy, Genocide in Late Ottoman, Russian, and Habsburg Spheres*, ed. Christin Pschichholz
   (Berlin: Duncker and Humblot, 2020), 135–58.
37 Reinhard Günste [Rifat Gozdović Pascha pseud.], "Wie ich den Mehrer Montenegros kennen lernte," *Wiener Sonn- und Montags-Zeitung*, January 19, 1914, 3.
38 F. Michael Florer, "Kriegsaufzeichnungen," AT-OeStA/KA NL 654 (B), Kriegsarchiv Vienna, 675–677.

sented this in terms of conflict between a loyal father and a "good for nothing" (*Taugenichts*) son, the story could also be interpreted in terms of a political choice between two countries.[39] For Vukmanović, dressing as a Montenegrin represented freedom and pride rather than subjection.[40]

The successes of the combined Montenegrin and Serbian forces (as well as the militaries of Greece and Bulgaria) in 1912–1913 meant that Ottoman power in Europe was reduced to a small area of land around Edirne. The Habsburg Monarchy had withdrawn its right to garrison Sandžak in 1908, which was then wrested from the Ottomans and divided as spoils by Montenegro and Serbia in 1913. In Bosnia and Hercegovina, the authorities started to be even more concerned about the true loyalty of their own Orthodox population. Oskar Potiorek became Governor (*Landeschef*) of Bosnia and Hercegovina in May 1911, remaining in post for a crucial period until December 1914. In May 1913 he declared a state of emergency and targeted socialist and Orthodox organizations, leaving Muslim, Catholic, and "Habsburg" organizations to continue as normal.[41] Potiorek also created a new paramilitary border guard (*Grenz-Schutzkorps*), who could avoid regular military service. The *Schutzkorps* specifically excluded Orthodox men and drew its cohort from local Muslims and Catholics.[42] Although the creation of a group of soldiers without rank preceded the events of June 1914, they were immediately brought into service at the outbreak of war.[43]

---

39 On the political choice between Serbia and the Ottoman Empire made by a soldier called Şerefeddin who became Milan Milovanović, see Jovo Miladinović, "Heroes, Traitors, and Survivors in the Borderlands of Empires: Military Mobilizations and Local Communities in the Sandžak (1900s–1920s)" (Ph.D. diss., Humboldt University, Berlin, 2022), 424–30.

40 On the complex factors within the army that led to the development of national consciousness, see Christa Hämmerle, "Die k. (u.) k. Armee als 'Schule des Volkes'? Zur Geschichte der Allgemeinen Wehrpflicht in der multinationalen Habsburgermonarchie (1866–1914/1918)," in *Der Bürger als Soldat: Die Militarisierung europäischer Gesellschaften im langen 19. Jahrhundert; Ein internationaler Vergleich*, ed. Christian Jansen (Essen: Klartext, 2004), 175–213.

41 Grunert, "The Inner Enemy in Wartime," 254; Vojislav Bogićević, "'Iznimne mjere' u Bosni i Hercegovini u maju 1913 godine," *Godišnjak društva istoričara Bosne i Hercegovine* 7 (1955): 209–18.

42 Schachinger, *Die Bosniaken kommen*, 53–56.

43 Res. Nr. 31, "Verwendung der freiwillig Einrückenden," Sarajevo, July 29, 1914, AT-OeStA/KA FA NFA (Bileća 309), Kriegsarchiv, Vienna.

Although the relationship between Franz Joseph and his heir Franz Ferdinand was often fraught, the latter's death in 1914 came at a time when the political direction of the state was undecided. Franz Ferdinand had been interested in a possible "Trialist" solution that would have given the Slavs more steer within the Monarchy and he had enemies within his own ranks, including Conrad von Hötzendorf. Arriving on an official visit, Franz Ferdinand had spent June 27 on military maneuvers while his wife Sophie had been welcomed by Bishop Ivan Šarić at the Catholic Cathedral. As they left the predominantly Orthodox village of Ilidža close to the source of the Bosna River on June 28, they had notably light personal security and traveled through the city along the Appelquai in an open-top car.[44] The streets of Sarajevo were thinly lined with welcoming crowds: the regime wished to demonstrate that it ruled by consent rather than coercion. A small group of *Mlada Bosna* activists had gathered in Sarajevo after making the journey across the Serbian border with weapons that they had acquired in Belgrade. After the first bomb was thrown by Nedeljko Čabrinović, several of the retinue were injured and the rattled royal party arrived at Vijećnica, the Sarajevo city hall. The security arrangements were Oskar Potiorek's responsibility. Even after the first attempt on Franz Ferdinand's life, Potiorek insisted that the existing security forces were sufficient and the army's field exercises should not be disrupted by bringing them onto the streets of Sarajevo. As Franz Ferdinand's car set off for the hospital to visit Potiorek's injured adjutant Merizzi, Gavrilo Princip opened fire when the car stalled, and killed the royal couple. Princip had not intended to shoot Sophie, but instead was aiming for Potiorek, a figure of absolute contempt for *Mlada Bosna* activists.

The reaction of the non-Orthodox subjects across Bosnia and Hercegovina to the royal deaths was rapid and devastating and the atmosphere deteriorated rapidly.[45] Trebinje also became the focus of media attention because of the Čabrinović family connection. Josip Vancaš, the deputy mayor of Sarajevo, spoke to crowds on June

---

44 Named after Johann Freiherr von Appel (1826–1906), Governor of Bosnia from 1882–1903. Army Inspector Michael Ludwig Edler von Appel (1856–1915) was his son.

45 "Grosse serbenfeindliche Demonstration in Sarajevo," *Sarajewoer Tagblatt*, June 29, 1914, 1.

29, 1914, just before they rioted.[46] Hotel Evropa, which had been designed by Karel Pařík, was virtually demolished at the hands of an angry mob.[47] Other buildings were gutted. Demonstrations occurred in other regional centers. In Travnik, demonstrators broke into a school and attacked an Orthodox priest.[48] In Trebinje, a crowd gathered outside the mosque in the *kaštel* and had to be broken up and dispersed by imposing Viennese officer Karl Rost.[49] The crowd paraded with a picture of Franz Ferdinand wrapped in black, shouted insults, and had intended to attack Orthodox properties, including an ironmongery owned by Vaso Babić as well as church buildings. A Polish officer, Michał Potuczko, also stopped the rioters, and the priest Stevan Pravica tried to prevent any further violence in the city.[50] In Trebinje at least, soldiers from the garrison kept the peace on the streets, albeit temporarily. Exceptional measures were introduced by the Legislative Order of the National Government of July 26, 1914, which extended state powers.[51]

The assassination of the heir to the Habsburg Monarchy in 1914 set off a diplomatic flurry across Europe now known as the "July Crisis." Chief of the Armed Forces Conrad von Hötzendorf supported a rapid punitive war against Serbia, as did Oskar Potiorek. Officers in the Habsburg army moved quickly toward a war footing while effectively accusing the Serbian government of complicity with Gavrilo Princip; they issued an ultimatum to Belgrade on July 23, which was printed verbatim in most of the empire's daily newspapers. The demands of the ultimatum were mostly conceded by the Serbian government, but it could not agree to a Habsburg military presence on their sovereign territory (and in this respect, Serbia was supported

---

46 Robert J. Donia, *Sarajevo: A Biography* (Ann Arbor: University of Michigan Press, 2006), 124.
47 Andrej Mitrović, *Serbia's Great War, 1914–1918* (London: Hurst, 2007), 18. Its owner was Gligorije Jevtanović, a Habsburg-loyal Orthodox patrician of the city.
48 "Serbenfeindliche Demonstrationen," *Pester Lloyd*, July 1, 1914, 6.
49 Popović, *Patnje i žrtve Srba*, 10–11. Karl Rost's funeral in Vienna at the age of seventy-seven was well attended by mourners. His obituary remembered his "kind and dignified" manner as well as his imposing stature. See O. K., "In Memoriam: Oberst d. R. Karl Rost," *Danzers Armee-Zeitung*, January 21, 1938, 6; also Novottny, "Erinnerungen," AT-OeStA/KA NL 417: 12, 232.
50 Grunert, *Glauben im Hinterland*, 511. He was also known as Leo Michael. See also Novottny, "Erinnerungen," AT-OeStA/KA NL 417: 12, 203.
51 Zijad Šehić, "Atentat, mobilizacija, rat," *Prilozi*, no. 34 (2005): 29.

by its allies). The Trebinje garrison received the order to mobilize on the morning of July 26: military personnel were increased to more than 10,000 and the available cash within the Trebinje garrison complex was doubled to 200,000 Kronen.[52] Preparing for war on July 27, the families of officers were evacuated from the garrisons in both Bileća and Trebinje.[53] When Richard Neutra arrived in Trebinje from Vienna via Sarajevo with a copy of the ultimatum in his rucksack, he recalled a febrile atmosphere:

> ...night had fallen when the train stopped at the track's end. A crowd of people had gathered at the simple station, sleeping beside their baggage—women and children waiting for a train to take them north. Evacuation!... The fortress had just been alerted, put on war footing.... I squeezed through the crowd and grabbed a *Droschke*....[54] It was hellishly hot, even by night.... Lots of people were on the street, and many officers in the dim lobby; everywhere excitement dominated.... It happened to be a sleepy hot fortress, alerted only a few hours ago.[55]

As a result of its failure to comply in full with the ultimatum, the Habsburg Monarchy declared war on Serbia on July 28. This action cemented the alliances that had been developing across Europe for several years. France, Montenegro, Russia, and Britain (and eventually Italy in 1915) supported Serbia against Germany, Austria-Hungary, Bulgaria, and the Ottoman Empire. Within the Habsburg Monarchy, war unleashed a kind of euphoria mixed with hate: "it was precisely the intellectual impulse for war that allowed the tremendous enthusiasm for the conflict to emerge."[56] Propaganda went

---

52 Volker Konstantin Pachauer, "Trebinje: Austro-Hungarian Garrison and Fortress 1878–1918," *Tribunia: Prilozi za istoriju, arheologiju, etnologiju, umjetnost i kulturu* 13 (2014): 184.

53 Šehić, "Atentat, mobilizacija, rat," 31.

54 Either a motorized or horse-drawn open-top cab, similar to a Fiaker.

55 Neutra, *Life and Shape*, 101–2. Later in the war, Antonio Budinich also commented that the train to Trebinje was "crowded with soldiers and overloaded with war material: cannons, ammunition, military supplies"; see Budini, *Le memorie di guerra*, 39.

56 Manfried Rauchensteiner, *The First World War and the End of the Habsburg Monarchy 1914–1918* (Vienna: Böhlau, 2014), 138; Mark Cornwall, "The Spirit of 1914 in Austria-Hungary," *Prispevki za Novejšo Zgodovino* 55, no. 2 (2015): 7–21.

hand in hand with policy. British Ambassador Maurice de Bunsen described the "extreme ... anti-Servian feeling prevalent in Vienna" in a concerned telegram to Sir Edward Grey on July 30.[57] The liberal politician Ivan Hribar, who was interned between 1914 and 1917 for his opposition to the war, remembered the "shameful" slogan as "*Srbe na vrbe*" ("Hang Serbs on the willows").[58]

Just a few weeks before the crisis, Leo Weirather was arrested and tried for espionage for the Montenegrin state. Weirather had married in November 1913 and resigned from the postal service in the Trebinje garrison. He aimed to make a living by selling fossils and specimens from the caves, which his wife helped him to prepare. At the end of December 1913, Weirather had written to Karel Absolon and told him of his plans to explore the caves around Grahovo in Montenegro. He evidently found the colder weather got in the way of his plans and he could hardly wait to get back to his research.[59] He was driven by the idea that there were still many caves to be explored on the border regions. Weirather came under the suspicion of the military authorities in early 1914 and was placed under arrest in the Trebinje garrison. Military personnel were forbidden to communicate with him during the investigations.[60] In the middle of May, his case was moved to Sarajevo.[61] Despite resigning from his official role, Weirather continued to maintain very close working relationships with officers in the Trebinje garrison and to follow events there, as did Absolon.[62] The extensive field notes were sometimes written in his own, almost inscrutable, scientific shorthand which raised suspicion.[63] Just prior to his trial, he had been denounced to the military

57 Thomas G. Otte, *July Crisis: The World's Descent into War, Summer 1914* (Cambridge: Cambridge University Press, 2014), 373.

58 Ivan Hribar, *Moji Spomini*, vol. 2 (Ljubljana: Merkur, 1928), 69. The phrase "*Srbe na vrbe*" has appeared regularly since this date in graffiti and social media.

59 Leo Weirather to Karel Absolon, December 29, 1913, Sbirka Karla Absolona, Pavilon Anthropos, Moravské zemské muzeum, Brno.

60 "Ein Höhlenforscher unter geverdacht," *Pester Lloyd*, May 5, 1914, 6.

61 "Ein Spionageprozeß in Sarajevo," *Reichspost*, May 14, 1914, 10.

62 Jovan Cvijić to Karel Absolon, June 27, 1914. Cvijić was on vacation in Karlovy Vary when he wrote to Absolon on Friday, June 26, 1914 (postmarked Saturday).

63 This shorthand was only later cracked by his colleague Egon Pretner (who proved their purely scientific content). See Egon Pretner, "Die Verdienste von Leo Weirather um die Biospeläologie, insbesondere Jugoslawiens, sein Höhlenkataster und seine Sammelplätze," *Berichte des Naturwissenschaftlich-medizinischen Vereins in Innsbruck* 97 (2011): 85–234.

authorities by an Orthodox assistant, but the process failed to find anything that would have been of any obvious military interest to the Montenegrins.[64] It was soon established that Weirather was only interested in the caves, not their strategic or military potential, and he was released without charge only days before the looming crisis.[65]

FIGURE 24. Richard Neutra as a Habsburg soldier. Courtesy of his son Raymond Neutra.

Violence in the Rimland

Even though the Habsburg Army played such an important part in the life of the state and dominated the lives of young men, it was inexperienced in combat, especially compared with the other European powers. For many officers, it was their first chance to go into battle for a generation. Richard Neutra described the welcome he received when he arrived to meet the Trebinje garrison's commander: "General Major Braun, an old-timer with a drooping gray mustache, told me with scarcely subdued excitement in his voice that every man ... was welcome at this crucial moment."[66] The Trebinje garrison was always at the heart of the policy to contain the Orthodox population. Rudolf Braun implemented distinctive local tactics, but overall strategy was devised by Oskar Potiorek. Accompanying Archduke Leopold Salvator and the Minister for War Alexander von Krobatin, Potiorek had visited Trebinje just ten days before the Sarajevo assassination to review security on the eastern border.[67]

Montenegro mobilized before its own declaration of war on August 6. The French, Russian, and British diplomatic representatives

---

64 "Verhaltungen unter Spionageverdacht," *Tages-Post*, June 10, 1914, 3.
65 "Spionageprozeß," *Pester Lloyd*, May 14, 1914, 11; "Die Verhaftung des Höhlenforschers," *Neues Wiener Tagblatt (Tages-Ausgabe)*, June 27, 1914, 14.
66 Neutra, *Life and Shape*, 104.
67 "Potiorek ist gestern aus Trebinje nach Sarajevo zurückgekehrt," *Fremden-Blatt*, June 19, 1914, 7.

in Cetinje had warned Montenegrin King Nikola not to get directly involved in the conflict, but he did have some specific territorial aims around the 1912 border with Albania and the Bojana river. The Montenegrins also regarded the approximate area between Zubci and the confluence of the Drina and Lim rivers as "unredeemed territory" primarily inhabited by kinsmen. Even more optimistic war aims included plans to take the Dalmatian coast helped by the French and British, at least according to the Russian military attaché Nikolai Potapov.[68] Although he was a great admirer of the elderly Franz Joseph, Nikola felt duty bound to support Serbia in its war with the Habsburg Monarchy. The Serbian regent Aleksandar was Nikola's grandson, born in the Montenegrin capital Cetinje. As the lines of division hardened, the Hercegovinian Orthodox population on the border was left dangerously exposed.

The border garrisons in Bosnia and Hercegovina began to review security arrangements even before the declaration of war; Montenegrins were to be expelled immediately if there was any question about their loyalty.[69] One Trebinje garrison memo on July 29, 1914, described the population of Dubočani close to the Montenegrin border as both "hostile and unreliable" and called for a guard to be mounted close to Kosijerevo.[70] On July 30, 1914, Gajo Gudelj was arrested for tending his cattle at night with a candle (and thus allegedly signaling to the Montenegrins): for this, he was executed.[71] There had been a long tradition of armed Montenegrins crossing the border under cover of night to avoid import taxes on their cattle in the Trebinje market, so it is possible that if Gudelj was out with a candle, he was communicating about livestock. On August 4, it was forbidden to burn lanterns during the night. The security of transport, especially bridges and

---

68 Radoslav Raspopović, ed., *N. M. Potapov: Ruski vojni agent u Crnoj Gori; Dnevnik 1906–07, 1912, 1914–15* (Podgorica: Istorijski institut Crne Gore, 2003), vol. 2: 507; Dragoljub R. Živojinović, "King Nikola and the Territorial Expansion of Montenegro, 1914–1920," *Balcanica* 14 (2014): 353–68.

69 "Montenegriner Behandlung," Verfügung des Armeekommandos Res. Nr. 94 v. 1/ 8, Mostar, August 4, 1914, AT-OeStA/KA FA NFA (Trebinje 50), Kriegsarchiv, Vienna.

70 "feindselig" and "unverlässlich," in "Allgemeine Situation in Montenegro," Trebinje, July 29, 1914, AT-OeStA/KA FA NFA (Trebinje 50), Kriegsarchiv, Vienna.

71 Ćorović, *Crna knjiga*, 124.

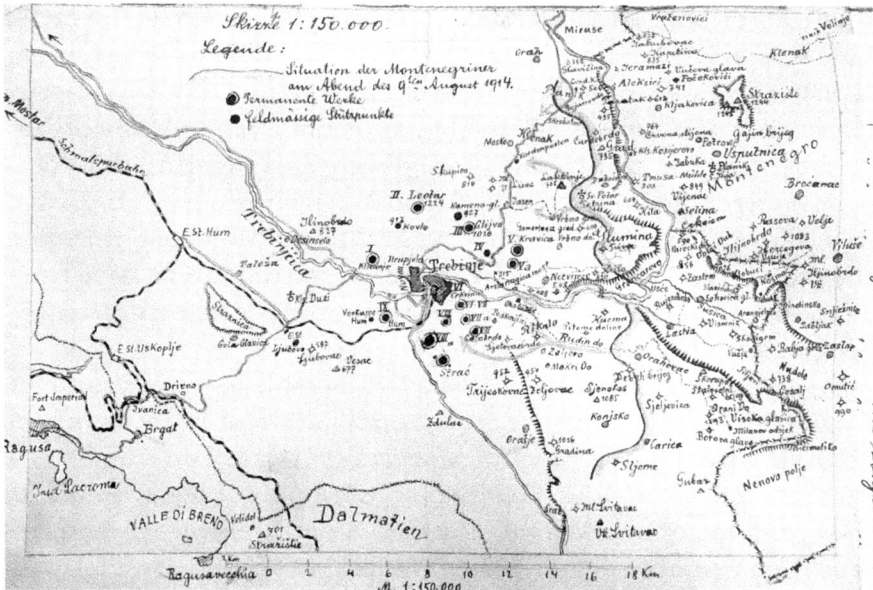

FIGURE 25. Montenegrin positions on August 9, 1914, drawn by Karl Novottny. Kriegsarchiv Vienna, Austrian State Archives.

railway stations, was judged to be imperative.[72] Shepherds had continued to lead their flocks over the mountainous passes which constituted the 1878 state borders, but this practice ended abruptly during the war. By 1914, mistrust of the population in Hercegovina was an old, well-established phenomenon. In 1882, insurgents had lit fires to communicate with each other across the hills,[73] sheltering and concealing their leaders. At that time, it was argued that those who had supported the insurgency "with bread, wine, and meat" should feel the force of military judgement against them.[74] But at that time, official policy lent toward amnesty with conspicuous punishment for ringleaders only, but among the military, hostility rumbled on for a generation and was quickly remobilized in 1914.

After August 6, the Montenegrins advanced over the border in small battalions and temporarily occupied several villages close to

---

[72] "An der Bezirksamt in Trebinje," Op. Nr. 9, August 4, 1914, AT-OeStA/KA FA NFA (Trebinje 50), Kriegsarchiv Vienna.

[73] "Von Metkovich nach Domanovic," *Neue Freie Presse (Abendblatt)*, February 14, 1882, 2.

[74] "Auf dem Aufstands-Gebiete," *Welt Blatt*, March 30, 1882, 9.

the frontier, capturing Habsburg soldiers. Their immediate tactic seems to have been to damage infrastructure and undermine Habsburg morale in the border forts and garrisons, but this alacrity left border populations vulnerable to retributive punishments. In October 1914, troops on the ground were still insisting that local people were signaling at night to Montenegrin troops.[75] In Lastva, Petar Radoman was reported to have greeted the Montenegrins when they took over the village.[76] A friendly greeting might have been a rational response to any armed invader, but it cost this priest his life in 1916 when he was recaptured.

As a garrison, Trebinje was always vulnerable to water shortages. In 1882, during the insurgency, floodwater had been drunk in Trebinje through necessity.[77] A Montenegrin attack on August 8–9, 1914, attempted to block Trebinje's water supply at Oko, which led the garrison commanders to establish new defensive lines to the south and east of Lastva.[78] Officer Wenzel Marschalek assembled fifteen soldiers and fifty-five local armed men to ensure the continuation of the water supply to Trebinje.[79] Richard Neutra remembered the incident well after he accidentally flooded his floor in his billet by leaving the faucet open:

> ...I learned that there was a great water shortage in the fortress. Water was released by the pumping station at 4.00am and turned off in the early afternoon. Two days later the Montenegrins took over the pumping station somewhere near the village of Lastva, a few kilometers from the frontier, and had to be driven off by a fairly frightened garrison.[80]

In 1858 at Grahovac, Montenegrin forces led by Mirko Petrović Njegoš had granted an honorable four-hour ceasefire because the Ot-

75 Memo dated October 4, signed by Rudolf Braun, Feldpostamt 305, AT-OeStA/KA FA NFA (Trebinje 50), Kriegsarchiv Vienna.
76 Mitrović, *Serbia's Great War*, 75.
77 "Inland," *Grazer Volksblatt*, February 25, 1882, 2.
78 Pachauer, "Trebinje: Austro-Hungarian Garrison," 184.
79 Schachinger, *Die Bosniaken kommen*, 54.
80 Neutra, *Life and Shape*, 103.

toman troops had run out of water,[81] so this attack on Oko in 1914 indicates a discernible strategic shift by the Montenegrins when dealing with the Habsburg threat. Fear of Montenegrin incursions was very real: it was reported in 1915 that a captured soldier had been dragged along by a horse while still alive.[82] Folksinger Đula Dizdarević, interviewed in 1935, remembered the sound of cannon at Plana. The terror of the gunfire made her family abandon their house without securing the lock or closing the door, and they ran barefoot to Zagradci and then to the nearby mountain for safety.[83] In October 1914, four men from the 9th Landsturm infantry regiment were killed close to the border and their bodies were stripped of uniforms.[84] It was assumed that Montenegrins would disguise themselves as Habsburg soldiers and slip in among troops in the field undetected. Montenegrins were also supposed to be trigger-happy; Alice Schalek described the Montenegrins who "know and love" their guns and fire them often "just to keep their hands warm."[85] In the Trebinje garrison, Rudolf Braun asked for evidence of atrocities by Montenegrins to be collected and photographed.[86] Emil Stettner and his colleagues at the Bileća garrison began to document war crimes and torture. When they found the corpse of a dead comrade, they deduced he had had a fire lit under his head.[87]

Before the outbreak of the First World War, a series of buildings were erected, including the fortress at Strač (or Srač), a watch tower on Mount Leotar, and a battery beside the ruins of Tvrdoš. An enormous but incomplete complex with numerous rooms and very thick walls, Strač had clear views of the surrounding settlements. Its guns

---

81 "Montenegro," *Pester Lloyd*, June 6, 1858, 2–3.
82 Schalek, "An der montenegrinischen Grenze," November 14, 1915, 2.
83 HadžiMuhamedović, *Waiting for Elijah*, 80.
84 Worm, "Auf Feldwache vor der Festung Trebinje," 5.
85 "Jeder Mann im Lande hat ein Gewehr, das er kennt und liebt. Er schießt ja oft nur, um sich die Hände zu wärmen." Schalek, "An der montenegrinischen Grenze," November 14, 1915, 2.
86 Memo dated November 30, 1914, Feldpostamt 305, AT-OeStA/KA FA NFA (Trebinje 50), Kriegsarchiv Vienna.
87 "Celui-ci avait vrai semblablement été dépouillé de ses habits—comme c'est l'habitude des Monténégrins—puis on l'avait martyrisé jusqu'à ce que mort s'ensuivît, en allumant du feu sous sa tête," in Ministerium des K. und K. Hauses und des Äussern, *Recueil de témoignages concernant les actes deviolation du droit des gens commis par les États en guerre avec l'Autrice-Hongrie* (Berne: K. J. Wyss, 1915), 161.

were designed by the Mladá Boleslav-based Škoda, the largest arms manufacturing company in the Monarchy; they were powerful enough to hit ships in the Adriatic, more than twenty-five miles away. By 1916, the fortifications had been greatly improved, by which time howitzer turrets had been constructed in Trebinje, Crkvice, Bileća, and Avtovac.[88] The indefensibility of the coastline with its numerous coves and landing points was a strategic preoccupation during the First World War.[89] The threat was seen to be imminent on August 18, 1914, as the Trebinje urban population were celebrating *Kaisertag*, and Rudolf Braun told his men:

> "The combined English-French Mediterranean fleet is steering up the Adriatic Sea at full force." They might use the Emperor's birthday as the occasion for a show of strength, or they might take advantage of the festivities to attempt a landing. The artillery staff officer placed a map before me on the table and showed me a route from our position in the fortress toward the coastal mountains.... "Leave the fortress in thirty minutes. You must find and alert your men wherever they are in the festive crowd."[90]

To improve border security and control the local population, *Schutzkorps* combatants were assembled.[91] They could move quickly, were loyal,[92] knew the terrain even better than the regular Habsburg army, and were not so obviously bound by years of training or international humanitarian law. In August 1914, the forts of Konjsko and Grab were reinforced and *Schutzkorps* troops operated in that region.[93] They also looted. In 1914 in Taleža, *Schutzkorps* troops stole folk costumes and jewelry for their financial value before setting

---

88 Pachauer, "Austro-Hungarian Fortification," 151.
89 Op. No. 668. "Küstenschutz im Abschnitt Ragusa–Gravosa," October 15, 1914, AT-OeStA/KA FA NFA GAK Balkan-Russland Küsten Rayonskommando Mostar 907, Kriegsarchiv Vienna.
90 Neutra, *Life and Shape*, 109.
91 "Verwendung der freiwillig Einrückenden," Res. No. 31, Trebinje, August 3, 1914, AT-OeStA/KA FA NFA (Trebinje 50), Kriegsarchiv Vienna.
92 "Mobile Reserve," Res. No. 232, October 27, 1914, AT-OeStA/KA FA NFA GAK (Mostar 907), Kriegsarchiv Vienna.
93 Memo dated August 25, 1914, signed by Rudolf Braun, AT-OeStA/KA FA NFA (Trebinje 50), Kriegsarchiv Vienna.

the village on fire.[94] In Velimlje in Montenegro in 1916, Richard Neutra encountered two "refugee" priests from Kosijerevo, who stated that the village where they were temporarily residing had been plundered just the evening before.[95] Recruited and resourced by the state, *Schutzkorps* were not uniformed and could even resemble insurgents. Such was the confusion about their role and actions that at the outbreak of war, army personnel were cautioned not to fire accidentally on the *Schutzkorps* (who would be wearing yellow armbands) and to proceed with "cold-blooded care."[96]

Paramilitary groups consisted of local Muslims and Catholics.[97] This helped to demarcate and exacerbate lines of division between local people, especially in the border regions. Orthodox people became more isolated and vulnerable. Richard Neutra purchased watermelons en route to Lastva in July 1914 from "some peasants sitting at the roadside," unaware that "the sellers and their wares [were] out of bounds and medically contraindicated."[98] Muslim-Orthodox relations were already weakened by decades of violence and reports from the Balkan Wars, so the outbreak of war brought matters to a head: the mosque in Lastva was badly damaged by artillery fire during Montenegrin incursions.[99] On July 30, 1914, one hundred rifles were ordered specifically for the Muslim population in the Lastva area.[100] Muslim looters followed the Habsburg army when it crossed the Drina into Serbia in 1914.[101] In December 1914, Braun recorded that there were five hundred *Schutzkorps* from Tuzla at the Trebinje garrison.[102] There was a crude and ludic element to the war-

94 Popović, *Patnje i žrtve Srba*, 14.
95 "In der vorhergehenden Nacht wurde der Ort von einer Bande geplündert," Neutra, Diary, 1915–16, Richard and Dion Neutra Papers, vol. 4, 31–32.
96 Auf Op. Nr. 43 v. 31/7 Mostar, August 4, 1914, des 6 Armeekmdo, AT-OeStA/KA FA NFA (Trebinje 50), Kriegsarchiv Vienna.
97 "Verwendung der freiwillig Einrückenden," Res. Nr 31, Trebinje, August 3, 1914, AT-OeStA/KA FA NFA (Trebinje 50), Kriegsarchiv Vienna.
98 Neutra, *Life and Shape*, 106.
99 Schalek, "An der montenegrinischen Grenze," December 15, 1915, 4.
100 Memo dated July 30, 1914, signed by Rudolf Braun, AT-OeStA/KA FA NFA (Trebinje 50), Kriegsarchiv Vienna.
101 Rudolphe A. Reiss, *Report upon the Atrocities Committed by the Austro-Hungarian Army during the First Invasion of Serbia* (London: Simpkin, Marshall, Hamilton, Kent, and Co, 1916), 147.
102 Memo dated December 20, 1914, signed by Rudolf Braun, Op. Nr. 558, K. u. K. Festungskommando in Trebinje, AT-OeStA/KA FA NFA (Trebinje 50), Kriegsarchiv Vienna.

time violence: in 1916, Richard Neutra recorded that a sow was led through a Montenegrin village just for fun (*"zum Spaß"*) by his fellow soldiers with a rope tied around each leg.[103] When about forty Orthodox men, including Vidak Parežanin, were taken in 1914 from the border regions to Trebinje,[104] two sows were also put in the wagon with the prisoners.[105] While this may have been intended as a humiliation, alternatively it could have been a seizure of assets, already a widespread garrison practice.

Rural communities felt the impact of violence from both the *Schutzkorps* and regular forces.[106] The small settlement of Taleža, on the edge of Popovo polje, was razed to the ground on August 12, 1914, because the local people were suspected of trying to sabotage the railway line by throwing stones.[107] Fires destroyed rural settlements along the border, echoing the destructive attacks of 1876 and 1882. The Montenegrin advance to Lastva on August 8–9 resulted in fierce fighting which led directly to the immolation of a settlement called Ljeskovac, close to Gornji Orahovac, where the "local population had made common cause with the invader" and their homes had been used to store weapons.[108] These fires were started by the Habsburg soldiers for strategic reasons, but evidently not all the men supported the strategy. As his battalion came to arrest the priest Sava Danilović in Zubci in July 1914, a Ruthene soldier quietly concealed a religious book he had found under his shirt. As the soldiers left, the Ruthene returned the book to the priest's wife with instructions to burn it. The houses in the villages were later torched and the remaining inhabitants forced to flee.[109] A memo sent by Rudolf Braun in late August 1914 suggested that the commanders in Grab and Kon-

---

103 Neutra, Diary, 1915–16, Richard and Dion Neutra Papers, vol. 4, 43.

104 Karl Novottny, "Denkschrift über den Verlauf der gesamtenn Ausrüstung der Festung Trebinje und deren Mitwirkung bei den Kriegserreignissen in den Jahren 1914 bis 1916," ATOeStA/KA NL 417, 1-5, 26, Kriegsarchiv Vienna.

105 Ćorović, *Crna knjiga*, 124.

106 Schachinger, *Die Bosniaken kommen*, 53–56.

107 Ćorović, *Crna knjiga*, 77.

108 Schachinger, *Die Bosniaken kommen*, 54–55.

109 Predrag Puzović, "Stradanje sveštenstva Zahumsko-hercegovačke eparhije tokom Prvog svetskog rat," *Bogoslovlje*, no. 1 (2016): 22–23.

jsko were unwilling to deport the local people "of Serb Orthodox faith" to Montenegro, which he dismissed as a small matter.[110]

In 1914, a scorched-earth strategy of burning frontier settlements extended right along the border regions. In early August, Oskar Potiorek had commanded that "around Avtovac a number of Hercegovinian villages should be set alight."[111] The Russian military attaché in Cetinje, Nikolai Potapov, recorded in his diary for August 11, 1914, that villages around Gacko were reported to have been "attacked and burned every day."[112] The areas targeted correlate with the settlements that were considered the most troublesome in the 1880s.[113] Richard Neutra witnessed a number of fires from a small fort at Kravica near the border, but attributed their origin to the Montenegrins:

We began to climb into the mountains to the left of the valley, and at last reached a desolate, neglected spot, a building with four ancient 70mm field guns standing forlorn and out of order, at the side of an emplacement under construction. We were on an exposed point opposite a savage guerrilla-trained enemy. The night had fallen overhead before we reached the mountaintop, and down in the dark valleys we saw the frontier hamlets go up in fires laid by our Montenegrin adversaries.[114]

A similar "rationale" was applied more cautiously by Antonio Budinich, who thought that Habsburg forces had immolated troublesome settlements: "in the early days of the war, there had been frequent attacks on the railways of Bosnia and Hercegovina by Orthodox revolutionaries: some bombers had been caught and nat-

110 Memo 192/2 dated August 25, 1914, signed by Rudolf Braun, AT-OeStA/KA FA NFA (Trebinje 50), Kriegsarchiv Vienna.
111 Ludwig von Thallóczy noted in his diary on August 17, 1914: "Potiorek telegraphiert, daß man bei Avtovac eine ganze Menge hercegovinischer Dörfer anzünden mußte"; see Grunert, *Glauben im Hinterland*, 523.
112 "Zatim je pozvao mene, Jankovića i Rista Popovića kod sebe u kabinet i upitao Jankovića šta da odgovori Mitru Martinoviću na njegovu molbu da mu se dozvoli da Austrijance kod Gacka nauči pameti, jer oni svakodnevno napadaju i pale pogranična sela," in Raspopović, *N. M. Potapov*, vol. 2: 533.
113 Kraljačić, *Kalajev režim*, 106.
114 Neutra, *Life and Shape*, 106.

urally hanged immediately; *in retaliation*, many villages were set on fire."[115] The Habsburg reserve officer Sekulović led operations over the border which, according to Nikolai Potapov, "mostly pillaged and burned abandoned villages."[116] Habsburg troops had used fire to weaken insurgency before. On Christmas Eve 1878, Jernej Andrejka and his men discovered an encampment which the *"hajduks"* had abandoned. Their boots were encrusted with snow, making a crunching noise as they marched, which gave the *hajduks* a few moments to get away. A fight ensued as night fell and there were fatal injuries. The soldiers stayed in the *hajduk* camp until morning, ate all the roasted lamb and drank their red wine. As they left the following morning, they burned the remaining encampment.[117]

"Actions" were discussed in the press: writing in 1915, Karl Nowak reported on the complete destruction of one Orthodox village in Hercegovina and the evacuation of others.[118] It is very clear, therefore, that the burning down of settlements on the border was well-known within Habsburg circles and not carefully concealed, although perhaps sometimes attributed to enemy combatants. The family of a soldier named Josef Worm published his letter in November 1914: "our artillery worked splendidly and destroyed some Montenegrin houses that burned down, giving us a gruesome spectacle in the evening."[119] War correspondent Alice Schalek noticed burned-out homes close to the Montenegrin frontier in 1915, which she thought had been destroyed "by our own vengeful troops," targeting those residents who had fled to Montenegro at the beginning of the war.[120] Christine Morscher and Ray Galvin have assessed Schalek's "double message" here: on the one hand, she was fiercely

---

115 My emphasis; see Budini, *Le memorie di guerra,* 132.
116 Raspopović, *N. M. Potapov,* vol. 2: 516.
117 "Sveti večer v hajduškem brlogu," Andrejka, *Slovenski fantje,* 275–80.
118 "Einmal im Anfang hatte sich ein serbisches Dorf erhoben. Das Dorf verschwand vom Erdboden. Die serbischen Dörfer wurden überhaupt evakuiert." Nowak, "Bosnische Grenzfahrt," 11.
119 "Unsere Artillerie arbeitete prächtig und zerstörte manche montenegrinischen Häuser, die brannten und abends ein grausiges Bild gaben." Worm, "Auf Feldwache vor der Festung Trebinje," 5.
120 "Diese Häuser sind nicht niedergeschossen, sondern niedergebrannt worden—und zwar von unseren eigenen strafenden Truppen." Alice Schalek, "An der montenegrinischen Grenze: Von Avtovac nach Stepen," *Neue Freie Presse,* December 11, 1915, 2.

against the Montenegrins, but on the other, she knew that war crimes were being committed by Habsburg troops.

> ...her writing style was too richly laced with feeling to provide the military chiefs with the wooden caricature of truth they wanted for their propaganda machine. While her earliest war reporting displays a naïve and unqualified support for her country, she became far more critical of the war in the light of what she saw of it up close as time went by.[121]

Other elements of traditional life were under threat after 1914. Initially churches were deemed suspicious because bells could be used to warn enemy forces.[122] This kind of security policy move was not unique to the Habsburg Monarchy: in Britain, the Defence of the Realm Act, which became law on August 8, 1914, similarly outlawed lighting bonfires, fireworks, trespassing on railway lines, and ringing church bells. Monasteries (including Dobrićevo and Duži) were used by the Habsburg army to store weapons and grain or used as stables. Eventually church bells and copper roofs were confiscated and repurposed.[123] Kosijerevo and Dobrićevo were regarded as particular security risks,[124] especially as they were both located in a relatively open border area.[125] In a raid on Kosijerevo on August 18, 1914, books and manuscripts were burned.[126] *Schutzkorps* leader Abaz Bijedić from Bihovo swam across the Trebišnjica from a point near Mosko with four other men to set fire to the monastery on the opposite bank.[127] An important spiritual site, a human bridge between Hercegovina and the Kingdom of Montenegro, it was an obvious target.[128] On August 13, 1915, Kosijerevo was blown up by

---

[121] Christine Morscher and Ray Galvin, "Alice Schalek's War: The Story of Austria-Hungary's Only Woman War Correspondent in the First World War," online at http://justsolutions. eu/resources/AliceSchaleksWar.pdf, accessed August 18, 2021.

[122] Gumz, *Resurrection and Collapse*, 38.

[123] Grunert, *Glauben im Hinterland*, 525.

[124] "Allgemeine Situation in Montenegro," Memo dated July 29, 1914, AT-OeStA/KA FA NFA (Trebinje 50), Kriegsarchiv Vienna.

[125] Novottny "Erinnerungen," AT-OeStA/KA NL 417: 12, 220–22.

[126] Schachinger, *Die Bosniaken kommen*, 53–56; Korać, *Trebinje: Istorijski pregled* vol. 2, part 2, 360.

[127] Popović, *Patnje i žrtve Srba*, 13.

[128] "Unsere Offiziere," *Pester Lloyd*, November 26, 1915, 9.

FIGURE 26. Kosijerevo Monastery in ruins in 1916. Photo by Antonio Budinich, courtesy of Piero Budinich.

Sapper Captain Guido Györgypál from Csíktaploca. He was subsequently decorated with a cross for military merit for this action.[129] Surveying the ruins of Kosijerevo, Antonio Budinich spoke to an Orthodox monk still living there in a "little house that remained intact ... the monk who guided me among the ruins and pointed out the places where the horrible atrocities had taken place, said to me: '...we have suffered a lot, but deserved it because we have committed horrendous acts.'"[130]

A mixture of fear and euphoria created a new wartime culture. On December 2, 1914, officers from Trebinje including Rudolf Braun and Karl Novottny went to Dubrovnik to celebrate the Emperor's Jubilee in another opportunity for the local population to express their loyalty to the regime. Wearing traditional uniforms, the Dubrovnik *Schutzkorps* paraded through the city with their standard. The streets were lined with older men wearing bowler hats, eager boys in sailor suits, and a few women and girls. A banquet for dig-

---

[129] Emil Woinovich et al, eds., *A mi hőseink*, vol. 1, *Tisztjeink hőstettei a világháborúban* (Budapest: Franklin-Társulat, 1916), 14. Many thanks to József Litkei for finding this reference for me.

[130] Budini, *Le memorie di guerra*, 152.

nitaries was held in the old city and Dr. Renkin, the local governor, toasted the "heroic Croatian people."[131] On the same day back in Trebinje, the garrison orchestra "played pieces by Beethoven, Svendsen, and Grieg, and 1,200 Krone was collected for charity."[132] On December 14, the Dubrovnik-based *Schutzkorps* marched to Trebinje on foot to begin service there.[133]

Within the garrisons, the urban population clustered around the army and individuals threw in their lot with the side they thought would win. Officer Gustav Müller recalled a letter being passed to him "from an unknown friend" in Trebinje in "either September or October 1914" which gave details of the position of Montenegrin forces. This leaked intelligence allowed the trapped 18th Infantry Division to survive a Montenegrin assault and get back across the border to Gacko safely.[134] In Bileća, the capture of a Montenegrin field gun, the so-called "long [Langer] Tom," in September 1914 was greeted with a parade with flags and eager spectators watching at the windows.[135] Women in the town had decked the "victors" with gold-embroidered silk cravats.[136] After the laurel-entwined field gun and soldiers marched through Bileća, "long Tom" was taken to Vienna and displayed on the Schwarzenbergplatz.[137] They were "as proud as Spaniards" as they celebrated, as one officer recalled: only later did he see "long Tom" again in an illustrated newspaper.[138]

Pacifist Richard Bermann had noted (perhaps ironically) in 1915 that the forts along the Montenegrin border "were operating in a Homeric mode since the outbreak of fighting in the war."[139] By the time

---

131 Novottny, "Erinnerungen," AT-OeStA/KA NL 417: 12, 224–45.

132 James Lyon, *Serbia and the Balkan Front, 1914: The Outbreak of the Great War* (London: Bloomsbury, 2015), 221. Trebinje garrison music master Hugo Riedel had already advertised for two first violinists in *Fremdenblatt* on July 2, 1914, 50.

133 "Küstenschutz Verlegung," December 14, 1914, K. u. K. Festungskommando in Trebinje, Op. Nr. 526, AT-OeStA/KA FA NFA (Trebinje 50), Kriegsarchiv Vienna.

134 Gustav Müller, "Spionage in der alten Monarchie," *Freie Stimmen*, April 2, 1935, 5.

135 "Ob mejni boji proti Črnogorcem," *Štajerc*, September 20, 1914, 3.

136 "Offizielle Karte für Rotes Kreuz, Kriegshilfs-Büro des k.k. Ministeriums des Innern," in Branko Dželetović, *Bileća kroz ratove i događaje u XX vijeku* (Bileća: Srpsko prosvijetno i kulturno društvo "Prosvjeta," 2004), 66.

137 Schalek, "An der montenegrinischen Grenze," December 15, 1915, 3.

138 "Der Entsatz bei Bilek: Skizzen aus dem Tagebuche eines Offizieres," *Fremden-Blatt*, April 23, 1915, 6.

139 Bermann, *Die Fahrt auf dem Katarakt*, 151.

FIGURE 27. "Long Tom," captured in Bileća in the first weeks of the war. Muzej Hercegovine, Trebinje.

he arrived in Bileća at the end of 1915, the female population had been evacuated, relocated to safer places.[140] War correspondent Karl-Hans Strobl was also posted close to Vardar in the early years of the conflict, where he wrote for the newspaper *Fremden-Blatt*. In his evocative short story "Die Bogumilenstein,"[141] first published in 1917, the motifs of dread and uncertainty in the border region were woven through, including military life, fear of irregular troops,[142] the spirit life of the ancient battle grounds,[143] ancient gravestones,[144] lost empires, and latent hostility to the *Švabe*.[145]

War had an immediate impact on the urban space in Trebinje as Rudolf Braun ordered gallows to be erected in the center of the city.

---

[140] Richard A. Bermann writing as Arnold Höllriegel, "Der Krieg im Steinmeer," *Tagliches Cincinnatier Volksblatt*, December 15, 1915, 8.

[141] Karl-Hans Strobl, *Lemuria: Seltsame Geschichten* (Munich: Heliakon, 2022), 337–43.

[142] Strobl used the word *Streifuni*, which appears to be a Germanization of the Bosnian word *Štrafuni* (itself a version of *Streifkorps*).

[143] Presumably this represented nearby Vučji Do, the scene of the devastating battle in 1876. In Strobl's short story, the battlefield corpses are female.

[144] The Bogumilenstein that comes to life in the story represented the white marble gravestones (*stećci*), commonly found in the region.

[145] On Strobl, see Clemens Ruthner, *Habsburgs "Dark Continent": Postkoloniale Lektüren zur österreichischen Literatur und Kultur im langen 19. Jahrhundert* (Tübingen: Narr Francke Attempto, 2018), 300.

Once again, the Habsburg military created a stark differentiation between the garrison and its rural hinterland. Across Bosnia and Hercegovina, political surveillance of local people was regularly undertaken and there were further trials.[146] In December 1914, a group of Trebinje students who were studying in Sarajevo, as well as several students still in their home city, were brought to court for sedition.[147] Vaso Milišić from Trebinje was shot in Dubrovnik on April 10, 1915, for incitement of hatred against the monarchy.[148] Although the Trebinje garrison complex never came as close to a siege as Przemyśl on the Eastern Front, the dominance of a crude kind of military culture, intermixed with the arbitrariness of wartime justice, certainly took hold. Despite the visibility of the executed people, garrison staff continued to live and eat in comfort. In late 1915, Richard Bermann was posted to Hercegovina but lost his appetite at the prospect of a banquet:

> As we war correspondents drove into ... Trebinje to reach the commander's house, we inquired, to whom we had to report. A non-commissioned officer told us ... "You cannot miss the house because there is a large gallows in front of it." ... To my horror, twenty-one Serbian men and women had been hanged upon it as a warning to the locals. Inside the house, a welcome meal [*Festmahl*] had been arranged ... but it did not taste good to me.[149]

For more than a millennium in Europe, the visible sight of gallows had marked out the authority of the state and the city against the surrounding countryside. They were usually located in open spaces to limit any chance of ambush and rescue: in the Ragusan Republic the gallows (*vješalima*) were close to Gradac, and there were gallows at Arslanagić most during the Ottoman era. In Southeastern Europe, especially close to imperial borders, the public execu-

---

146 Milorad Ekmečić, "Žalosna baština iz godine 1914: Političke namjene sudskih procesa u Bosni i Hercegovini za vrijeme prvog svjetskog rata," in *Veleizdajnički proces u Banjaluci*, ed. Galib Šljivo (Banja Luka: Institut za istoriju, 1987), 13–41.
147 Sivrić, "Radnički pokret u Trebinju," 111.
148 Ćorović, *Crna knjiga*, 158.
149 Bermann, *Die Fahrt auf dem Katarakt*, 151.

tion of a bandit or *hajduk*, many of whom were trying to avoid military service or arbitrary treatment, reinforced the power of urban government. The Habsburg state had regularly displayed the bodies of nationalists who had defied it, especially in the early days of the reign of Franz Joseph. In 1849, as the recently crowned monarch put his stamp on the realm, thirteen rebel Hungarian generals were hanged in Arad:[150] they were executed on rows of wooden pillars, similar in design to those found in Trebinje. In 1852, the former priest and nationalist Enrico Tazzioli had been ritually defrocked before he was hanged on the city walls at Belfiore, outside Mantua. The Habsburg Monarchy was not alone in demonstrating its real political vulnerability through excessive violence. The hubris of the British Empire in India from 1856–58, in response to the mutinies among the Santal people and the Sepoys in the army, probably damaged the state much more than the fear inspired by the retribution. Mass shootings in villages were reported and images of public hangings were circulated as a reminder of the atrocities.[151]

Whereas the executions in Arad and Mantua were carried out beyond the city gates, in Trebinje the central position of the gallows shocked visitors. Arriving there in 1916, Fritz Telmann hinted at the dissonance: "a line of gallows, six in a row, neatly aligned."[152] On February 19, 1916, nine people aged between forty-five and sixty-six had been hanged in Trebinje, adding to the dozens already executed.[153] Hanging had the function of stripping its victim of their dignity and was undertaken in public to shame, humiliate, and deter. This strategy was employed in 1869, when men from Risan who had dared to defy the state were hanged in public.[154] And the full meaning of this dishonor was not lost on local people. As one newspaper

---

150 "It was intended to be humiliating." Rady, *Habsburgs*, 254–55.
151 Felice Beato, born a Habsburg subject in Venice in 1832, took a stark photograph of a public hanging of rebels in Northern India which was frequently reproduced in later publications; see Akshaya Tankha and Rahaab Allana, "Photographs of the Aftermath, 1857," *India International Centre Quarterly* 34, no. 1 (2007): 24.
152 "eine Allee von Galgen: je sechs in einer Reihe, säuberlich ausgerichtet." Fritz Telmann, "Feldgerichtserinnerungen," *Prager Tagblatt*, September 7, 1924, 4. This figure of six gallows was also given by Ćorović, *Crna knjiga*, 123.
153 "Noch immer die Selbstbesudlung," *Wiener Neueste Nachrichten*, September 22, 1919, 4.
154 "Der Aufstand in Dalmatien, Korrespondenten-Bericht vom 13. November 1869 (aus Cattaro)," *Neue Freie Presse*, November 20, 1869, 3. See also Grandits, *End of Ottoman Rule*, 48.

FIGURE 28. Gallows and crowds of soldiers in Trebinje in August 1914. Wikimedia Commons.

reported in 1882 about the men of Krivošije: "They are not afraid of the bullet because it is not shameful for them to be shot; they fear the gallows more, for it is shameful to be hanged."[155] The fact that the executions were rapid and summary in Trebinje, despite Karl Novottny's emphasis on their legality, and that the hangings took place in public, suggests they were primarily designed to scare the remaining local population.[156]

Bodies of people condemned by the state had begun to disappear slowly from European landscapes and cityscapes as part of a gradual movement that preceded the abolition of the death penalty in almost all the states on the continent of Europe. Public executions had also become less frequent in the Habsburg Monarchy by the twentieth century, but the shock, anger, and opportunity structure that opened up in 1914 took the state back to its stark repressiveness, thereby canceling out one of the most fundamental achievements of the Enlightenment.[157] Hanging remained the standard form of

155 "Aus der Crivoscie," *Innsbrucker Nachrichten*, March 8, 1882, 816.
156 Novottny, "Erinnerungen," AT-OeStA/KA NL 417: 12, 26.
157 On Habsburg retributive public violence, see Vanda Wilcox, "The Execution of Cesare Battisti: Loyalty, Citizenship and Empire in the Trentino in World War I," in *1916 in Global Context: An Anti-Imperial Moment*, ed. Enrico Dal Lago, Róisín Healy, and Gearóid Barry (London: Routledge, 2017), 173–87.

legal execution in the Habsburg Monarchy in 1914, but could only be inflicted on those over twenty: Danilo Ilić and Veljko Čubrilović were hanged after the assassination of Franz Ferdinand, while Gavrilo Princip and Nedeljko Čabrinović were imprisoned. When Rudolf Braun signed the death penalty in Trebinje for a young Orthodox man who was eighteen in August 1914, he sidestepped established Habsburg law for the sake of wartime contingency.[158] According to local methods, hanging was a very swift procedure because of the use of a device intermediate between the garrote and traditional gallows. Furthermore, only a close examination of a corpse could determine whether the act was self-inflicted or not. In Trebinje, the public hangings drew in crowds that are visible in the surviving photographs. There was spitting and shouting at the Orthodox people brought to Trebinje for trial, accompanied by a loud drumroll.[159] Elsewhere there was crowd participation: Risto Bjeletić from Sutorina was imprisoned in Bileća in the summer of 1914 and then transported to Arad in January the following year. As he left the garrison prison, he was cursed, stoned, had his beard pulled, and was spat at by the assembled crowd.[160]

Defiance by prisoners was noted by observers: Rade Vučković from Bogojević Selo was executed in August 1914 and was stabbed with bayonets, but shouted out: "I am not sorry I'm dying, but I am sorry I will not witness the retribution!"[161] An elderly priest is reported to have sung Serb popular songs "in a raucous [or hoarse] voice" on his route from the prison to the scaffold.[162] Stevan Pravica was present to give the last rites to the priest Vidak Parežanin; the body was buried "in the vicinity" of the Toplivsko cemetery after the priest's execution.[163] Like the insurgent Luka Sjenić, it seems that the condemned were also deliberately dumped in the city's public waste disposal to further dishonor their bodies in 1914, at least

158 Parežanin, *Die Attentäter*, 144.
159 Ćorović, *Crna knjiga*, 123.
160 Puzović, "Stradanje sveštenstva Zahumsko-hercegovačke Eparhije," 30.
161 Popović, *Patnje i žrtve Srba*, 21.
162 "d'une voix rauque"; Pierre de Lanux and Milan Toplitza, "L'Autriche-Hongrie: en guerre contre ses sujets," *La Revue hebdomadaire*, September 24, 1915, 63. This was probably Vidak Parežanin.
163 Grunert, *Glauben im Hinterland*, 517.

according to Vidak's son Ratko Parežanin.[164] In the circumstances, it is probable that most people were scared rather than defiant. Stevan Pravica wrote about the mood among the Orthodox in and around Trebinje after the tumultuous first weeks of the war: "in this situation, it is impossible to celebrate church services in the surrounding small chapels, but also because the district administration ... has forbidden holding church meetings in the open air and the chapels barely have room for twenty people. The people who came would be weak in any case, as they are afraid because of the many executions. Here twenty-four have been hanged so far."[165] Men from the Bay of Kotor were also regarded as a security risk, while the vale of Sutorina remained part of Hercegovina and therefore under the direct military control of the Trebinje garrison. In Španjola, Milan Srzentić and Filip Hadžija were executed on September 17, 1914.[166] A system of collective punishment was continued in occupied Montenegro between 1916 and the end of the war: men from Hercegovina who had fled across the border in 1914 were hanged in Trebinje.[167] After Radomir Vešović escaped from arrest by killing a Habsburg official, "half the inhabitants of his hometown of Kolašin were executed or jailed."[168]

There was also some more silent or passive resistance to Habsburg rule. In the absence perhaps of a common language, many felt they saw mistrust in the eyes of local people of Hercegovina.[169] This was not a new accusation; staring had been a common complaint before the war. Antonio Budinich was put in charge of defiant Orthodox prisoners:

I ... had these hostages in my charge many times—the silent people, they called them—who boarded the train car with chains on their hands and feet: they were all Orthodox, proud types who displayed great indifference.... I remember one ... with a very in-

---

164 Parežanin, *Die Attentäter*, 144. This was also the fate of the bodies of those who had committed suicide in eighteenth-century France; see Hunt, *Inventing Human Rights*, 74.
165 Grunert, *Glauben im Hinterland*, 526.
166 Tepavčević, "Boka Kotorska," 1.
167 Ćorović, *Crna knjiga*, 158.
168 Reber, "The Experience of Borders," 204.
169 "Tagebuch eines Mobilisirten," 5.

telligent face, and he spoke a little Italian; we almost became friends and often had long conversations. But neither he nor I ventured to discuss politics openly: it would have been too dangerous for him and could have cost him his life, but we understood each other with veiled words and looks.[170]

The cruelty and dissonance of the hangings clearly weighed heavily on many combatants, and this may account for the photographs that were taken by soldiers of the executions, although it might also be interpreted in terms of vicarious brutality or curiosity.[171] The publication of *Dei delitti e delle pene* (On crimes and punishments) by Milanese jurist Cesare Beccaria in 1765, himself a subject of the Habsburg crown, created a powerful language of rational dissent against the death penalty and spectacle of the public execution. Although this dissenting idea grew rapidly, it remained a minority faith, competing with a much older belief in physical punishment, especially toward traitors, however defined. The Enlightenment project was fragile in 1914 and it competed with archaic worldviews which had resurfaced in the name of national or racial pride. Rudolf Braun's decision to display hanged bodies in the center of Trebinje while he invited guests to dine with him harked back to older values; they were a reminder that conquest involved complete bodily subjection, disrespect, scorn, and triumphalism. In some respects, the public executions were a continuation of the harshness and inflexibility of a military regime that had forced its men to march in baking heat in 1903, or had bayoneted them on the spot in 1878.[172] Even so, Braun's orders look like a radical break from military severity, turning the urban space into a charnel house. Furthermore, Braun was always clear that command responsibility in the Trebinje garrison rested with him.[173]

---

170 Budini, *Le memorie di guerra*, 38.
171 Anton Holzer, *Das Lächeln der Henker: Der unbekannte Krieg gegen die Zivilbevölkerung 1914–1918* (Darmstadt: Primus, 2014), 10.
172 Charles St John to the Marquis of Salisbury, Dubrovnik, September 4, 1878. FO7 940, National Archives, London.
173 "Ganz abgesehen davon kann es in einer Festung nur <u>einen</u> Komandanten, aber nicht deren zwei geben." Rudolf Braun, Memo 291 to the Gendarmariekorpskommando Sara-

There is a sadness in many of the contemporary sources because emerging humanitarian views also coincided with the older religious admonitions against killing, which reinforced the essential dissonance of the act. Dione Neutra recalled her husband's hatred of the retribution against local people in an interview conducted in 1978 after his death: "He talked about the people he met [in Trebinje] ... how his commander was a sadist, who was able to play out his sadistic tendencies.... He was just a small-town clerk in Vienna,[174] but then he became his commander ... apparently he [i.e., Neutra] felt a great feeling of injustice about things, executions which he commandeered [sic] of the native population and so on."[175] Private disquiet about the executions seems to have been widespread.[176] Protests leaked out while the war was still being fought and evidence of crimes was collected. The Serbian newspaper *Politika* published a front-page article on the gallows in Zubci in September 1915.[177] The same month, the Paris-based journal *La Revue hebdomadaire* carried a story about the mass hangings in Trebinje, allegedly leaked by a Czech driver.[178] A December 1917 newspaper report in *Böhmerwald Volksbote* struck a critical note: "immediately after the outbreak of war, dungeons were placed in the fortress area of Trebinje and filled with respected citizens. At the time of their incarceration, they were threatened with execution.... The main reason for this was the orders of General Braun, who is still on active service. The district captain, who stood up for the victims, had to be transferred from Trebinje immediately."[179] In 1917, the Dalmatian writer Ante Tresić-Pavičić made a speech in the *Reichsrat* listing the eighty-two Ortho-

---

jevo, October 14, 1914, AT-OeStA/KA FA NFA (Trebinje 50), Kriegsarchiv Vienna. Underlined in the original.

174 This probably refers to Captain Endlicher, who had worked for the fire brigade in Vienna before the war; see Neutra, *Life and Shape*, 106–7.

175 "To tell the truth: oral history transcript," BANC MSS 84/85 c, 33.

176 Polish minister Leon Biliński (1846–1923) noted the "whole alleys of gallows in Trebinje" and the demand from the bereaved relatives for recompense, comparing their predicament with the execution of Poles in Galicia, see his translated memoir, *Bosna i Hercegovina u Uspomenama Leona Bilińskog* (Sarajevo: Institut za istoriju, 2004), 100.

177 "Vešala u Zupcima," *Politika*, September 8, 1915, 1.

178 Pierre de Lanux and Milan Toplitza, "L'Autriche-Hongrie: En guerre contre ses sujets," *La Revue hebdomadaire*, September 24, 1915, 63.

179 Presumably this captain was Michał Potuczko; see "Die Sünden des Militarismus," *Böhmerwald Volksbote*, December 23, 1917, 1.

dox hanged at Zubci, 103 in Trebinje, as well as the deaths in the internment camp at Arad: "the whole of the border area with Serbia and Montenegro, like the Palatinate under Louis XIV, was almost depopulated and turned into a desert."[180] The speech was reported in the media far beyond Central Europe.[181] The historian Vladimir Ćorović recounted how he collected photographic evidence of war crimes in 1918 and smuggled them out to Paris via Prague.[182] The Habsburg army "outlived the empire which it had been defending," but only just.[183] It was only in the last days of the Habsburg Monarchy in 1918 that the Trebinje gallows were hastily removed. Without the actual wooden structures, it would have been harder to string up any remaining Habsburg soldiers spontaneously. Perhaps recalling the fate of Hasan in the Biblical book of Esther, who was hanged high up on a structure of his own devising, a "clever Viennese" officer had the gallows dismantled, lest the victors be tempted to hang them from it in retribution.[184] The Trebinje gallows became part of an emerging narrative that condemned the old monarchy for its violence. In 1929, a photograph of Bosnian Governor Stjepan Sarkotić standing in front of hanged men on a row of gallows was reprinted in the Viennese newspaper *Der Kuckuck*.[185] Rebecca West was shown photographs of the hanged when she visited Trebinje in 1937: "Most of them wore an expression of astonishment. I remember one priest who was being led through a double line of gibbets to his own; he looked not horrified but simply surprised. That indeed was natural enough, for surprise must have been the predominant emotion of most of the victims."[186]

---

180 "beinahe entvölkert und in eine Wüste verwandelt." Holzer, *Das Lächeln der Henker*, 71–72. Ante Tresić-Pavičić (1867–1949), originally from Hvar, was a writer known for travel and historic themes.

181 "Slav Deputy details Austrian Atrocities: Serb Civilians Made to Dig Own Graves and Lie in Them to be Killed," *New York Times*, December 22, 1917, 3.

182 Ćorović, *Crna knjiga*, 5.

183 Norman Stone, "Army and Society in the Habsburg Monarchy," *Past and Present*, no. 33 (1966): 95.

184 Telmann, "Die letzen Tage von Trebinje," 1.

185 "Die Bravos der Frau Zita: Politik der Deklallierten," *Der Kuckuck*, December 1, 1929, 3.

186 Rebecca West, *Black Lamb and Grey Falcon: A Journey through Yugoslavia* (Edinburgh: Cannongate, 1993), 375.

In addition to execution, villages were swiftly cleared as a means of controlling the frontier.[187] In military communications, this was presented as contingency: Rudolf Braun considered that the "evacuation of all settlements east of the line Bileća-Trebinje-Grab of all their inhabitants would be best to preserve calm and order."[188] In demographic terms, this was more significant than public executions and the most significant depopulation since the turbulence in 1875-6, 1878, and 1882. By early 1916, thousands of Orthodox men, women, and children had been sentenced to expulsion and had their property expropriated.[189] The evacuations were accompanied by violence. In Zubci, Vasa Đurić was beaten and robbed of his watch and money, before being sent to Arad.[190] In the Neckenmarkt (Sopronnyék) internment camp, over sixty non-combatants from five months to eighty years old died from "Bezirk Trebinje" alone between June 4, 1916, and February 1, 1918.[191] The *Sterbregister* records the death of individuals from the same extended family, including the infant Vida Vukalović on June 4, 1916, twelve-year-old Jovana Vukalović on June 24, 1916, and eight-year-old Avdja Vukalović on July 23, 1916.[192] In August 1914, Pero Zurić, Obren Sredanović, Vujoš Vukalović, Mato and Rade Vukalović, Rade Vučković, and Vidak Simović, all from Bogojević Selo, were executed in Trebinje.[193] The following year, on November 29, 1915, Ahmet Cevo stated that he had killed seventeen

---

187 Dželetović, *Bileća kroz ratove*, 63–82.
188 "durch die Räumung aller Ortschaften östlich der Linie BILECA-TREBINJE-GRAB von der Bevölkerung, wohl am besten für die Aufrechthaltung der Ruhe und Ordnung gesorgt." Rudolf Braun, Memo 291 to the Gendarmariekorpskommando Sarajevo, October 14, 1914, AT-OeStA/KA FA NFA (Trebinje 50), Kriegsarchiv Vienna.
189 Wayne Vucinich considered the fate of his relatives: "When World War I broke out and Austria-Hungary invaded Serbia in 1914, families in Bileća Rudine were faced with special hardships. At the beginning of the war, Austria-Hungary ordered frontier villagers to withdraw into the interior." Vucinich, "Transhumance," 69.
190 Ćorović, *Crna knjiga*, 127.
191 "Sterbregister des Kriegsgefangenenlagers in Sopronyek (2/7/1916–18/4/1918)," Burgenländisches Landesarchiv, Eisenstadt. On this point, see Nenad Lukić and Walter Mentzel, "Popis umrlih Srba u logoru Šopronjek/Nekenmarkt 1915–1918. godine," *Godišnjak za istraživanje genocida* 8 (2016), 15–16.
192 "Sterbregister des Kriegsgefangenenlagers in Sopronyek (2/7/1916–18/4/1918)," Burgenländisches Landesarchiv, Eisenstadt.
193 Ćorović, *Crna knjiga*, 127.

people from Bogojević Selo. This was carried out on the orders of the officer Radovan Stankov, who was Orthodox by religion.[194]

Between the mid-nineteenth century and the end of World War One, the populations of Korjenići, including the Banjani and Zubčani, were devastated by a series of assaults on the traditional economy and their ancient way of life.[195] The Vukalović family and near relatives in their rebel nest of Bogojević Selo were decimated during the First World War, in a series of actions designed to eliminate them and their children. Although people from these border settlements were in a position to offer resistance to the state before the spring of 1882, they had not posed a viable threat to Habsburg power for more than thirty years. Mark Levene's theory about violent "psychosis" against transgressive minorities seems particularly applicable here.[196] Although extended families from Bogojević Selo might have seemed threatening to army commanders looking back to their last combat experience around Mount Orjen in 1882, a generation later they were far less powerful. Nonetheless, the specter of their threat was still potent.[197] Although the Montenegrins and any local supporters could mount raids and terror attacks, they were not in a position to make significant long-term territorial gains. Rudolf Braun gave a short account of the fighting and the losses the garrison had sustained by November 1915, which included five officers dead, fifteen wounded, a hundred soldiers dead, three hundred and thirty-one wounded, and sixty-one missing. He also listed the garrison's prisoners of war which included one officer, fifty-two men, and two insurgents.[198]

How, then, can we account for the persecution of villagers along the Montenegrin border in 1914 and 1915? If the Trebinje garrison was militarily secure during these years, it may be necessary to look

---

194 "Im Dorfe Bogojević habe ich auf Befehl des Hptm. Stankov 17 Bauern welche anscheinend nach Montenegro fluchten und ihr Vieh mitreiben wolten, teils ich selbst niedergemacht, teils durch meine Leute niedermachen lasse." Ćorović, *Crna knjiga*, 126.

195 Milan Šantić, "Kraj koji ima bogatu prošlost a tešku sadašnjicu," *Politika*, December 15, 1935, 13.

196 Levene, *The Crisis of Genocide*, vol. 1: 90.

197 This case study has parallels with the perceived threat of the *franc-tireurs* in Belgium in 1914; see John N. Horne and Alan Kramer, *German Atrocities, 1914: A History of Denial* (New Haven, CT: Yale University Press, 2001).

198 Rudolf Braun, "Kurzer Gefechtsbericht über die Kämpfe im November 1915 bei Trebinje," NL Karl Novottny AT-OeStA/KA NL 417, 2, Kriegsarchiv Vienna.

beyond contingency. Among army veterans, a very specific anger existed against Orthodox people: the assassination of Franz Ferdinand in 1914 by pro-Serbian youths gave these officers a chance to settle old scores once and for all. That same year also marked a deterioration of order and standards on other fronts. During the Drina Campaign in mid-August 1914 when Serbia was attacked, Oskar Potiorek had commanded his troops to "wipe out villages that harbored *komitadjis* and publicize the event,"[199] an order that led directly to widespread atrocities against civilians in the Mačva region. Writing about 1882 some forty-five years later, Stjepan Sarkotić reflected upon how leniently the Orthodox insurgents had been treated: "at that time, out of humanitarian considerations, *no one among us* thought of a confinement or even of a deportation of the male population into the interior of the country."[200] By 1914, much more drastic measures came to be taken.

From Victory to Defeat, 1915–1918

Oskar Potiorek was encouraged to step down as Bosnian Governor three days before Catholic Christmas in 1914, after the military defeats at Cer Planina and Kolubara in Serbia. His position was filled by Stjepan Sarkotić, who visited Trebinje within weeks of his appointment.[201] Posted to the city as a young soldier in the days of Djuro Babić, he knew the region well.[202] Sarkotić already knew Rudolf Braun,[203] and while in the city, he enjoyed a reception at the Hotel Naglić,[204] for so long a "strategic asset"[205] of the regime and a patriotic safe space. By

199 Wawro, *A Mad Catastrophe*, 142. "*Komitadjis*" was a commonplace term for Serb insurgents, especially after 1912.
200 My emphasis. Sarkotić, "Aus meinen Erinnerungen," 2–3. Elsewhere, Sarkotić commented on the leniency (*Milde*) of Habsburg military law; Florer, "Kriegsaufzeichnungen," AT-OeStA/KA NL 654 (B), Kriegsarchiv Vienna, 626.
201 "Der bosnische Landeschef in der Herzegowina," *Villacher Zeitung*, January 17, 1915, 3.
202 Sarkotić, "Aus meinen Erinnerungen," 2–3.
203 Željko Karaula, "Posljednja crnogorska bitka—Dnevnik austro-ugarskog generala Stjepana Sarkotića," *Montenegrin Journal for Social Sciences* 3, no. 1 (2019): 133.
204 Telmann, "Die letzen Tage von Trebinje," 1.
205 Kenneth Morrison, *Sarajevo's Holiday Inn on the Frontline of Politics and War* (London: Palgrave Macmillan, 2016), 15.

1915, the Habsburg Monarchy was in a challenging position. The Montenegrins had been successfully contained, but elsewhere the Habsburg army was experiencing mixed fortunes. On the Eastern Front, Przemyśl was besieged for months before its surrender to the Imperial Russian forces in March 1915, and over 100,000 Habsburg soldiers were taken as prisoners of war. The Russians had encircled the fortress in November 1914 and waited for the trapped population to run out of supplies. Possible traitors and Ruthenian peasants who were suspected of being pro-Russian were executed.[206] The defeat, which occurred despite many efforts to relieve the fortress, caused great soul-searching among Habsburg subjects and local acts of revenge. Cvijeta Pažin, originally from Zubci, was denounced by a forestry worker named Omeragić from Čičevo, who overheard her singing in her cow pen when the Russians captured Przemyśl. She was hanged for this offense.[207] Montenegrins could be heard over the border with Hercegovina celebrating the fall of Przemyśl with shouts of "živio."[208] The idea that Montenegrins celebrated Habsburg misfortune or taunted their neighbors was an old accusation that predated the war and highlighted the problems caused by a border that was intimate and approximate in so many places. One soldier stationed on the border near Bileća recalled that a Montenegrin officer had said to him in 1898: "Why has great Austria built so many fortifications against little Montenegro? Are you perhaps afraid of us?"[209]

Individuals from Hercegovina fled to Montenegro and Serbia; the *Bosnische Post* published lists of people who had forfeited their status as Habsburg subjects, which was republished in Britain by R. W. Seton-Watson.[210] Most of the confiscated land was close to Bileća and Trebinje, and these areas contained the largest number of volunteers in the Serbian and Montenegrin armies.[211] After severe bombing,

---

206 Alexander Watson, *The Fortress: The Great Siege of Przemyśl* (London: Allen Lane, 2019), 46.
207 Popović, *Patnje i žrtve Srba*, 23–24.
208 Schalek, "An der montenegrinischen Grenze," November 14, 1915, 2.
209 Josef Berger, "Neuer Kurs und Neue Bahnen in Bosnien," *Danzers Armee-Zeitung*, August 1, 1912, 11.
210 R. W. Seton-Watson, "Frightfulness in Bosnia," *Times*, March 30, 1915, 11.
211 Tomislav Kraljačić, "Austrougarski planovi o stvaranju etničkog zida u istočnoj Bosni u Prvom svetskom ratu," *Srbi u BIH*, https://srbiubih.com/austrougarski-planovi-o-stvaranju-etnickog-zida-u-istocnoj-bosni-u-prvom-svjetskom-ratu/ (accessed May 5, 2024).

Belgrade was taken in December 1914, but subsequently lost by the Habsburg forces and only retaken in October 1915. The Serbian army retreated to the Ionian Islands, and the Habsburg Monarchy took over Serbia imposing a new type of rule in the country. This victory allowed the Habsburg Monarchy to focus on conquering Montenegro. Italy had initially remained neutral against the Habsburg Monarchy in 1914, in return for a guarantee of no direct attack on Montenegrin territory and further assurance of its own security in the Adriatic.[212] When Italy entered the war in May 1915, Nikola's small kingdom became extremely vulnerable. The Montenegrins had been using Italian-made artillery, which depended on uninterrupted Adriatic shipping.[213] By November 1915, there was general confidence in the Trebinje garrison that their own troops controlled the entire border region.[214] When Montenegro was finally invaded in January 1916, the victorious attack was launched from the network of garrisons in Hercegovina, including Trebinje, where the lights could go back on after more than a year of nighttime curfews.[215] Montenegro was subdued in just over a week and the task of imposing Habsburg "civilization" then commenced. Civilians and potential combatants were punished and war crimes were committed. Prisoners were taken back to the Trebinje garrison to be interrogated. Richard Neutra recorded sexual abuse by troops against Montenegrin women and specifically mentioned that this was carried out by "lads from Dalmatia, Bosnia, and Hercegovina."[216]

Antonio Budinich recalled that the punishment of Orthodox men was not simply a military tactic because it carried on even after the swift victory against Montenegro:

---

212 "Italien hat Neutralität erklärt," Telegramme August 5, op. Nr 107, AT-OeStA/KA FA NFA (Trebinje 50), Kriegsarchiv Vienna.
213 Johann F., "Über die letzten Kämpfe mit den Montenegrinern und die Zurückweisung ihrer Einfälle," *Österreichische Volkszeitung*, November 25, 1914, 7.
214 Rudolf Braun, "Festungskommando Nr. 119 Trebinje, am 16. November 1915," NL Karl Novottny AT-OeStA/KA NL 417: 2, Kriegsarchiv Vienna.
215 Worm, "Auf Feldwache vor der Festung Trebinje," 5.
216 "Vom Sattel an werfen wir das Geschütz förmlich abwärts. Zum Vergnügen der Grenzjäger, in die sich jedes Mädel gern verlieben könnte. Jungen aus Dalmatien, Bosnien und Herzegowina," Neutra, Diary, 1915–16, Richard and Dion Neutra Papers, vol. 4, 43.

FIGURE 29. Antonio Budinich as a Habsburg soldier. Courtesy of Piero Budinich.

In the month of February [1916] an espionage trial took place and three Hercegovinians from near Bileća were sentenced to death for high treason.... Since the war with Montenegro was over, it was generally assumed that they would be pardoned. Instead [Emil] Stettner confirmed the sentence and, one afternoon in mid-February, at 2:00pm, the three wretches were hanged in a field a few meters from the town. I did not want to go and witness the horrible scene, but to my surprise many other officers did ... toward sunset, passing that way by chance, I happened to see the unfortunate men who still hung from the gallows, their bodies rocked by the wind: heroes of an idea, killed by the ruthless reason of state![217]

Hunger had started to have an impact on the Trebinje region by the fall of 1916, not least because the pastoral year and transhumance had been disrupted.[218] A community that had once lived in a semi-

217 Budini, *Le memorie di guerra*, 132.
218 Vucinich, "Transhumance," 71.

autonomous manner while supplying the markets with food had
been decimated by persecution and imprisonment. Requisitions had
started in 1914 and involved large numbers of animals being seized
from settlements along the border with Montenegro. Chaos ensued
as the cattle were moved. A telegram sent from the Trebinje garrison to Herceg Novi recorded that four hundred oxen were driven
to Trebinje on both August 1 and 2, 1914, and another two hundred
on August 3. The division responsible requested that cattle be taken
"daily" to the Dalmatian border.[219] Another telegram sent to the
Trebinje garrison from Gacko on August 21 stated that their troops
had "confiscated all livestock" from the local insurgent population
and intended to deport people to Montenegro. Presented as a legitimate financial compensation to the regime, they claimed that this
process had been already "radically applied" (*"radikal beantragt"*).[220] In
Trebinje, smaller livestock were packed into the city walls, but these
animals had to be fed. Garrison staff suggested that cattle should be
released into the city's parks, which became a wasteland within a few
hours.[221] Rudolf Braun complained about the excessive number of
animals within the Trebinje garrison, requesting that small cattle,
goats, and sheep be moved to other locations.[222]

Requisitions were carried out by the garrison troops both within
Hercegovina and after the invasion of Montenegro. Notes were
handed out to those individuals who had had livestock appropriated.
Richard Neutra recalled how a young girl wept when his battalion
took her family's cattle; he was also ashamed because Captain Endlicher told the officers not to issue compensatory notes if they could
avoid doing so.[223] This was emphatically not the first time that
Habsburg troops had forced people in occupation zones to give up
provisions in exchange for promissory notes or even for nothing.
In 1878, troops had confiscated large numbers of livestock, includ-

219 Telegramme Op. Nr. 65/1 Festungskomando Trebinje, undated but circa August 4, 1914, AT-OeStA/KA FA NFA (Trebinje 50), Kriegsarchiv Vienna.
220 "Gendarmerieszugskommando Gacko nach Festungskommando Trebinje," August 21, 1914, AT-OeStA/KA FA NFA (Trebinje 50), Kriegsarchiv Vienna.
221 Popović, *Patnje i žrtve Srba*, 31.
222 Memo dated August 1, 1914, Nr 63/4, written by Rudolf Braun, AT-OeStA/KA FA NFA (Trebinje 50), Kriegsarchiv, Vienna.
223 Neutra, Diary, 1915–16, Richard and Dion Neutra Papers, vol. 4, 26–27.

ing goats and sheep.[224] This usually occurred because Habsburg soldiers were short of funds and plundered to supplement their rations during times of crisis simply because they were hungry, but the August 1914 requisitions exceeded Habsburg severity and led eventually to a regional food crisis. Alice Schalek was always aware of the impact of war on nature and the land.[225] In her series of dispatches from the front, she noted: "In Lastva, there was a viticulture training college and a wine tasting facility before the war. The Montenegrins, driven by their own ideas, destroyed everything and no grape has ripened this year ... you can see the settlements reduced to rubble, the devastated vineyards, the deep hanging clouds and the brown, naked mountain slopes..."[226]

Antonio Budinich kept a pig which he fed with scraps: "part of the meat I ate myself with the officers, and the rest I gave to the sergeants and to the few non-commissioned officers and Christian soldiers, but Muslim soldiers would not have eaten pork even if it meant dying of hunger."[227] Requisitions robbed local people of their means to feed themselves and they were beginning to become more visibly discontented with the regime.[228] Orthodox priest Stevan Pravica recalled this terrible time: "In 1916 I had to bury four hundred and seventy-one children, of whom over four hundred died of hunger; your heart is oppressed, but you cannot help them."[229] The health of all of the population declined sharply during the second half of the war. Food parcels containing jam, meat, and sugar were sent home by Antonio Budinich during the war: the army was well-provisioned until the summer of 1918, but he was aware that there were food shortages among civilians. Budinich paid "homage to the exemplary regularity and accuracy of the Austrian postal service because a parcel was never lost or tampered with," adding that the in-

---

224 Andrejka, *Slovenski fantje*, 255.
225 Elisabeth Klaus, "Rhetoriken über Krieg: Karl Kraus gegen Alice Schalek," *Feministische Studien* 26, no. 1 (2008): 70.
226 Schalek, "An der montenegrinischen Grenze," December 15, 1915, 4.
227 Budini, *Le memorie di guerra*, 143–44.
228 Hamdija Kapidžić, *Bosna i Hercegovina u vrijeme austrougarske vladavine: (članci i rasprave)* (Sarajevo: Svjetlost, 1968), 216.
229 Grunert, "The Inner Enemy in Wartime," 272, footnote 77.

FIGURE 30. Elsa Novottny and Adolf Kutzlnigg are standing forward in the center of the crowd at Christmas 1916 at the Garrison Hospital, Trebinje. Kriegsarchiv, Vienna, Austrian State Archives.

dividuals delivering the parcels "must have been suffering from hunger themselves and yet discipline did not break down."[230]

Scientists were mobilized to break the shortages and many saw the opportunity to do research despite the crisis. Karel Absolon was in Krivošije and Grahovo in 1917 and in Gatačko polje the following year, working alongside men in uniform.[231] Camillo Praschniker and Arthur Haberlandt, both army officers, were permitted to carry out a scientific expedition into the newly conquered territories in Montenegro in the summer of 1916.[232] An ethnographer by training, Haberlandt had been wounded twice during his military service in Trebinje, but still produced research work during his fieldwork in 1916.[233] Jiří Daneš, who had written a short monograph on Hercegovina in 1903, was sent back by the army during the war to

---

230 Budini, *Le memorie di guerra*, 54–55.
231 Karel Absolon to Leo Weirather, Brno, October 1, 1922, Collections Leo Weirather, Muséum d'histoire naturelle de Genève.
232 Marchetti, "Austro-Hungarian *Volkskunde* at War," 220.
233 Arthur Haberlandt, "Bericht über die ethnographischen Arbeiten im Rahmen der historisch-ethnographischen Balkanexpedition," *Mitteilungen der Geographischen Gesellschaft in Wien* 59 (1916): 736–42.

investigate organic sediments in caves. This was because nitrogen fertilizers, deemed essential for mass farming, were in very short supply by the second year of the war. The droppings in caves were viewed as a possible alternative chemical source.[234]

The weather did not help morale and in late July 1918, Trebinje was again unbearably hot.[235] By the fall of 1918, serious fraud was committed against the Trebinje garrison by a deserter who went under the name of Böla Obendorfer. Provisions that had been ordered were not delivered.[236] Incipient malnutrition and tuberculosis began to have a deep impact on the health of both soldiers and civilians. As Habsburg power began to falter, other possible centers of power emerged. A Serbian government led by Nikola Pašić was set up in exile and over the next few months, it started to claim a role as the voice for all South Slavs. King Nikola had fled from Montenegro in January 1916, moving eventually to France where he died in 1921; the Petrović dynasty was never restored. In May 1917, the leader of the Slovene People's Party, the Catholic priest Anton Korošec, pressed for greater rights for the monarchy's South Slavs. In July 1917, the Dalmatian politician Ante Trumbić issued the Corfu Declaration, which anticipated the postwar unification of the South Slavs of Serbia, Montenegro, and the Habsburg Monarchy. By January 1918, the American President Woodrow Wilson was expressing support for national autonomy for the peoples of the Habsburg Monarchy. In early 1918, there was a short-lived mutiny in the Bay of Kotor among sailors who were inspired by the Soviets in Petrograd. Although the mutiny was quickly suppressed, and four sailors were shot on February 11, the revolt indicated that the regime was losing ground among servicemen. As they had in 1882, the pathways of Krivošije formed an escape route for some of the mutineers.[237] Serbia was retaken by its army in September 1918 after the collapse of the Bulgarian military regime. The country had been devastated by

---

234 Daniel Hanták, "Jiří Václav Daneš (1880–1928)" (BA thesis, Charles University, Prague, 2013), 10.
235 "Aus dem Hinterland," *Kriegszeitung des A.T.V. Graz*, August 4, 1918, 1235.
236 "Lebensmittelschwindel," *Pester Lloyd*, October 11, 1918, 9.
237 F. Michael Florer, "Kriegsaufzeichnungen," AT-OeStA/KA NL 654 (B), Kriegsarchiv Vienna, 605–6.

the years of occupation and illnesses such as typhus. On October 29, 1918, a new state of Serbs, Croats, and Slovenes was proclaimed. In Bosnia and Hercegovina, the Habsburg Monarchy had its rule terminated gradually between the end of October and mid-November 1918. Emperor Karl relinquished his role at the time of the Armistice of November 11, 1918. Exiles returned to the region from across the Allied territories where they had taken refuge, and the task of reconstruction began.

The Habsburg withdrawal from Hercegovina was generally orderly, in part because of the dire collapse of infrastructure and war fatigue, although it was undoubtedly tumultuous and confusing on a personal level. Jiří Daneš disappeared for several days during the handover to the Serbian Army between November 16 and 18 in Sarajevo: he may have slipped and fallen while walking around Mount Trebević.[238] Trebinje made a swift transition to the new state authorities when an officer named Kutzelnik officially handed over the authority of the city on November 5.[239] Mitar Goranović, himself a former Habsburg officer, took a vow of loyalty to the new Karadjordjević authorities and he and his fellow soldiers took over the Trebinje garrison.[240] The Serbian Army arrived in Trebinje on November 13 (October 31 in the Orthodox calendar) and received a "jubilant reception."[241] Celebrations took place in the Hotel Naglić. The following day, a parade was organized through the streets. Orthodox priests in full vestments walked through the crowds and the remaining political prisoners were released. There were similar celebrations on the streets in Bileća,[242] and the hospital there was blown up.[243] In

---

238 Hanták, "Jiří Václav Daneš," 12.
239 "Note from the Austrian Delegation concerning the return of the Fortress of Trebinje to the Yugo-Slavs to the Secretariat General of the Peace Conference," Paris, June 28, 1920, FO 893/7, National Archives, London. This is likely to have been Adolf Kutzlnigg.
240 Marijan Sivrić, "Osnivanje i rad Kotarskog odbora Narodnog Vijeća z ujedinjenje u Trebinju u Novembru i Decembru 1918. godine," *Tribunia: Prilozi za istoriju, arheologiju, etnologiju, umjetnost i kulturu,* nos. 7–8 (1984): 65–72.
241 "Südslawisches," *Pester Lloyd (Abendblatt),* November 19, 1918, 2; Dragan Bakić, "Transition from Austria-Hungary to Yugoslavia: The Serbian Army's Occupation of Bosnia and Herzegovina in Late 1918," in *Finir la Grande guerre dans les Balkans 1918–1923,* ed. Vojislav G. Pavlović (Belgrade: Institut des Études balkaniques, 2022), 108.
242 Dželetović, *Bileća kroz ratove,* 81–82.
243 Telmann, "Die letzen Tage von Trebinje," 1.

the last months of the war and afterward, banditry was widespread as Montenegrins raided border settlements in Hercegovina and targeted Muslim villagers.[244] Personal property was not returned to departing Habsburg officers.[245] American Red Cross volunteer Henry Rushton Fairclough drove between Bileća and Trebinje in 1919, which he described as "a lonely region infested by *komitadjis*."[246]

In September 1919, the Treaty of St. Germain-en-Laye officially dissolved the Habsburg Monarchy. Many who had served in the Habsburg armies were now a very long distance from their former postings. The new Yugoslav state was free from the burden of reparations which weighed down post-war Austria and post-Trianon Hungary. Initially called the Kingdom of Serbs, Croats, and Slovenes, the regent Aleksandar became king when his father Petar died in 1921. The new state included all of Hercegovina and Montenegro, but some South Slav lands remained under Italian control. War came with a huge cost to all the people of Hercegovina and returning natives found a very different place. Miloš Šaraba, born in 1894, from the village of Turmenti in Zubci, left the region as a young man, but returned from the United States to fight with the Serbian army on the Salonika Front. When he returned to his village, his old home was destroyed, and he was forced to start again from scratch.[247] The reconstruction effort of 1918 was not dissimilar to that of 1878: farms and crops were again devastated.[248] The new Sarajevo authorities expressed deep concern for the nutritional health of the people in Zubci and Korjenići in December 1918 and grain was distributed to

---

244 A report written on January 4 in Mostar for the newly established Karadjordjević Ministry of Defense stated that "Montenegrin raiders came to the counties of Trebinje, Bileća, Gacko, Nevesinje, Ljubinje, and plundered all Muslim villages." Quoted in Bakić, "Transition from Austria-Hungary to Yugoslavia," 125.

245 "Austro-Hungarian ex-officers should be able to take their effects away from Trebinje. In spite of this decision ... it has not been possible, up to now, to take back and transport ... the effects in question." "Note from the Austrian Delegation," Paris, June 28, 1920, FO 893/7, National Archives, London.

246 Henry Rushton Fairclough, *Warming Both Hands: The Autobiography of Henry Rushton Fairclough, Including His Experiences under the American Red Cross in Switzerland and Montenegro* (Redwood City, CA: Stanford University Press, 1941), 371. In the original, it is spelled "comitadjis."

247 Rade Vučurović, "Osvrt na Ratni Dnevnik Miloša Šarabe," *Tribunia: Prilozi za istoriju, arheologiju, etnologiju, umjetnost i kulturu*, no. 2 (1976): 10–13.

248 "Repatriirung," *Grazer Volksblatt*, May 31, 1879, 5.

these areas.[249] The impact of war, especially on cattle breeding, as well as the production of wine, wheat, and potatoes, was still evident in 1932.[250]

Initially the war had impacted people living on the border, but by 1916 the whole region and all its inhabitants were suffering. Life in Hercegovina depended on a delicate ecological balance even in peacetime, but war left civilians without food and both civilians and soldiers without water. Habsburg officers had confidently expected to win the local war, but Richard Bermann, Fritz Telmann, and the unknown Ruthene soldier, among many others, give us a glimmer of quite radical doubt. It is possible that the wartime orders and propaganda had not completely destroyed love of the land or its people. Some Habsburg soldiers ventured to return to the new South Slav state, but there were risks involved. The Belgrade authorities issued an extradition list of military personnel, which included Rudolf Braun, Oskar Potiorek, and Paul von Salis-Soglio.[251] Captain Theodor Karlik was arrested in Kotor in 1921, supposedly for his role in the execution of two hundred villagers in Hercegovina and the expropriation of cattle.[252] He had served in Herceg Novi from the beginning of the war until January 15, 1915, and wrote to Karl Novottny to try and help him clear his name.[253] Diplomatic pressure was levied on the Belgrade government to release Karlik.[254] However, his having been stationed in Herceg Novi neither confirms nor invalidates the charges against Karlik, since the coastal garrison operated very closely with the Trebinje authorities after July 1914. Although the formal processes to punish those guilty for wartime catastrophes were limited, many years of suffering—or, at the very least, anger or disappointment—followed on both sides.

---

249 Sivrić, "Osnivanje i rad Kotarskog odbora," 65–72.

250 "Die Herzegowina hungert," *Innsbrucker Nachrichten*, March 26, 1932, 6.

251 Paul von Salis-Soglio (1861–1938) was the younger son of Daniel. "Die jugoslawische Auslieferungsliste: Etwa 300 Namen," *Neues Wiener Tagblatt*, September 5, 1920, 5.

252 "Verhaftung eines österreichischen Majors in Cattaro," *Reichspost*, February 2, 1921, 6.

253 Theodor Karlik to Karl Novottny, February 21, 1921, Bundesministerium für Heerwesen Abteilung 2. Zahl 700/1921. NL Karl Novottny AT-OeStA/KA NL 417: 12, Kriegsarchiv, Vienna.

254 "Ein österreichischer Offizier in Jugoslavien verhaftet," *Arbeiter Zeitung*, February 16, 1921, 4.

Epilogue
VICTORS AND VANQUISHED AFTER 1918

The new South Slav kingdom attempted to bring together a population with a shared experience of death, disease, and privation, but
had come to loathe and fear each other during the war. What looked
like a victory in 1918 for the Serb Orthodox peoples also looked like
a defeat for those Catholics and Muslims in Hercegovina who had
so wholeheartedly supported the Habsburg war effort. Natives who
had emigrated years earlier began to establish contact with Trebinje
again. The monastery at Tvrdoš was a picturesque ruin before the
First World War, but its restoration was financed by American Nikola
Runjevac in 1928, who had left his home village of Poljice years earlier. Others also made the journey home. Jovo Krstovich had left for
Gary, Indiana in 1903. In 1907, he had founded a grocery shop with
Mato Chuck, John Wuletich, and Theodore Komenich, and was active in the Sokol Lodge and Sloboda Society, but went back to Trebinje
in 1921 to get married.[1] The Serb Orthodox population asserted its
presence and newfound hegemony. New research, with distinct paradigm shifts, was undertaken, while the *Landesmuseum/Zemaljski muzej*
in Sarajevo was newly led by Serb Orthodox directors. Milenko
Filipović began his fieldwork in the 1920s around Popovo polje, extending some of the research interests of Vejsil Ćurčić. Jovan Dučić,
born in Trebinje but for so long absent, served as a Yugoslavian dip-

---

1   Lane, *City of the Century*, 76–77.

FIGURE 31. Trebinje in 1938, with soldiers of the Royal Yugoslav Army. Fortepan, 191413, Gyula Kieselbach.

lomat before moving to the United States. A statue of the Montenegrin poet and ruler Petar II Petrović Njegoš by the Split-born sculptor Toma Rosandić was erected in 1934 in the center of Trebinje, under the auspices of Dučić and at his expense. The Petrović dynasty had had an enormous role in shaping both local and national consciousness before 1914, but by this time Trebinje was part of the banovina of Zeta, which included Nevesinje, Dubrovnik, Novi Pazar, and Kotor, with its capital in Cetinje.[2] Four years later in 1938, Dučić returned to his hometown to celebrate the opening of a new gymnasium and the unveiling of a striking memorial to commemorate the victims of the First World War, which he called "a symbol of the past and of the martyrdom of this land."[3] It depicted an angel of peace and now stands among the plane trees in the market square.

---

2   *Ranjeni Orao*, the 1936 novel by Milica Jakovljević which was turned into a popular television series filmed in Trebinje, has led to an increased sense of pride, connection, and belonging, as well as a nostalgia for the Zetska banovina years during the Kingdom of Yugoslavia.

3   Puvačić, *Balkan Themes*, 50.

Trebinje's urban identity was therefore inextricably linked to the wartime executions of the local people.

The collapse of the Habsburg state meant that many soldiers were deprived not only of victory despite so many triumphs in the field, but also of the comforts of military honors and veteran associations. Personal connections helped to make the transition easier for some. In the spring of 1919, Richard Neutra traveled to a small village near Zürich, where he stayed in a guesthouse owned by the nurse Elsa Tekely, aunt of his friend and fellow officer Dr. Endre Aladár (Bandy) Ungár.[4] Years later, Neutra met Bandy Ungár again in Mexico where he was a pharmaceutical consultant, and they kept in touch.[5] Despite suffering from the consequences of malaria for years after his military service, Neutra's style of architecture took off in California, giving him an enduring international reputation. He died in 1970 but seems to have had great nostalgia for Hercegovina, despite the malarial flashbacks: "I remembered more and more ... the landscape around it and the two years I lived there, from my twenty-second to my twenty-fourth year. Trebinje is surely the most romantic place in which I ever lived."[6] Other soldiers did not fare so well. In July 1918, the *Pilsner Tagblatt* carried an obituary for Reinhard Günste, observing that Bosnia and Hercegovina had been his "second home."[7] Fritz Telmann, a popular writer whose deprecating style pointed to the tyranny of the gallows in Trebinje, returned to Vienna where he took up heavy drinking and committed suicide in 1929.[8] After the war Jiří Daneš had a remarkable, but brief career serving as a diplomat for Czechoslovakia, but was run over in a motor accident in 1928.[9]

Rudolf Braun passed away at the age of fifty-nine in 1920, remaining at liberty and dying in his bed even before he was named by the Belgrade authorities. He had been posted to the Eastern Front in the

---

4 Dione Neutra and Richard Neutra, *Promise and Fulfillment, 1919–1932: Selections from the Letters and Diaries of Richard and Dione Neutra* (Carbondale, IL: Southern Illinois University Press, 1986), xv.
5 "To tell the truth: oral history transcript," BANC MSS 84/85c, 33.
6 Neutra and Neutra, *Promise and Fulfillment*, 67.
7 "Rifaat Gozdović Pascha," *Pilsner Tagblatt*, July 28, 1918, 2.
8 "Die Leiche des Schriftstellers Telmann agnosziert," *Wiener Zeitung*, May 29, 1929, 4.
9 "Ein Prager Gelehrter in Los Angeles tödlich verunglückt," *Neue Freie Presse (Abendblatt)*, April 13, 1928, 2.

later years of the war and never had to face justice for the damage he had caused in Hercegovina. Originally from České Budějovice (Budweis), he went to Vienna at the end of the war.[10] His loyal officer Karl Novottny also died in Vienna in 1931. Stjepan Sarkotić, the former Governor of Bosnia and Hercegovina, had done his initial military service under the command of Djuro Babić.[11] After the war he also lived in Vienna and kept in touch with other veterans in local coffeehouses.[12] A figure of some controversy in the Republic of Austria because of the war, Sarkotić died in 1939. Oskar Potiorek returned to his native Carinthia where he lived quietly and died in 1933. Anton Galgóczy lived to a patriarchal age, dying in 1929 at ninety-two, and was compared to Josef Radetzky in one of his obituaries.[13] Antonio Budinich survived the war and died at the age of ninety-four in Trieste in 1972, the year that Marie Marvánková also passed away in Prague. Georg Veith's research continued to thrive after 1918, and he remained a well-known personality, but he was murdered in Turkey in 1925 during a fieldwork trip. Veith's close friend, the museum curator Carl Patsch, left Sarajevo after the war, but remained in touch with friends and colleagues from that era. Karel Vandas, the botanist who had been so warmly welcomed by Djuro Babić in Trebinje as a young scholar, was shot and died from his wounds while on fieldwork in Skopje in 1923.[14] Emil Lilek, who had been a high school teacher in Sarajevo while he undertook his significant research, died almost four decades later in Celje in 1940. Jernej Andrejka survived the First World War and lived to see the creation of an enlarged Karadjordević state, but died in Ljubljana in 1926.

After 1918, Leo Weirather returned to work full time on collecting specimens from caves (especially beetles/coleoptera) in the karst.[15] He continued to finance his research by selling specimens on the pri-

---

10 "Kleine Chronik," *Wiener Zeitung*, April 17, 1920, 6.
11 Dinko Čutura, *Stjepan Sarkotić, posljednji poglavar Bosne i Hercegovine* (Zagreb: AGM, 2019), 37.
12 Sarkotić, "Aus meinen Erinnerungen," 2–3; Bauer, *Der letzte Paladin*, 154–55.
13 "Feldz[e]ugmeister Galgotzy gestorben: Ein populärer General des alten Oesterreich-Ungarn," *Neue Freie Presse*, November 6, 1929, 2.
14 Pavel Křivka and Vojtěch Holubec, "The Balkan Collections in the Main Czech Herbaria," *Phytologia Balcanica* 16, no. 2 (2010): 218.
15 Leo Weirather, "Diaries of a Biospeleologist at the Beginning of the XX Century," ed. Pier Mauro Giachino and Enrico Lana, *Fragmenta Entomologica* 37, no. 2 (2005): 1–264.

vate market: he is credited with discovering dozens of new species, several of which are named after him. He often used local people (including adolescents who were shorter in stature) as cave guides and recorded the stories they told him. In 1922, Karel Absolon returned to Trebinje.[16] There, he visited the popular hotelier Ivan Naglić,[17] as well as the grave of his scientific companion, Lucijan Matulić, who had died in 1917. He confided in a letter to Leo Weirather that this once "cheerful city" (*heitere Stadt*) was now "dead" and that he had spent the minimum possible time there.[18] Both men missed the privileges and freedoms that they had enjoyed before the collapse of the Habsburg Monarchy. Absolon's local expertise was not forgotten in the meantime, and he was contacted in 1938 by Stevan Marković, who worked for the municipal electrical company, with a question about the Ombla river.[19] Weirather kept in touch with Absolon until the latter's death in 1960. Their friendship was a remarkable testament to scientific comradeship. Although they were separated by the fault lines of the Cold War after 1945, in many ways, they were men of an earlier era, haunted by memories of what Weirather called "the beautiful and evil times."[20] Friendship was an abiding theme in Absolon's life, and he was an inveterate correspondent.[21]

Leisure travel to the region recommenced quickly after the end of the war and the new Yugoslav state encouraged tourism; the term "Turkish Trebinje" was still regularly used in the press, with a trip there still presented as a "fairy tale" trip to the Orient.[22] Over

---

16 Absolon had planned to return in 1921 but found the bureaucratic obstacles of traveling by car too unpalatable; see Karel Absolon to Jovan Cvijić, Brno, August 11, 1921, Sbirka Karla Absolona, Brno.
17 Naglić was described as "diminutive, affectionate, gray-bearded." Oransz, "Die Gesellschafts-Radreise," August 15, 1903, 8.
18 Karel Absolon to Leo Weirather, Brno, October 1, 1922, Collections Leo Weirather, Muséum d'histoire naturelle de Genève.
19 Stevan Marković to Karel Absolon, September 2, 1938, Sbirka Karla Absolona, Brno.
20 "Ich bin gerade bei den Räumen um Trebinje, denke oft an Sie und Ihre Aufsammler, an schöne und an üble Tage." Leo Weirather to Karel Absolon, January 8, 1961, Sbirka Karla Absolona, Brno. The postcard sadly arrived after Absolon had passed away; Weirather died in 1965.
21 Petr Zajiček, Martin Oliva, and Petr Kostrhun, *Karel Absolon: Objevitel, manažer, vědec* (Prague: Academia, 2021), 327–41.
22 Josef Friedrich Perkonig, "Zwischen Abend und Morgen: Ein östliches Märchen," *Neues Wiener Journal*, March 21, 1932, 4.

the years, many former soldiers, including the artist Ludwig Heßhaimer, remembered their compulsory billet with fondness: "I rushed in for the first time as a cheerful lieutenant, coming from Trebinje with a comrade on a bike at night under a full moon. I have been there several times in later years, and it has always enchanted me."[23] Having been banned from the Habsburg Monarchy in 1882, Arthur Evans returned to Yugoslavia in 1930 at the age of eighty. There, he promised to visit his old home in Dubrovnik every fifty years![24] His "intimate" friend Spiridion Gopčević, who had spent time in jail alongside Evans in 1882, died in 1929, but had long since turned his attention away from politics and toward astronomy.

Many looked back on the forty years of Habsburg rule with wistfulness rather than anger. Writing in 1919, Fritz Telmann described how the young Trebinje *kafedži* (café owner) Alija broke down and wept when he heard the Habsburg Monarchy had collapsed: "the Austrians made everything beautiful for us, the streets, the railway, and our children could learn in school."[25] In 1940, the ethnologist Vera Stein Erlich stated that:

From all conversations with the peasants, a nostalgia for old times can be heard. It is remarkable that the Muslims, the Catholics, and the Orthodox all speak in the same way, constantly pointing out how things used to be in the Austrian times. I now heard the same words repeated in tiny houses on the Romanija Mountain as well as in the surroundings of Jajce, at the market, in the courtrooms of Visoko, in the health centers of Herzegovina and in the *avlije* (courtyards) of Banja Luka. They constantly repeat how it was easier to live before, how life [had been] well ordered.[26]

---

23 Ludwig Heßhaimer "Wiedersehen mit Dalmatien," *Danzers Armee-Zeitung*, August 30, 1935, 5.
24 Kirigin, *Arthur Evans in Dubrovnik*, 11.
25 Telmann, "Die letzen Tage von Trebinje," 1. This was probably Alija Šuljak (1901–1992), born in Zasad, whose family owned a café close to the market in Trebinje. Telmann remembered that this young man was handsome and popular with the female market traders, "who decked him with roses."
26 Bojan Baskar, "Austronostalgia and Bosnian Muslims in the Work of Croatian Anthropologist Vera Stein Erlich," in *Imagining Bosnian Muslims in Central Europe: Representations, Transfers and Exchanges*, ed. František Šístek (Oxford: Berghahn, 2021), 159.

Even the *Mlada Bosna* conspirator Vaso Čubrilović, whose brother Veljko had been hanged in 1915, admitted that he had helped to "destroy a beautiful world that was lost forever due to the war that followed."[27] Was this really a "beautiful world" or was Čubrilović just forgetting the rage that he and his friends felt in 1914? In answer, it would be fair to say that the Habsburg regime was both oppressive and progressive. It shaped Bosnia and Hercegovina through radical infrastructural development and by injecting capital, but the insolent stare of people indicated that many thought they would be better off without the *Švabe* amongst them in their ancestral lands. As one correspondent remarked of local people in Trebinje during the uprising of 1882: "their expressions of untamed defiance and stubbornness show only too clearly that they have not stopped hating."[28]

Alija Šuljak, an important Ustaša nationalist ideologue, returned to Trebinje and chose the Hotel Naglić as his meeting venue for the Croat and Muslim supporters of Ante Pavelić in 1941.[29] From this base in Trebinje and from Gacko, Šuljak spearheaded the regional persecution of Serbs in 1941. After the end of the Second World War, he left the region and relocated to Istanbul, where he died in 1992. During the Second World War, the Orthodox and Jewish communities were persecuted by the new Ustaša regime: many were murdered in their villages or taken to the death camp at Jasenovac. While the Orthodox were targeted en masse in Gacko, Trebinje, and Stolac in Spring 1941, the men of Bileća seem to have used their proximity to Italian-occupied Montenegro to hide in the mountains.[30] In 1941, the remobilization of old divisions from the First World War was "pivotal" in determining who would be victimized.[31] In Trebinje, the Ustaša specifically attacked two hundred supporters of the "old regime" and targeted up to seventy villagers from Pridvorci,

---

27 He died in 1990 at the age of ninety-three. Peter F. Sugar, *East European Nationalism, Politics and Religion* (Farnham: Ashgate, 1999), 70.
28 C. M., "Aus Trebinje," *Neue Freie Presse (Abendblatt)*, February 24, 1882, 2.
29 Savo Skoko, *Pokolj i hercegovačkih Srba '41* (Belgrade: Stručna knjiga, 1991), 32.
30 Tomislav Dulić, *Utopias of Nations: Local Mass Killing in Bosnia and Herzegovina, 1941–42* (Uppsala: Uppsala Universitet, 2005), 124–75.
31 Newman, *Yugoslavia in the Shadow of War*, 3.

Arslanagić most, Gorica, Hrupjela, Mostaći, (Donje or Gornje) Police, and Zasad.[32]

Many Jews who had been important in the making of Habsburg Trebinje and notable for their humane rejection of national extremes found their lives under threat during the Second World War. Dora Münch, who had visited Trebinje in 1912 and written a series of articles about the region, was taken from her home in Brno in 1941 and transported to the Minsk ghetto where she died.[33] Dr. Moritz Oransz, who wrote such a vivid account of his cycling tour around Trebinje, was born in 1866 in Świdnica. By 1905, he had established a thermal spa hotel in Grado, a town which later became part of Italy. He received the Ritterkreuz of the Franz Joseph Order in February 1918 in recognition of his bravery as a garrison doctor for Regiment no. 106. He was transported to Auschwitz in 1943, where he perished at the age of seventy-seven with his wife Sophie Leim, who was sixty-nine.[34] The former garrison doctor Alois Pick remained in Vienna and survived the Holocaust, as did Alice Schalek, who fled from Austria. Sigmund Freud and Richard Bermann also left Austria but died before the outbreak of war. Dr. Rudolf Löwy (also known as Levi in local sources), originally from Mladá Boleslav in Bohemia, worked in Trebinje from 1898 onwards, survived the war, and was buried in the Jewish cemetery in Dubrovnik in 1951. Many local Jewish families in Hercegovina did not survive the turbulent 1940s. Boris Dubelier, the clockmaker who owned a jewelry shop in the city that was popular with Habsburg officers, died in Auschwitz in December 1944, but his children survived the war.[35]

At the same time that Jews were being systematically targeted, nationalist Četnici took over parts of Hercegovina and persecuted Muslims; many thousands were killed.[36] In turn, the victorious Partisans hunted down both Ustaša and Četnici and attempted to eliminate their personnel and ideologies. Political instability had led almost

---

32 Dulić, *Utopias of Nations*, 126, footnotes 17 and 19. The source quoted by Dulić spelled the villages as Zasade, Rupjeli, and Gorice.
33 Also written in Czech as Muenchova; see her entry in the database of victims of the Holocaust at https://collections.yadvashem.org/en/names
34 Also sometimes written as Maurizio.
35 His surname was sometimes also written as Dubeljer.
36 Dulić, *Utopias of Nations*, 194–215.

inexorably to war and interethnic conflict. After 1945, damaged by the war years, Trebinje resumed another long stretch as a garrison city, but this time for the Yugoslav National Army.[37] New generations of soldiers came to love or loathe their posting. Trebinje also served as a center for the Bosnian Serb Army during the Civil War of 1992–95. By the time the Dayton Peace Treaty was signed in 1995, most of the remaining Muslim population had left Trebinje by force or to avoid force.[38] Despite the "right to return" stipulated in the 1995 peace treaty, most of Trebinje's Bosniaks did not go back to their home city. Since the mid-1990s, Trebinje has had an overwhelmingly Serb Orthodox population that leans toward kindred spirits in Serbia and Montenegro as part of the Republika Srpska of Bosnia and Hercegovina. "Turkish Trebinje" now only survives through political connection to the Bosnian state, the memories of the people who once lived there, and through cultural artefacts such as the Osman-paša Mosque, now only intermittently open. The past is a foreign country. Trebinje has reinvented itself as a "sunny city" (*grad sunca*) in the twenty-first century with an emphasis on high-quality food and wine as well as leisure facilities. In 2000, the city was able to repay its debt to Jovan Dučić when he was laid to rest in a new monastery on Crkvina, close to where bonfires had once been lit on Kaisertag. The Muzej Hercegovine (Museum of Hercegovina) is housed in a centrally located former Habsburg military building. Hotel Naglić is now an apartment block close to the Hotel Platani: visitors to the bustling market can get a cup of coffee there.

In Hercegovina, everything begins and ends with the land and the water, dictating so much about the course of life, events, and peoples. As with so many other breakthroughs in scientific knowledge, the role of local people was profoundly instrumental in the codification of knowledge about insects, caves, fishing, snakes, plants, and disease. Before 1918, Hercegovina was a home to a complex, intricate and ancient set of beliefs about the natural world. Incomers were struck by the exuberance of clothes, of embroidery, and the

---

37 The city, army life, and the garrison are a central feature in Dejan Šorak's 1989 film *Najbolji*.
38 Ivana Nizich, *War Crimes in Bosnia-Hercegovina*, vol. 2 (Washington, DC: Human Rights Watch, 1992), 382–91.

extravagant use of flowers as decoration, even in the humblest homes. Festivals brought people of all denominations together to feast and sing at the top of their voices. But the Habsburg soldiers had also arrived in a recent war zone, already gravely damaged by 1878. Although the transfer of power to the new Habsburg authorities was swift, Hercegovina was almost irreparably divided. Direct challenges to the Habsburg state were repressed very brutally, but many incomers cared about the lives of local people, admired their culture, respected their right to live in a particular way, and tapped into their ancient wisdom about the climate, land, and botany.

The Habsburg Monarchy under Franz Joseph and Karl was highly dependent on its vast army. A short decisive military intervention made the army feel successful and confident in 1878. The evident "primitiveness" of the persistently rebellious local people in 1882 made the army staff feel as if their "civilizing mission" was beneficial and necessary, not only to themselves but also to the Muslims, Catholics, and numerous Orthodox people who also supported the regime. Arguably, this confidence lasted until 1916, by which time morale was knocked by military defeats but conversely strengthened by victories, such as the rapid conquest of Montenegro, which occurred in a matter of days. Collapse was infrastructural rather than political or on the battlefield, but when it came, it was total. The persecutions in the summer of 1914 were initiated by Oskar Potiorek and ruthlessly carried out on the ground by local commanders like Rudolf Braun. Within the top brass of the army, perhaps most notably from the head of the armed forces, Conrad von Hötzendorf, dislike of Orthodox people and distrust of the states of Serbia and Montenegro had been simmering for many years, and the assassination of Franz Ferdinand provided a pretext to attack the frontier settlements as well as to invade Serbia. This led directly to a war so injurious that it set off a demographic catastrophe which destroyed the essential character of a rimland, namely the border region between Hercegovina and Montenegro. The mosque in Lastva was riddled with artillery damage, children were evacuated to internment camps, houses were burned down, cattle appropriated, old orchards and vineyards were destroyed, and heads of families were hanged in public. Years of chaos laid the foundations for prolonged resentment between the South Slavs as the survivors remembered the war guilt or collaboration of their neighbors in this wave of destruction. *Divide et impera*. The extensive violence committed during the First World War had long term consequences which still rebound to this day.

Bibliography

Archives

Austria
    Kriegsarchiv, Vienna
    Nachlass Hans Wagner-Schönkirch, Österreichische Nationalbibliothek, Vienna
    Burgenländisches Landesarchiv, Eisenstadt
Bosnia and Hercegovina
    Arhiv Bosne i Hercegovine, Sarajevo
    Arhiv Hercegovine, Mostar
    Muzej Hercegovine, Trebinje
Czechia
    Sbirka Karla Absolona, Pavilon Anthropos, Moravské zemské muzeum, Brno
Germany
    Südost-Institut, Munich
Hungary
    Hadtörténeti Intézet és Múzeum, Budapest
Switzerland
    Muséum d'histoire naturelle de Genève
    Staatsarchiv Graubünden, Chur
United Kingdom
    Royal Anthropological Institute, London
    British Library Manuscripts, London
    National Archives, Kew, London
    Royal Geographical Society, London
United States
    The Bancroft Library, University of California, Berkeley
    Richard and Dion Neutra Papers, UCLA Library Special Collections, Charles E. Young Research Library, Los Angeles

Printed Primary Sources

Newspapers

Agramer Zeitung, Arbeiter Zeitung, Der Bezirksbote für den politischen Bezirk Bruck an der Leitha, Bosnische Post, Bregenzer Tagblatt, The Caian, Tagliches Cincinnatier Volksblatt, Club-Organ des Oesterreichischen Touring-Club, The Daily Telegraph, Danzers Armee-Zeitung, Epoche, The Fleetwood Chronicle, Freie Stimmen, Die Friedens-Warte, Grazer Volksblatt, Innsbrucker Nachrichten, Das interessante Blatt, Jagd-Zeitung, Klagenfurter Zeitung, Kremser Volksblatt, Kriegszeitung des A.T.V. Graz, Der Kuckuck, Leitmeritzer Zeitung, Linzer Volksblatt, Mährisch-Schlesische Presse, The Manchester Guardian, Marburger Zeitung, Militär-Zeitung, Morgen-Post, Murtaler Zeitung, Neue Freie Presse, Neue Illustrirte Zeitung, Neues Wiener Journal, Neues Wiener Tagblatt, The New York Times, Nordböhmisches Volks-

blatt, Österreichische Illustrierte Zeitung, Österreichische Volkszeitung, Pester Lloyd, Politika, Prager Abendblatt, Prager Tagblatt, Die Presse, Reichspost, Salzkammergut-Zeitung, Slovenski Narod, Štajerc, Steirische Alpenpost, Steyrer Zeitung, Südsteirische Post, Tages-Post, Tagblatt, Teplitz-Schönauer Anzeiger, Time, The Times, Das Vaterland, Die Vedette, Verkehrs-Zeitung, Villacher Zeitung, Welt Blatt, Weiner Abendpost, Wiener Allgemeine Zeitung, Wiener Bilder, Wiener Landwirtschaftliche Zeitung, Wiener Salonblatt, Wiener Zeitung, Wiener Neueste Nachrichten, Die Zeit

Books and authored articles

A., R. "Cannosa." *Prager Tagblatt*, February 12, 1898, 1–4.

"A Summer Holiday." *The Caian* 18 (1908): 142–56, 211–13.

Abtheilung für Kriegsgeschichte des K. K. Kriegs-Archivs. *Die Occupation Bosniens und der Hercegovina durch K. K. Truppen im Jahre 1878.* Vienna: Verlag des K.K. Generalstabes/Seidel und Sohns, 1879.

Absolon, Karel. "Výsledky výzkumných cest po Balkáně: Část třetí." *Časopis moravského musea zemského* (1914): 216–22.

———. "Z výzkumných cest po krasech Balkánu: S 33 původními obrázky dle snímků a mikrofotografií pí. Marie Absolonové." *Zlatá praha* 33, no. 48 (1916): 574–76; no. 49: 586–88; no. 50: 597–600; no. 51: 609–12; no. 52: 622–24.

Andrejka, Jernej. *Slovenski fantje v Bosni in Hercegovini 1878.* Klagenfurt: Družba sv. Mohorja, 1904.

The Annual Register: A Review of Public Events at Home and Abroad for the Year 1878. London: Rivingtons, 1879.

Asbóth, János. *An Official Tour through Bosnia and Herzegovina with an Account of the History, Antiquities, Agrarian Conditions, Religion, Ethnology, Folk Lore, and Social Life of the People.* London: Swan Sonnenschein, 1890.

"Aus einem Feldpostbriefe," *Nordböhmisches Volksblatt*, October 4, 1878, 1–2.

B. "Der Kronprinz in der Herzegowina." *Neues Wiener Tagblatt*, April 4, 1886, 3.

Bäenitz, Carl. "Botanische Reisen." *Österreichische Botanische Zeitschrift* 47, no. 7 (1897): 270.

Bailey, William Frederick. *The Slavs of the War Zone.* New York: E. P. Dutton, 1916.

Ballif, Philipp. *Wasserbauten in Bosnien und der Hercegovina.* Vol. 1, *Meliorationsarbeiten und Cisternen im Karstgebiete.* Vienna: A. Holzhausen, 1896–1899.

B[eranek], J[ulius]. "Eine Fahrt durch die Suttorina." *Wiener Landwirtschaftliche Zeitung*, October 21, 1885, 1.

B[eranek], Julius. "Ein Todessprung: Erinnerungen an die Occupation der Herzegowina." *Reichspost*, December 19, 1896, 1.

Beranek, Julius. "Der neue Compagnie-Commandant: Erinnerung eines Veteranen." *Reichspost*, December 25, 1900, 23–25.

Berger, Josef. "Neuer Kurs und Neue Bahnen in Bosnien." *Danzers Armee-Zeitung*, August 1, 1912, 10–12.

Bermann, Richard A. [Arnold Höllriegel pseud.]. *Die Fahrt auf dem Katarakt: Eine Autobiographie ohne einen Helden.* Edited by Hans-Harald Müller. Vienna: Picus, 2021.

———. "Der Krieg im Steinmeer." *Tagliches Cincinnatier Volksblatt*, December 15, 1915, 8.

Besarović, Risto. *Kultura i umjetnost u Bosni i Hercegovini pod Austrougarskom upravom.* Vol. 4. Sarajevo: Arhiv BiH, 1968.

Bock, Hermann. "Die Knöchenhöhle im Pratschaltale und die neuentdeckte Tropf-steingrotte." *Pester Lloyd*, September 25, 1913, 1-3.

Broemel, Francis. "Auf grünen Felsen." *Wiener Allgemeine Zeitung*, November 25, 1880, 1-2.

Broucek, Peter, ed. *Feldmarschalleutnant Alfred Jansa: Ein österreichischer General gegen Hitler; Erinnerungen.* Vienna: Böhlau: 2011.

Brunner, Alfred. "Über Maltafieber." *Wiener Klinische Wochenschrift*, February 15, 1900, 149-53.

Budini, Antonio. *Le memorie di guerra di papà.* Trieste: Beit Storia, 2013.

Bukowski, Gejza von. "Beitrag zur Geologie der Landschaften Korjenici und Klo-buk in der Hercegovina." *Jahrbuch der Kaiserlich-Königlichen Geologischen Reichs-sanstalt* 51 (1901): 159-69.

Capus, Guillaume. *A travers la Bosnie et l'Herzégovine: Études et impressions de voyage.* Paris: Librairie Hachette, 1896.

Conrad von Hötzendorf, Franz. "Einiges über den südherzegowinischen Karst in militärischer Hinsicht." *Organ der militär-wissenschaftlichen Vereine* 24, no. 1 (1882): 1-46.

———. *Mein Anfang: Kriegserinnerungen aus der Jugendzeit 1878-1882.* Berlin: Verlag für Kulturpolitik 1925.

Coote Lake, E. F. "The Dance of the Spirit of the New Corn in Cattaro." *Folklore* 77, no. 1 (1966): 31-40.

Cotton Minchin, James George. *The Growth of Freedom in the Balkan Peninsula: Notes of a Traveller in Montenegro, Bosnia, Servia, Bulgaria, and Greece, with Historical and Descriptive Sketches of the People.* London: John Murray, 1886.

Cruger Coffin, Marian. "Where East Meets West: A Visit to Picturesque Dalma-tia, Montenegro and Herzegovina." *National Geographic*, May 1908, 309-44.

Ćurčić, Vejsil. *Narodno ribarstvo u Bosni i Hercegovini.* Sarajevo: Zemaljska štamparija, 1910.

Cvitković, Johann. "Eine Adriareise." *Neue Freie Presse*, May 28, 1914, 25-28.

Daneš, Georg V. *Bevölkerungsdichtigkeit der Hercegovina.* Prague: E. Leschinger, 1903.

Davis, W. M. "An Excursion in Bosnia, Hercegovina and Dalmatia." *Bulletin of the Geographical Club of Philadelphia*, no. 2 (1901): 21-50.

Dedijer, Jevto. "Bilećke Rudine." *Srpski etnografski zbornik* 5 (1903): 669-899.

———. "La transhumance dans les pays dinariques." *Annales de Geographie* 25, no. 137 (1916): 347-65.

Defterdarović, Ibrahim. "Stare listine porodice Resulbegović." *Glasnik Zemaljskog muzeja u Bosni i Hercegovini*, April 1, 1897, 193-226.

Delić, Stevan R. "Ćuprija na Mostu." *Glasnik Zemaljskog muzeja u Bosni i Hercegovini*, April 1, 1891, 116-19.

"Die Gährung in der Herzegovina." *Pester Lloyd*, December 18, 1881, 2.

Dillinger, Andreas. "Ragusa." *Dillingers Reise- und Fremdenzeitung*, March 10, 1897, 3-5.

Doerr, Robert. *Das Pappatacifieber: Ein endemisches Drei-Tage-Fieber im adriatischen Küstengebiete Österreich-Ungarns.* Vienna: Deuticke, 1909.

Dombrowski, Ernst. "Ein verlorenes Jagdparadies." *Neues Wiener Tagblatt*, April 5, 1914, 45-46.

———. "Auf heißem Boden." *Neues Wiener Tagblatt*, February 22, 1914, 40.

Durham, Mary Edith. *Through the Lands of the Serb.* London: Edward Arnold, 1904.

————. *Twenty Years of Balkan Tangle.* London: George Allen Unwin, 1920.

Ebenhoch, Alfred. "Aus meinem Tagebuche in der Herzegowina." *Mühlviertler Nachrichten*, September 21, 1889, 1–2; September 28, 1889, 1–2; October 5, 1889, 1–2.

Evans, Arthur J. *Through Bosnia and the Herzegovina on Foot during the Insurrection, August and September 1875, with an Historical Review of Bosnia, and a Glimpse at the Croats, Slavonians, and the Ancient Republic of Ragusa.* London: Longmans, Green and Co, 1876.

————. "The Austrian Mission in Bosnia and the Balkans." *Manchester Guardian*, March 6, 1880, 9.

————. "The Austrian War Against Publicity." *Contemporary Review* 42 (September 1882): 383–99.

————. "Austria's Difficulties in Bosnia and Herzegovina." *Manchester Guardian*, March 27, 1880, 7.

————. "Christmas and Ancestor Worship in the Black Mountain." *Macmillan's Magazine* 43 (1881): 219–33.

————. "With the Bocchese Insurgents." *Manchester Guardian*, December 12, 1881, 5.

F., Johann. "Über die letzten Kämpfe mit den Montenegrinern und die Zurückweisung ihrer Einfälle." *Österreichische Volkszeitung*, November 25, 1914, 7.

Fairclough, Henry Rushton. *Warming Both Hands: The Autobiography of Henry Rushton Fairclough, Including His Experiences under the American Red Cross in Switzerland and Montenegro.* Redwood City, CA: Stanford University Press, 1941.

Francis. "Wir war'n beim k. u. k. Infanterie-regiment: Der letzte Traum der Reservisten." *Neues Wiener Journal*, November 9, 1930, 7.

Freeman, Edward A. *Sketches from the Subject and Neighbour Lands of Venice.* London: Macmillan, 1881.

Friedrich, Theodor. "Bosnische Eindrücke I." *Pester Lloyd*, July 20, 1901, 3; "Bosnische Eindrücke II." *Pester Lloyd*, July 21, 1901, 3.

Freshfield, Douglas W. "The Southern Frontiers of Austria." *The Geographical Journal* 46, no. 6 (December 1915): 414–33.

Freud, Sigmund. *Zur Psychopathologie des Alltagslebens (Über Vergessen, Versprechen, Vergreifen, Aberglaube und Irrtum).* Berlin: S. Karger, 1904.

————. *Die Traumdeutung.* Leipzig/Vienna, 1914.

Fromm, Karl J. "Reisen in Bosnien und der Herzegowina." *Die Zeit*, September 1, 1910, 13.

Formánek, Edvard. "Beitrag zur Flora von Bosnien und der Hercegovina." *Österreichische Botanische Zeitschrift* 39, no. 4 (April 1889): 145–47.

Funder, Friedrich. "Im Kampf mit den Räubern." *Reichspost*, July 17, 1903, 1–2.

G., D. "Die Eröffnung der neuen herceg-dalmatinischen Eisenbahn." *Agramer Zeitung*, July 16, 1901, 5–6.

Gatti, Major R. "Der Übergang der Mittelcolonne über die Orjenska lokva, 9. bis 11. März 1882: Aus meinem Tagebuch." *Danzers Armee-Zeitung*, May 1, 1902, 4.

Gayersperg, Franz Xaver von. "Neue Eisenpfade." *Welt Blatt*, August 9, 1901, 7–8; part IV, *Welt Blatt*, August 18, 1901, 7–8.

Glaise von Horstenau, Edmund. *Ein General im Zwielicht: Die Erinnerungen Edmund Glaise von Horstenau K. u. K. Generalstabsoffizier und Historiker.* Vol. 1. Edited by Peter Broucek. Vienna: Böhlau, 1980.

Gregory, John Walter. "Pseudo-Glacial Features in Dalmatia." *The Geographical Journal* 46, no. 2 (1915): 105–17.

Günste, Reinhard [Rifat Gozdović Pascha pseud.]. "Als ich das zweitemal einen Vortrag hielt." *Pilsner Tagblatt*, September 6, 1914, 2–3.

——— [Rifaat Gozdović Pascha pseud.]. "Aus den Erinnerungen eines Pilsner Kindl's." *Pilsner Tagblatt*, July 24, 1910, 1–6.

——— [Rifat Gozdović Pascha pseud.]. "Aus einem Feldzugstagebuch." *Pilsner Tagblatt*, May 7, 1911, 3.

——— [Rifât Effendija Gozdović pseud.]. "Bosniens römische Katholiken." *Reichspost*, October 27, 1906, 1–2.

——— [Rifaat Gozdović Pascha pseud.]. "Das Popovo Polje." *Pilsner Tagblatt*, July 27, 1910, 3–5.

——— [Rifât Effendija Gozdović pseud.]. "Die bosnische Ostbahn." *Reichspost*, March 27, 1906, 1–3.

——— [Rifat Gozdović Pascha pseud.]. "Die Pekingenten." *Pilsner Tagblatt*, May 23, 1915, 2–6.

——— [Rifaat Gozdović Pascha pseud.]. "Eine Jagd am Utovo Blato." *Pilsner Tagblatt*, July 31, 1910, 4–5.

——— [Rifat Gozdović Pascha pseud.]. "Heitere Erinnerungen aus ernster Zeit." *Pilsner Tagblatt*, January 17, 1915, 2–5.

——— [Rifat Gozdović Pascha pseud.]. "Huflattich." *Pilsner Tagblatt*, March 12, 1916, 18.

——— [Rifat Gozdović Pascha pseud.]. "Paschastreiche." *Pilsner Tagblatt*, August 11, 1912, 1–4.

——— [Rifat Gozdović Pascha pseud.]. "Schloß Starislano: Eine hercegowinische Spukgeschichte." *Pilsner Tagblatt*, March 3, 1912, 2.

——— [Rifat Gozdović Pascha pseud.]. "Wie ich den Mehrer Montenegros kennen lernte." *Wiener Sonn- und Montags-Zeitung*, January 19, 1914, 1–3.

——— [Rifat Eff. Gozdović pseud.]. "Zavala, das herzegowinische Athoškloster und die Vjetrinicahöhle." *Deutsches Volksblatt*, December 2, 1906, 21.

Günthersen, Alexander. "Erinnerungen an Feldzeugmeister Galgotzy." *Reichspost*, November 7, 1929, 7.

H., H. "Der Zug über den Orien." *Der Vaterland*, April 16, 1882, 9–11.

H., H. "Der Übergang über den Orien." *Die Vedette*, April 30, 1882, 2–3; May 3, 1882, 2–3; May 7, 1882, 2–3; May 10, 1882, 2–3.

H., K. "Das Hajdukenthum." *Die Presse*, July 28, 1891, 1–4.

Haberlandt, M[ichael], Dr. "Aus Bosnien." *Wiener Zeitung*, June 25, 1895, 5–7; "Aus Bosnien II." *Wiener Zeitung*, June 26, 1895, 2–3.

Haberlandt, Arthur. "Bericht über die ethnographischen Arbeiten im Rahmen der historisch-ethnographischen Balkanexpedition." *Mitteilungen der Geographischen Gesellschaft in Wien* 59 (1916): 736–42.

Hankenstein, Karl Hanke von. "Weihnachten am Kordon." *Teplitz-Schönauer Anzeiger*, December 25, 1909, 1–3.

Hartenstein, Gabriele. "Die Ruine: Ein Erlebnis in der Herzegowina." *Reichspost*, May 27, 1927, 1–3.

Hassert, Kurt. *Reise durch Montenegro, nebst Bemerkungen über Land und Leute.* Vienna: Hartleben, 1893.

Heimfelsen, Sepp. "Reisebriefe aus Bosnien, Herzegovina und Dalmatien." *Der Fremdenverkehr*, April 19, 1914, 7–8.

"Heinz." "Das Lager auf der Visoka Glavica." *Militär-Zeitung*, September 18, 1885, 2–5.

Heller, Franz. "Vor Dreißig Jahren." *Salzburger Volksblatt*, August 14, 1908, 3–4.

Hetz, Felix. "'Ronde': Bilder aus Österreich-Ungarns Vergangenheit." *Der Österreichischer Kamerad (Neues Wiener Journal)*, January 6, 1937, 15.

Heßhaimer, Ludwig. "Wiedersehen mit Dalmatien." *Danzers Armee-Zeitung*, August 30, 1935, 5.

Himmel, Hauptmann. "Opanken: Keine Militär-Beschuhung," *Die Vedette*, March 4, 1883, 134–35.

Hochbichler, Conrad. "Aus den schwarzen Bergen." *Ischler Wochenblatt*, April 27, 1890, 1–2 (part I); May 4, 1890, 1–2 (part II); May 11, 1890, 1–2 (part III).

Holbach, Maude. *Bosnia and Herzegovina: Some Wayside Wanderings*. London: J. Lane, 1910.

———. *Dalmatia: The Land Where East Meets West*. London: J. Lane, 1910.

Hoernes, Moriz. *Dinarische Wanderungen: Cultur- und Landschaftsbilder aus Bosnien und der Hercegovina*. Vienna: C. Graeser, 1888.

Hopffgarten, M. von. "Bericht über eine entomologische Reise nach Dalmatien, der Herzegowina und Montenegro im Jahre 1880." *Entomologische Nachrichten* 6 (1880): 101–30.

Hörmann, Kosta. *Narodne pjesne Muhamedovaca u Bosni i Hercegovini*. Sarajevo: Zemaljska štamparija, 1888–89.

Hribar, Ivan. *Moji Spomini*. Vol. 2. Ljubljana: Merkur, 1928.

Hubka von Czernczitz, Gustav Ritter. *Geschichte des k. und k. Infanterie-Regiments Graf von Lacy Nr. 22 von seiner Errichtung bis zur Gegenwart*. Zadar: Verlag des Regiments, 1902.

Hugonnet, Léon. *La Turquie Inconnue: Roumanie, Bulgarie, Macédoine, Albanie*. Paris: L. Frinzine, 1886.

Humpelstetter, Z.-A. Michel. "Osterreise 1912 des Österreichischen Toüristen-Klubs nach Bosnien, der Herzegowina und Dalmatien." *Österreichische Touristenzeitung*, June 1, 1912, 133–39.

Hutchinson, Frances Kinsley. *Motoring in the Balkans: Along the Highways of Dalmatia, Montenegro, the Herzegovina and Bosnia*. Chicago: A. C. McClurg, 1909.

Ivanetič, Franz. "Allerlei aus Trebinje." *Grazer Volksblatt*, November 25, 1879, 5–6.

———. "Arzloin Agič Most." *Klagenfurter Zeitung*, September 28, 1879, 1–2.

———. "Aus Trebinje." *Klagenfurter Zeitung*, August 23, 1879, 1.

Jackson, Frederick Hamilton. *The Shores of the Adriatic, the Austrian side, the Küstenlande, Istria, and Dalmatia... Fully Illustrated with Plans, Drawings, by the Author, and Photographs Taken Specially for This Work*. London: J. Murray, 1908.

K., H. "Ein Kaisertag in der Heimat des Bombenwerfers: Eindrücke aus Trebinje." *Reichspost*, July 10, 1914, 7–8.

K., O. "In Memoriam: Oberst d. R. Karl Rost." *Danzers Armee-Zeitung*, January 21, 1938, 6.

Kählig, Eduard von. "Eine Erinnerung an die Bekämpfung des Aufstandes in der Herzegowina 1882." *Danzers Armee-Zeitung*, February 21, 1907, 1–5.

Kasch, Igo. "Skizzen aus Süddalmatien." *Badener Zeitung*, October 3, 1906, 1–4.

Kennedy, Robert J. *Montenegro and its Borderlands*. London: Hatchards, 1894.

King, Edward. *Descriptive Portraiture of Europe in Storm and Calm: Twenty Years' Experiences and Reminiscences of an American Journalist.* Springfield, MA: C. A. Nichols and Co, 1888.

Kriechbaum, Eduard. "Dalmatien." *Neue Warte am Inn,* March 4, 1927, 8–9.

Kutschbach, A. "Erinnerungen eines Mitkämpfers an die Insurrektion in der Herzegowina 1875." *Allgemeiner Tiroler Anzeiger,* January 15, 1909, 1–4.

Lahner, Georg. "Eindrücke von der Forschungsreise des Vereines für Höhlenkunde nach Bosnien und Hercegovina." *Wiener Abendpost,* March 17, 1914, 1–3.

———. "Lebend begraben: Warnende Betrachungen zum Üngluck in der Frauenmauer-Höhle." *Linzer Volksblatt,* January 6, 1929, 5.

Lanin, E. B [Emile J. Dillon]. "Bosnia and Herzegovina." *Contemporary Review* 65 (May 1894): 735–60.

L., P. "Ein Mann der Zukunft." *Mährisches Tagblatt,* April 7, 1887, 1–3.

Lanux, Pierre de, and Milan Toplitza. "L'Autriche-Hongrie: En guerre contre ses sujets." *La Revue hebdomadaire,* September 24, 1915, 43–69.

Lilek, Emilian. "Familien- und Volksleben in Bosnien und in der Herzegowina." *Österreichische Zeitschrift für Volkskunde* 6 (1900): 23–30, 53–72, 164–72, 202–20.

"Lilienstengel." "Meine Erinnerungen an die Kämpfe in Süddalmatien im Jahre 1882." *Danzers Armee-Zeitung,* March 14, 1907, 1–3.

Lukas, Georg A. "Bosnische Eindrücke." Part 1. *Grazer Tagblatt,* October 9, 1909, 1–2.

Lyde, Lionel W. *A Military Geography of the Balkan Peninsula.* London: A. and C. Black, 1905.

M., C. "Jovanović Armeebefehl." *Neue Freie Presse (Abendblatt),* February 23, 1882, 2.

M., C. "Das Gefecht auf der Kobila-Glava." *Neue Freie Presse (Abendblatt),* February 23, 1882, 2.

M., C. "Aus Trebinje." *Neue Freie Presse (Abendblatt),* February 24, 1882, 2.

M., C. "Der Aufstand." *Neue Freie Presse (Morgenblatt),* March 7, 1882, 2.

M., F. von. "Über Ragusa nach Trebinje." *Wiener Zeitung,* March 19, 1886, 2–4; March 20, 1886, 2–4.

M., F. von. "Die Culturarbeit der österreichischen Armee (Hercegovina)." *Wiener Zeitung,* June 10, 1886, 2–4; June 11, 1886, 2–4; June 12, 1886, 2–4.

M., F. von. "Auf Cordon." *Wiener Abendpost,* March 4, 1887, 1–3; March 5, 1887, 1–2.

Magyar, Ludwig. "In den Schwarzen Bergen." *Mährisches Tagblatt,* November 13, 1915, 2.

Marge, Pierre. *Voyage en Dalmatie, Bosnie-Herzégovine et Monténégro.* Paris: Plon-Nourrit, 1912.

Marich, John T. *Memoirs of John T. Marich, 1881–1965.* Gary, IN: n.p., 1968.

Martiny, Hugo von. "Wie Mihalčić es erzählte." *Die Quelle: Sonntag-Beiblatt der Reichpost,* May 1, 1932, 17–18.

Michel, Robert. "Der Deserteur." *Pilsner Tagblatt,* December 13, 1914, 2–6.

———. "Meine erste Fahr im Auto." *Der Abend,* December 13, 1930, 9–10.

Mihajlović, Hristifor. "Manastir Zavala i Vjetrenica pećina." *Glasnik Zemaljskog muzeja u Bosni i Hercegovini* 2, no. 2 (1890): 130–43.

Miller, William. *Travels and Politics in the Near East.* London: T. F. Unwin, 1898.

Ministerium des K. und K. Hauses und des Äussern. *Recueil de témoignages concernant les actes deviolation du droit des gens commis par les États en guerre avec l'Autrice-Hongrie.* Berne: K. J. Wyss, 1915.

Morokutti, Josef. "Der Aufstand im Süden der Okkupationsgebietes im Jahre 1882." *Kärntner Zeitung*, October 5, 1907, 2–4.

Möser, Alfred. "Feldpostbriefe." *Leitmeritzer Zeitung*, October 14, 1914, 10.

Müller, Gustav. "Spionage in der alten Monarchie." *Freie Stimmen*, April 2, 1935, 5.

Münch, Dora. "Ein Erlebnis in Trebinje." *Bukowinaer Post*, July 7, 1912, 1–4.

N., Clotilde. "Erinnerung an Dalmatien." *Vorarlberger Landes-Zeitung*, June 13, 1888, 1–2.

N., N. "Brief eines Grenzsoldaten." *Österreichische Volkszeitung*, January 12, 1909, 1–3.

N., S. "Eine hercegovinische Idylle." *Agramer Zeitung*, 1908, 1–5.

Neutra, Dione, and Richard Neutra. *Promise and Fulfillment, 1919–1932: Selections from the Letters and Diaries of Richard and Dione Neutra*. Carbondale, IL: Southern Illinois University Press, 1986.

Neutra, Richard. *Life and Shape*. Los Angeles: Atara Press, 2009.

Neweklowsky, Ernst. "Volkskundliches aus Westmontenegro." *Österreichische Zeitschrift für Volkskunde* 23 (1917): 59–69.

Njegoš, Mirko Petrović. *Junački spomenik, pjesne o najnovijim Tursko-Crnogorskim bojevima*. Cetinje: U knjažeskoj štampariji, 1864.

Novotni, Vjekoslav. "Iz Zagreba preko Orjena do Kotora." *Hrvatski Planinar* 7, nos. 3–4 (1904): 20–27.

Nowak, Karl. "Bosnische Grenzfahrt." *Prager Tagblatt*, December 8, 1915, 11.

Oeser, Reinhold. "Die Blitzsicherung der Militär-Telephonanlage in Trebinje." *Mitteilungen über Gegenstände des Artillerie- und Geniewesens*, 1894, 541–50.

———. "Ein Ausflug zu Rad von Ragusa nach Trebinje." *Club-Organ des Oesterreichischen Touring-Club*, no. 10 (1899): 5.

Oransz, [Moritz] Dr. "Die Gesellschafts-Radreise des 'Ö.T.-C.' nach Kroatien, Dalmatien, Herzegowina und Bosnien im Juli 1902." *Club-Organ des Oesterreichischen Touring-Club*, part 8, August 15, 1903, 7–8; part 9, September 15, 1903, 4–8; part 10, October 15, 1903, 3–6.

Otte, Thomas G., ed. *An Historian in Peace and War: The Diaries of Harold Temperley*. London: Routledge, 2014.

Passarge, Ludwig. *Dalmatien und Montenegro: Reise- und Kulturbilder*. Leipzig: B. Elischer Nachfolger, 1904.

Patsch, Carl. *Historische Wanderungen im Karst und an der Adria*. Vol. 1, *Die Herzegowina einst und jetzt*. Vienna: Forschungsinstitut für Osten und Orient, 1922.

Penck, Albrecht. "Geomorphologische Studien aus der Herzegowina." *Zeitschrift des deutschen und österreichischen Alpenvereins*, no. 31 (1900): 25–41.

Perkonig, Josef Friedrich. "Markt in Banjaluka." *Völkischer Beobachter*, August 7, 1943, 4.

———. "Zwischen Abend und Morgen." *Neues Wiener Tagblatt*, December 10, 1942, 2–3.

———. "Zwischen Abend und Morgen: Ein östliches Märchen." *Neues Wiener Journal*, March 21, 1932, 4.

Petermann, Reinhard E. "Auf den Orjen." *Österreichische Touristenzeitung*, October 16, 1901, 229–31.

———. "Bergfahrt." *Neues Wiener Tagblatt*, August 30, 1901, 1–3.

———. "Mit der Eisenbahn in die Bocche di Cattaro." *Neues Wiener Tagblatt*, July 16, 1901, 1–2.

Pfeffer, Rudolf. *Geschichte des k. u. k. Infanterieregiments Freiherr Kray Nr. 67: Erster Band 1860–1910.* Vienna: Im Selbstverlage des Regiments, 1912.

Pichler, Josephine. "Quer durch Montenegro: Trebinje-Draga Obrenov Han." *Agramer Zeitung,* December 23, 1905, 17–21.

Pick, Alois. "Zur Pathologie und Therapie einer eigenthümlichen endemischen Krankheitsform." *Wiener Medizinische Wochenschrift,* no. 33 (1886): 1141–45.

Popović, Vladimir J. *Patnje i žrtve Srba sreza trebinjskoga 1914–1918.* Trebinje na Vidovdan, 1929.

Preindlsberger-Mrazović, Milena. *Bosnisches Skizzenbuch: Landschafts und Kultur Bilder aus Bosnien und der Hercegovina.* Dresden: Pierson, 1900.

Radiczky, Eugen von. "Nevisinje-Trebinje." *Wiener Landwirtschaftliche Zeitung,* February 9, 1907, 1–2.

Raspopović, Radoslav, ed. *N. M. Potapov: Ruski vojni agent u Crnoj Gori; Dnevnik 1906–07, 1912, 1914–15.* Vol. 2. Podgorica: Istorijski institut Crne Gore, 2003.

Rebel, H. "Studien über die Lepidopterenfauna der Balkanländer. II. Teil. Bosnien und Herzegowina." *Annalen des Naturhistorischen Museums in Wien* 19, nos. 2–3 (1904): 97–377.

Renner, Heinrich. *Durch Bosnien und die Hercegovina kreuz und quer.* Berlin: D. Reimer, 1897.

Röhrich, Helene. "Von Mostar nach Ragusa." *Salzburger Fremden-Zeitung,* February 16, 1901, 4–5.

Ružička, Adolf. "Bosnien–Herzegowina–Cettinje: Ein Ausflug dahin." *Kaufmännische Zeitschrift,* July 1, 1901, 107–9.

Salis-Soglio, Daniel Freiherr von. *Mein Leben und was ich davon erzählen will, kann und darf.* Vol. 2. Stuttgart/Leipzig: Deutsche Verlags-Anstalt, 1908.

Šantić, Milan. "Kraj koji ima bogatu prošlost a tešku sadašnjicu." *Politika,* December 15, 1935, 13.

Sarkotić, Stefan Freiherr von. "Aus meinen Erinnerungen." *Danzers Armee-Zeitung,* April 8, 1927, 2–3.

Schalek, Alice. "An der montenegrinischen Grenze." *Neue Freie Presse,* November 14, 1915, 2–3.

———. "An der montenegrinischen Grenze: Von Avtovac nach Stepen." *Neue Freie Presse,* December 11, 1915, 1–4.

———. "An der montenegrinischen Grenze: Von Bilek nach Lastva." *Neue Freie Presse,* December 15, 1915, 1–4.

———. "An der montenegrinischen Grenze: Ein Idyll." *Neue Freie Presse,* December 23, 1915, 1–4.

Sch., A. "Zum fünfzigjährigen Gedenke." *Danzers Armee Zeitung,* March 4, 1932, 2.

———. "Vor fünfzehn Jahren: Aus dem Tagebuch eines Kriegsteilnehmers." *Danzers Armee Zeitung,* March 11, 1932, 5–6.

Schneeweiß, Edmund. "Volksnahrung im Plivatal (Bosnien)." *Österreichische Zeitschrift für Volkskunde* 24, no. 4 (1918): 81–97.

Schweiger-Lerchenfeld, [Amand von]. "Aus der Herzegowina." *Die Presse,* September 11, 1875, 1–2.

Seeliger, Emil. "General Galgotzy—der eisener General." *Wiener Sonn- und Montags-Zeitung,* August 20, 1923, 4–5.

Seton-Watson, R. W. "Frightfulness in Bosnia." *The Times,* March 30, 1915, 11.

Souvan, Ivan. "Fastnachtsspiel in der Hercegovina." *Agramer Zeitung*, November 23, 1893, 1–2.

Stenzel, Vera. "In der südlichen Herzegowina: Erinnerung aus Österreich." *Arbeiter Zeitung*, August 18, 1928, 6.

Stephens, W. R. W. *The Life and Letters of Edward A. Freeman*. London: Macmillan, 1895.

Stern, Alexander. "Aus aller Welt." *Tagblatt*, August 30, 1930, 3.

———. "Aus B. H. D." *Donauland*, 1917, 1122–25.

———. "B. H. D." *Der Kuckuck*, July 31, 1932, 12.

Stillman, William J. *Herzegovina and the late Uprising: The Causes of the Latter and Remedies*. London: Longmans, Green and Co, 1877.

Stillman, William J. *The Autobiography of a Journalist*. Vol. 2. London: Grant, 1901.

———. "The late Baron Jovanovich." *The Times*, December 12, 1885, 3.

Strobl, Karl-Hans. *Lemuria: Seltsame Geschichten*. Munich: Heliakon, 2022.

"Tagebuch eines Mobilisirten," *Pester Lloyd*, January 25, 1882, 3.

Telmann, Fritz. "Als Mitglied des Feldgerichts in Trebinje." *Neues Wiener Journal*, August 15, 1924, 8.

———. "Die letzen Tage von Trebinje." *Die Zeit*, May 30, 1919, 1.

———. "Feldgerichtserinnerungen." *Prager Tagblatt*, September 7, 1924, 4.

Teschenburg. "Was schreibt man über Neu-Oesterreich?" *Das Vaterland*, October 22, 1899, 1–2.

Teuber, Oskar. "Eine Ungarn-Kolonie in der Herzegovina." *Pester Lloyd*, November 4, 1896, 3–4.

"The Austrians in Herzegovina." *The Times*, October 6, 1883, 7.

Thomson, Harry Craufuird. *The Outgoing Turk: Impressions of a Journey through the Western Balkans*. New York: D. Appleton, 1897.

"Unsere Soldaten an der Grenze." *Der Bezirksbote für den politischen Bezirk Bruck an der Leitha*, March 14, 1909, 2.

Vandas, K[arel]. "Beiträge zur Kenntniss der Flora von Süd-Hercegovina." *Österreichische botanische Zeitschrift* 39 (1889): 266–69.

Vavrović, Josip. "Nešto o Vjetrenici pećini." *Glasnik Zemaljskog muzeja u Bosni i Hercegovini* 5, no. 4 (1893): 709–15.

Veith, Georg. *Der Feldzug von Dyrrhachium zwischen Caesar und Pompejus*. Vienna: L. W. Seidel 1920.

———. "Die Reptilien von Bosnien und der Herzegowina." Edited by F. Tiedemann and F. Grillitsch. *Herpetozoa* 3, nos. 3–4 (1991): 97–196; and vol. 4, nos. 1–2 (1991): 1–96.

W., C. "Trebinje: Cultur nach Osten tragen." *Militär-Zeitung*, April 24, 1885, 246.

W., H. "Wilde Rosen: Skizze aus der Herzegowina." *Reichspost*, July 30, 1905, 1–2.

Waldmann, C. H. "Ein lockendes Reiseziel für Naturfreunde: Nach Erinnerungen ausgezeichnet." *Salzburger Wacht*, July 9, 1930, 7–8.

Wartburg, Dr. I. Rudolph von. "Meine Erinnerungen an die Kämpfe um Trebinje 7. bis 29. September 1878." *Salzburger Volksblatt*, September 23, 1908, 1–3.

Weirather, Leo. "Diaries of a Biospeleologist at the Beginning of the XX Century." Edited by Pier Mauro Giachino and Enrico Lana. *Fragmenta Entomologica* 37, no. 2 (2005): 1–264.

Went von Römö, Karl. "Aus dem südöstlichen Theile des Occupationsgebietes." *Österreichisch-ungarische Revue* 17 (1894–95): 18–40.

Werner, Franz von [Murad Efendi, pseud.]. *Türkische Skizzen.* Leipzig: Dürr, 1877.

West, Rebecca. *Black Lamb and Grey Falcon: A Journey through Yugoslavia.* Edinburgh: Cannongate, 1993.

Wester, Josip. "Dr. Sketova pisma iz Bosne." *Ljubljanski Zvon* 35, no. 3 (1915): 136–39.

———. "Tri pisma o Bosni." *Ljubljanski Zvon* 30, no. 11 (1910): 653–62.

Wettstein, Otto. "Oberst Veith, der Schlangensammler." *Neues Wiener Tagblatt*, November 1, 1925, 6–7.

Wieman, Bernard. *Bosnisches Tagebuch.* Kempten: Kösel'schen Buchhandlung, 1908.

Winter, Carl. "Das herzegowinische Paris." *Neues Wiener Tagblatt*, August 21, 1885, 1–2.

Wirth, C. "Fahrt durch Montenegro." *Neue Freie Presse*, February 11, 1916, 1–4.

Woinovich, Emil et al, eds. *A mi hőseink*, vol. 1, *Tisztjeink hőstettei a világháborúban.* Budapest: Franklin-Társulat, 1916.

Worm, Josef. "Auf Feldwache vor der Festung Trebinje." *Österreichische Volkszeitung*, November 3, 1914, 5.

Yriarte, Charles. *Bosnie et Herzégovine: Souvenirs de voyage pendant l'insurrection.* Paris: Plon, 1876.

Zuccaci, Maria. "Markttag in Trebinje: Ein Stück Orient in Jugoslawien." *Neues Wiener Journal*, September 6, 1930, 8.

Secondary Sources

Aleksov, Bojan. "The Serbian Orthodox Church." In *Orthodox Christianity and Nationalism in Nineteenth-Century Southeastern Europe*, edited by Lucian N. Leustean, 65–100. New York: Fordham University Press, 2014.

Aličić, Ahmed S. *Pokret za autonomiju Bosne od 1831. do 1832. godine.* Sarajevo: Orijentalni Institut, 1996.

Andrijašević, Živko M., and Šerbo Rastoder. *Crna Gora i velike sile.* Podgorica: Zavod za Udžbenike i Nastavna Sredstva, 2006.

Arnautović, Esad. "Austrougarska okupacija Trebinja." In *Prilozi za istoriju Trebinja u XIX stoljeću*, edited by Esad Arnautović, 9–23. Trebinje: Opštinska zajednica culture, 1986.

———. "Izvještaji austrijskog Vicekonzula iz Trebinja Vuka Vrčevića 1875–1878. godine." In *Prilozi za istoriju Trebinja u XIX stoljeću*, edited by Esad Arnautović, 24–121. Trebinje: Opštinska zajednica culture, 1986.

Arslanagić, Hamdija, and Adem Arslanagić. *Arslanagići i Arslanagića most.* Sarajevo: Maore, 1998.

Bakić, Dragan. "Transition from Austria-Hungary to Yugoslavia: The Serbian Army's Occupation of Bosnia and Herzegovina in Late 1918." In *Finir la Grande guerre dans les Balkans 1918–1923*, edited by Vojislav G. Pavlović, 91–139. Belgrade: Institut des Études balkaniques, 2022.

Bandžović, Safet. "Ratovi i demografska deosmanizacija Balkana (1912.–1941.)." *Prilozi*, no. 32 (2003): 179–229.

Baric, Daniel. "Archéologie classique et politique scientifique en Bosnie-Herzégovine habsbourgoise: Carl Patsch à Sarajevo (1891–1918)." *Revue germanique internationale* 16 (2012): 73–89.

Bartov, Omer. *Anatomy of a Genocide: The Life and Death of a Town Called Buczacz.* New York: Simon and Schuster, 2018.

Bartulović, Alenka. "'We Have an Old Debt with the Turk, and It Best Be Settled': Ottoman Incursions through the Discursive Optics of Slovenian Historiography and Literature and Their Applicability in the Twenty-First Century." In *Imagining "the Turk"*, ed. Božidar Jezernik, 111–37. Newcastle-upon-Tyne: Cambridge Scholars, 2010.

Baskar, Bojan. "Austronostalgia and Bosnian Muslims in the Work of Croatian Anthropologist Vera Stein Erlich." In *Imagining Bosnian Muslims in Central Europe: Representations, Transfers and Exchanges*, edited by František Šístek, 155–69. Oxford: Berghahn, 2021.

———. "Southbound, to the Austrian Riviera: The Habsburg Patronage of Tourism in the Eastern Adriatic." *Anthropological Notebooks* 16, no. 1 (2010): 9–22.

Bassett, Richard. *For God and Kaiser: The Imperial Austrian Army 1619–1918*. New Haven, CT: Yale University Press, 2015.

Bauer, Ernest. *Der letzte Paladin des Reiches: Generaloberst Stefan Freiherr Sarkotić von Lovćen*. Graz: Styria, 1988.

Baumann, Alexander. "Das 2. Bosnisch-hercegovinische Infanterieregiment in Graz Die öffentliche Wahrnehmung der Bosniaken." BA thesis, Karl-Franzens-Universität Graz, 2017.

Bencze, László. *The Occupation of Bosnia and Herzegovina in 1878*. New York: Columbia University Press, 2005.

Berdan, Helga. "Die Machtpolitik Österreich-Ungarns und der Eisenbahnbau in Bosnien Herzegowina." Master's thesis, University of Vienna, 2008.

Bjelić, Dušan I. *Normalizing the Balkans: Geopolitics of Psychoanalysis and Psychiatry*. Farnham: Ashgate, 2011.

Bojić, Mehmedalija. "Svrgavanje turske vlasti i odbrambeni rat Bosne i Hercegovine protiv austrougarske invazije 1878. godine." In *Naučni skup Otpor austrougarskoj okupaciji 1878. godine u Bosni i Hercegovini*, edited by Milorad Ekmečić, 71–94. Sarajevo: Akademija nauka i umjetnosti Bosne i Hercegovine, 1979.

Branković, Jasmin. *Mostar 1833–1918: Upravni i politički položaj grada*. Sarajevo: University Press Magistrat, 2009.

Brendel, Heiko. "'Our land is small, and it's pressed on all sides. Not one of us can live here peacefully': Population Policy in Montenegro from the Long Nineteenth Century to the End of the First World War." In *The First World War as a Caesura? Demographic Concepts, Population Policy, Genocide in Late Ottoman, Russian, and Habsburg Spheres*, edited by Christin Pschichholz, 135–58. Berlin: Duncker and Humblot, 2020.

Brixel, Eugen. "Es rauscht Musik, der Trommelwirbel hallet Versuch einer Militärmusikgeschichte der Garnison Graz." In *Graz als Garnison: Beiträge zur Militärgeschichte der steirischen Landeshauptstadt*, edited by Wilhelm Steinböck, 194–209. Graz: Leykam, 1982.

Carmichael, C. "'Za filozofa preveč romantičnega pridiha': Nekaj zapazanj o Valvasorjevi etnografiji." *Traditiones* 24 (1995): 95–107.

Charlesworth, Andrew. "The Topography of Genocide." In *The Historiography of the Holocaust*, edited by Dan Stone, 216–52. Basingstoke: Palgrave Macmillan, 2004.

Cole, Laurence, and Daniel L. Unowsky, eds. *The Limits of Loyalty: Imperial Symbolism, Popular Allegiances, and State Patriotism in the Late Habsburg Monarchy*. New York: Berghahn, 2007.

Cole, Laurence. *Military Culture and Popular Patriotism in Late Imperial Austria.* Oxford: Oxford University Press, 2014.

Cornwall, Mark. "The Spirit of 1914 in Austria-Hungary." *Prispevki za Novejšo Zgodovino* 55, no. 2 (2015): 7–21.

Ćorović, Vladimir. *Crna knjiga: Patnje Srba Bosne i Hercegovine za vreme svetskog rata 1914–1918. godine.* Belgrade: Izdanje I. Đurđevića, 1920.

———. *The Relations between Serbia and Austria-Hungary in the 20th Century.* Belgrade: Archives of Yugoslavia, 2018.

Ćutura, Dinko. *Stjepan Sarkotić, posljednji poglavar Bosne i Hercegovine.* Zagreb: AGM, 2019.

Cvijić, Siniša, and Jasna Guzijan. "Urban Regeneration as an Instrument of Identity Preservation: A Case Study of Trebinje's Krš District." *Arhiv za Tehničke Nauke/Archives for Technical Sciences*, no. 14 (2016): 19–27.

Damjanović, Dragan. "Austro-ugarska okupacija Bosne i Hercegovine gledana očima hrvatskog slikara: Prijelaz Save kod Broda Ferdinanda Quiquereza." *Radovi Instituta za povijest umjetnosti* 41 (2017): 199–214.

Deák, István. *Beyond Nationalism: A Social and Political History of the Habsburg Officer Corps 1848–1918.* Oxford: Oxford University Press, 1990.

Dedijer, Vladimir. *The Road to Sarajevo.* New York: Simon and Schuster, 1966.

Djokić, Dejan. *A Concise History of Serbia.* Cambridge: Cambridge University Press, 2023.

Donia, Robert J. *Islam under the Double Eagle: The Muslims of Bosnia and Hercegovina 1871–1914.* New York: Eastern European Monographs, 1981.

———. *Sarajevo: A Biography.* Ann Arbor: University of Michigan Press, 2006.

———. "The Habsburg Imperial Army in the Occupation of Bosnia and Hercegovina." In *Insurrections, Wars, and the Eastern Crisis in the 1870s,* edited by Bela K. Kiraly and Gale Stokes, 375–91. Boulder, CO: Social Science Monographs, 1985.

Dredger, John A. *Tactics and Procurement in the Habsburg Military 1866–1918: Offensive Spending.* Cham: Palgrave Macmillan, 2017.

Duančić, Vedran. *Geography and Nationalist Visions of Interwar Yugoslavia: Modernity, Memory and Identity in South-East Europe.* Cham: Palgrave Macmillan, 2020.

Dulić, Tomislav. *Utopias of Nations: Local Mass Killing in Bosnia and Herzegovina, 1941–42.* Uppsala: Uppsala Universitet, 2005.

Duranović, Amir. "The Aggressiveness of Bosnian and Herzegovinian Serbs in the Public Discourse during the Balkan Wars." In *War and Nationalism: The Balkan Wars, 1912–1913 and Their Sociopolitical Implications,* edited by M. Hakan Yavuz and Isa Blumi, foreword by Edward J. Erickson, 371–98. Salt Lake City: University of Utah Press, 2013.

Džaja, Srećko. *Bosnien-Herzegowina in der österreichisch-ungarischen Epoche (1878–1918): Die Intelligentsia zwischen Tradition und Ideologie.* Munich: Oldenbourg, 1994.

Dželetović, Branko. *Bileća kroz ratove i događaje u XX vijeku.* Bileća: Srpsko prosvjetno i kulturno društvo "Prosvjeta," 2004.

Ekmečić, Milorad. *Ustanak u Bosni: 1875–1878.* Sarajevo: Veselin Masleša, 1973.

———. "Ustanak u Hercegovini 1882. i istorijske pouke." *Prilozi*, no. 19 (1982): 9–74.

———. "Žalosna baština iz godine 1914: Političke namjene sudskih procesa u Bosni i Hercegovini za vrijeme prvog svjetskog rata." In *Veleizdajnički proces u Banjaluci,* ed. Galib Šljivo, 13–41. Banja Luka: Institut za istoriju, 1987.

Evans, Joan. *Time and Chance: The Story of Arthur Evans and His Forebears.* London: Longmans, Green and Company, 1943.

Fahey, John E. *Przemyśl, Poland: A Multiethnic City During and After a Fortress, 1867–1939.* West Lafayette, IN: Purdue University Press, 2023.

Figurić, Ante. *Trebinje nekada i danas.* Ljubljana: Tiskarna Slovenija, 1930.

Fine, John V. A. "The Medieval and Ottoman Roots of Modern Bosnian Society." In *The Muslims of Bosnia-Herzegovina: Their Historic Development from the Middle Ages to the Dissolution of Yugoslavia*, edited by Mark Pinson, 1–21. Cambridge, MA: Harvard University Press, 1996.

Flamm, Heinz. "Aufklärung des Pappataci-Fiebers durch österreichische Militärärzte." *Wiener Klinische Wochenschrift*, no. 120 (2008): 198–208.

Fontana, Nicola. "Trient als Festungs- und Garnisonsstadt: Militär und Zivilbevölkerung in einer k. u. k. Festungsstadt, 1880–1914." In *Glanz—Gewalt—Gehorsam: Militär und Gesellschaft in der Habsburgermonarchie (1800 bis 1918)*, edited by Laurence Cole, Christa Hämmerle, and Martin Scheutz, 177–98. Essen: Klartext, 2011.

Foster, Samuel. *Yugoslavia in the British Imagination: Peace, War and Peasants before Tito.* London: Bloomsbury, 2021.

Fuchs, Brigitte. "Orientalizing Disease: Austro-Hungarian Policies of 'Race,' Gender and Hygiene in Bosnia and Herzegovina, 1874–1914." In *Health, Hygiene and Eugenics in Southeastern Europe to 1945*, edited by Christian Promitzer, Sevasti Trubeta, and Marius Turda. Budapest–New York: Central European University Press, 2011.

Furneaux, Holly. *Military Men of Feeling: Emotion, Touch and Masculinity in the Crimean War.* Oxford: Oxford University Press, 2016.

Gerwarth, Robert. *The Vanquished: Why the First World War Failed to End, 1917–1923.* London: Penguin, 2017.

Giomi, Fabio. *Making Muslim Women European: Voluntary Associations, Gender, and Islam in Post-Ottoman Bosnia and Yugoslavia (1878–1941).* Budapest–New York: Central European University Press, 2021.

Glenny, Misha. *The Balkans, 1804–2012: Nationalism, War and the Great Powers.* London: Granta, 2020.

Gjivoje, Marinko. "Prilog historijatu speleologije u Hrvatskoj." *Speleolog: Časopis za Speleologiju* 2, no. 2 (1954): 49–51.

Göderle, Wolfgang. "The Habsburg Anthropocene: Vipers and Mongooses in Late Habsburg Southern Dalmatia." *Südost-Forschungen* 79, no. 1 (2020): 215–40.

———. "Materializing Imperial Rule? Nature, Environment, and the Middle Class in Habsburg Central Europe." *Hungarian Historical Review* 11, no. 2 (2022): 445–76.

Gojković, Milan. "Arslanagića most kod Trebinja." *Zbornik zaštite spomenika*, no. 14 (1963): 21–38.

Grandits, Hannes. *The End of Ottoman Rule in Bosnia: Conflicting Agencies and Imperial Appropriations.* London: Routledge, 2021.

———. *Herrschaft und Loyalität in der spätosmanischen Gesellschaft: Das Beispiel der multikonfessionellen Herzegowina.* Vienna: Böhlau, 2008.

———. "Violent Social Disintegration: A Nation-Building Strategy in Late-Ottoman Herzegovina." In *Conflicting Loyalties in the Balkans: The Great Powers, the Ottoman Empire and Nation-Building*, edited by Hannes Grandits, Nathalie Clayer and Robert Pichler, 110–33. London: I. B. Tauris, 2011.

Greble, Emily. *Muslims and the Making of Modern Europe.* Oxford: Oxford University Press, 2021.

Grunert, Heiner. *Glauben im Hinterland: Die Serbisch-Orthodoxen in der habsburgischen Herzegowina 1878–1918.* Göttingen: Vandenhoeck and Ruprecht, 2016.

———. "The Inner Enemy in Wartime: The Habsburg State and the Serb Citizens of Bosnia-Herzegovina, 1913–1918." In *Sarajevo 1914: Sparking the First World War,* edited by Mark Cornwall, 253–73. London: Bloomsbury, 2020.

Gumz, Jonathan E. *The Resurrection and Collapse of Empire in Habsburg Serbia, 1914–1918.* Cambridge: Cambridge University Press, 2009.

Hadžibegović, Iljas. *Bosanskohercegovački gradovi na razmeđu 19. i 20. Stoljeća.* Sarajevo: Institut za istoriju, 2004.

Hadžijahić, Muhamed. "Emigracije muslimana Bosne i Hercegovine u Tursku u doba austro-ugarske vladavine 1878.–1918. god." *Historijski zbornik* 3 (1950): 70–75.

HadžiMuhamedović, Safet. *Waiting for Elijah: Time and Encounter in a Bosnian Landscape.* Oxford: Berghahn, 2018.

Hadžismailović, Vefik. "Edmund Misera." *Behar* 109 (2013): 65–66.

Hajdarpašić, Edin. *Whose Bosnia? Nationalism and Political Imagination in the Balkans, 1840–1914.* Ithaca, NY: Cornell University Press, 2015.

Hanták, Daniel. "Jiří Václav Daneš (1880–1928)." BA thesis, Charles University, Prague, 2013.

Hämmerle, Christa. "Die k. (u.) k. Armee als 'Schule des Volkes'? Zur Geschichte der Allgemeinen Wehrpflicht in der multinationalen Habsburgermonarchie (1866–1914/1918)." In *Der Bürger als Soldat: Die Militarisierung europäischer Gesellschaften im langen 19. Jahrhundert; Ein internationaler Vergleich,* edited by Christian Jansen, 175–213. Essen: Klartext, 2004.

———. *Ganze Männer? Gesellschaft, Geschlecht und Allgemeine Wehrpflicht in Österreich-Ungarn (1868–1914).* Frankfurt: Campus, 2022.

Happ, Helga, and Paul Mildner. "Georg Veith—Herpetologe, Altertumsforscher und Soldat." *Rudolfinum: Jahrbuch des Landesmuseums für Kärnten* (2003): 435–43.

Harari, Yuval Noah. *Renaissance Military Memoirs: War, History and Identity, 1450–1600.* Woodbridge: Boydell, 2004.

Hauptmann, Ferdinand. *Die Österreichisch-ungarische Herrschaft in Bosnien und der Hercegovina, 1878–1918: Wirtschaftpläne und Wirtschaftsentwicklung.* Graz: Institut für Geschichte an der Universität Graz, 1983.

———. "General Rodić i politika austrijske vlade u krivošijskom ustanku 1869/70: (Uz dnevnike generala Gabrijela Rodića)." *Godišnjak društva istoričara Bosne i Hercegovine* 13 (1962): 53–91.

Hartmuth, Maximilian. "The Habsburg Landesmuseum in Sarajevo in its ideological and architectural contexts: a reinterpretation." *Centropa* 12, no. 2 (2012): 194–205.

Hauser, Bernd. "Ein autobiographisches Fragment von Leo Weirather (1887–1965), dem Tiroler Pionier der biospeläologischen Erforschung des Balkans." *Contributions to Natural History: Scientific Papers from the Natural History Museum Bern,* no. 12 (2009): 603–13.

Hecht, Dieter J. "Bosnische Impressionen: k.k. Soldaten als Tourismuspioniere vor dem Ersten Weltkrieg." In *Zwischen Exotik und Vertrautem: Zum Tourismus in der Habsburgermonarchie und ihren Nachfolgestaaten,* edited by Peter Stachel and Martina Thomson, 201–16. Bielefeld: Transcript, 2014.

Healy, Roísín. "From Travel to Mobility: Perspectives on Journeys in the Russian, Central and East European Past." In *Mobility in the Russian, Central and East European Past*, edited by Roísín Healy, 1–14. London: Routledge, 2019.

Healy, Maureen. "Europe on the Sava: Austrian Encounters with 'Turks' in Bosnia." *Austrian History Yearbook* 51 (2020): 73–87.

Holzer, Anton. *Das Lächeln der Henker: Der unbekannte Krieg gegen die Zivilbevölkerung 1914–1918.* 2nd ed. Darmstadt: Primus, 2014.

Horel, Catherine. "Franz Joseph's Tafelspitz: Austro-Hungarian Cooking as an Imperial Project." In *Food Heritage and Nationalism in Europe*, edited by Ilaria Porciani, 138–54. London: Routledge, 2019.

Horne, John N., and Alan Kramer. *German Atrocities, 1914: A History of Denial.* New Haven, CT: Yale University Press, 2001.

Hukić, Mirsada, and Irma Salimović-Besić. "Sandfly-Pappataci fever in Bosnia and Herzegovina: The New-Old Disease." *Bosnian Journal of Basic Medical Sciences* 9, no. 1 (2009): 39–43.

Hutečka, Jiří. *Men Under Fire: Motivation, Morale, and Masculinity among Czech Soldiers in the Great War, 1914–1918.* Oxford: Berghahn, 2020.

Hunt, Lynn. *Inventing Human Rights: A History.* New York: Norton, 2007.

Ilić, Ninoslav. "Revitalisation of k.u.k. fortifications in Trebinje: Design sample; Fort Kličanj." BA thesis, Institute for Architecture and Design, University of Vienna, 2017.

Isnard, Hildebert. "Notes sur la transhumance pastorale en Herzégovine." *Méditerranée* 2, no. 2 (1961): 37–55.

Jelavich, Charles. "The Revolt in Bosnia-Hercegovina, 1881–2." *The Slavonic and East European Review* 31, no. 77 (1953): 420–36.

Jelić, Djoko, Matjaž Jeršić, Jože Lojk, and Metod Vojvoda. "The Cadastrian Commune of Trebijovi in the Karstland of Hercegovina." *Geographia Polonica* 5 (1965): 267–84.

Jeřábek, Rudolf. *Potiorek: General im Schatten von Sarajevo.* Graz: Styria, 1991.

Jezernik, Božidar. *Jugoslavija, zemlja snova.* Belgrade: Biblioteka XX vek, 2018.

———. *Wild Europe: The Balkans in the Gaze of Western Travellers.* London: Saqi, 2004.

Jovanović, Jovan. "Izvještaj Atanasija Vasiljevića Vasiljeva o Završetku Hercegovačkog Ustanka 1875–1878. godine." *Prilozi*, no. 13 (1977): 328–33.

Judson, Pieter. *The Habsburg Empire: A New History.* Cambridge, MA: Harvard University Press, 2016.

Juvanec, Borut. "Popovo polje, a different view." *Acta Carsologica* 45, no. 3 (2016): 275–83.

Juzbašić, Dževad. "Austrougarski planovi gradnje strateških željeznica na Balkanu u oči kretske krize i izgradnja željezničke pruge prema Boki Kotorskoj, Trebinju i Dubrovniku." *Prilozi*, no. 8 (1972): 11–32.

Kamberović, Husnija. *Begovski Zemljišni posjedi u Bosni i Hercegovini od 1878. do 1918. godine.* Zagreb: Hrvatski institut za povijest, 2003.

Kapel, Anton. "Contribution to the History of the Explorations of the Cave Vjetrenica in Zavala to 1914." *Acta Carsologica* 26, no. 2 (1997): 95–98.

Kapidžić, Hamdija. *Bosna i Hercegovina u vrijeme austrougarske vladavine: (članci i rasprave).* Sarajevo: Svjetlost, 1968.

———. *Hercegovački ustanak 1882 godine.* Sarajevo: Veselin Masleša, 1958.

Karaula, Željko. "Posljednja crnogorska bitka—Dnevnik austro-ugarskog generala Stjepana Sarkotića." *Montenegrin Journal for Social Sciences* 3, no. 1 (2019): 115–42.

Karan, Isidora. "The Significance of the Topographic Element of Hill in the Modern Urban Context: Crkvina and Jablanica." *SPATIUM International Review* 31 (July 2014): 7–13.

———. "Trebinje on the Border between East and West: Heritage and Memory of Trebinje Bosnian-Herzegovinian Town." *Revista Bitácora Urbano Territorial* 24, no. 2 (2014): 31–40.

Kirigin, Branko. *Arthur Evans in Dubrovnik and Split (1875–1882)*. Oxford: Archaeopress, 2015.

Klaus, Elisabeth. "Rhetoriken über Krieg: Karl Kraus gegen Alice Schalek." *Feministische Studien* 26, no. 1 (2008): 65–82.

Korać, Vojislav. *Trebinje: Istorijski pregled*, vol. 2, parts 2 and 3. Trebinje: Zavičajni muzej, 1971.

Kostrhun, Petr. "Prehistorie v obdobi Československé republiky: Rozvoj moravské paleolitické archeologie mezi léty 1918–1938." Ph.D. diss., Institute of Archeology and Museology, Masaryk University, Brno, 2013.

Kostrhun, Petr, and Martin Oliva. *K. Absolon: Fotografie z evropských jeskyní a krasů.* Brno: Moravské zemské muzeum, 2010.

Ković, Miloš. "The Beginning of the 1875 Serbian Uprising in Herzegovina: The British Perspective." *Balcanica* 41 (2010): 55–72.

Kraljačić, Tomislav. "Austrougarski planovi o stvaranju etničkog zida u istočnoj Bosni u Prvom svetskom ratu." *Srbu u BIH*, https://srbiubih.com/austrougarski-planovi-o-stvaranju-etnickog-zida-u-istocnoj-bosni-u-prvom-svjetskom-ratu/, accessed May 5, 2024.

———. *Kalajev režim u Bosni i Hercegovini (1882–1903)*. Sarajevo: Izdavačko Veselin, 1987.

Kramer, Alan. *Dynamic of Destruction: Culture and Mass Killing in the First World War.* Oxford: Oxford University Press, 2007.

Krivec, Jaroš. "Pogled na drugega: Podobe Bosne in Hercegovine in njenih prebivalcev med 1878 in 1918." MA thesis, University of Ljubljana, 2021.

Křivka, Pavel, and Vojtěch Holubec. "The Balkan Collections in the Main Czech Herbaria." *Phytologia Balcanica* 16, no. 2 (2010): 215–20.

Lane, James B. *City of the Century: A History of Gary, Indiana.* Bloomington: Indiana University Press, 1978.

Lange, Frederik. "Kooperation und Konfrontation—Der Grenzstreit in der habsburgisch-serbischen Kontaktzone Drina-Becken, 1878–1914." *Storia e regione* 31, no. 2 (2022): 91–110.

Lefnaer, Stefan. "Erhaltene Galgen in Österreich." *Richtstättenarchäologie* 3 (2010): 214–69.

Leidinger, Hannes. "Suizid und Militär: Debatten—Ursachenforschung—Reichsratsinterpellationen, 1907–1914." In *Glanz—Gewalt—Gehorsam: Militär und Gesellschaft in der Habsburgermonarchie (1800 bis 1918)*, edited by Laurence Cole, Christa Hämmerle, and Martin Scheutz, 337–58. Essen: Klartext, 2011.

Levene, Mark. *The Crisis of Genocide*, vol. 1, *Devastation: The European Rimlands 1912–1938*. Oxford: Oxford University Press, 2014.

Lučić, Iva. "Law of the Forest: Early Legal Governance in Bosnia-Herzegovina during the Inter-Imperial Transition between Ottoman and Austro-Hungarian Rule 1878–1901." *Slavic Review* 81, no. 3 (2022): 585–608.

Lučić, Ivo. "Povijest poznavanja Dinarskog krša na primjeru Popova polja." Ph.D. diss., Nova Gorica University, 2009.

Lučić, Ivo. "Shafts of Life and Shafts of Death in Dinaric Karst, Popovo Polje Case (Bosnia and Herzegovina)." *Acta Carsologica* 36, no. 2 (2007): 321–30.

Lukić, Nenad and Walter Mentzel. "Popis umrlih Srba u logoru Šopronjek/Neckenmarkt 1915–1918. godine." *Godišnjak za istraživanje genocida* 8 (2016): 15–69.

Luković, Petko. "Slovenci i hercegovački ustanak protiv Austro-Ugarske 1882. godine." *Zgodovinski časopis* 36, nos. 1–2 (1982): 45–83.

Lupić, Ivo. "Arthur Evans and the Illyrian Parnassus." *Dubrovnik Annals* 25 (2021): 149–88.

Lyon, James. *Serbia and the Balkan Front, 1914: The Outbreak of the Great War.* London: Bloomsbury, 2015.

Mader, Brigitta. "Zu Arthur J. Evans' Ausweisung und Verhaftung in Ragusa aus den Geheimakten der k. k. Statthalterei für Dalmatien in Zara 1880 und 1882." *Eteokriti: Verein zur wissenschaftlichen Erforschung Kretas und der Ägäis*, no. 3 (2013): 8–20.

Madžar, Božo. "Istorijat Gradskog Vodovoda u Trebinju." *Tribunia: Prilozi za istoriju, arheologiju, etnologiju, umjetnost i kulturu*, nos. 7–8 (1984): 51–64.

Malečková, Jitka. *"The Turk" in the Czech Imagination (1870s–1923).* Leiden: Brill, 2020.

Malešević, Siniša. "Forging the Nation-Centric World: Imperial Rule and the Homogenisation of Discontent in Bosnia and Herzegovina (1878–1918)." *Journal of Historical Sociology* 34, no. 4 (2021): 665–87.

Marchetti, Christian. "Austro-Hungarian Volkskunde at War: Scientists on Ethnographic Mission in World War I." In *Doing Anthropology in Wartime and War Zones: World War I and the Cultural Sciences in Europe*, edited by Reinhard Johler, Christian Marchetti, and Monique Scheer, 207–30. Berlin: De Gruyter, 2014.

Mašić, Izet. "One Hundred Fifty Years of Organized Health Care Services in Bosnia and Herzegovina." *Medical Archives* 72, no. 5 (2018): 374–88.

Mattes, Johannes. *Reisen ins Unterirdische: Eine Kulturgeschichte der Höhlenforschung in Österreich bis in die Zwischenkriegszeit.* Vienna: Böhlau, 2015.

McCarthy, Justin. "Archival Sources concerning Serb Rebellions in Bosnia 1875–76." In *Ottoman Bosnia: A History in Peril*, edited by Markus Koller and Kemal H. Karpat, 141–45. Madison: University of Wisconsin Press, 2004.

Melichar, Peter. "Ästhetik und Disziplin: Das Militär in Wiener Neustadt 1740–1914." In *Die Wienerische Neustadt: Handwerk, Handel und Militär*, edited by Sylvia Hahn and Karl Flanner, 283–336. Vienna: Böhlau, 1994.

Meyer, Anna-Maria. "Was ist Armeeslavisch?" In *Linguistische Beiträge zur Slavistik*, edited by Ivana Lederer, Anna-Maria Meyer, and Katrin Schlund, 63–88. Berlin: Peter Lang. 2020.

Mijušković, Slavko. *Ustanak u Boki Kotorskoj 1869.* Kotor: Centar za kulturu, 1970.

Miklobušec, Valentin. "Od Trebinja do stratišta: O. Josip Müller DI (1883–1945)." *Obnovljeni Život: časopis za filozofiju i religijske znanosti* 69, no. 2 (2014): 193–219.

Miladinović, Jovo. "Heroes, Traitors, and Survivors in the Borderlands of Empires: Military Mobilizations and Local Communities in the Sandžak (1900s–1920s)." Ph.D. diss., Humboldt University, Berlin, 2022.

Milošević, Vlado. "Tambura i harmonika u bosanskom varoškom pjevanju." *Zbornik Krajiških muzeja* 1 (1962): 132–35.

Mitrović, Andrej. *Serbia's Great War, 1914–1918*. London: Hurst, 2007.

Morrison, Kenneth. *Sarajevo's Holiday Inn on the Frontline of Politics and War*. London: Palgrave Macmillan, 2016.

Morscher, Christine and Ray Galvin. "Alice Schalek's War: The Story of Austria-Hungary's Only Woman War Correspondent in the First World War." Cambridge, 2006. Online at http://justsolutions.eu/resources/AliceSchaleksWar.pdf.

Mulaomerović, Jasminko. "Caves as Illustrations in Popular and Scientific Articles." In *Proceedings of the International Symposium on History of Speleology and Karstology in Alps, Carpathians and Dinarides, ALCADI 2018*, 50–61. Sarajevo: Center for Karst and Speleology, 2019.

Naletilić, Marija. "O povijesti duhana u Hercegovini do kraja Prvoga svjetskoga rata." *Godišnjak Centra za balkanološka ispitivanja* 39 (2010): 189–97.

Newman, John Paul. *Yugoslavia in the Shadow of War: Veterans and the Limits of State Building, 1903–1945*. Cambridge: Cambridge University Press, 2015.

Nikolić, Anja. "Similarities and Differences in Imperial Administration: Great Britain in Egypt and Austria-Hungary in Bosnia-Herzegovina 1878–1903." *Balcanica* 47 (2016): 177–95.

Nizich, Ivana. *War Crimes in Bosnia-Hercegovina*, vol. 2. Washington, DC: Human Rights Watch, 1992.

Okey, Robin. *Taming Balkan Nationalism: The Habsburg "Civilizing Mission" in Bosnia 1878–1914*. Oxford: Oxford University Press, 2007.

Oršolić, Tado. "Sudjelovanje dalmatinskih postrojbi u zaposjedanju Bosne i Hercegovine 1878." *Radovi Zavoda za povijesne znanosti HAZU u Zadru*, no. 42 (2000): 287–308.

Otte, Thomas G. *July Crisis: The World's Descent into War, Summer 1914*. Cambridge: Cambridge University Press, 2014.

Pachauer, Volker Konstantin. "Austro-Hungarian Fortification in Bosnia-Herzegovina and Montenegro: Cultural Heritage between Value, Touristic Potential and Extinction." *International Journal of Heritage Architecture* 2, no. 1 (2018): 149–58.

———. "Trebinje: Austro-Hungarian Garrison and Fortress 1878–1918." *Tribunia: Prilozi za istoriju, arheologiju, etnologiju, umjetnost i kulturu* 13 (2014): 175–89.

Pachauer, Volker Konstantin, and Filip Suchoń. "Typy zieleni i elementy wodne w przestrzeni dawnego miasta-twierdzy Trebinje/Types of greenery and water features in the space of the former fortress-city of Trebinje." *Środowisko Mieszkaniowe*, no. 24 (2018): 82–88.

Papić, Mitar. "Prve Škole u Trebinju." *Tribunia: Prilozi za istoriju, arheologiju, etnologiju, umjetnost i kulturu*, no. 2 (1976): 97–103.

Parežanin, Ratko. *Die Attentäter: Das junge Bosnien im Freiheitskampf*. Munich: L. Jevtić, 1976.

Pederin, Ivan. "Vojne operacije domaršala baruna Stjepana Jovanovića u Hercegovini 1878. i u Krivošijama 1882." *Bosna Franciscana*, no. 35 (2011): 123–32.

Pennanen, Risto Pekka. "Immortalised on Wax—Professional Folk Musicians and their Gramophone Recordings Made in Sarajevo, 1907 and 1908." In *Europe and its Others: Notes on the Balkans*, edited by Božidar Jezernik, Rajko Muršič, and Alenka Bartulović, 107–48. Ljubljana: Filozofska fakulteta, 2007.

Preljević, Vahidin. "'Zauberhafte Mischung' und 'reine Volksseele': Literatur, Kultur und Widersprüche der imperialen Konstellation im habsburgischen Bosnien-Herzegowina um 1900." In *Bosnien-Herzegowina und Österreich-Ungarn, 1878–1918: Annäherungen an eine Kolonie*, edited by Clemens Ruthner and Tamara Scheer, 373-91. Tübingen: Narr Francke Attempto, 2018.

Pretner, Egon. "Die Verdienste von Leo Weirather um die Biospeläologie, insbesondere Jugoslawiens, sein Höhlenkataster und seine Sammelplätze." *Berichte des Naturwissenschaftlich-medizinischen Vereins in Innsbruck* 97 (2011): 85-234.

Puskar, Samira. *Bosnian Americans of Chicagoland*. Charleston, SC: Arcadia, 2007.

Puvačić, Dušan. *Balkan Themes: Tradition and Change in Serbian and Croatian Literature*. Paris: Éditions Ésopie, 2013.

Puzović, Predrag. "Stradanje sveštenstva Zahumsko-hercegovačke eparhije tokom Prvog svetskog rat." *Bogoslovlje*, no. 1 (2016): 22-32.

Rady, Martyn. *The Habsburgs: The Rise and Fall of a World Power*. London: Allen Lane, 2020.

Rauchensteiner, Manfried. *The First World War and the End of the Habsburg Monarchy 1914-1918*. Vienna: Böhlau, 2014.

Reber, Ursula. "The Experience of Borders: Montenegrin Tribesmen at War." In *Doing Anthropology in Wartime and War Zones: World War I and the Cultural Sciences in Europe*, edited by Reinhard Johler, Christian Marchetti, and Monique Scheer, 191-206. Berlin: De Gruyter, 2014.

Redžić, Sulejman. "Wild Edible Plants and their Traditional Use in the Human Nutrition in Bosnia-Herzegovina." *Ecology of Food and Nutrition* 45, no. 3 (2006): 189-232.

Reynolds Cordileone, Diana. "Swords into Souvenirs: Bosnian Arts and Crafts under Habsburg Administration." In *Doing Anthropology in Wartime and War Zones: World War I and the Cultural Sciences in Europe*, edited by Reinhard Johler, Christian Marchetti, and Monique Scheer, 169-90. Berlin: De Gruyter, 2014.

Roper, Michael. *The Secret Battle: Emotional Survival in the Great War*. Manchester and New York: Manchester University Press, 2009.

Rothenberg, Gunther. *The Army of Francis Joseph*. West Lafayette, IN: Purdue University Press, 1976.

Ruthner, Clemens. "Die Invasoren und Insurgenten des Okkupationsfeldzugs 1878 im kulturellen Gedächtnis." In *Bosnien-Herzegowina und Österreich-Ungarn, 1878-1918: Annäherungen an eine Kolonie*, edited by Clemens Ruthner and Tamara Scheer, 123-46. Tübingen: Narr Francke Attempto, 2018.

———. *Habsburgs "Dark Continent": Postkoloniale Lektüren zur österreichischen Literatur und Kultur im langen 19. Jahrhundert*. Tübingen: Narr Francke Attempto, 2018.

Šarić, Salko. "Sigmund Freud u Trebinju 1898. godine." *Most*, no. 175 [85] (2004), online at https://www.most.ba/085/095.aspx.

Sattler, Gernot. "Vorwart." *Herpetozoa* 3, nos. 3-4 (1991): 99-102.

Šćekić, Milan. "Crnogorski dobrovoljci u prvom svjetskom ratu (1914-1916)." *Matica crnogorska*, no. 66 (2016): 223-56.

Schachinger, Werner. *Die Bosniaken kommen: Elitetruppe in der k.u.k. Armee, 1879-1918*. Graz: Stocker, 1994.

Scheer, Tamara. *Die Sprachenvielfalt in der österreichisch-ungarischen Armee (1867-1918)*. Vienna: Heeresgeschichtliches Museum, 2022.

———. *"Minimale Kosten, absolut kein Blut!": Österreich-Ungarns Präsenz im Sandžak von Novipazar (1879–1908)*. Frankfurt: Peter Lang, 2013.

———. *Von Friedensfurien und dalmatinischen Küstenrehen: Vergessene Worte aus der Habsburgermonarchie*. Vienna: Amalthea Signum, 2019.

Schindler, John R. "Defeating Balkan Insurgency: The Austro-Hungarian Army in Bosnia-Hercegovina, 1878–82." *Journal of Strategic Studies* 27, no. 3 (2004): 528–52.

Šehić, Zijad. "Atentat, mobilizacija, rat." *Prilozi*, no. 34 (2005): 23–38.

———. "Vojni imami u bosanskohercegovačkim jedinicama u okviru austrougarske armije 1878–1918." *Godišnjak BZK Preporod*, no. 1 (2006): 309–21.

Sivrić, Marijan. "Osnivanje i rad Kotarskog odbora Narodnog Vijeća z ujedinjenje u Trebinju u Novembru i Decembru 1918. godine." *Tribunia: Prilozi za istoriju, arheologiju, etnologiju, umjetnost i kulturu*, nos. 7–8 (1984): 65–72.

———. "Radnički pokret u Trebinju od konca 19. stoljeća do 1918. godine." *Tribunia: Prilozi za istoriju, arheologiju, etnologiju, umjetnost i kulturu*, no. 6 (1982): 95–112.

Skoko, Savo. *Pokolji hercegovačkih Srba '41*. Belgrade: Stručna knjiga, 1991.

Šljivo, Galib. *Klek i Sutorina u međunarodnim odnosima 1815–1878*. Belgrade: Filozofski fakultet, 1977.

Smajić, Ramiza. "Migracijski tokovi, društveno-političke prilike u Bosanskom ejaletu (1683.–1718.)." Ph.D. diss., University of Zagreb, 2019.

Sparks, Mary. *The Development of Austro-Hungarian Sarajevo, 1878–1918: An Urban History*. London: Bloomsbury, 2015.

Sondhaus, Lawrence. *Franz Conrad von Hötzendorf: Architect of the Apocalypse*. Leiden: Brill, 2000.

Standeker, Borut Rudolf. "Die Rolle des Feuilletons während des Zweiten Weltkrieges in der deutschsprachigen Presse in Oberkrain und der Untersteiermark Fallbeispiele *Marburger Zeitung* und *Karawanken Bote*." BA thesis, University of Ljubljana, 2020.

Stergar, Rok. *Slovenci in vojska, 1867–1914: Slovenski odnos do vojaških vprašanj od uvedbe dualizma do začetka 1. svetovne vojne*. Ljubljana: Oddelek za zgodovino Filozofske fakultete, 2004.

———. *"Vojski prijazen in zaželen garnizon": Ljubljanski častniki med prelomom stoletja in prvo svetovno vojno*. Ljubljana: Zveza zgodovinskih društev Slovenije, 1999.

Stone, Norman. "Army and Society in the Habsburg Monarchy." *Past and Present*, no. 33 (1966): 95–111.

Sugar, Peter F. *East European Nationalism, Politics and Religion*. Farnham: Ashgate, 1999.

———. *Industrialization of Bosnia-Hercegovina, 1878–1918*. Seattle: University of Washington Press, 1963.

Suppan, Arnold. "Aussen- und militärpolitische Strategie Österreich-Ungarns vor Beginn des bosnischen Aufstandes 1875." In *Međunarodni naučni skup povodom 100-godišnjice ustanka u Bosni i Hercegovini, drugim balkanskim zemljama i istočnoj krizi 1875–1878. godine*, vol. 1, edited by Rade Petrović, 159–77. Sarajevo: Akademija nauka i umjetnosti Bosne i Hercegovine, 1977.

Šuško, Dževada. "Bosniaks and Loyalty: Responses to the Conscription Law in Bosnia and Hercegovina 1881/82." *Hungarian Historical Review*, no. 3 (2014): 529–59.

Swales, Peter. "Freud, Death and Sexual Pleasures: On the Psychical Mechanism of Dr. Sigmund Freud." *Arc de Cercle*, no. 1 (2003): 4–74.

Talam, Jasmina. *Folk Musical Instruments in Bosnia and Herzegovina*. Newcastle-upon-Tyne: Cambridge Scholars, 2013.

Talam, Jasmina, and Tamara Karača Beljak. "Matija Murko and His Researches in Bosnia and Herzegovina." In *"Music in Society": The Collection of Papers* (Sarajevo: Musicological Society of the Federation of Bosnia and Herzegovina Academy of Music, University of Sarajevo, 2016), 549–60.

Tankha, Akshaya, and Rahaab Allana. "Photographs of the Aftermath, 1857." *India International Centre Quarterly* 34, no. 1 (2007): 8–24.

Tepavčević, Ivan. "Boka Kotorska at the Beginning of the 20th Century." *Montenegrin Journal for Social Sciences* 3, no. 1 (2019): 101–15.

Terzić, Velimir, Dragić Vujošević, Ilija Jovanović, and Uroš Kostić. *Operacije crnogorske vojske u prvom svetskom ratu*. Belgrade: Vojno Delo, 1954.

Tomović, Nada. "Saradnja muslimanskog i pravoslavnog stanovništva u toku austrougarske okupacije Bosne i Hercegovine 1878–1882. godine." *Almanah*, nos. 81–82 (2019): 65–74.

Treadway, John D. *The Falcon and the Eagle: Montenegro and Austria-Hungary 1908–1914*. West Lafayette, IN: Purdue University Press, 1998.

Trode, Rachel. "The Sarajevo Tobacco Factory Strike of 1906: Empire and the Nature of Late Habsburg Rule in Bosnia and Herzegovina." *Central European History* 55, no. 4 (2022): 493–509.

Turhan, Fatma Sel. *The Ottoman Empire and the Bosnian Uprising: Janissaries, Modernisation and Rebellion in the Nineteenth Century*. London: I. B. Tauris, 2014.

Velagić, Adnan. "Atentat u Sarajevu i njegove refleksije na području Hercegovine." *Historijski pogledi*, no. 2 (2019): 174–93.

Verginella, Marta. "La mobilità femminile tra confini politici e nazionali nell'area alto-adriatica tra Ottocento e Novecento." *DEP*, no. 38 (2018): 69–82.

Vidović, Domagoj. "Toponimija sela Zavala, Golubinac, Belenići i Kijev Do u Popovu." *Folia onomastica croatica*, no. 20 (2011): 207–48.

Viktořík, Michael. *Hinter den Wällen der Festungsstadt: Ein Beitrag zu Alltagsleben, Organisation und Einrichtung der Festungsstadt im 19. Jahrhundert (am Beispiel der Festung Olmütz)*. České Budějovice: Bohumír Němec-Veduta, 2018.

Vogrič, Ivan. "Zasedba Bosne in Hercegovine leta 1878 v pismih Ivana Mankoča." *Zgodovinski časopis* 70, nos. 3–4 (2026): 314–36.

Vojinović, Miloš. "Political Ideas of Young Bosnia: Between Anarchism, Socialism, and Nationalism." In *The First World War and the Balkans: Historic Event, Experience, Memory/Der Erste Weltkrieg auf dem Balkan: Ereignis, Erfahrung und Erinnerung*, Südosteuropa-Jahrbuch 42, edited by Wolfgang Höpken and Wim van Meurs, 162–96. Berlin: Peter Lang, 2018.

Volarić, Klara. "Under a Gun: Eugen Kumičić on the Austria-Hungarian Occupation of Bosnia and Herzegovina." In *European Revolutions and the Ottoman Balkans: Nationalism, Violence and Empire in the Long Nineteenth Century*, edited by Dimitris Stamatopoulos, 183–98. London: Bloomsbury, 2019.

Vucinich, Wayne. *A Study in Social Survival: The Katun in Bileća Rudine*. Denver: University of Denver, 1975.

———. "Transhumance." In *Yugoslavia and Its Historians: Understanding the Balkan Wars of the 1990s*, edited by Norman M. Naimark and Holly Case, 66–92. Stanford, CA: Stanford University Press, 2003.

Vučurović, Rade. "Osvrt na Ratni Dnevnik Miloša Šarabe." *Tribunia: Prilozi za istoriju, arheologiju, etnologiju, umjetnost i kulturu*, no. 2 (1976): 10–13.

Vulić, Slaviša M. "Austrougarska okupacija Bosne i Hercegovine i prve godine uprave (1878–1882)." Ph.D. diss., University of Belgrade, 2021.

Watson, Alexander. *The Fortress: The Great Siege of Przemyśl*. London: Allen Lane, 2019.

Wawro, Geoffrey. *A Mad Catastrophe: The Outbreak of World War I and the Collapse of the Habsburg Empire*. New York: Basic Books, 2014.

Welter, Volker M. "From the Landscape of War to the Open Order of the Kaufmann House: Richard Neutra and the Experience of the Great War." In *The Good Gardener? Nature, Humanity, and the Garden*, edited by Annette Giesecke and Naomi Jacobs, 216–33. London: Black Dog, 2014.

Wiggermann, Frank. *K.u.K. Kriegsmarine und Politik: Ein Beitrag zur Geschichte der italienischen Nationalbewegung in Istrien*. Vienna: Österreichische Akademie der Wissenschaften, 2004.

Wilcox, Vanda. "The Execution of Cesare Battisti: Loyalty, Citizenship and Empire in the Trentino in World War I." In *1916 in Global Context: An Anti-Imperial Moment*, edited by Enrico Dal Lago, Róisín Healy, and Gearóid Barry, 173–87. London: Routledge, 2017.

Wingfield, Nancy. "The Enemy Within: Regulating Prostitution and Controlling Venereal Disease in Cisleithanian Austria during the Great War." *Central European History* 46, no. 3 (2013): 568–98.

Wölfl, Adelheid. "Wiederherstellungsprojekt: Aufruf zu Hilfe für bosnisches Archiv; Brand vor einem Jahr—Österreichische Akten vernichtet." *Der Standard*, February 10, 2015.

Zagmajster, Petra. "Flucht aus der Realität: Das Feuilleton der Laibacher Zeitung im Ersten Weltkrieg (1914–1918)." MA thesis, University of Ljubljana, 2019.

Zajiček, Petr, Martin Oliva, and Petr Kostrhun. *Karel Absolon: Objevitel, manažer, vědec*. Prague: Academia, 2021.

Zorić, Damir. "Način života u istočnoj Hercegovini sredinom XIX stoljeća." *Studia ethnologica Croatica*, no. 1 (1989): 99–120.

Živojinović, Dragoljub R. "King Nikola and the Territorial Expansion of Montenegro, 1914–1920." *Balcanica* 14 (2014): 353–68.

Index

Milton Keynes UK
Ingram Content Group UK Ltd.
UKHW021459230924
448659UK00008B/88

9 789633 867709